SECURITY MANAGEMENT OF NEXT GENERATION TELECOMMUNICATIONS NETWORKS AND SERVICES

SECURITY MANAGEMENT OF NEXT GENERATION TELECOMMUNICATIONS NETWORKS AND SERVICES

Stuart Jacobs

IEEE Press
Series on
Networks and
Services Management

Thomas Plevyak and
Veli Sahin, *Series Editors*

Sponsored by

IEEE
COMMUNICATIONS
SOCIETY

IEEE Press

Library of Congress Cataloging-in-Publication Data:
Jacobs, Stuart.
  Security management of next generation telecommunications networks and services / Stuart Jacobs.
    pages   cm
  ISBN 978-0-470-56513-1 (hardback)
1. Computer networks–Security measures.   I. Title.
  TK5105.59.J329 2013
  005.8–dc23
                        2013011611

ISBN: 9780470565131

10 9 8 7 6 5 4 3 2 1

This book is dedicated to my wife, Eileen,
for her patience with my spending so much time at the
keyboard rather than with her.

CONTENTS

3 SECURITY MANAGEMENT IN CURRENT AND FUTURE NETWORKS   139

4 RISK MANAGEMENT IN CURRENT AND FUTURE NETWORKS   191

PREFACE

This book focuses on the management of information security in next generation networks from the viewpoint of a telecommunications service provider, commercial enterprise or any other type of networked organization as a governance issue that needs to follow the "Plan, Do, Check and Act" approach promulgated by W. Edwards Deming and captured in ISO Standard 27001 as it applies to the management of security. Following a review of the evolution of standardized network management concepts and how networking concepts and context have grown in complexity over the last 20 years, the need for security governance is discussed. Under governance, not only are current management frameworks considered, the need for well-organized information security policies, security organizational structures, approaches for establishing security procedures, and development of security requirements are discussed. Risk management, a core component of information security governance, is then covered starting with asset inventory capture and categorization through vulnerability identification, threat determination, risk mitigation, and prioritization of mitigation plans. The subject of operations security (OPSEC) is then dealt with as OPSEC is where the Deming "Act" and "Check" aspects are most fully realized. The security governance concepts presented herein are equally applicable to both legacy and next generation network environments. A significant number of appendices useful to industry professionals and students are included, which provide examples of information security policies, detailed security requirements derivation, request for proposal security material, evaluation of proposal security submissions, security statements of work for contracts, and operations security procedures for auditing and platform hardening. Three appendices provide overviews covering the role of cryptography in information security, authentication of subjects, network security mechanisms, and securing network protocols.

ORGANIZATION

Chapter 1 discusses:

- How the very concept of networking has evolved over time;
- The evolution of network security concepts from a standards perspective;
- Network and security management systems;
- The evolution of network and security management concepts; and
- How the management of information security needs have changed over time.

Chapter 2 discusses:

- How modern networks have evolved over time;
- Common network organizations including wired, wireless metropolitan area, wide area, Supervisory Control and Data Acquisition (SCADA), sensor networks and clouds;
- Next Generation Network framework and architecture concepts; and
- The evolving Internet Protocol (IP) Multimedia Subsystem organization of services.

Chapter 3 discusses:

- How cybercrime has become a significant information security driver;
- The evolution of Information Security Governance into a core organizational management component;
- The primary Information Security management frameworks and the relative advantages/disadvantages to each framework; and
- A holistic information security management approach leveraging the strengths of existing frameworks.

Chapter 4 discusses:

- Asset identification and developing an inventory of organizational assets;
- Analyzing the impact when organizational assets are damaged, lost, or made unavailable due to accidental or malicious human activities;
- Procedural risk mitigation controls;
- Technical risk mitigation controls acquisition or development; and
- Risk mitigation controls deployment testing.

Chapter 5 discusses:

- Security within Element and Network Management Systems;
- Telecommunications Management Network Security;
- Operations Support Systems Security Needs;
- A Security Management Framework as defined by ITU-T Recommendation M.3410;
- Operational Security Compliance Programs;
- Security Operations Reviews and Audits;
- Security Event Response and Incident Management;
- Penetration Testing;
- Common Criteria Evaluated Systems;
- Accreditation and Certification; and
- Withdrawal from service.

Also included are a variety of appendices as follows:

Appendix A   provides a synopsis of basic cryptography concepts, explores major aspects of crypto-analysis and key management, and describes the primary approaches for cryptographically based authentication.

Appendix B   describes the Kerberos authentication system, public key management via Public Key Infrastructures (PKI), reviews issues associated with human authentication, and describes the capabilities of RADIUS-, LDAP- and Diameter-based authentication.

Appendix C   reviews the Data Link Layer Security Mechanisms (IEEE 802.1q, IEEE 802.1x, IEEE 802.11i), the IP Security (IPsec) inter-networking security mechanism, network authorization and access control mechanisms (Firewalls, Application-level Gateways, and IPS/IDS), Transport protocol security mechanisms (TLS, DTLS, SSL, and Secure Shell), Application Security Mechanisms, Web application Security Mechanisms (XML, SOA, SOAP, and SAML), and Anti-Malware Applications, Host-based Firewalls, Modification Scanners, and Host-based IPS/IDS.

Appendix D   provides an example Organization security policy document based on the ISO/IEC 27002 standard that can serve as a starting point for developing customized policy documents.

Appendix E   provides an example decomposition of the example security policy document in Appendix D into detailed enterprise security functional requirements that can serve as a starting point for developing customized policy documents.

Appendix F   provides an overview of commonly used networking protocols in the data link, inter-networking, transport, and application layers along with known attacks that leverage vulnerabilities within different protocols.

Appendix G   provides a comparison of security functionality covered by ITU-T Recommendations M.3400 and M.3050.

Appendix H   lists the state level personally identifiable information privacy—breach notification laws enacted within the United States as of 2010.

Appendix I   provides an example set of detailed information security-related functional requirements that can be used in Requests for Proposals (RFPs).

Appendix J   provides an example Microsoft Excel spreadsheet that can be used for evaluating supplier proposals based on the requirements found in Appendix I.

Appendix K   provides an example Security Statement of Work that can be used in contract negotiations.

Appendix L   provides an example set of Solaris Operating System security audit procedures.

Appendix M   provides an example set of Microsoft XP Operating System security hardening procedures.

Appendix N   provides an example set of network security audit procedures.

Appendix O   provides an example set of generic Unix Operating System security audit procedures.

TARGET AUDIENCE

The major audiences for this book are:

* Graduate students studying Computer/Information Sciences/Engineering, Systems Engineering, and Technology/Business Management, and
* Professionals in the telecommunications field that rely on reliable and trustable information processing and communications systems and infrastructures.

ABOUT THE AUTHOR

Stuart Jacobs holds the position of Lecturer on the faculty in the Boston University Metropolitan College Computer Science (MET CS) department. Stuart's responsibilities include teaching graduate courses on "Enterprise Information Security," "Network Security," and "Network Forensics" along with serving as the MET CS department security curriculum coordinator with responsibility for all MET CS security courses.

Stuart has served as an Industry Security Subject Matter Expert for the Alliance for the Telecommunications Industry Solutions (ATIS) and has served as the Technical Editor of the ATIS Technical Report "Information & Communications Security for NGN Converged Services IP Networks and Infrastructure" and as the Technical Editor of ITU-T M.3410, "Guidelines and Requirements for Security Management Systems."

Stuart retired from Verizon Corporation in 2007 where he was a Principal Member of the Technical Staff with responsibility for security architecture development, security requirements analysis, and standards development activities. As Verizon's lead security architect, Stuart was the lead engineer for security on numerous Verizon network equipment RFPs and provided security consulting on wireless and wired networks, SS7, CALEA/LI, vulnerability analysis, intrusion detection, and systems engineering methodologies. Additionally, Stuart served as Verizon's security subject matter expert for ANSI-ATIS, ITU-T, TMF, OIF, MSF, OMG, and IETF activities. In addition to his other duties, Stuart has also pursued applied research in network design and security, in particular wireless networks, public key infrastructures, network authentication schemes, distributed computing security mechanisms (including autonomous agent systems, authentication mechanisms for Mobile IP, Mobile Ad-Hoc Self Organizing Networks, and Intelligent Agents) for government and commercial organizations and agencies.

Stuart holds an MSc. degree and CISSP certification; he is completing a Ph.D. degree in Information Systems with a concentration in security and is a member of the:

* Institute of Electrical and Electronics Engineers (IEEE),
* IEEE Computer Society,
* Association for Computing Machinery (ACM), Senior Member,
* International Information Systems Security Certification Consortium (ISC)^2, and
* Information Systems Security Association (ISSA), Senior Member.

ACKNOWLEDGMENTS

I would like to thank Thomas Plevyak for encouraging me to write this book; Thomas Plevyak and Veli Sahin, the IEEE Press Network Management Series Editors, for all their constructive comments and suggestions; the anonymous reviewers for their comments and advice; my former Verizon co-workers; and members of the New England chapter of the ISSA.

1

INTRODUCTION

At the very outset of this book, questions worth asking are:

- What is the author referring to by the word "security?"
- What is the author referring to by the words "security management?"
- What are next-generation networks and services?

Security is a word whose meaning seems to change depending on the context where it is used and by the "mindset" or background of the individual. Some people think security is solely about "chain-link" fences, security guards, burglar alarms/video cameras, etc. Other people think security is about the use of encryption, login passwords, "firewalls," etc. Then there are those who believe security is only an issue for military-intelligence type organizations and of no importance, or a hindrance, to commercial and other enterprises, as allegedly overheard at a meeting of security people (Kaufman et al., 2002):

Speaker: Isn't it terrifying that on the Internet we have no privacy?
Heckler 1:   You mean confidentiality. Get your terms straight.
Heckler 2:   Why do security types insist on inventing their own language?
Heckler 3:   It's a denial of service attack.

Security Management of Next Generation Telecommunications Networks and Services,
First Edition. Stuart Jacobs.
© 2014 The Institute of Electrical and Electronics Engineers, Inc. Published 2014 by John Wiley & Sons, Inc.

The aforementioned simply exemplifies how words become confused, misused, or ambiguous, when talking about security.

This problem just grows when the phrase "security management" appears. Does security management refer to:

- the management of technology related to security?
- the management of security activities?
- security for information processing management activities?
- security of organizational management activity?

    or

- all of the above?

Again it depends on the individual as to which of the aforementioned is germane.

Then there is the term "Next-Generation Network," usually abbreviated as NGN. What is an NGN? What technologies are used by an NGN? How does an NGN differ from today's Internet Protocol (IP)-based networks and the existing Public Switched Telephone Networks (PSTNs)? A wide number of subjects need to be considered to answer the previous questions and should be addressed in an order that builds upon a number of foundation concepts.

The goal of this book is to provide an answer to these questions.

This chapter discusses:

- How the very concept of networking has evolved over time;
- The evolution of network security concepts from a standards perspective;
- Network and security management systems;
- The evolution of network and security management concepts;
- How the management of information security needs have changed over time.

Chapter 2 discusses:

- How modern networks have evolved over time;
- Common network organizations including: wired, wireless, metropolitan area, wide area, Supervisory Control and Data Acquisition (SCADA), sensor networks, and clouds;
- Next-Generation Network framework and architecture concepts;
- The evolving IP Multimedia Subsystem (IMS) organization of services.

Chapter 3 discusses:

- How cybercrime has become a significant information security driver;
- The evolution of information security governance into a core organizational management component;

- The primary information security management frameworks and the relative advantages/disadvantages to each framework;
- A holistic information security management approach leveraging the strengths of existing frameworks.

Chapter 4 discusses:

- Asset identification and developing an inventory of organizational assets;
- Analyzing the impact when organizational assets are damaged, lost, or made unavailable due to accidental or malicious human activities;
- Procedural risk mitigation controls;
- Technical risk mitigation controls acquisition or development;
- Risk mitigation controls deployment testing.

Chapter 5 discusses:

- Security within Element and Network Management Systems (EMS/NMS);
- Telecommunications Management Network (TMN) Security;
- Operations Support Systems (OSSs) Security Needs;
- A Security Management Framework as defined by ITU-T Recommendation M.3410;
- Operational Security Compliance Programs;
- Security Operations Reviews and Audits;
- Security Event Response and Incident Management;
- Penetration Testing;
- Common Criteria Evaluated Systems;
- Accreditation and Certification;
- Withdrawal from service.

Also included are a wide variety of appendices including:

Appendix	Presents
A	Provides a synopsis of basic cryptography concepts;
	Explores major aspects of crypto-analysis and key management; and
	Describes the primary approaches for cryptographically based authentication.
B	Describes the Kerberos and Public Key Infrastructure (PKI) authentication systems;
	Reviews issues associated with human authentication;
	Describes the capabilities of RADIUS-, LDAP- and Diameter-based authentication.
C	The Data Link Layer Security Mechanisms IEEE 802.1q, IEEE 802.1x, IEEE 802.11i;
	The IP Security (IPsec) inter-networking Security Mechanism;
	Network Authorization and Access Control mechanisms for: Firewalls, Application-level Gateways and IPS/IDS;
	Transport protocol security mechanisms: TLS, DTLS, SSL and Secure Shell (SSH);
	Application Security Mechanisms;
	The Web application Security Mechanisms: XML, SOA, SOAP and SAML; and

(*continued*)

Appendix	Presents
	Anti-Malware Applications for malware and spyware Scanning, Host Based Firewalls, Modification Scanners and Host Based IPS/IDS.
D	An example Organization security policy document based on the ISO/IEC 27002 standard that can serve as a starting point for developing customized policy documents.
E	An example decomposition of the example security policy document in Appendix D into detailed enterprise security functional requirements that can serve as a starting point for developing customized policy documents.
F	An overview of commonly used networking protocols in the data link, internetworking, transport, and application layers along with know attacks that leverage vulnerabilities within different protocols.
G	A comparison of security functionality covered by ITU-T Recommendations M.3400 and M.3050.
H	The state level personally identifiable information privacy—breach notification laws enacted within the United States as of 2010.
I	An example set of detailed information security related functional requirements that can be used in Requests for Proposals (RFPs).
J	An example Microsoft Excel spreadsheet that can be used for evaluating supplier proposals based on the requirements found on Appendix I.
K	An example Security Statement of Work (SOW) that can be used in contract negotiations.
L	An example set of Solaris Operating System security audit procedures.
M	An example set of Microsoft XP Operating System security hardening procedures.
N	An example set of network security audit procedures.
O	An example set of generic Unix Operating System security audit procedures.

1.1 EVOLUTION OF NETWORKING CONCEPTS

Through the 1960s and 1970s, there were two approaches to networking:

- the Public Switched Telephone Network (PSTN), commonly referred to as telephony, and
- computer/data communications networks.

Each approach evolved independently of the other and represented very different views regarding how devices should communicate and who should control the technology.

1.1.1 The Public Switched Telephone Network

The Public Switched Telephone Network (PSTN) was a government-sanctioned and regulated monopoly of "telephone companies" with about 65% owned and operated by AT&T,[1] about 30% owned and operated by GTE,[2] with the remaining 5% by some 20 very small independent owners/operators. As AT&T represented the largest PSTN

---

[1] American Telephone & Telegraph Corporation (AT&T), also referred to as the Bell System.

[2] General Telephone & Electronics (GTE).

operator, its Bell Laboratories was the driving force for the development of most PSTN technologies (especially network interfaces and protocols), since the other much smaller operators all had to interconnect with AT&T's infrastructure. Only following the 1968 U.S. Supreme Court "Carterphone" decision (and FCC ruling 13 F.C.C.2d 420), regarding modems,[3] were devices not supplied by the telephone company allowed to be interconnected to telephone networks. Even after the "Carterphone" decision, up through the 1990s, PSTN technology evolution was primarily controlled by PSTN operating companies and their equipment suppliers. Starting in the 1990s, Standards Development Organizations (SDOs) and industry forums began to have a major impact on PSTN technology. The major SDOs and forums impacting PSTN technology development have been the:

- International Telecommunication Union-Telecommunications (ITU-T) Standardization Sector whose predecessor was the International Telegraph and Telephone Consultative Committee (CCITT);
- Telecommunications Industry Association (TIA);
- Alliance for Telecommunications Industry Solutions (ATIS);
- European Telecommunications Standards Institute (ETSI);
- International Standards Organization (ISO); and
- 3rd Generation Partnership Project (3GPP).

Presently, these and numerous other organizations have assumed a significant role in defining how telephony-related technology should evolve.

1.1.2 Computer/Data Communications Networks

Computer/data communications network technology through the 1960s and 1970s was predominately controlled by computer manufacturers who developed network capabilities specifically to support their proprietary product lines. During this era, IBM[4] represented over 70% of all computers sold; consequently, other computer manufacturers routinely provided some degree of interoperability with IBM's networking technology. Virtually all of these proprietary computer networking capabilities were based on bit synchronous link protocols and used of an end-to-end connection approach between end computer systems. Each computer manufacturer developed their unique networking capabilities according to a proprietary network architecture[5] that was not subject to non-company external review or approval. In the 1980s, work on the concept of connectionless packet networking, independent of any single computer manufacturer, started to mature with the publication of the U.S. Government Defense Advanced Research Projects Agency sponsored, and in many cases Internet

---

[3] A modem (modulator-demodulator) is a device used for converting digital signals into, and recovering them from, quasi-analog signals suitable for transmission over analog communications channels such as the PSTN.

[4] IBM was the common abbreviation for the International Business Machine Corporation.

[5] A network architecture specifies the design of a communications network via a framework for the specification of a network's physical components, functional organization, protocols, data/message formats, and operational principles and procedures.

Engineering Task Force published, Request for Comments (RFCs) 791,[6] 792,[7] and 793[8] (defining IPv4, ICMPv4, and TCPv4) that are the foundation protocols for the modern Internet Suite of protocols and defined basic packet internetworking and end-to-end transport capabilities for generalized connectionless networking. By the early 1990s, IPv4 and TCPv4 had become de facto standards for computer-to-computer communications with the responsibility for these, and many other protocols, under the control of the Internet Engineering Task Force (IETF). Virtually all computers now include native Internet Protocol (IP-) and Transmission Control Protocol (TCP)-based communications capabilities. It must be noted that IETF protocol development does not follow any formalized network architecture beyond relying on the use of IP, TCP, and User Datagram Protocol (UDP).

1.1.3 Network Architectures

The first approach to developing a non-proprietary network architecture resulted in the publication by the ISO of document ISO/IEC 7498-1[9] in 1984, known as the Open System Interconnect (OSI) model.[10] It was quickly followed by three other standards, ISO/IEC 7498–2,[11] ISO/IEC 7498–3,[12] and ISO/IEC 7498-4.[13] The major contributions of these standards have been:

- Formal introduction of the concept of layering protocols, that operate on an end-to-end basis upon other protocols that provide interconnection/forwarding capabilities that provide basic communications link functions;
- The concept that a protocol should only utilize information about another protocol (either above it or below it) that is available via a well-defined interface, thereby allowing the internal structure or operation of a protocol to be changed without negatively impacting other protocols; and

[6] RFC 791, INTERNET PROTOCOL DARPA INTERNET PROGRAM PROTOCOL SPECIFICATION, September 1981.

[7] RFC 792 INTERNET CONTROL MESSAGE PROTOCOL DARPA INTERNET PROGRAM PROTOCOL SPECIFICATION, September 1981

[8] RFC 793, TRANSMISSION CONTROL PROTOCOL DARPA INTERNET PROGRAM PROTOCOL SPECIFICATION, September 1981

[9] ISO/IEC 7498–1:1984, "Information technology – Open Systems Interconnection – Basic Reference Model: The Basic Model" International Standards Organization (ISO), 1984. A revised version was published by ISO as 7498–1:1994 and by ITU-T as X.200 in 1994.

[10] The OSI model goal was to get industry participants to agree on common network standards to provide multi-vendor interoperability.

[11] ISO/IEC 7498–2:1989, "Information technology – Open Systems Interconnection – Basic Reference Model: Part 2: Security Architecture" International Standards Organization (ISO), 1989 and published by the ITU-T as X.800 in 1994.

[12] ISO/IEC 7498–3:1989, "Information technology – Open Systems Interconnection – Basic Reference Model: Naming and addressing" International Standards Organization (ISO), 1989.

[13] ISO/IEC 7498–4:1989, "Information technology – Open Systems Interconnection – Basic Reference Model – Part 4: Management Framework" International Standards Organization (ISO), 1989 and published by the ITU-T as X.700 in 1992.

- Recognition that more than just protocols are necessary for a network architecture, namely, it:
  - provided formalized descriptions of protocol concepts for multiple protocol layers (ISO/IEC 7498–1);
  - introduced a standardized approach for the consideration of communications security capabilities (ISO/IEC 7498–2);
  - recognized the need for standardized naming, addressing, and directory capabilities (ISO/IEC 7498–3); and
  - presented a framework and basic concepts for the management of communications components, features, and services (ISO/IEC 7498–4).

Although the seven protocol layers and specific protocols specified within these ISO standards have not been widely adopted, the general concepts from:

- ISO/IEC 7498–1 (aka ITU-T X.200) of protocol layering and well-defined interprotocol interfaces are widely accepted;
- ISO/IEC 7498–2 (aka ITU-T X.800) for communications security services, security mechanisms, and the management of security mechanisms are considered the de jure definitions for security; and
- ISO/IEC 7498–4 (aka ITU-T X.700) for the management of communications devices, in the form of Fault, Configuration, Accounting, Performance, and Security Management (the "FCAPS" of management), are considered the de jure areas that network management focuses upon.

Figure 1.1 highlights the relationship of protocol layer within the OSI protocol model versus the Internet Suite of protocols. Some consider Internet Suite application protocols to constitute layer 5 protocols.

Protocol layer	OSI	TCP/IP	Protocol layer
OSI 7	Application	Application	
OSI 6	Presentation		
OSI 5	Session		
OSI 4	Transport	Transport	4
OSI 3	Network	Internet	3
OSI 2	Data link	Data link	2
OSI 1	Physical	Physical	1

Figure 1.1. OSI Model and Internet Suite Protocol Layers.

1.1.4 Data Network Complexity

Since the aforementioned ISO standards were published, the complexity of deployed networks has vastly grown. Chapter 2 will explore this increasing complexity in more detail. Up through the 1980s, computer-oriented networks were primarily single facility/location oriented with computers either directly interconnected or connected to a local area network (LAN) that may have included a number of segments interconnected by bridging devices (e.g., Ethernet layer 2 bridges). Interfacility/location interconnection of computers or LANs relied on the use of modems to attach the local network to the PSTN via a modem and dial-up lines/services or a channel service unit to a PSTN-operator-supplied leased line.[14]

A "sea change" occurred in computer-data-networking with the concept of a router[15] which was under development through the 1970s and 1980s based on the use of minicomputers. These minicomputer router capabilities were, in this time frame, primarily limited to academic, government, and industrial research networks, given their expense and complexity. In the late 1980s, stand-alone multi-protocol connectionless routers became commercially available. These routing devices radically altered how computer networks were structured. From the late 1980s up to the present, router-based networks frequently utilize multiple routers to structure facility/location networks into logically separate subnets and tie multiple facility/location networks into enterprise networks that span geographic regions. High capacity versions of these routers have been instrumental to the evolution and growth of the Internet, which is really the router-based interconnection of a number of very large corporate or other enterprise-operated router networks. Figure 1.2 depicts the concept of a number of core (backbone) networks operated by AT&T, Verizon Business (formally MCI), Quest, Sprint, Level 3 Communications (L3), NTT Communications (NTTC) and Global Crossing (GBLX), "Tier 1" Internet Service Providers (ISPs), and an example set of commercial/residential access ISPs (the terms "alpha," "bravo," "delta," "echo," "tango," and "zulu" are used rather than actual company names for these example commercial/residential access ISPs). The term wide area network (WAN) represents Tier 1 ISP-routed networks that span wide geographic regions, and the term "IP Metro Network" represents access ISP-routed networks that span metropolitan-size geographic areas. As shown in Figure 1.1, the "Internet" is not a single network but many interconnected networks used to interconnect millions of other networks and computers.

Another area of complexity not considered by the ISO standards is at layer 2 of the OSI model. At the time when the ISO standards were published, the OSI layer 2 for local networks was considered to be a simple ability to interconnect two devices in either:

• a point-to-point manner (also called direct connection) as shown in Figure 1.3;

---

[14] A PSTN-operator-supplied leased line is a dedicated circuit between two different facilities at the link layer providing 56Kbps, 1.544 Mbps or sometimes 45 Mbps of bandwidth.

[15] A router is a networking device tailored to the tasks of routing and forwarding information between two or more networks based on layer 3 protocol information unlike a bridge or layer 2 switch that forwards information between two or more network segments based on layer 2 protocol information.

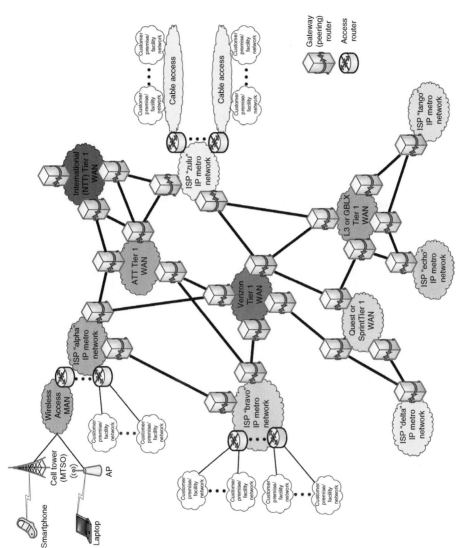

Figure 1.2. The Internet Concept of Core and Access ISP Networks.

- a multi-drop manner where a number of devices are interconnected to a common physical medium such as with the early versions of Ethernet (i.e., 10base5 "thick-wire" and 10base2 "thin-wire" coaxial cabled Ethernet) as shown in Figure 1.4; or
- a "star" manner where a number of devices are interconnected to a common device such as with hubbed or switched versions of Ethernet (i.e., 10baseT over-twisted pair cabling) as shown in Figure 1.5.

Interconnection of LANs was expected to rely on some form of intermediate packet switching network, such as a commercially available X.25 network. During the 1990s timeframe, significant layer 2 technological developments resulted in the availability of Synchronous Optical Network (SONET) and Asynchronous Transfer Mode (ATM) layer 2 networking along with continued use of X.25 and its commercial successor Frame Relay networking. These developments resulted in interfacility interconnection of facility/location LANs often using two or three protocols below the layer 3 protocol (routinely IPv4). For example, an organization interconnecting routed subnets at three

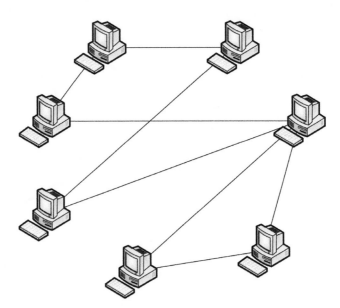

Figure 1.3. Direct Interconnection of Computers.

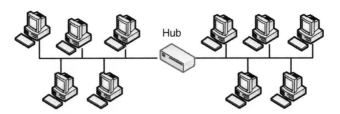

Figure 1.4. Multi-drop Interconnection of Computers.

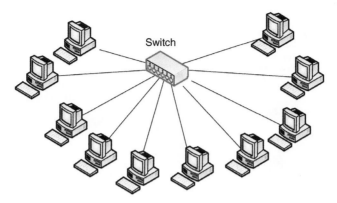

Figure 1.5. "Star" Interconnection of Computers.

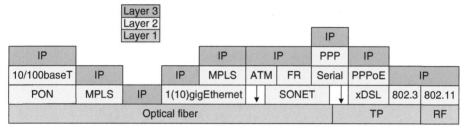

Figure 1.6. Current Complexity of Protocols in Layer 2.

locations would configure their routers to use SONET links over which ATM would be used to transport Ethernet frames that carried IP packets. Figure 1.6 depicts various arrangements for layering protocols within layer 2.

In Figure1.6:

- PON represents Passive Optical Networking
- MPLS represents Multi-protocol Label Switching
- xDLS represents various forms of Digital Subscriber Line technologies
- FR represents Frame Relay
- Serial represents asynchronous dial-up PSTN access
- 802.3 represents Ethernet
- 802.11 represents Wireless Ethernet (aka "WiFi")
- PPP represents Point-to-Point Protocol
- PPPoE represents Point-to-Point Protocol over Ethernet.

What needs to be pointed out is that:

- SONET technology is not a simple direct-connect, multi-drop, or star technology but actually provides the ability to interconnect many devices in what are called

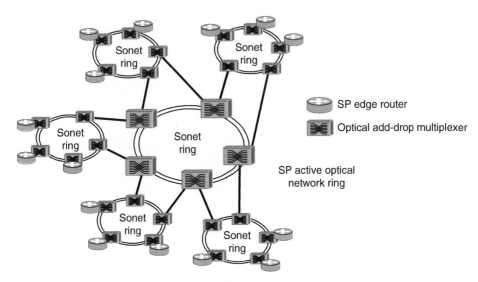

Figure 1.7. Example Sonet Rings.

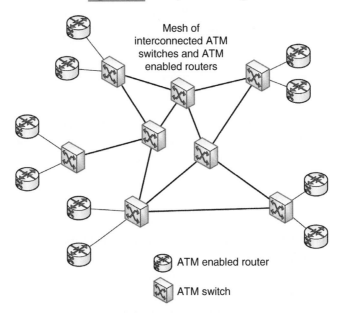

Figure 1.8. Example ATM Network.

rings and even interconnect these rings into more complex organizations as
shown in Figure 1.7; and

• ATM technology is also not a simple direct-connect, multi-drop, or star technology but actually provides the ability to interconnect many devices in a meshed
manner, with multiple links exiting/entering each ATM switch allowing the con-
struction of complex ATM interconnections as shown in Figure 1.8.

ATM switches are routinely interconnected over SONET infrastructures, thus resulting in a complex organization of interconnected devices layered on top of another complex organization of interconnected devices.

As can be seen from the proceeding discussion, the standards describing network architectures have not kept pace with the various technologies deployed and the corresponding complexity of modern networks. For this reason, we start our discussion by considering how security, and its management, has been viewed from a standards perspective. We will also discuss some of the typical security technologies deployed in today's network infrastructures.[16]

1.2 A NETWORK SECURITY HISTORICAL PERSPECTIVE

To properly discuss what security management focuses on, it is helpful to understand where the very concept of network management began and how the issue of managing security has evolved over the decades. The first effort to formalize network management concepts resulted in the development and publication of ISO/IEC 7498–4. Prior to the publication of ISO/IEC 7598–1, network management (and security) were proprietary capabilities of both the PSTN and computer manufacturer products and services. However, during the 1980s, many in telecommunications-related industries began to recognize that network management activities could be grouped into the five areas of:

- **F**ault management;
- **C**onfiguration management;
- **A**ccounting management;
- **P**erformance management; and
- **S**ecurity management.

As organized in ISO/IEC 7498–4, these areas are typically referred to collectively as FCAPS (an acronym based on the first letter of each area). The subject of security management was further expanded upon in ISO/IEC 7498–2. When ISO published ISO/IEC 7498–4, the subject of security management was limited to simply noting that security management exists to support the application of security policies by functions concerned with:

- creation, deletion, and control of security services and mechanisms;
- distribution of security-relevant information; and
- reporting of security-relevant events,

and then directs the reader back to ISO/IEC 7498–2 for additional information on management functions within the ISO security architecture. Therefore, to understand the

---

[16] A network infrastructure is the basic physical (communications links/media), technical (hardware, software, and protocols), and organizational (policies, processes, and procedures) structures needed for the operation of an enterprise communications network that delivers services and facilities to the enterprise, its customers/ users, and other interconnected networks.

roots of security management concepts, we need to further examine ISO/IEC 7498–1 and ISO/IEC 7498–2.

The aforementioned ISO standards ISO/IEC 7498–1, ISO/IEC 7498–2, and ISO/IEC 7498–4 have served as cornerstone documents and even adopted directly by the ITU-T as ITU-T X.200 (ISO/IEC 7498–1), ITU-T X.800 (ISO/IEC 7498–2), and ITU-T X.700 (ISO/IEC 7498–4). It is worth taking a look at these documents.

1.2.1 ISO/IEC 7498–1 (ITU-T X.200) Coverage of Management

ISO/IEC 7498–1 (X.200) focuses on the formal architecture of networks and the control of network components/devices (assets); however, only about 2 pages, out of some 60 plus pages, are devoted to the management of network assets. This document defines a number of concepts, specifically:

1. application management functions are concerned with managing application processes, and application management software provide application management functions;
2. systems management functions are concerned with the management of various network resources, and their status across all protocol layers of a network architecture, and system management software provide system management functions; and
3. protocol layer management functions reside within each layer for activities such as activation and error control and are partly performed as a subset of systems management.

ISO/IEC 7498–1 (X.200) then states that only management-related communication between management functions within networked devices is of concern within the network architecture, and that management activities local to specific networked devices are out of scope as the standard only considers network resources involved with data processing and data communication. Application management is discussed as the management of network application processes and includes activities such as:

a. initialization of parameters;
b. initiation, maintenance, and termination of applications;
c. allocation and de-allocation of network resources;
d. detection and prevention of network resource interference;
e. integrity and commitment controls;
f. security controls; and
g. application checkpoint and recovery control.

The activities of application security controls are not further explained or defined within the standard. Systems management is discussed as the management of network resources across all protocol layers, and such activities include:

a. activation/deactivation management, including activation, maintenance, and termination of network resources, program loading functions, control of connections between management entities, and parameter initialization/ modification;

b. monitoring, including reporting status, status changes, and statistics; and

c. error control, including error detection, diagnostic functions, reconfiguration, and restart.

The protocols used for systems management are considered application layer protocols. Protocol layer management activities such as activation and error control are considered to occur within each protocol layer, whereas other layer management activities are viewed as part of systems management. ISO/IEC 7498-1's consideration of management and security subjects is so general as to be almost useless. Five years would pass before network management and security were given any serious consideration with the publication of ISO/IEC 7498–4 (X.700) and ISO/IEC 7498–2 (X.800).

1.2.2 ISO/IEC 7498–4 (ITU-T X.700) Coverage of Security Management

ISO/IEC 7498–4 (ITU-T X.700) devotes a single paragraph to the subject of security management which simply says that this area focuses on:

* creation, deletion, and control of security services and mechanisms;
* distribution of security-relevant information; and
* reporting of security-relevant events.

Nowhere in this document are these concepts further discussed other than to refer the reader to ISO/IEC 7498–2 (X.800).

1.2.3 ISO/IEC 7498–2 (ITU-T X.800) Coverage of Security and Management

For the sake of simplicity, and because the ITU-T published standards tend to be more frequently referenced than the ISO/IEC versions, we will hence forward reference X.200, X.700, and X.800 rather than the ISO/IEC versions.

Although frequently referred to as a "security architecture," the main value of ITU-T X.800 is the introduction and definition of:

* five primary network security services;
* a set of specific network security mechanisms;
* a number of non-specific (general) device resident security mechanisms; and
* a description of management mechanisms for controlling deployed security mechanisms.

ITU-T X.800 is concerned only with those visible aspects of communications that permit networked elements to achieve the secure transfer of information between them. It does not attempt to provide any kind of detailed descriptions or requirements, nor does it provide the means to assess conformance of any implementation to this or any other security standard. Additionally, it does not indicate, in any detail, the additional security mechanisms needed within networked elements to ensure reliable, secure computer operation.

1.2.3.1 X.800 Security Services. Security services are abstract functional capabilities which can counter security threats. In practice, these services are invoked at appropriate protocol layers and within computing elements, and in different combinations, to satisfy organizational security policies, requirements, and operational rules. Practical realizations of systems may implement particular combinations of the basic security services for direct invocation. Historically, there were considered to be five fundamental security services: Authentication (three variations), Access Control, Confidentiality (four variations), Integrity (five variations), and Non-repudiation (two variations). Standardized definitions of these historical security services were provided in ITU-T X.800-1991 and presented in Table 1.1.

X.800 then goes on to say that these security services would be instantiated via the deployment of security mechanisms, which are then discussed next as either specific security mechanisms or pervasive security mechanisms.

1.2.3.2 X.800 Specific Security Mechanisms. The specific security mechanisms X.800 considers appropriate for providing the aforementioned security services, which may be implemented (provided) within individual protocol layers, are presented in Table 1.2.

Appendix A of this book, "Role of Cryptography in Information Security," provides an overview of cryptographic hash algorithms and both symmetric and asymmetric cryptography along with how this technology may be used to provide:

- both Peer-entity and Data-origin authentication;
- different forms of confidentiality and integrity; and
- non-repudiation via digital signatures.

Appendix B of this book, "Authentication of Subjects," provides an overview of the different approaches for both cryptographic and non-cryptographic authentication of subjects (both human and machine).

1.2.3.3 X.800 General Security Mechanisms. ITU-T X.800 also describes a number of non-specific (general or pervasive) security mechanisms that all networked devices should include. These pervasive security mechanisms are expected to be independent of any network services, rather general capabilities of a network attached device, be it a router, switch server, workstation, etc. The intent of these mechanisms is to provide a secure execution environment for protocol-related security mechanisms.

TABLE 1.1. X.800 Security Services.

Service Group	Specific Service	Service Purpose or Capability
Authentication	**Peer-entity authentication**	A service for confirming the identities of subjects communicating with each other and provides confidence that a subject is not attempting to masquerade as some other subject.
	Data-origin authentication	A service for corroborating the source subject from which data are received and does not necessarily provide protection against duplication or modification of data.
	User authentication	A service for confirming/validating the identity of a human subject when the subject logs into a computer system and provides confidence that a human subject is not attempting a masquerade as a different human subject.
Access control		A service that provides protection against unauthorized use or access to communications resources (objects) and may be applied to various types of access to a resource.
Confidentiality	**Connection confidentiality**	A service that provides for the confidentiality of all data (objects) on a protocol connection being used by two communicating subjects.
	Connectionless confidentiality	A service that provides for the confidentiality of all data (objects) transferred by a protocol being used by two communicating subjects over a protocol exchange between the two subjects where the protocol uses a connectionless, or best effort/datagram, exchange method.
	Selective field confidentiality	A service that provides for the confidentiality of selected data (objects) transferred by a protocol regardless of whether the protocol operates in a connection-oriented or connectionless manner.
	Traffic flow confidentiality	A service that provides for the protection of information which might be derived from observation of the existence of communications activities between two subjects.
Integrity	**Connection integrity with recovery**	A service that provides the ability to detect the occurrence of unauthorized modification of all data (objects) on a protocol connection being used by two communicating subjects and should an unauthorized modification be detected, this service includes the ability to effect retransmission of the modified object(s).

(continued)

TABLE 1.1. *(cont'd)*

Service Group	Specific Service	Service Purpose or Capability
	Connection integrity without recovery	A service that provides the ability to detect the occurrence of unauthorized modification of all data (objects) on a protocol connection being used by two communicating subjects and does not include the ability to effect retransmission of the modified object(s).
	Selective field connection integrity	A service that provides the ability to detect the occurrence of unauthorized modification of selected data (objects) on a protocol connection being used by two communicating subjects and does not include the ability to effect retransmission of the modified object(s).
	Connectionless integrity	A service that provides the ability to detect the occurrence of unauthorized modification of all data (objects) on a protocol connection being used by two communicating subjects where the protocol uses a connectionless, or best effort/datagram, exchange method.
	Selective field connectionless integrity	A service that provides the ability to detect the occurrence of unauthorized modification of selected data (objects) on a protocol connection being used by two communicating subjects where the protocol uses a connectionless, or best effort/datagram, exchange method.
Non-repudiation	**Non-repudiation with proof of origin**	A service that provides a receiving subject of data with proof of the origin (sending subject) of data/object. This will protect against any attempt by the sender (sending subject) to falsely deny sending the object or its contents.
	Non-repudiation with proof of delivery	A service that provides a sender (sending subject) of data with proof of delivery of object to the receiving subject. This will protect against any subsequent attempt by the recipient to falsely deny receiving the data or its contents.

Unfortunately, ITU-T X.800 does not provide any in-depth discussion or description of these pervasive security mechanisms beyond a general definition of each (Table 1.3).

1.2.3.4 X.800 Security Management Mechanisms.

ITU-T X.800 management of security focuses specifically on managing, controlling, configuring, and monitoring security services and mechanisms within network protocols and securing network management functionality; any consideration of managing general security capabilities within devices is considered out of scope of the document. A key concept introduced in X.800 is that of a "Security Domain" wherein all "subjects" are expected to adhere to

TABLE 1.2. **X.800 Included Specific Security Mechanisms.**

Security Mechanism	Mechanism Purpose or Capability
Encipherment	Encipherment mechanisms are based on encryption to provide confidentiality of either data or traffic flow information. Applicable encryption algorithms include symmetric (i.e., secret key) encryption and asymmetric (e.g., public key) encryption, and the use of an encryption mechanism implies the use of a key management mechanism.
Digital signatures	Digital signature mechanisms are based on asymmetric encryption and include procedures for signing data and verifying the signature of signed data. The basic characteristic of a digital signature mechanism is that the signature can only be produced using the signer's private information.
Access control mechanisms	Access control mechanisms rely on some combination of: • authenticated identity of an entity; • information about an entity; • capabilities of an entity; • time of attempted access; • route of attempted access; and • duration of access, in order to determine if access by the entity will be allowed to a resource.
Data integrity mechanisms	Data integrity mechanisms provide the ability to detect any accidental or intentional modifications. These mechanisms rely on the use of information (a secret key) shared by only the sending and receiving entities involved in an interaction.
Authentication exchange mechanisms	Authentication exchange mechanisms provide the ability to verify a claimed identity. These techniques may use cryptographic mechanisms, characteristics, or possessions of the requesting entity. These mechanisms may be combined with "handshaking" protocols.
Traffic padding mechanisms	Traffic padding can be used to provide some degree of protection against traffic analysis by obscuring the actual size of information being exchanged when used with encryption mechanisms.
Routing control mechanisms	Routing control mechanisms and systems are used to instruct a network SP to establish a connection via a specific route so as to bypass known/suspected malicious intermediate systems or to pass through certain sub-networks, relays, or links.
Notarization mechanisms	Notarization mechanisms are used to provide assurance of properties (such as data integrity, origin, time, and destination) about the data communicated between entities via a trusted third-party notary.

TABLE 1.3. X.800 Pervasive Security Mechanisms.

Trusted functionality	The intent of this mechanism is to ensure that security functions will perform as expected and not be affected by non-security-related functions within the device. However, the document does not provide any further elaboration on this subject.
Security labels	The intent of this mechanism is that software and data elements (resources) within a device may have a label associated with them such that the label indicates the "sensitivity" of the associated resource. These labels could be used to control access to a resource. The document does not provide any further elaboration on this subject.
Event detection	The intent of this mechanism is that apparent violations of security should be detectable and may also include detection of non-violation events, such as successful log-on or log-off. Events related to network activities and non-network activities should be detectable. This mechanism should also cover event reporting and event logging along with the syntactic and semantic definitions associated with these activities. The document does not provide any further elaboration on this subject.
Security audit trail	The intent of this mechanism is the ability to review security audit trails and provide a valuable capability to detect and investigate security breaches via subsequent security audits. Security audits require the recording of security relevant information in a security log file or equivalent form. Analysis and report generation from event and audit logs is considered a security management function. The document does not provide any further elaboration on this subject.
Security recovery	The intent of this mechanism is the ability to respond to requests from mechanisms such as event handling and management functions and either initiate or recommend recovery actions that isolate or mitigate the impact of security-violation-related events. The goal of this mechanism is the restoration of reliable normal functionality. The document does not provide any further elaboration on this subject.

a common set of security policy statements (requirements) as specified by a single "authority." The authority is the organization that controls or is responsible for network services and identifies who may interact with what services and functions via statements within the security policy. As stated in X.800, security management is concerned with the management of communications security services and mechanisms and spans both the configuration of these services and mechanisms and collection of information concerning the operation of these services and mechanisms. Some of the configuration control responsibilities of communications security management include:

- distribution of cryptographic keys ("Key management");
- the setting of security-related parameters ("Configuration management");
- monitoring of both normal and abnormal security-related events ("Event–Fault management");
- generation and processing of audit trails ("Audit management"); and
- both security service/mechanism activation and deactivation.

In X.800's view, security management does not address how security mechanisms in protocols actually provide specific security services. Another basic concept introduced by X.800 is that of a Security Management Information Base (SMIB), which serves as a repository for security-relevant information. No specific approach, or other details, for the storage of the information is discussed; yet each networked device is expected to maintain that local information necessary for the device to enforce applicable security policy statements. The SMIB is expected to be:

- essentially distributed across those devices within a "Security Domain," and
- likely included in any general Management Information Base (MIB) within and maintained by each device.

X.800 aggregates security management activities into three categories:

- network security management;
- network security service management;
- network security mechanism management.

Network security management functionality is expected to typically include:

- overall network security policy management;
- interaction with other network management functions;
- interaction with network security service management and network security mechanism management;
- network security event management spans those aspects of event handling and the remote reporting of apparent attempts to violate network security and the modification of thresholds used to trigger event reporting;
- network security audit management is responsible for:
  - the selection of events to be logged and/or remotely collected;
  - the enabling and disabling of audit trail logging of selected events;
  - the remote collection of selected audit records; and
  - the preparation of security audit reports;
- network security recovery management is responsible for:
  - maintenance of the rules used to react to real or suspected security violations;
  - the remote reporting of apparent violations of system security; and
  - security administrator interactions.

Network security service management focuses on specific network security services and is expected to typically (but not exhaustively) include the following activities on a per service basis:

- determination and assignment of the target security protection for the service;
- assignment and maintenance of rules for the selection (where alternatives exist) of the specific security mechanism to be employed to provide the requested security service;

- negotiation (locally and remotely) of available security mechanisms which require prior management agreement;
- invocation of specific security mechanisms via the appropriate security mechanism management function, for example, for the provision of administratively imposed security services; and
- interaction with other security service management functions and security mechanism management functions.

Network security mechanism management focuses on specific network security mechanisms and is expected to typically (but not exhaustively) include the following activities on a per mechanism basis:

- key management is responsible for:
  ○ generating keys;
  ○ deciding which entities should receive a copy of each key; and
  ○ making available, or distributing keys, in a secure manner.
    While noting that some key management functions, such as the physical distribution of keys, may occur outside of network security management functions, the exchange of session keys used during an association is a normal protocol layer function and utilize a key distribution center (KDC) or functions pre-distributed via management protocols.
- encipherment management is responsible for:
  ○ interaction with key management;
  ○ establishment of cryptographic parameters; and
  ○ cryptographic synchronization;
- digital signature management is responsible for:
  ○ interaction with key management;
  ○ establishment of cryptographic parameters and algorithms; and
  ○ use of protocols between communicating entities and possibly a third party;
- access control management is responsible for distribution of security attributes and parameters along with access control lists (ACLs) or capabilities lists;
- data integrity management is responsible for:
  ○ interaction with key management;
  ○ negotiation of cryptographic parameters and algorithms; and
  ○ use of protocol between communicating entities;
- authentication management is responsible for distribution of descriptive information, passwords, or keys to entities required to perform authentication;
- traffic padding management is responsible for maintenance of rules used for traffic padding, such as data rates, message characteristics (i.e., length), and variation of these rules based on attributes such as time of day or calendar;
- routing control management is responsible for definition of links or sub-networks considered to be either secured or trusted with respect to particular criteria; and

- notarization management is responsible for distribution of information about notaries and the protocols and interactions between notaries and a notary and other entities.

Although X.800 was developed specifically as a communications security architecture, the underlying concepts have broader applicability representing the first international consensus on the definitions of basic security services (Authentication, Access Control, Data Confidentiality, Data Integrity, and Non-repudiation) along with more general (pervasive) services such as Trusted Functionality, Event Detection, and Security Audit and Recovery.

Following the development of X.800, the need for additional related communications security standards was identified. As a result, work on a number of supporting standards and complementary architectural recommendations was initiated. Some of these recommendations are discussed next.

1.2.4 The Security Frameworks (ITU-T X.810–ITU-T X.816)

The security frameworks were developed to provide comprehensive and consistent descriptions of the security services defined in X.800. They were intended to address all aspects of how the X.800 security services could be applied in the context of a specific security architecture, including possible future security architectures. The frameworks focus on providing protection for systems, objects within systems, and interaction between systems. They do not address the methodology for constructing systems or security mechanisms.

The frameworks address both data elements and sequences of operations (excluding protocol elements) that are used to obtain specific security services. These services may apply to the communicating entities of systems as well as to data exchanged between, and managed by, systems.

1.2.4.1 The Security Framework Overview (X.810).[17] The Security Framework Overview introduces the other frameworks and describes common concepts, including security domains, security authorities, and security policies that are used in all the frameworks. It also describes a generic data format that can be used to convey both authentication and access control information securely.

1.2.4.2 The Authentication Framework (X.811).[18] The Authentication Framework occupies a position at the top of a hierarchy of authentication standards that provide concepts, nomenclature, and a classification for authentication methods. This framework defines the basic concepts of authentication, identifies possible classes of authentication mechanism, defines the services for these classes of mechanism, identifies functional requirements for protocols to support these classes of mechanism, and identifies the general management requirements for authentication.

---

[17] ITU-T Recommendation X.810, Information technology – Open Systems Interconnection – Security frameworks in open systems: OVERVIEW, 11/95

[18] ITU-T Recommendation X.811, Information technology – Open Systems Interconnection – Security frameworks in open systems: AUTHENTICATION Framework, 04/95

1.2.4.3 The Access Control Framework (X.812).[19] The Access Control Framework describes a model that includes all aspects of access control in Open Systems, the relationship to other security functions (such as Authentication and Audit), and the management requirements for Access Control.

1.2.4.4 The Non-repudiation Framework (X.813).[20] The Non-repudiation Framework extends the concepts of non-repudiation security services as described in X.800 and provides a framework for the development of these services. It also identifies possible mechanisms to support these services and general management requirements for non-repudiation.

1.2.4.5 The Confidentiality Framework (X.814).[21] The purpose of the confidentiality service is to protect information from unauthorized disclosure. The Confidentiality Framework addresses the confidentiality of information in retrieval, transfer, and management by defining the basic concepts of confidentiality, defining the possible classes of confidentiality and the facilities required for each class of confidentiality mechanism, identifying the management and supporting services required, and addressing the interaction with other security services and mechanisms.

1.2.4.6 The Integrity Framework (X.815).[22] The Integrity Framework addresses the integrity of data in information retrieval, transfer, and management. This recommendation defines the basic concepts of integrity, identifies possible classes of integrity mechanism and the facilities for each class of mechanism, identifies management required to support each class of mechanism, and addresses the interaction of the integrity mechanism and the supporting services with other security services and mechanisms.

1.2.4.7 The Audit and Alarms Framework (X.816).[23] The Audit and Alarms Framework defines the basic concepts and provides a general model of security audit and alarms, identifies the criteria for a security audit and for raising alarms, identifies possible classes of audit and alarm mechanisms, defines the services for these classes of mechanisms, identifies functional requirements to support these mechanisms, and identifies general management requirements for security audit and alarms.

1.2.4.8 Applicability of the ITU-T Security Frameworks. Unfortunately, these seven documents have received little attention since they were published. What has happened is that only the concepts directly contained within the original X.800 document have received general acceptance. In 2003, the ITU-T published X.805 as an updated

---

[19] ITU-T Recommendation X.812, Information technology – Open Systems Interconnection – Security frameworks in open systems: ACCESS CONTROL Framework, 11/95

[20] ITU-T Recommendation X.813, Information technology – Open Systems Interconnection – Security frameworks in open systems: NON-REPUDIATION Framework, 10/96

[21] ITU-T Recommendation X.814, Information technology – Open Systems Interconnection – Security frameworks in open systems: CONFIDENTIALITY Framework, 11/95

[22] ITU-T Recommendation X.815, Information technology – Open Systems Interconnection – Security frameworks in open systems: INTEGRITY Frameworks, 11/95

[23] ITU-T Recommendation X.816, Information technology – Open Systems Interconnection – Security frameworks in open systems: SECURITY AUDIT and ALARMS Framework, 11/95

security architecture meant to supersede X.800, and most standards developed after this document routinely reference and build upon X.805 rather than X.800 or the X.810 through X.816 framework documents. So we need to examine X.805.

1.2.5 The ITU-T X.805 Approach to Security

ITU-T X.805[24] attempts to define a security architecture for providing end-to-end network security by building on some of the concepts of X.800. The functionality of the basic security services of X.800 (Access Control, Authentication, Data Confidentiality, Data Integrity, and Non-repudiation) matches the functionality of what X.805 refers to as Security Dimensions. However, X.805 proceeds to introduce three new Communications Security, Availability, and Privacy Security Dimensions that are not consistent with X.800. Nor does X.805 build on, use, or even reference the security frameworks (X.810–X.816). X.805 relies on two major concepts: layers and planes.

The three layers are Infrastructure layer, Services layer, and Applications layer. The Infrastructure layer consists of the network transmission facilities as well as individual network elements (NEs). Examples of components that belong to the Infrastructure layer are individual routers, switches and servers, as well as the communication links between them. The Services layer addresses security of network services that are offered to customers. The Application layer addresses requirements of the network-based applications used by the customers.

X.805 also defines three Security planes to represent the three types of protected activities that take place on a network, namely, (i) the Management plane, (ii) the Control plane, and (iii) the End-User plane. These Security planes address specific security needs associated with network management activities, network control or signaling activities, and end-user activities correspondingly. The Management plane is concerned with Operations, Administration, Maintenance, and Provisioning (OAM&P) activities such as provisioning a user or a network, etc. The Control plane is associated with the signaling aspects for setting up (and modifying) the end-to-end communication through the network irrespective of the medium and technology used in the network. The End-User plane addresses security of access and use of the network by customers as well as protecting end-user data flows. However, X.805 cannot:

- be used as the basis of a security assessment as X.805 only talks about generic security objectives, not security requirements; nor does it provide any specific criteria for such an assessment;
- be used for maintaining, or reviewing, a security program over time as a specific security environment changes; also, it does not provide any specific criteria for security program review; and
- assist in the management of security policies and procedures, incident response and recovery plans, and technology architectures as it does not discuss security policy, operational procedures, business continuity, or technology architectures in a detailed manner.

---

[24] ITU-T Recommendation X.805, Security architecture for systems providing end-to-end communications, 10/2003

1.3 NETWORK AND SECURITY MANAGEMENT SYSTEMS

From the 1960s up to almost the end of the 1980s, data network and computer management was considered a local computer administrative activity with virtually no capabilities for remote administration. This was not an unreasonable view considering that commercial/business computer-oriented networking was primarily a computer-to-computer activity with little network-oriented equipment being used beyond modems throughout this period. However, by 1989, there were four commercial products that targeted the management of networks:

- International Business Machine's (IBM) Netview;
- Digital Equipment Corporation's (DEC) Enterprise Management Architecture (EMA);
- American Telephone & Telegraph (**AT&T**) Bell Laboratory's Unified Network Management Architecture (UNMA); and
- Hewlett Packard Corporation's (HP) OpenView.

Netview was primarily IBM System Network Architecture (SNA) network centric with meager management capabilities for non-SNA network technologies. DEC's EMA was primarily a Digital Networking (DECnet) tool along with providing a framework that could incorporate third-party management and interface functionality. AT&T's UNMA never progressed much beyond initial product introductions. HP's OpenView was based on the use of the IETF's Simple Network Management Protocol (SNMP) to make it vendor independent and has evolved into one of the more commercially successful heterogeneous management products available.

1.3.1 Element and Network Management Systems

During the 1990s, with the growth of LAN deployments, two categories of packet network applications evolved: the Element Management System (EMS) and the Network Management System (NMS). EMS products are typically developed by network equipment manufacturers for the remote administration of their own products and usually products with identical capabilities (as shown in Figure 1.9), whereas NMS products are intended

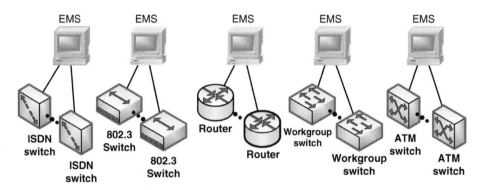

Figure 1.9. EMSs Dedicated to Specific Device Types.

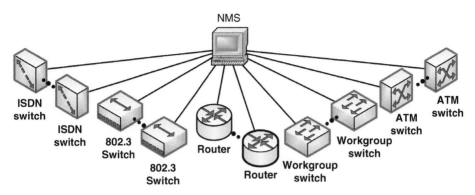

Figure 1.10. NMS Managing Different Types of Devices.

for the administration products from diverse manufacturers (as shown in Figure 1.10). These EMS and NMS applications were initially designed to execute on "minicomputers" and workstations and are now frequently found on personal computer systems.

1.3.2 Operations Support Systems

Within the PSTN world, administration was primarily a local telephone switch activity. Not until the late 1980s did telephone network operating companies begin to deploy intelligent networking equipment such as subscriber line/loop concentrators and remote switching units outside of the telephone central office (CO) where the main telephone switch was located. The major public telephone companies developed a number of mainframe-computer-based applications for managing their deployed telephone switch assets, access circuits, inter-CO links, directories, billing, and expansion planning. Some of these administrative applications included, just to name a few:

- TIRKS, LFACS, SWITCH for Inventory Control;
- SOAC for Service Request and Performance Administration; and
- LMOS and MLT for Trouble Resolution.

(Note that these are defined in Table 1.5.)

These administrative applications were routinely referred to as Operations Support Systems (OSSs) and provided multiple, and sometimes over-lapping, capabilities and complex interfaces, as depicted in Figure 1.11. Although a number of international standards documents have introduced the term Operations System (OS), many people use the term OSS, and this book follows the OSS convention, especially since the term OS is routinely associated with operating systems.

Many of these OSSs were created in the early to mid-1980s and continue as "cornerstone" management, administrative, and control systems.

Telecommunications Service Providers (SPs) developed a diverse suite of management systems (OSSs) over the last 25 plus years to support the major PSTN Operation, Administration, Maintenance and Provisioning (OAM&P) activities, where:

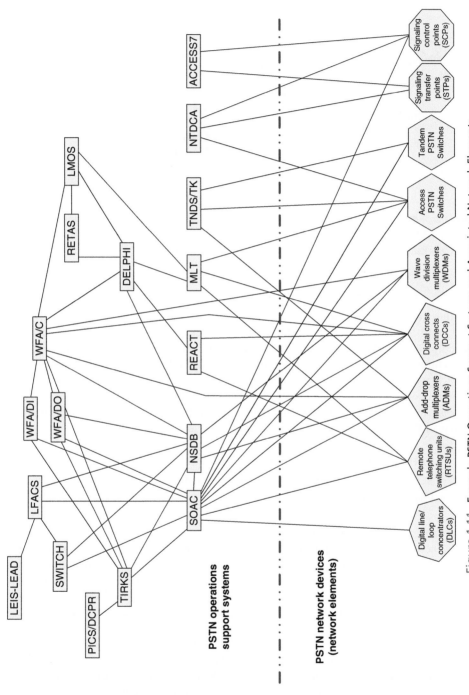

Figure 1.11. Example PSTN Operations Support Systems and Associated Network Elements.

Operations refers to the processes and procedures used to manage and control telecommunications network devices and telecommunications management network (TMN)-related devices;

Administration refers to activities that ensure that the network resources are used efficiently and service-quality objectives met;

Maintenance refers to activities, such as tests, measurements, replacements, adjustments, and repairs, necessary to restore or maintain a network resource in a specified state so that the resource can perform its required functions; and

Provisioning refers to the process of preparing and equipping a network to allow it to provide services to its users.

In a traditional telecommunications network infrastructure, there is no distinction made between telecommunications transport services and "higher-level" application services, and therefore provisioning has spanned configuring systems, providing users with access to data and resources, and refers to all enterprise-level information resource management involved. Most PSTN SPs organize their OSSs as shown in Table 1.4.

As can quickly be seen in Table 1.4, many of these OSSs are involved in a number of different functional activities, such as TIRKS and SWITCH. Table 1.5 provides brief description of the more common OSSs used by PSTN Service Providers (SPs).

1.4 EVOLUTION OF NETWORK AND SECURITY MANAGEMENT CONCEPTS

How have management concepts evolved from those first presented in X.800. It was recognized that management systems need to be deployed in an organized manner. Figure 1.11 illustrates how the companies responsible for the PSTN had developed numerous management systems which frequently included proprietary functions and interfaces to the devices they were responsible for controlling and managing. This recognition was a driving factor for the development of ITU-T M.3010[25] in 1996 and ITU-T M.3400[26] in 1997 (both revised in 2000).

1.4.1 Telecommunications Management Network

ITU-T M.3010 introduced the concept that management of a telecommunications (PSTN) infrastructure is basically a distributed information processing application spread across a set of management OSSs that interact with a vastly larger set of communication devices within the PSTN, usually referred to as Network Elements (NEs) or Managed

[25] ITU-T M.3010, "SERIES M: TMN AND NETWORK MAINTENANCE: INTERNATIONAL TRANSMISSION SYSTEMS, TELEPHONE CIRCUITS, TELEGRAPHY, FACSIMILE AND LEASED CIRCUITS: Telecommunications management network: Principles For A Telecommunications management network", INTERNATIONAL TELECOMMUNICATION UNION TELECOMMUNICATION STANDARDIZATION SECTOR, 02/2000

[26] ITU-T M.3400, "SERIES M: TMN AND NETWORK MAINTENANCE: INTERNATIONAL TRANSMISSION SYSTEMS, TELEPHONE CIRCUITS, TELEGRAPHY, FACSIMILE AND LEASED CIRCUITS: Telecommunications management network: TMN management functions", INTERNATIONAL TELECOMMUNICATION UNION TELECOMMUNICATION STANDARDIZATION SECTOR, 02/2000

TABLE 1.4. Example Well-Known OSSs Used by Many SPs.

Functional Area	Functional Activities	Well-Known Example OSSs
Infrastructure Provisioning Systems	Forecasting	TNDS/TK
	Planning	LEIS–LEAD
	In-place Network Inventory	LEIS–LEAD and TIRKS
	Inventory Management	PICS/DCPR, TIRKS, CMA, CRIS
	Network Request Entry/ Management	CRIS
	Operations Performance Reporting	CRIS and LEIS–LEAD
	Design	CRIS
Service Provisioning Systems	TN/Address Inventory	FACS and SWITCH
	Operations Performance Reporting	Varies by SP
	Assignable Inventory	LFACS, SWITCH, and TIRKS
	Service Fallout & Resolution	Varies by SP
	Service/ Inventory Management	LFACS, SWITCH, and TIRKS
	Design & Assign	LFACS, SWITCH, and TIRKS
	Activation	Varies by SP
	Service Request & Performance Management	SOAC
Service Assurance Systems	Trouble Entry	RETAS
	Trouble Management	WFA/C and LMOS
	Operations Performance Reporting	Varies by SP
	Performance Monitoring & Trend Analysis	NTDCA
	Circuit Inventory	TIRKS, NSDB, LMOS
	Fault Location & Integrated Testing	DELPHI and MLT
	Proactive Fault Discovery	NFM and NMA
	Network Management & Reconfiguration	ACCESS7
	Traffic Data Collection	TNDS/TK, NDS–TIDE, and NTDCA
	Billing Data Collection	Varies by SP
Administration Systems	Billing	BOSS, CRIS, and CABS
	Field Access	Varies by SP
	Workforce Management	WFA/DI and FWA/DO

TABLE 1.5. Example OSS Brief Descriptions.

OSS	Description, Purpose, or Usage
ACCESS7	A distributed OSS that collects and analyzes messages from SS7 links. It is totally switch independent, providing a comprehensive, impartial view of what is happening on the network even during fault conditions.
BOSS	BOSS (Billing and Order Support System) allows access to and contains bill and credit information, equipment information, carrier billing information, customer contact notes, and payment history.
CABS	Carrier Access Billing System (CABS) is a system for billing interexchange carriers and other SPs for network access.
CRIS	Customer Record Information System (CRIS) contains the customer billing database and is used in the customer billing process.
DELPHI	The Delphi system provides connectivity to test systems.
EADAS/ EADAS/ NM	Engineering and Administrative Data Acquisition System (EADAS), used since the late 1970s, is the major data collecting system of TNDS and is used by network administrators to determine QoS and to identify switching problems. It also makes additional real-time information available to these administrators by providing traffic data history that covers up to 48 hours. EADAS/NM uses data directly from EADAS as well as receiving data from switching systems which do not interface with EADAS. It is used to analyze problems in near real time to determine their location and causes.
LEIS–LEAD	The Loop Engineering Information System (LEIS) is a family of applications that is made up of multiple modules that contain multiple databases. The Loop Engineering Assignment Data (LEAD) module of LEIS contains a separate database for each wire center.
LFACS	Loop Facilities Assignment and Control System (LFACS) maintains an inventory of local loop access facilities with automated assignment of customer access circuits and support of maintenance and engineering activities. LFACS also assigns outside loop plant facilities to requests received from SOAC as a result of customer service order activity.
LMOS	The Loop Maintenance Operations System (LMOS) is a trouble ticketing system that plays an essential part in the act of repairing local loops (telephone lines). LMOS is responsible for trouble reports, analysis, and similar related functions. LMOS started as a mainframe application in the 1970s and was one of the first telephone company operations support systems to be ported to the UNIX operating system.
MLT	Mechanized Loop Test (MLT) is a system that tests subscriber access lines (local loops), which is comprised of the wires and equipment used to provide dial tone/calling service to end users. MLT hardware is located in a repair service center, and test trunks connect MLT hardware to the telephone exchanges or wire centers, which in turn connect with subscriber loops.
NFM	Network force management (NFM) is a system that provides awareness screens that depict alarm condition descriptions for switch and facility alarms.
NMA	Network Monitoring and Analysis (NMA) is a system for monitoring all network facilities for abnormalities and provides transport of trouble alarm information.
NSDB	Network and service database (NSDB) is a repository for line record, customer, circuit, and call service data.

(*continued*)

TABLE 1.5. (cont'd)

OSS	Description, Purpose, or Usage
NTDCA	Network Traffic Data Collection & Analysis (NTDCA) is used to warehouse data collected by TDMS; NTDCA allows for long-term data storage of trunk capacity and overflow information.
PICS/DCPR	PICS is the mechanized operations system developed for the efficient management of large amounts of equipment inventories. It assists with both inventory and materials management and the introduction of new types of equipment while phasing out older types and sets utilization goals that balance service objectives and carrying charges on spare equipment. PICS/DCPR (PICS with Detailed Continuing Property Records) administers all types of PSTN Central Office (CO) equipment. The DCPR portion of PICS/DCPR serves as a detailed investment database supporting accounting records for all types of CO plug-in and "hardwired" equipment.
PREMIS	Premises Information System (PREMIS) is a geographical database that allows SP employees to perform customer lookups by telephone number (CNA), check for multiple subscribers at an address (upstairs/downstairs), and view account status. It has three mechanized databases: address data, a credit file, and a list of available telephone numbers.
RETAS	The Repair Trouble Administration System (RETAS) is a front-end tool that allows Competitive Local Exchange Carriers to interface with an SP's OSS maintenance and repair systems.
SOAC	Service Order Analysis and Control (SOAC) is an OSS for coordinating the provisioning order management process. SOAC schedules and manages tasks performed by provisioning systems such as facility assignment, circuit design, and network activation.
SWITCH	Switch/Frame Operations Management System (SWITCH) maintains the inventory of equipment inside PSTN switching COs.
TIRKS	Trunks Integrated Record Keeping System (TIRKS), used since the late 1970s, provides inventory and order control management of interoffice trunk circuits that interconnect telephone switches, supporting circuits from Plain Ordinary Telephone Service (POTS) and 150 baud modems up through T1, DS3, SONET, and DWDM. TIRKS consists of five major interacting component systems: Circuit Order Control system (COC), Equipment system (E1), Facility system (F1), Circuit system (C1), and Facility and Equipment Planning System (FEPS).
TNDS	TNDS is a set of coordinated systems which support a broad range of activities that depend on accurate traffic data. TNDS supports operations centers responsible for administration of the trunking network, network data collection, daily surveillance of the load on the switching network, the utilization of equipment by the switching network, and the design of local and CO switching equipment to meet future service needs.
WFA/C	Workforce Administration/Control (WFA/C) stores trouble tickets by circuit number and includes location, trouble history, and connections to other circuit details.
WFA/DI/DO	Workforce Administration/Dispatch In (WFA/DI) and Workforce Administration/Dispatch Out (WFA/DO) are OSSs supporting COs and field activities that include coordinating, assigning, dispatching, and tracking work requests.

Network Elements (MNEs). ITU-T M.3400 focuses on expanding the initial FCAPS management concept areas introduced in ITU-T X.700.

1.4.1.1 Basic TMN Concepts. M.3010 describes a Telecommunication Management Network (TMN) architecture to support the management needs of PSTN SPs in the planning, provisioning (configuring), installation, maintenance, operation, and administration of telecommunication networks and the services delivered over these networks. The basic concept of the TMN is to provide an organized approach for the interconnection between various types of OSSs and telecommunications equipment (devices) using an architecture with standardized interfaces defining protocols and messages. In defining the concept of the TMN, M.3010 was written to accommodate not just a complex infrastructure of OSSs, networks, and devices already deployed but also provide access to, and display of, management information contained within the TMN to service customers/users. Figure 1.12 shows the general relationship between a TMN and a telecommunications network which it manages. Most PSTN SPs implement their TMNs as a physically separate set of network links that interface telecommunications network devices at multiple points for information transfer and operational control. The parallel and separate TMN implementation is common to enhance TMN availability and ensure that the TMN is operational even when managed telecommunications network links and devices are experiencing congestion, overload, or even failures.

The goal of the TMN concept is to provide a framework for telecommunications management. By introducing the concept of generic network models for management, it is possible to perform general management of diverse equipment, networks, and services using generic information models and standard interfaces. A key component of the TMN concept is the ability to support a wide variety of management areas, such as infrastructure planning, equipment installation, ongoing operations and administration of devices and services, device maintenance, and service provisioning of telecommunications networks and services. The TMN functional architecture presented in ITU-T M.3010 provided a decomposition of management functionality into the following categories:

- Operations Systems functions;
- Management Application functions;
- Network Element to Management Application interaction functions;
- Transformation functions; and
- Workstation to Management Application interaction functions.

Another aspect of the TMN is the identification of reference points which delineate external views of management functionality. These TMN reference points can represent the interactions between a particular pair of management functions. The reference point concept is considered important as it represents the aggregate of all of the abilities that a particular management function seeks from another particular management function.

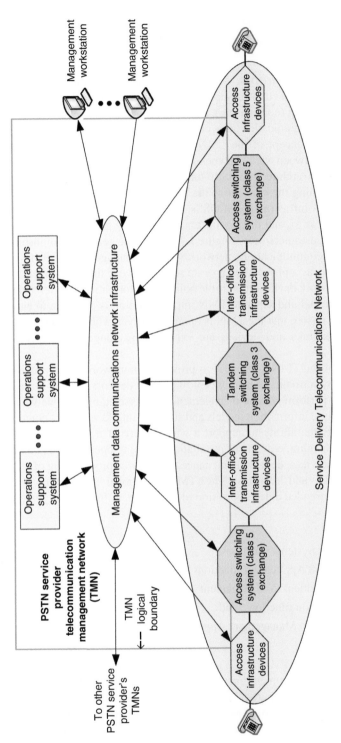

Figure 1.12. Major TMN Components.

It also represents the aggregate of all of the operations and/or notifications (such as alarms and alerts) that a management function can provide to a requesting management function. These TMN-specified reference points usually correspond to a physical interface if and only if the management functions are implemented in different devices.

The TMN concept deals with the complexity of telecommunications management, by partitioning management functionality into logical layers which organizes management functions into groups and describes the relationship between layers. A logical layer reflects particular aspects of management arranged by the following different levels of abstraction:

- business management;
- service management;
- network management;
- element management; and
- network elements.

Element Management Layer (EML) systems (EMSs) manage NEs on an individual or group basis. Within the EML, there may be one or more EMSs that are individually responsible for some subset of NEs.

According to the TMN, an EMS within the EML has the following three principal roles:

1. Control and coordination of a subset of NEs on an individual NE basis. In this role, an EMS is intended to support interaction between network management layer (NML) systems and NE layer devices by processing management information being exchanged between NML systems and individual NEs. EMSs are expected to provide full access to NE functionality.
2. An EMS may also control and coordinate a subset of NEs on a collective basis.
3. An EMS should maintain statistical, log, and other data about NEs within its scope of control.

The majority of commercially available EMS products provide extensive management capabilities over NEs but frequently are not designed to be subservient to NML systems beyond reporting log information, alarm notifications, and event forwarding to these NML systems. The primary management functionality of these EMSs focus on NE Fault, Configuration, and Performance management via the SNMP's[27] "set", "get", and "trap" commands. Rarely is security management available beyond what can be provided by Fault reporting and Configuration change. Another problem with today's EMS products is that these products are rarely designed to manage a heterogeneous collection of NEs. Routinely, a manufacturer will develop and sell an EMS that is only capable of working with that manufacturer's products and even limited to a subset of these products.

[27] RFC 1157, "A Simple Network Management Protocol (SNMP)," Internet Engineering Task Force, May 1990; RFC 1446, "Security Protocols for version 2 of the Simple Network Management Protocol (SNMPv2)," Internet Engineering Task Force, April 1993; RFC 3414, "User-based Security Model (USM) for version 3 of the Simple Network Management Protocol (SNMPv3)," Internet Engineering Task Force, December 2002.

Network Management Layer (**NML**) systems (NMSs) have the responsibility for the management of a variety of network devices. The TMN identifies an NMS as addressing the management of devices and EMSs over a wide geographical area. Complete visibility of the whole network is expected, and an NMS is supposed to provide a technology-independent view to service management layer (SML) systems. According to the TMN, an NMS has the following five principal roles:

1. Control and coordination of the network view of all NEs within the NMS's scope or domain;
2. Provision, cessation, or modification of network capabilities for the support of services to customers;
3. Maintenance of network capabilities;
4. Maintenance of statistical, log, and other data about the network and interaction with service manager layer systems on performance, usage, availability, etc.; and
5. May manage interaction between and connectivity with other NMSs.

TMN NMSs are intended to manage a network by coordinating activity across all network devices to support the "network" demands made by SML systems. These NMSs are expected to know what network resources are available, how these resources are interrelated, and how these resources can be controlled. Systems within this layer are identified as responsible for the performance of the network and control available network resources to provide necessary accessibility and quality of service (QoS).

Unfortunately, commercially available NMS products provide extensive management capabilities over diverse NEs but are rarely designed to be subservient to SML systems; nor do they actually understand the relationship between network resources and service establishment, access, or service quality. As with EMSs, available NMSs primarily focus on NE Fault, Configuration, and Performance management via SNMP's "set", "get", and "trap" commands. Also, these NMSs have minimum specific security management capabilities beyond what can be provided by Fault reporting and Configuration change capabilities, especially as security-related parameters should be identified and managed as specifically security related. The primary difference between typical NMS products and typical EMS products is that NMS products are usually designed to manage a heterogeneous collection of NEs whereas the EMS products are not.

As defined within the TMN architecture, Service Management Layer (**SML**) systems focus on the administrative aspects of services that are being provided to customers. Some of the main functions provided by systems within this layer are service order handling, complaint handling, and invoicing/billing. These SML systems are expected to:

1. provide support for customer service personnel for all service transactions including service ordering, provisioning, modification and termination of services, account administration, QoS, and fault reporting, etc.;

2. interface with SML systems of other SPs; and
3. maintain service-oriented statistical data for ensuring QoS/performance commitments are met.

Historically, these SML systems were directly developed by PSTN SPs in-house with no regard for security issues beyond basic administrative and user login authentication. Throughout much of the twentieth century, very few PSTN-offered services included any form of security capabilities resulting; therefore, security management capabilities for service-related security have been basically non-existent.

The TMN **Business Management Layer (BML)** is described as having responsibility for the total enterprise with BML systems accessing information and functionality in other management layer systems. Systems in this layer are expected to carry out "goal setting tasks rather than goal achievement but can become the focal point for action in cases where executive action is called for."[28]

M.3010 goes on to say that the main functions of the BML systems are for optimizing investment and use of new SP resources and support:

1. the decision-making process for the optimal investment and use of new telecommunications resources;
2. the management of OA&M-related budget;
3. the supply and demand of OA&M-related manpower; and
4. aggregation of data about the total enterprise.

Table 1.6 provides a snapshot of the functionality within each TMN layer and other details.

EML and NML management systems rarely provide management of functionality above the transport protocol (layer 4), or Transport Stratum. SML management systems either rely on EML/NML systems for direct administration of elements or some may subsume EML and NML capabilities internally. Many SP SML systems fall into the latter type and are referred to as OSSs. The TMN approach to organizing management systems and functionality served well for many years, yet has led to a series of separate TMNs, with each TMN supporting a specific business/service activity. These separate TMNs evolved over time with little concern for cross-resource management among all products/services and as such are colloquially called "siloed" systems as they are totally stand-alone as a grain silo on a farm, as represented in Figure 1.13.

So long as business/organizations focused only on a single type of service, having siloed management was not an issue. With convergence of services onto common communications infrastructures (CCIs) and consolidation of businesses offering integrated services, siloed management now represents an operational inefficiency, likely source of coordination problems, security vulnerabilities, and even loss of actual or potential revenue. This reality has led to further study of the necessary management functions, and their organization, for economical, secure, and efficient management of multiple services. The TeleManagement Forum (TMF) has been working on the "Next Generation

[28] Section 9.5.1.4 of ITU-T M.3010.

TABLE 1.6. **TMN Management Layers.**

TMN Layers	Role/Purpose
BML systems	Provide high-level planning, budgeting, goal setting, decision support, and business level agreements. These are proprietary in design and frequently "home-grown," geographically redundant, typically deployed following a client–server approach, and usually utilize CORBA, DCE, XML, .NET, and SNMP protocols.
SML systems	Rely on information presented by NML systems to manage contracted for services of existing and potential customers. Provides basic point of contact support with customers for provisioning, accounts, QoS, and fault/performance management. SML systems are also a key point for SP interaction with other PSTN administrative domains. These systems may be quasi standards based, geographically redundant, and using a distributed deployment design, and usually utilize CORBA, TL1,[29] DCE, XML, .NET, and SNMP protocols.
NML systems	Responsible for management of heterogeneous collections of NEs frequently co-located or integrated into a service or organization security domain. These are usually standards based, geographically distributed, typically designed to use a client–server architecture, and usually utilize SNMP, TMF-814,[30] and sometimes XML and telnet protocols.
EML systems	Responsible for management of homogeneous collections of NEs. These are usually vendor specific, geographically distributed, typically designed to use a client–server architecture, and usually utilize SNMP and sometimes TL1, XML, and telnet protocols.
NEL systems	Devices that provide transport, application, and infrastructure services within a network infrastructure.

Operations Systems and Software" (NGOSS) program to address these very issues. Before considering NGOSS components, we will first review how the TMN deals with the management of security.

1.4.1.2 TMN Security Management Concepts.
The management of security outlined in ITU-T X.800 is further developed in ITU-T M.3400 by mapping the services defined in ITU-T X.800 for authentication, access control, data confidentiality, data integrity, and non-repudiation using the perspective of a set of functional capabilities organized around:

- Prevention;
- Detection;
- Containment and recovery; and
- Security administration.

ITU-T M.3400 notes that security of management is necessary for all TMN management functional areas and transactions that occur during communications between

---

[29]TL1 messages are used to accomplish specific functions between an OSS and an NE. TL1 is defined in Telcordia Technologies (formerly Bellcore) Generic Requirements document GR-831-CORE.

[30] TMF 814, "Multi-Technology Network Management Solution Set, NML-EML Interface Version 2.0", TeleManagement Forum, 2001.

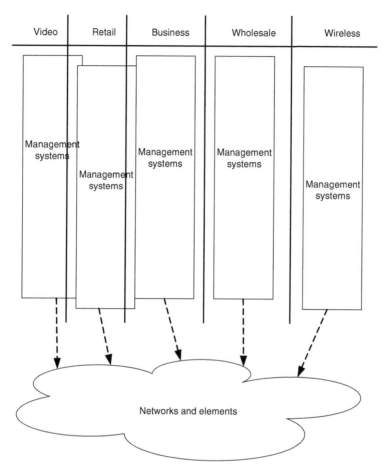

Figure 1.13. Siloed Management System Structuring.

systems, between customers and systems, and between internal users and systems. The set of pervasive security mechanisms discussed in ITU-T X.800 (i.e., event detection, security audit trail management, and security recovery) are also considered applicable to any network communication activities so that security event detection and reporting are communicated to higher security management systems of any activity that may be a security violation (e.g., unauthorized user or access attempt, logical or physical tampering with equipment, network traffic indicative of malicious behavior or actions, etc.).

1.4.1.2.1 TMN PREVENTION SECURITY CONCEPTS. The Prevention functions are organized into sets of capabilities identified as those needed to prevent intrusions. The TMN Prevention concepts span the following activities:

- Legal review of corporate documents and service offerings;
- Physical access controls to enterprise facilities and areas within these facilities;

- Human access monitoring and inspection of packages/containers entering/leaving enterprise facilities;
- Personnel controls focusing on checking the trustworthiness of employees and other personnel that access enterprise facilities for business purposes; and
- Customer verification of the ability to pay for services ordered/purchased as well as determining that a customer is legally permitted access to requested services or products.

These capabilities are primarily procedural in nature, rather than technology focused. However, these are not the only Prevention capabilities an enterprise would or should deploy.

Prevention is the act of limiting the occurrence of unauthorized or potentially harmful behavior or activities. Thusly, there are a large number of authentication and authorization access control capabilities that should be deployed such as:

- IEEE 802.1x for Peer-entity or Data-origin authentication and authorization for link layer usage;
- IPsec (especially ESP-nul) for Peer-entity and Data-origin authentication, authorization, and optional confidentiality of both network and host packet flows;
- transport layer security (i.e., TLS, SSL, DTLS, SSH) for Peer-entity and/or Data-origin authentication, authorization, and confidentiality of application communications flows; and
- device operating system and application hardening for user/administrator authentication, authorization, and access control.

From an access control perspective, an enterprise should be deploying mechanisms such as firewalls, Intrusion Prevention Systems, and Session Border Controls. Anti-malware (viruses, worms, keyboard scanners, root-kits, Trojans, etc.) scanners should be included within the Prevention area as these products are designed to remove, not just identify the presence of, malware. Unfortunately, the ITU-TM series recommendations do not provide any procedural and technical details of these prevention security mechanisms that necessitate some level of security administration.

1.4.1.2.2 TMN DETECTION SECURITY CONCEPTS. The TMN Detection functions are organized into sets of capabilities identified as those needed to detect intrusions. The TMN procedurally oriented Detection capabilities are:

- revenue pattern analysis for significant shifts in revenue that might indicate fraud or theft of service;
- determination of need for, including monitoring and analysis of, security alarm systems and alarms indicating power or HVAC (heating, ventilation, and air conditioning) failures in addition to the occurrence of fire, flood, and open doors or cabinets/chassis; and
- investigation of fraud or theft of service by customer and internal users based on usage patterns.

These procedural Detection capabilities will certainly require information processing resources; yet it is primarily personnel who are responsible to ensure the pre-requisite analyses, determinations, and investigations occur consistent with approved enterprise security policy and procedures within the context of the enterprise's overall security governance program.

The TMN service-oriented Detection capabilities are:

- Customer access to SP security alarm information that indicates security attacks on a customer's network infrastructure, and
- Collection and analysis of customer usage data profiles to identify anomalies and irregularities indicative of a security breach or theft of service.

SPs may, or may not, consider informing their customers that these customers are under some form of attack; however, this capability will be likely based on SP service design and market considerations, and not a general offering by all SPs. It is more likely that an SP will track customer service usage as one way to perhaps identify a security breach or theft of service. The use of this capability will be affected by the budget limitations the SP places on allocation of personnel and Information Technology (IT) resources to such data collection and analysis along with any decided upon follow-up actions.

The TMN SP infrastructure-oriented Detection capabilities are:

- data collection and analysis of network traffic and activity patterns to identify anomalies, abnormalities, or actual activity indicative of a security breach or attack;
- capabilities to receive, store, correlate, and analyze audit trail log information from:
  - network intrusion detection systems (IDS);
  - network traffic and activity pattern analysis systems (i.e., NetFlow[31]);
  - NE IDS (host IDS);
  - NE security alarm management systems (SEMs[32]); and
  - NE log and audit trail management systems (such as syslog[33]) for the purposes of identification, reporting, and recording of anomalies or abnormalities;

[31] Although initially implemented by Cisco, the NetFlow protocol, described in RFC 3954 has been superseded by Internet Protocol Flow Information eXport (IPFIX), described in RFC 5101 and RFC 5102, with network product vendors adding IPFIX support to their devices. With IPFIX, a router will output a flow record when it determines that a unique flow of packets has ended.

[32] A security event manager (SEM) is an application used to centralize the storage and interpretation of events generated by other networked devices. The SEM concept is about 10 years old and still evolving. Some of these products are called security information managers (SIMs) or security information and event managers (SIEMs).

[33] Syslog is a standard (RFC 5424) for logging program logging message by separating the system that generates messages from the system that stores them and the software that reports and analyzes them. Syslog can be used for device management and security auditing and is supported by a wide variety of devices and receivers across multiple platforms. Because of this, syslog can be used to integrate log data from many different types of systems into a central repository.

- capabilities to receive, store, correlate, and analyze security alarms generated by NML, EML, and NE systems from:
  - network IDS;
  - network traffic and activity pattern analysis systems;
  - NE IDS;
  - NE SEMs; and
  - NE log and audit trail management systems;
- reporting and display of security alarm information that indicate the occurrence of network security violations indicative of a security breach or attack.

The deployment of any of the aforementioned detection mechanisms will be affected by the budget constraints the SP has on the allocation of personnel and IT resources to such data collection and analysis along with any decided upon follow-up actions. All deployed procedural and technical detection security mechanisms necessitate some level of security administration that is not covered by the TMN recommendations.

1.4.1.2.3 TMN CONTAINMENT AND RECOVERY SECURITY CONCEPTS. The TMN discussed Containment and Recovery functions are organized into sets of capabilities identified as those needed to deny access to an intruder, to repair damage done by an intruder, and to recover losses. The TMN information-protection-oriented Containment and Recovery capabilities are:

- access and management mechanisms to protect storage of business, customer, network configuration, and NE configuration data;
- maintaining backup copies of data; and
- monitoring for data corruption.

Protection of stored information on customers, the enterprise, and enterprise infrastructure components should not be considered part of Containment and Recovery but rather as a Prevention capability. The protection mechanisms would include use of access control lists (ACLs), assignment of access rights to customers, and internal users commensurate with each subject's authorized "need to know" rights/privileges. Maintaining backup copies of information necessary for enterprise continued operation is just sound business continuity policy and should not be described as primarily a security capability. However, monitoring for data integrity is a valid security concern and is properly a Prevention function, especially when provided by the use of mechanisms such as Tripwire.[34]

The TMN containment-oriented Containment and Recovery capabilities are:

- isolation of equipment or data so that corruption is not propagated;
- remove/revoke of customer or internal user access privileges; and

---

[34] Tripwire is a software security and data integrity tool useful for monitoring and alerting on specific file change(s) within systems. An available open-source version detects changes to file system objects serving purposes, such as integrity assurance, change management, and policy compliance. Other open-source projects exist that provide similar functionality. Examples include OSSEC, AIDE, and Samhain.

- severance of either internal user or customer connections to limit data and system corruption as the result of a detected security violation.

These are quite properly containment-type capabilities. However, action to effect device isolation, access privilege revocation, or connection termination routinely requires human interaction via generalized configuration management system functions. Some industry designers consider it desirable to have security management software be able to automatically perform isolation, revocation, and termination actions; yet, there are others who believe that a human needs to be part of the decision-making "loop" and argue for automation of these capabilities with humans making the decision to initiate the corresponding action.

The TMN identifies a number of forensic- and legal-involvement-oriented Containment and Recovery capabilities including:

- cooperation with law enforcement agencies against a perpetrator of an illegal action;
- forensic investigation of a detected, or suspected, security violation;
- assistance to law enforcement agencies in apprehending an intruder including identification of an intruder via actions such as analyzing security logs, monitoring targets of intrusion, or feeding misinformation to a suspected intruder; and
- ability to initiate litigation against a perpetrator of an illegal action.

Cooperation with law enforcement agencies and the ability to litigate perpetrators are actually security governance capabilities, and not security management capabilities. The performance of forensic investigations necessitates an enterprise possess personnel qualified and trained in forensic investigation procedures and procedurally required to act as "first responders" whenever an actual, or suspected, security breach occurs or some type of abnormal event occurs.

The TMN recovery-oriented Containment and Recovery capabilities are:

- restoration of backed up data upon request;
- backup and restoration of stored data in support of intrusion recovery;
- service intrusion recovery that supports requests to access backup files in order to restore service after detection of a security violation;
- network intrusion recovery that supports requests for restoration of the network configuration after detection of a security violation; and
- NE intrusion recovery that provides access to backup files in order to restore NE or element management information after detection of a security violation.

The secure and routine creation of data backup sets (regardless of contents) should be a standardized part of general enterprise operations, and not just a part of security management. The creation, transportation (physical or electronic), storage, and restoration of data backup sets should always be subject to appropriate authentication, authorization, integrity, and confidentiality mechanisms and operational procedures.

The TMN authentication-and–authorization-revocation-oriented Containment and Recovery capabilities are identified as the ability to:

- revoke network device public key, customer public key, and employee public key certificates used for NE or service access that are known as, or suspected of being, invalid due to a security violation resulting in suspected private key theft, or the private key is no longer available due to it being modified or lost while stored in an encrypted form;
- revoke network device public key, customer public key, and employee public key certificates used for NE or service access due to administrative procedures (e.g., a system has been replaced, a customer has moved elsewhere, an EMS or NE has been replaced, etc.);
- revoke network device, customer, and employee access control certificates used for NE or service access that are known as, or suspected of being, invalid due to a security violation;
- revoke network device, customer, and employee access control certificates used for NE or service access due to administrative procedures (e.g., a system has been replaced, a customer has moved elsewhere, an EMS or NE has been replaced, etc.); and
- revoke or replace shared secret keys known as, or suspected of being, invalid due to security violation (e.g., theft of secret keys, actual or suspected breach, or KDC system, etc.).

Whenever asymmetric encryption public keys are used within an enterprise, these public keys should only be stored, distributed, and used when embedded within ITU-T X.509 version 3 digital certificates issued by authenticated and authorized Digital Certificate Authorities that are part of a formally recognized Public Key Infrastructure (PKI) (see Appendix B). The certificate revocation capabilities contained within a PKI (whether use of CRLs[35] or OCSP[36]) should be the approach relied upon by enterprises regardless of the cause being: private key theft, private key loss, or revocation due to administrative decisions. These PKI revocation mechanisms can support both public-key-containing digital certificates as well as authorization (access control) digital certificates. The use of shared secret keys for symmetric encryption or secret-key-based message authentication (such as with HMAC[37] algorithms) should only be accomplished via a standardized KDC[38] (such as the Kerberos system), via secure dynamic key

[35] CRL stands for Certificate Revocation List which is a mechanism that allows for verifying whether a Certificate Authority (CA)-issued X.509 digital certificate has been revoked prior to its stated "Not After" date due to the corresponding private key either no longer available for use has actually been stolen or cannot be used for administrative reasons.

[36] OCSP represents the Online Certificate Status Protocol which provides the capability for a requester to make a query whether a specified X.509 digital certificate has been revoked.

[37] HMAC stands for Hash-Based Message Authentication Code. U.S. Federal Information Processing (FIPS) Publication 198 generalizes and standardizes the use of HMACs such as HMAC-SHA-1 and HMAC-MD5 which are used within the IPsec and TLS protocols.

[38] KDC stands for Key Distribution Center which is a facility responsible for the generation, storage, distribution, and revocation/destruction of shared symmetric secret encryption keys.

agreement algorithms such as the Internet Key Exchange and Internet Security Association Key Management Protocol within IPsec, or a secure Diffie–Hellman key negotiation within the context of TLS, SSL, DTLS, SSH protocols, or XML key management.

1.4.1.2.4 TMN SECURITY ADMINISTRATION CONCEPTS. The Security Administration function sets are those needed for planning and administering security policy and managing security-related information.

The planning- and analysis-oriented Administration capabilities include:

- Security policy that provides access to company guidelines for establishing and maintaining a secure environment for personnel, hardware, and software;
- Disaster recovery planning that supports access to methods and procedures to be used in restoring the network in the event of a security breach and the resulting corruption of data; and
- Assessment of corporate data integrity that provides access to information to determine the need for security, monitoring, and analysis of security measures instituted to protect corporate data from unauthorized access, altering, tampering, and/or corruption.

The procedure-oriented Administration capabilities include:

- Manage guards that provides access to information about the management of physical and mechanized devices used to provide security;
- Audit trial analysis that provides access to methods and procedures for audit trail information to be collected and evaluated to identify possible and/or potential security violations by individuals or groups of users; and
- Security alarm analysis that provides access to guidelines for monitoring, evaluating, and correlating security alarms.

The authentication-oriented Administration capabilities include:

- Administration of external authentication that supports requests for and distributes codes for verification that a customer or user of a peer Administration is who they present themselves to be. It also supports an authentication path involving external authenticators. If a customer has been authenticated by an authentication agent outside the TMN, this function supports the certification, if appropriate, that the external authentication agent is a valid entity for providing that kind of authentication.
- Administration of internal authentication that receives requests for and distributes codes for verification that internal users are who they present themselves to be.

The authorization-oriented Administration capabilities include:

- Administration of external access control that supports requests for and distributes permissions (in accordance with security policy) for control over what a customer or user of a peer Administration can do with any given resource and includes establishing and validating customer permissions and credentials.

- Administration of external certification that supports requests for and distributes permissions (in accordance with security policy) for control over what a customer or user of a peer Administration can do with any given resource and includes establishing and validating customer permissions and credentials.
- Administration of internal access control that supports requests for and distributes permissions (in accordance with security policy) for control over what an internal user can do with any given resource.
- Administration of internal certification that supports requests for and distributes Access Control Certificates that permit internal users access to previously agreed upon sets of capabilities.

The encryption-key-oriented Administration capabilities include:

- Administration of external encryption and keys that supports requests for and distributes encryption keys to be used in communications between an external customer or user of a peer Administration and a TMN (such keys may be used for authentication, integrity, confidentiality, and non-repudiation).
- Administration of internal encryption and keys that supports requests for and distributes encryption keys to be used in communications between internal users (such keys may be used for authentication, integrity, and confidentiality). It provides information on which encryption algorithms are to be used and in which mode.
- Administration of keys for NEs that supports requests for the generation of encryption keys to be used in communications between NEs or between an NE and an EMS or other building block. It also supports the distribution of these keys to NEs and communicating entities. Such keys may be used for authentication, integrity, and confidentiality.
- Administration of keys by an NE that supports requests for the generation of encryption keys within an NE to be used in communications between NEs or between an NE and an EMS or other building block. It also supports the distribution of these keys to communicating entities. Such keys may be used for authentication, integrity, and confidentiality.

The encryption-algorithm-oriented Administration capabilities include:

- Administration of external security protocols that provides for the management of joint implementation agreements with other jurisdictions to assure interoperability of security protocols. For example, it assures that both communicating parties use the same encryption algorithm with the same set of options and parameters. Further, it assures agreement on the kind of security information that shall be provided for authentication. It also provides for the administration of external security protocols.

The event- and alarm-oriented Administration capabilities include:

- Network security alarm management that supports the collection of security alarm information that indicates network security violations. It allows an internal user access to such data.
- NE(s) security alarm management that supports the collection of security alarms detected by lower level functions. It provides access to such information, possibly including information resulting from the correlation of such alarms.

The audit-oriented Administration capabilities include:

- Customer audit trial that allows a customer to establish and configure audit trails to obtain information about service usage. It allows a customer access to usage and security event information related to their portion of the network.
- Customer security alarm management that allows a customer access to security alarm information that indicates security attacks on their portion of the network.
- Testing of audit trail mechanism that supports testing to ascertain that designated events are recorded in a security log.
- Network audit trail management that allows for internal users, generally security personnel, to establish and configure audit trails to obtain information about network usage. This function collects and allows an internal user access to network usage and security event information.
- NE audit trail management that allows internal users, generally security personnel, to establish and configure audit trails to obtain NE usage data and reports on actions involving, for example, identification, authentication, user address space actions, and administrative data.

The TMN security mechanism management capabilities covered in ITU-T M.3400 are predominantly operational in nature and do not provide much guidance for the:

- planning of an information security management program;
- consideration of what organizational security capabilities are required;
- consideration of what technical security capabilities are required; or
- consideration of what operational security capabilities are required.

1.4.2 Next Generation Operations Systems and Software

The TeleManagement Forum (TMF[39]) has been evolving management concepts with its Next Generation Operations Systems and Software (NGOSS) activity that represents an industry-agreed set of frameworks driven and managed by the TMF that provide:

- Business process modeling that provides an industry agreed upon set of process definitions and an organization of these processes that reflect the relationship of these processes to each other;

[39] www.tmforum.org.

- Standard information and data models that provide an industry agreed upon set of information and data definitions furthering a common understanding as to what information business processes rely upon which furthers the interoperability of business process software applications from competing application system vendors;
- Systems architecture definition that provides an industry agreed upon architecture that identifies and describes how business process support applications should interact with each other which furthers the interoperability of business process software applications from competing application system vendors;
- Integration interfaces that provide an industry agreed upon set of definitions for the interfaces between business process support applications which furthers the interoperability of business process software applications from competing application system vendors; and
- Methodology for the application of the aforementioned process models, information and data definitions, systems architecture, and interfaces.

Five key NGOSS principles are:

1. Separation of Business Process from Component Implementation through the use of the enhanced Telecom Operations Map (eTOM) NGOSS business process framework.

2. A loosely coupled distributed Systems approach so that each application is relatively independent of the other applications in the overall system, thereby allowing that one application can be altered without the alteration necessarily affecting others.

3. A shared information model so that data can be shared between the applications where all applications know how other applications interpret the data that is shared via a common model of the shared data. Within the NGOSS, the Shared Information/Data Model (SID) provides this capability.

4. A CCI allowing OSSs to interface with the CCI rather than directly with each other as had been common since the mid-1980s. The CCI allows these applications to work together using the CCI so that each application only requires one interface instead of many application-specific interfaces reducing interface complexity.

5. Contract-defined interfaces that describe how applications interface to the CCI both in terms of the technology employed and the functionality of the application, the data used, the pre- and post-conditions, etc. These NGOSS contract specifications provide a means to document these interfaces and can be seen as extensions of Application Programming Interface specifications.

The NGOSS initiative is based on the following four interrelated frameworks that form the NGOSS program (depicted in Figure 1.14):

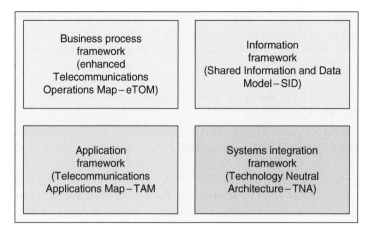

Figure 1.14. NGOSS Initiative Components.

- Business Process Framework—the eTOM[40];
- Enterprise-wide information framework—the SID;
- Systems Integration Framework—the TNA; and
- Telecom Applications Framework—the TAM.

The NGOSS perspective does not contradict the concepts put forth in prior ITU-T recommendations. Rather, ITU-TM.3200 and M.3400 provide a technology- and resource-oriented view of the management domain, which provides value when considering the structure and organization of a management solution. The eTOM framework provides a business-oriented viewpoint that is important in considering the business requirements of the enterprise and ensuring management functions are arranged in a meaningful and useful way reflecting how business is conducted. Where ITU-TM.3400 provides a detailed, functional view on the EMLs, NMLs, and SMLs, the ITU-TM.3050 series of

---

[40] M.3050.0, "eTOM – Introduction," International Telecommunication Union, TELECOMMUNICATION STANDARDIZATION SECTOR, March 2007; M.3050.1, "eTOM – The business process framework," International Telecommunication Union, TELECOMMUNICATION STANDARDIZATION SECTOR, March 2007; M.3050.2, "eTOM – Process decompositions and descriptions," International Telecommunication Union, TELECOMMUNICATION STANDARDIZATION SECTOR, March 2007; M.3050.3, "eTOM – Representative process flows," International Telecommunication Union, TELECOMMUNICATION STANDARDIZATION SECTOR, March 2007; M.3050.4, "eTOM – B2B integration: Using B2B inter-enterprise integration with the eTOM," International Telecommunication Union, TELECOMMUNICATION STANDARDIZATION SECTOR, March 2007; M.3050 Supplement 1, "eTOM – An Interim View of and Interpreter's Guide for eTOM and ITIL Practitioners," International Telecommunication Union, TELECOMMUNICATION STANDARDIZATION SECTOR, February 2007; M.3050 Supplement 2, "eTOM – Public B2B Business Operations Map (BOM)," International Telecommunication Union, TELECOMMUNICATION STANDARDIZATION SECTOR, February 2007; M.3050 Supplement 3, "eTOM to M.3400 mapping," International Telecommunication Union, TELECOMMUNICATION STANDARDIZATION SECTOR, May 2004; M.3050 Supplement 4, "eTOM – An eTOM Primer," International Telecommunication Union, TELECOMMUNICATION STANDARDIZATION SECTOR, February 2007.

recommendations provide the business view for those layers, and details of this relation are described in the M.3050 eTOM to M.3400 mapping supplement. It has been proposed that the eTOM level 1 horizontal functional process groupings correspond to the layering in M.3010 in that:

- the eTOM Service Management & Operations (SM&O) grouping corresponds to the M.3010 SML, and
- the eTOM Resource Management & Operations (RM&O) grouping corresponds to both the M.3010 NML and the EML.

Of the four NGOSS areas (eTOM, SID, TNA, and TAM), only the eTOM has progressed to a significant level of detail worth discussing from a security management perspective.

1.4.3 Enhanced Telecom Operations Map

The eTOM Business Process Framework is the ongoing TMF initiative to deliver a business process model, or framework, for describing the enterprise processes required by an SP, or any enterprise, with complex telecommunications and business processes. eTOM analyzes these enterprise processes to different levels of detail according to their significance and priority for the business. Figure 1.15 depicts the overall structure of the eTOM organization of functions.

A key concept with the eTOM is that there are four primary components to an enterprise:

- General Enterprise Management covering the general management and administrative activities that any enterprise needs to address independent of whatever products or services the enterprise provides. Put another way, any organization, be it an appliance manufacturer, telecommunications SP, hospital, university, or even government agency, has management responsibilities for most, if not all, of these activity sub-areas.
- Strategy, Infrastructure, and Product Management covering the management and administrative activities that focus on the planning, design, development, and supply chain required to product the products or services offered by the enterprise. Again most, if not all, of these activities are applicable to most any organization.
- Operations Management covering the management and administrative activities that focus on the delivery of products and services to customers. Again most, if not all, of these activities are applicable to most any organization.
- Customers that are, or should be, the focus of any enterprise, for without customers an enterprise has no reason to exist. One should remember that customers may come from the general population, could be other enterprises, or even be the employees of a larger organization of which the enterprise is part of (namely, an internal support organization).

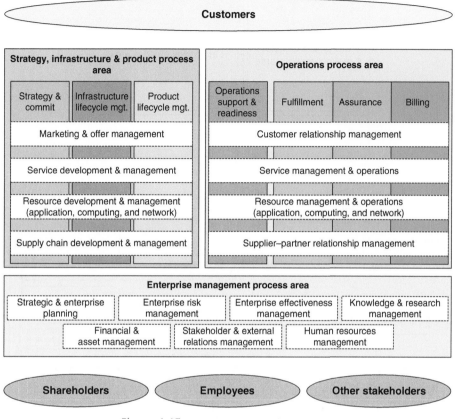

Figure 1.15. eTOM Structure of Functions.

The degree to which these management areas apply to any given enterprise will be primarily affected by the size of the enterprise, the complexity of its offered products or services, and its financial resources.

The eTOM begins at the Enterprise level and defines business processes in a series of groupings to structure business processes and define process descriptions, inputs and outputs, as well as other key elements for each process at each level. These groupings are organized around the three key enterprise areas (shown in Figure 1.16) of:

1. Strategy, Infrastructure, and Product (SIP) Process Area which is concerned with the activities necessary to develop services and resources;

2. Operations Process Area which is concerned with the activities necessary to operate and administer services and resources; and

3. Enterprise Management Process Area which is concerned with the core administrative activities of the enterprise.

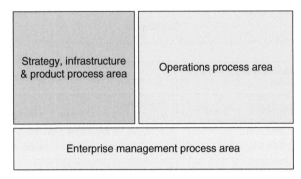

Figure 1.16. eTOM—Key Process Areas.

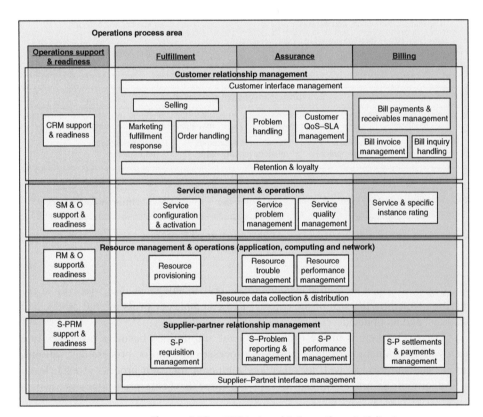

Figure 1.17. eTOM—Level 2 Operations Activity Areas.

The eTOM Framework contains seven vertical and four horizontal process groupings required to support customers and to manage the business. Under the Operations Process Area are the core customer-oriented operations processes of Operations Support and Readiness, Fulfillment, Assurance, and Billing (eTOM 2007 Process Area Identifier 1.1) as depicted in Figure 1.17.

The SIP Process Area (eTOM 2007 Process Area Identifier 1.2), shown in Figure 1.18, contains the Strategy and Commit verticals, as well as two Lifecycle Management verticals. The eTOM also includes horizontal views of functionality across an SP's organization. The horizontal functional process groupings span functional operations processes and other types of business functional processes, for example, Marketing versus Selling, Service Development versus Service Configuration, etc. Among these horizontal functional process groupings, those on the left (that cross the Strategy and Commit, Infrastructure Lifecycle Management, and Product Lifecycle Management vertical process groupings) enable, support, and direct the work in the Operations Process Area.

The Enterprise Management Process Area (eTOM 2007 Process Area Identifier 1.3), shown in Figure 1.19, contains the seven verticals spanning:

- Strategic and Enterprise Planning;
- Financial Asset Management;
- Enterprise Risk Management;
- Stakeholder and External Relations Management;
- Enterprise Effectiveness Management;
- Human Resource Management; and
- Knowledge and Research Management.

The eTOM also includes horizontal views of functionality across an SP's organization.

The mapping of the eTOM (M.3050 version 2007) security-related process areas to M.3400 security management function sets, as provided by M.3050Sup3,[41] is far from complete (see Appendix G for an augmented mapping). The following 14 eTOM clauses are simply mapped to the M.3400 Introduction clause (9) which provides no further specifics:

- Customer Relationship Management (clause 1.1.1);
- SM&O (clause 1.1.2);
- Design Solution (clause 1.1.2.2.1);
- Track & Manage Service Provisioning (clause 1.1.2.2.3);
- Issue Service Orders (clause 1.1.2.2.7);
- Create Service Trouble Report (clause 1.1.2.3.1);
- Diagnose Service Problem (clause 1.1.2.3.2);
- Correct & Resolve Service Problem (clause 1.1.2.3.3);
- Track & Manage Service Problem (clause 1.1.2.3.4);
- Report Service Problem (clause 1.1.2.3.5);
- Close Service Problem Report (clause 1.1.2.3.6);

---

[41] M.3050 Supplement 3, "eTOM to M.3400 mapping," International Telecommunication Union, TELECOMMUNICATION STANDARDIZATION SECTOR, May 2004.

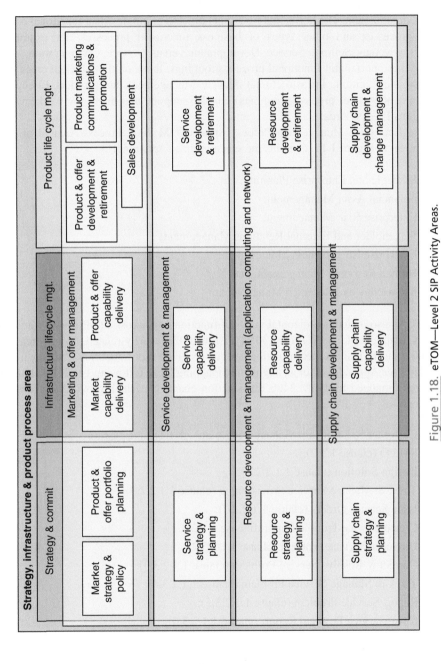

Figure 1.18. eTOM—Level 2 SIP Activity Areas.

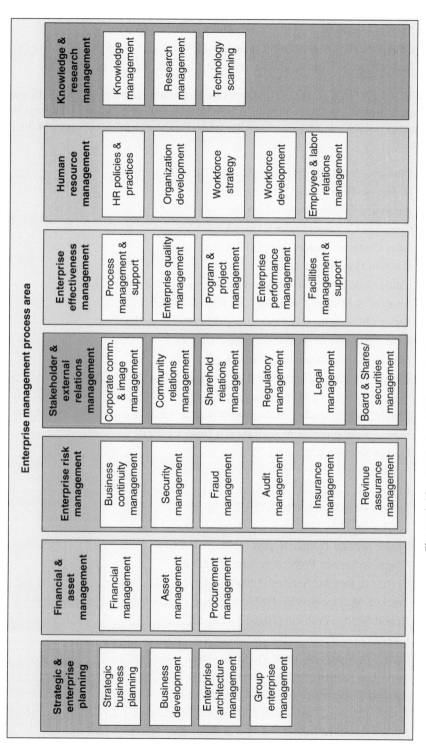

Figure 1.19. eTOM—Level 2 Enterprise Management Activity Areas.

- Survey & Analyze Service Problem (clause 1.1.2.3.7);
- Enterprise Risk Management (clause 1.3.2); and
- Stakeholder & External Relations Management (clause 1.3.6).

The following 39 (out of 212) eTOM Operations Support and Readiness, Fulfillment, Assurance, and Billing Area clauses are mapped to M.3400 Security Management sub-clauses which do not necessarily address the specifics of the M.3050-2 processes:

- Customer Relationship Management (clause 1.1.1);
- Order Handling (clause 1.1.1.5);
- Authorize Credit (clause 1.1.1.5.2);
- Complete Customer Order (clause 1.1.1.5.5);
- Issue Customer Orders (clause 1.1.1.5.6);
- Problem Handling (clause 1.1.1.6);
- Establish & Terminate Customer Relationship (clause 1.1.1.9.1);
- Analyze & Manage Customer Risk (clause 1.1.1.9.3);
- Service Management & Operation (SM&O) (clause 1.1.2);
- SM&O Support & Readiness (clause 1.1.2.1);
- Manage Service Inventory (clause 1.1.2.1.1);
- Enable Service Configuration & Activation (clause 1.1.2.1.2);
- Support Service Problem Management (clause 1.1.2.1.3);
- Enable Service Quality Management (clause 1.1.2.1.4);
- Service Configuration & Activation (clause 1.1.2.2);
- Design Solution (clause 1.1.2.2.1);
- Track & Manage Service Provisioning (clause 1.1.2.2.3);
- Implement, Configure, & Activate Service (clause 1.1.2.2.4);
- Issue Service Orders (clause 1.1.2.2.7);
- Service Problem Management (clause 1.1.2.3);
- Create Service Trouble Report (clause 1.1.2.3.1);
- Diagnose Service Problem (clause 1.1.2.3.2);
- Correct & Resolve Service Problem (clause 1.1.2.3.3);
- Track & Manage Service Problem (clause 1.1.2.3.4);
- Report Service Problem (clause 1.1.2.3.5);
- Close Service Problem Report (clause 1.1.2.3.6);
- Survey & Analyze Service Problem (clause 1.1.2.3.7);
- Service & Specific Instance Rating (clause 1.1.2.5);
- Analyze Usage Records (clause 1.1.2.5.3);
- Enable Resource Performance Management (clause 1.1.3.1.2);
- Enable Resource Data Collection & Processing (clause 1.1.3.1.4);

- Configure & Activate Resource (clause 1.1.3.2.2);
- Collect, Update & Report Resource Configuration Data (clause 1.1.3.2.4);
- Resource Data Collection & Processing (clause 1.1.3.5);
- Collect Resource Data (clause 1.1.3.5.1);
- Report Resource Data (clause 1.1.3.5.3);
- Audit Resource Usage Data (clause 1.1.3.5.4); and
- S/P Interface Management (clause 1.1.4.6).

The following 2 (out of 128) eTOM SIP Process Area clauses are mapped to M.3400 Security Management sub-clauses which do not necessarily address the specific details that the M.3050-2 processes would need:

- Resource Development & Management (clause 1.2.3), and
- Resource Strategy & Planning (clause 1.2.3.1).

The coverage of modern security management in the M.3400 and M.3050 documents is further compounded by M.3400[42] being predominantly operational in nature and does not provide much guidance for many of the processes discussed in eTOM. Given the deficiencies in M.3050 and M.3400, we will develop the details for security management in modern networking environments in Chapter 3. This development will consider not just ISO 27001 and 27002 but will also discuss Information Technology Infrastructure Library (ITIL), a set of concepts and practices for IT services management, and Control Objectives for Information and related Technology (COBIT), a set of best practices (framework) for IT management concepts for security management, and also consider concepts from ITU-T M.3401 and other documents.

1.5 HOW THE NEED FOR INFORMATION SECURITY HAS CHANGED

How has the need for security progressed over the last 10 years? One indication of the change in the security of networked systems can be seen by the statistics[43] developed by the CERT within the Software Engineering Institute at Carnegie Mellon University (shown in Table 1.7 of cataloged vulnerabilities in various systems). Although the table only covers up to October 2008, one can reasonably presume that not only will the number of vulnerabilities in 2008 exceed those cataloged in 2007 but the frequency of vulnerabilities in future years will be similar if not greater than those shown (note that more current data are discussed later). Many security events/attacks leverage system vulnerabilities; therefore, the magnitude of vulnerabilities is related to the frequency of security events.

---

[42] ITU-T M.3400, "SERIES M: TMN AND NETWORK MAINTENANCE: INTERNATIONAL TRANSMISSION SYSTEMS, TELEPHONE CIRCUITS, TELEGRAPHY, FACSIMILE AND LEASED CIRCUITS: Telecommunications Management Network: TMN management functions", INTERNATIONAL TELECOMMUNICATION UNION TELECOMMUNICATION STANDARDIZATION SECTOR, 02/2000

[43] CERT Statistics (n.d.). Retrieved October 11, 2011, from: http://www.cert.org/stats/

TABLE 1.7. CERT Cataloged Vulnerabilities.

Year	Total Vulnerabilities Cataloged	From Direct Reports
Q1–Q3, 2008	6058	310
2007	7236	357
2006	8064	345
2005	5990	213
2004	3780	170
2003	3784	191
2002	4129	343
2001	2437	153
2000	1090	—
1999	417	—
1998	262	—
1997	311	—
1996	345	—
1995	171	—
Total	44,074	

From http://www.cert.org/stats/

Notes: Year—This column represents the calendar year, not fiscal year.

Total Vulnerabilities Cataloged—This column reflects the total number of vulnerabilities that we have cataloged based on reports from public sources and those submitted to us directly. Storing the information in our database allows our analysts to systematically record vulnerability data; helps provide insight into significant preconditions, impacts, and scope; and gives us a way to validate reports and recognize new classes of vulnerabilities.

From Direct Reports—This column reflects the total number of vulnerabilities we have cataloged based on vulnerabilities reported directly to us. We encourage people to report vulnerabilities so we can coordinate with affected vendors to resolve vulnerabilities while minimizing the risk to all stakeholders. To determine an approximate number of vulnerabilities from public sources, subtract the number of direct reports from the total vulnerabilities cataloged. The actual number may differ slightly because, occasionally, vulnerabilities are reported directly to us and disclosed to the public at the same time.

Another source of information regarding the evolving need to security can be found in print/online media reports of security incidents between June 2008 and February 2011. One growing area is the concern over privacy which has mushroomed over the last decade with the rapid deployment of "high-speed" worldwide communications capabilities and now ubiquitous information services available to billions of individuals and organizations. In 2010 alone, there were over 4600 articles published in the popular and trade press (including online and print sources) reporting on privacy issues and privacy-related activities. Societies across the world have adopted many forms of IT and reliance on such technology. Another perspective is provided by William Norton (2011) where he cited the 2010 Security Report from Verizon Business that presented a couple of findings including:

- an increasing number of breaches originated from internal sources—mostly lower-level employees of the breached organizations with deliberate and malicious intentions, and

- confirmation that the largest number of compromised data records still result from outsider attacks.

The 2010 study, conducted in association with the U.S. Secret Service, analyzed 900 breaches and over 900 million compromised records. Norton went on to note that "Verizon found that of all organizations whose financial information had been breached, more than three-quarters had failed to comply with PCI DSS standards."

A small sample of other SP-related security issues reported upon includes the following:

- A blog by Dave Jevans discussed a data breach in April 2011 at the email service provider (ESP) Epsilon which revealed the names and email addresses of tens of millions of customers of banks and e-commerce companies, including CitiBank, Chase, Wal-Mart, U.S. Bank, Capital One, Ameriprise, Target, Kroger, TiVo, HSN, Disney, Walgreens, Best Buy, and many others. Jevans also noted that he has heard from industry sources that this was not the first major break-in to an ESP in 2011.
- Andrei Patrick (2011) discussed a massive distributed denial-of-service (DDoS) attack in 2010 brought down the voice-over-IP (VoIP) call processing supplied by TelePacific Communications and cost the VoIP provider hundreds of thousands of dollars. In the same article, Patrick noted the statements of a number of panelists/presenters at the 2011 Comptel Plus Conference:
  - "The pace of many types of DDoS attacks appears to be increasing," and "to this day, TelePacific is still fighting against denial-of-service attacks, which traffic comes from China and Africa" according to Don Poe, vice president of TelePacific Communications' network engineering.
  - The competitive communications services provider industry trade group Comptel said "it does believe its membership is seeing growth in DDoS attacks."
  - "Many cases of network attacks which the FBI works on do appear to involve a financial motive," according to Stacy Arruda, a supervisory FBI special agent of the Cybercrime division.
  - "Service providers need to remember that they are a target and they need to have a plan in place for this kind of problem," noted Patrick Gray, principal security strategist at Cisco Systems.
  - "DDoS attacks and SYN floods are extraordinarily common nowadays," said Stacy Griggs, senior director at Cbeyond Cloud Services.
- Ellen Messmer (2011), also covering the Comptel Plus Conference, noted that Don Poe stated "TelePacific sees a multitude of daily scans against its network, and low-level attacks can occur about twice a day."
- An article by securitywatch.eweek.com discussed Arbor Networks fifth annual Worldwide Infrastructure Security Report. The report included responses from 132 IP network operators from North America, South America, Europe, Africa, and Asia and reported that:

- The size of DDoS attacks hitting SP infrastructures did not increase as much between third quarter of 2008 and the third quarter of 2009 as it had in previous years.
- The size of the attacks still went up by more than 20%.
- SPs had reported in the past that peak DDoS attack rates were nearly doubling year over year.
- In 2010, the largest sustained attack rate was 49 Gbps (gigabit per second), a 22% increase over last year's peak of a 40 Gbps attack.
- The 2009 largest sustained attack rate represented a 67% increase over the largest attack reported in the 2007 survey.
- The Arbor Networks report went on to say that non-technical factors such as poorly defined operational policies and responsibilities are hurting efforts to strengthen security while "The complexity introduced by the continuing convergence of critical services onto IP networks and multi-tenant cloud-based solutions significantly increases the exposed risk profile of infrastructure and customer-visible services."

- A recent *New York Times* article by Riva Richmond (2011) focused on how digital certificates were fraudulently issued by the Comodo Group, an Internet security company. In the attack at Comodo, it was reported that the hackers were able to infiltrate an Italian computer reseller and use the reseller's access to Comodo's systems to automatically create certificates for websites operated by Google, Yahoo, Microsoft, Skype, and Mozilla. With the certificates, the attacker could then set up servers that appear to work for those sites. Quoting the article, "many security experts say the problems start with the proliferation of organizations permitted to issue certificates. Browser makers like Microsoft, Mozilla, Google and Apple have authorized a large and growing number of entities around the world—both private companies and government bodies—to create them. Many private 'certificate authorities' have, in turn, worked with resellers and deputized other unknown companies to issue certificates in a 'chain of trust' that now involves many hundreds of players, any of which may in fact be a weak link." This type of attack was targeting a foundation technology used by virtually all types of organizations with an Internet presence, not just SPs, and thusly could serve as a "stepping stone" to future attacks specifically targeting SP infrastructures.

- A more direct (i.e., physical) attack in April 2010 was discussed by Bruce Perens (2011) about how unidentified attackers cut eight fiber cables which caused the city of Morgan Hill and parts of three counties to lose 911 service, cellular mobile telephone communications, landline telephone, DSL Internet and private networks, central station fire and burglar alarms, ATMs, credit card terminals, and monitoring of critical utilities. The objective of the perpetrators was not known; yet this act demonstrated how metropolitan communications can be disrupted in the absence of physical monitoring of manhole-located communications links. Also noted in the report was the point that "networks, even those of emergency services providers, are rarely tested for operation while disconnected from the outside world. Many such networks depend on outside services to match host names to network addresses, and thus stop operating the moment they are disconnected from the internet." SP communications cables have been cut by accident over the years; yet this incident was intentional and raises concern over the need for security monitoring access to SP outside plant whether underground or on poles/towers.

The continuing growth of concern over how secure SP infrastructures are has led to the U.S. Federal Communications Commission (FCC) launching an inquiry seeking public comments regarding a proposed Cyber Security Certification Program for communications SPs in 2010. The proposed voluntary certification program would use either private sector auditors or the FCC to conduct security assessments of participating communications SPs' networks, including their compliance with stringent cyber security practices. SPs, whose networks successfully completed this assessment, would then be able to claim their networks complied with these FCC network security requirements. As noted, the aforementioned reports/articles represent just a small sampling of the extended discussion regarding SP security issues; a short amount of time spent searching the "web" can quickly find many more such posts and reports.

1.6 SUMMARY

In this chapter, we started with a review of how information security, and its management, were first defined and specified in a standardized manner. An overview was presented on how networks have been designed and developed over the last 30 years and the different standards used to define security within these networks. As noted, networks have evolved over time and now are significantly more complex than the base standards ever anticipated. Focus was then directed at the management of networks, especially security. Again the baseline standards failed to address management and security in a comprehensive manner, although important concepts were introduced, namely, FCAPS, technology-independent security services, and the need for both specific and pervasive security mechanisms. Then the most current standards for network management were reviewed for their treatment of security management and deficiencies noted.

Chapter 2 presents a review of the technologies used for constructing modern communications networks. Also considered is how NGNs and associated services are being defined and specified. This review is provided to further emphasize the growing need for a holistic approach toward managing security within, not just network infrastructures, but integrating security management into, and within, general organizational management activities and plans. Starting with Chapter 3, we discuss what efforts have been made to standardize an organizational approach for security management with a review of the four main methodologies in use currently.

FURTHER READING AND RESOURCES

FCC (2010) Notice of Inquiry for Public Comments On Proposed Cyber Security Certification Program For Communications Service Providers, Docket No. 10–93. Retrieved October 10, 2011, from http://hraunfoss.fcc.gov/edocs_public/attachmatch/FCC-10-63A1.pdf

Jevans, D. (2011) Privacy and Identity Theft. Retrieved October 10, 2011, from http://blog.ironkey.com/?p=1250

Kaufman, C., Perlman, R., Speciner, M. (2002) *Network Security—Private Communication in a Public World*. 2nd ed. Prentice-Hall

Messmer, E. (2011) Massive DDoS attacks threaten VoIP services, Network World Creator. Retrieved October 10, 2011, from http://www.itworldcanada.com/news/massive-ddos-attacks-threaten-voip-services/144077

Norton, W.K. (2011) 2010 Security Report from Verizon Reveals New Patterns of Cybercrime (n.d.). Baker, Donelson, Bearman, Caldwell and Berkowitz, P.C. Retrieved October 11, 2011, from http://www.bakerdonelson.com/2010-security-report-from-verizon-reveals-new-patterns-of-cybercrime-04–13–2011/

Patrick, A. (2011) Massive DDoS attacks a growing problem to VoIP providers. Retrieved October 10, 2011, from http://www.iptelephony.org/article/massive-ddos-attacks-growing-problem-voip-providers

Perens, B. (2011) A Cyber-Attack on an American City. Retrieved October 11, 2011, from http://perens.com/works/articles/MorganHill/

Richmond, R. (2011) Attack on Comodo Sheds Light on Internet Security Holes—NYTimes.com. Retrieved October 11, 2011, from http://www.nytimes.com/2011/04/07/technology/07hack.html

securitywatch.eweek.com (2010) Service Providers Face Security Challenges. Retrieved October 11, 2011, from http://securitywatch.eweek.com/ddos/service_providers_face_security_challenges.html

2

OVERVIEW OF CURRENT AND FUTURE NETWORKS

To understand the complexity of managing security in modern networks, some history needs to be covered as to how networks evolved from an architectural and protocol perspective. In this chapter, we consider these points along with:

- reviewing common network designs and organizations;
- discussing the protocols routinely used in modern networks; and
- exploring the structure and capabilities of next-generation networks (NGNs).

Throughout the discussions, we will also focus on the security mechanisms routinely deployed, and how security management of these security mechanisms is necessary.

2.1 A LITTLE NETWORK HISTORY

The following discussion is not intended to be comprehensive; it focuses on some of the more significant points in networking history. Over the last 50 years, computer communications (networking) design has evolved significantly since its introduction.

Security Management of Next Generation Telecommunications Networks and Services,
First Edition. Stuart Jacobs.
© 2014 The Institute of Electrical and Electronics Engineers, Inc. Published 2014 by John Wiley & Sons, Inc.

2.1.1 Point-to-Point Data Communications

In the early 1960s, computers (what were called "mainframes") started to be marketed that supported the attachment of "dumb" terminal devices using synchronous or asynchronous connections to small ancillary computing devices called data communications front-end processors. These terminals contained a display, keyboard, and logic, allowing them to communicate with the data communications front-end processors using manufacturer proprietary protocols. In the mid- to late 1960s, a new form of computer (called minicomputers) came into the market that migrated communications processing and interfaces into the primary minicomputer cabinets, thereby doing away with the need for a separate data communications front-end processor. Data communications front-end processors and minicomputers were interconnected via leased circuits (lines) provided by telephone companies (frequently at a bit rate of 56 Kbps) using manufacturer proprietary protocols. The primary manufacturer proprietary protocols were defined by manufacturer-designed network architectures, such as IBM's Systems Network Architecture, Burroughs network architecture, and Digital Equipment Corporation's DECnet. Figure 2.1 depicts examples of these common forms of terminal to computer and intercomputer interconnections. Remotely located terminals could be connected via modems over Public Switched Telephone Network (PSTN) circuits to either the data communications processors or minicomputers.

2.1.2 Early Commercial Packet Switching

In 1976, the ITU-T (formerly CCITT) published the CCITT Recommendation X.25 (1976 *Orange Book*) that defined a standardized approach for interconnecting computers called packet switching. Packet switching concepts existed prior to X.25 publication, such as proposed by Baran (1964). The general X.25 approach was to create a universal packet-switched network that provided rigorous error correction and efficient sharing of capital-intensive physical resources (leased lines and PSTN switched circuits) and allowed communication between systems produced by any manufacturer. International providers of X.25-based communications services referred to this technology as public data networking. Publicly accessible X.25 networks offered by a number of companies, such as Compuserve, Tymnet, Euronet, PSS, and Telenet, were set up in most countries during the 1970s and 1980s. Figure 2.2 depicts a number of systems and even terminals interconnected via an X.25 public data network.

2.1.3 The ARPANET: Internet

Another major networking activity, which actually preceded the X.25 work by about 10 years, was sponsored by the U.S. Department of Defense Advanced Research Projects Agency (DARPA), and was called the ARPANET. The ARPANET work started in the late 1960s as defense-oriented research on the feasibility of packet switching concepts. The ARPANET used a number of protocols, then settled upon the use of Internet Protocol version 4 (IPv4) in 1981 with the issuance of Request for Comment (RFC) 791 in September 1981 and a military standard (MIL-STD-1777) published in 1983. IPv4 was designed to support the forwarding (switching) of message packets not just between

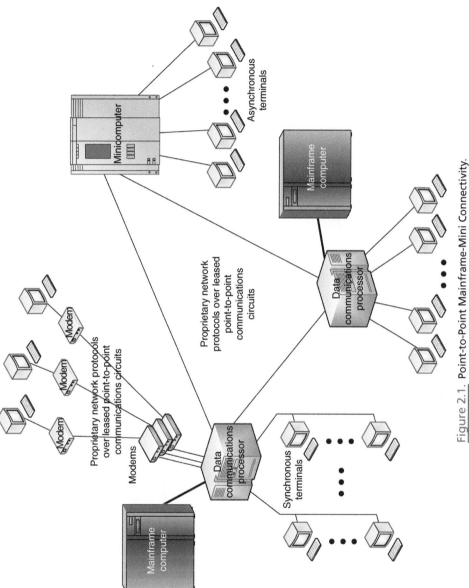

Figure 2.1. Point-to-Point Mainframe-Mini Connectivity.

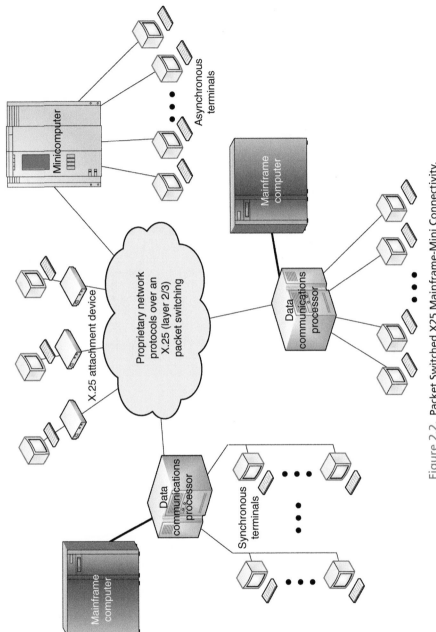

Figure 2.2. Packet Switched X25 Mainframe-Mini Connectivity.

computers attached to a common network but actually to provide forwarding between different networks using IPv4 (internetworking). Two protocols for end-to-end (computer-to-computer) communications were adopted in this timeframe: the User Datagram Protocol (UDP) in 1980 and the Transmission Control Protocol (TCP) in 1981. Figure 2.3 depicts an example set of computers and remote terminals logically interconnected via a set of point-to-point PSTN circuits.

Host computers and terminal devices attached to the ARPANET via small Interface Message Processors (called IMPs) that provided capabilities similar to early routers. These IMPs provided a store-and-forward packet switching function and were interconnected using modems and leased lines. Figure 2.4 shows the logical connection of computers to the ARPANET in 1977.

These aforementioned network technologies and concepts provided much of the context from which the first truly standardized concept of network architectures sprang, namely, ISO 7498-1 which was published in 1984 and later republished by the ITU-T as Recommendation X.200 in 1994. The layering of protocols in later ISO and ITU-T documents reflects those concepts first standardized in ISO 7498-1. Much of the work from the ARPANET was absorbed by the Internet Engineering Task Force (IETF) (formed in 1986) to develop and promote the TCP/IP-based network model and associated protocol standards now referred to as the Internet model. IETF-defined protocols only loosely follow the ISO layering concepts. RFC 3439 actually contains a section entitled "Layering considered harmful." The TCP/IP model does recognize four layers of functionality: the software application, the end-to-end transport connection, the internetworking range, and the direct links to other nodes on a local network.

However, the strict peer layering of the ISO Open Systems Interconnect (OSI) model, as usually described, is not necessarily followed by TCP/IP protocol usage since a number of these protocols include information utilized by lower layer protocols or protocols are used to carry lower layer protocols as upper layer protocol data units (PDUs). The use of tunneling protocols, which provide a Link Layer, Internetworking or application layer protocol capability, may well be an internetworking, transport, or application protocol in its own right. Some examples of tunneling protocols include FTP within HTTP, X-Windows within SSH, Internet Protocol version 6 (IPv6) within IPv4, IPv4 within IPv6, IPv6 within UDP, IPv4 within ATM, ATM within SONET, etc. Some of the key principles IETF protocol work follows are (as extracted from RFC 1958[1])

- "The community believes that the goal is connectivity, the tool is the Internet Protocol, and the intelligence is end to end rather than hidden in the network";
- "Connectivity is its own reward," and is more valuable than any individual application such as email or the World Wide Web;
- "The key to global connectivity is the inter-networking layer. The key to exploiting this layer over diverse hardware providing global connectivity is the 'end-to-end argument'";

---

[1] RFC 1958, "Architectural Principles of the Internet," Carpenter, B., Editor, Informational, June 1996

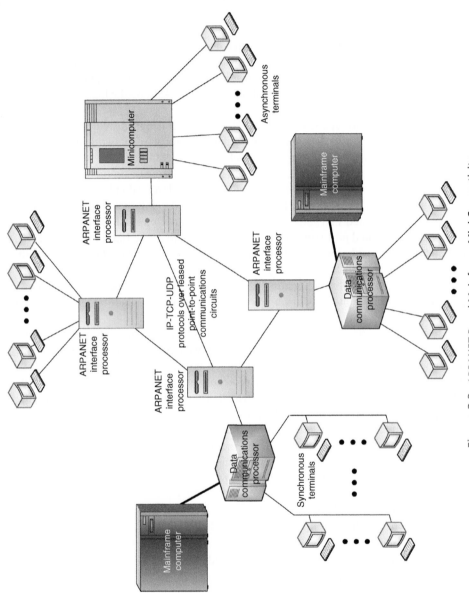

Figure 2.3. ARPANET-Based Mainframe-Mini Connectivity.

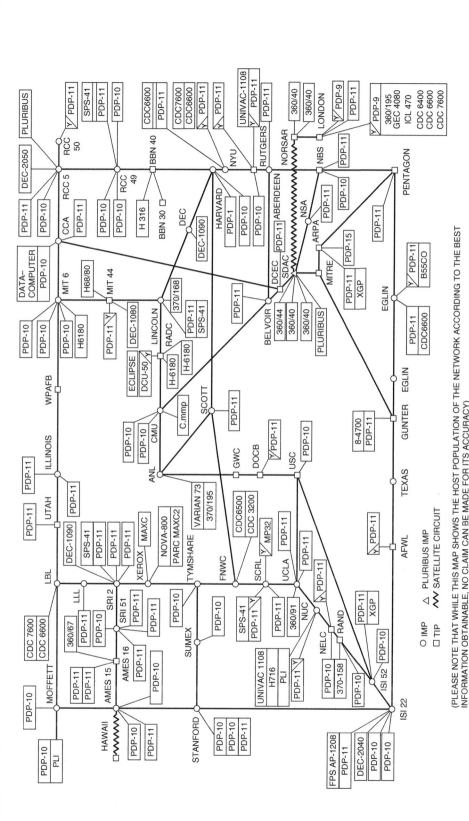

Figure 2.4. ARPANET Logical Map c.1977.

(PLEASE NOTE THAT WHILE THIS MAP SHOWS THE HOST POPULATION OF THE NETWORK ACCORDING TO THE BEST INFORMATION OBTAINABLE, NO CLAIM CAN BE MADE FOR ITS ACCURACY)

NAMES SHOWN ARE IMP NAMES. NOT (NECESSARILY) HOST NAMES

○ IMP   △ PLURIBUS IMP
□ TIP   ∿ SATELLITE CIRCUIT

- "It is also generally felt that end-to-end functions can best be realized by end-to-end protocols";
- "The end-to-end argument";
  - "The basic argument is that, as a first principle, certain required end-to-end functions can only be performed correctly by the end-systems themselves";
  - "An end-to-end protocol design should not rely on the maintenance of state (i.e., information about the state of the end-to-end communication) inside the network. Such state should be maintained only in the endpoints, in such a way that the state can only be destroyed when the endpoint itself breaks (known as fate-sharing). An immediate consequence of this is that datagrams are better than classical virtual circuits. The network's job is to transmit datagrams as efficiently and flexibly as possible";
- "Everything else should be done at the fringes";
- "To perform its services, the network maintains some state information: routes, QoS guarantees that it makes, session information where that is used in header compression, compression histories for data compression, and the like";
- "Nobody owns the Internet, there is no centralized control, and nobody can turn it off. Its evolution depends on rough consensus about technical proposals, and on running code. Engineering feedback from real implementations is more important than any architectural principles";
- "Multiple types of application protocol must be allowed for, ranging from the simplest such as remote login up to the most complex such as distributed databases."

Developers have consistently designed protocols with these principles in mind, resulting in the assumption that end computers/devices would solely engage in communication among themselves and expect minimal interaction with intermediate devices such as IP routers. For the most part, these requester/responder-type interactions have been viewed as the predominant form of computer-to-computer interactions with some secondary interactions between computers and networking support functions such as Domain Name Servers (DNS), authentication servers, and Dynamic Configuration servers. These principles have been followed into the current decade with IP-based networks operating over Ethernet, ATM, Frame Relay, serial connections, Token Ring, Fiber Distributed Data Interface (FDDI), Synchronous Optical Networking (SONET), multiple wireless technologies, and directly over fiber optics.

2.1.4 Ethernet and IEEE 802.3

In the mid-1970s, employees at Xerox Palo Alto Research Center (PARC) developed a new form of computer networking called Ethernet. In 1979, Xerox teamed up with Intel and Digital Equipment Corporation to promote Ethernet which led to the Institute of Electrical and Electronics Engineers (IEEE) publishing a draft standard in 1980 with a complete standard published in 1985 (IEEE 802.3); see Appendix F for further IEEE 802.3 Ethernet details. As initially specified, Ethernet was deployed over different forms of coaxial cabling and provided a maximum bandwidth of 10 Mbps. It uses

TABLE 2.1. Allocation of Routable IPv4 Addresses in 1992.

Routable Address Ranges	Total Defined	Total Allocated	Total Allocated as a % of Total Defined
Class A	126	49	38
Class B	16,383	7354	45
Class C	2,097,151	44,014	2

Extracted from RFC 1466.

a "contention"-type protocol for link access called Carrier Sense Multiple Access with Collision Detection (CSMA/CD) as the coaxial cabling ran from attached device to attached device in a "daisy-chained" manner, as shown in Figure 1.4. By the mid-1990s, Ethernet was predominantly deployed using twisted pair metallic wiring, as shown in Figure 1.5, in a star arrangement. Ethernet hardware is available for use at 100 Mbps and 1000 Mbps with 10 Gbps and 40 Gbps being worked on. Ethernet has become the predominant link layer technology for interconnecting computers within local areas, such as floors, buildings, and even campuses, as Local Area Networks (LANs) with IP used as the internetworking protocol. Ethernet and IP are now the de facto approach for constructing LANs/subnets that belong to individual organizations.

2.1.5 Network Address Translation

In 1992, the IETF published RFC 1466[2] noting that routable IPv4 addresses were being quickly assigned at an unacceptably high rate, as highlighted in the Table 2.1.

The IETF formed the IP Next-Generation (IPng) working group to address this issue and produced a new version of IP called IPv6, defined in a number of RFCs[3] in 1995, to address the expected exhaustion of available but not yet allocated IPv4 routable addresses. However, prior to the release of the IPv6 specifications, many organizations took advantage of a mechanism designed for use with non-routable IPv4 addresses. A number of specified non-routable ("private") address ranges existed for organizational use within private IP-based networks ("intranets"), and informational RFC 1597[4] was published in 1994 that defined how these non-routable addresses could be mapped to routable addresses, thereby allowing devices allocated non-routable addresses to communicate with devices outside of their intranets. The use of this Network Address Translation (NAT) capability resulted in a significant reduction in the demand for allocation of routable IPv4 address, and NAT usage has become commonplace within most organization intranets. NAT functions are installed in devices to allow the use of

---

[2] RFC 1466, "Guidelines for Management of IP Address Space", May 1993

[3] RFC 1885, "Internet Control Message Protocol (ICMPv6) for the Internet Protocol Version 6 (IPv6)", December 1995; RFC 1884, "IP Version 6 Addressing Architecture", December 1995; RFC 1883, "Internet Protocol, Version 6 (IPv6) Specification", December 1995

[4] RFC 1597, "Address Allocation for Private Internets", March 1994

private IP addresses on home and corporate networks (intra-networks or campus LANs) behind routers with a single public routable IP address facing the public Internet. The internal network devices are enabled to communicate with devices on external networks by altering the source address of outgoing IPv4 packets to that of the NAT device and relaying replies back to the originating device. However, NAT-enabled devices have no automatic method of determining the internal IPv4 address of the destination device of the incoming packets. There exists a NAT ingress problem that affects systems behind NAT-enabled devices for applications such as peer-to-peer (P2P) file sharing, Voice over Internet Protocol (VoIP) services, and online services to the current video game consoles which require client devices to act like servers and be able to receive unsolicited requests. It is this ability to receive unsolicited requests which poses the problem for devices behind NAT devices, as incoming requests cannot be easily correlated to the proper internal host device without an appropriate NAT table entry. Figure 2.5 provides a graphic example of a NAT function's placement and prototypical NAT table.

One common approach to the NAT ingress problem is to ensure that any requesting device can use the Fully Qualified Domain Name (FQDN[5]) of the destination device to reach the device even if it is behind a NAT function. When a device behind a NAT function needs to be able to receive unsolicited requests, an agent application can be installed in the device. The agent periodically polls the intranet router containing the NAT function for the current externally facing interface routable IPv4 address. Then the agent contacts a "Dynamic DNS" server to provide the appropriate IP address to translate FQDN queries. Agents usually provide DNS updates on a once every 5 minute basis.

2.2 COMMON NETWORK ORGANIZATIONS

There are a number of physical and logical organizations which modern network deployments utilize for the transport of IP-based internetworking, namely:

- Wired LANs;
- Wireless Networks;
- Metropolitan Area Networks (MANs); and
- Wide Area Networks (WANs).

In this section we will discuss these different organizations, their common usage, typical forms of attacks against such networks, network abuse, and the security technologies most effective in mitigating the aforementioned attacks and abuse. The purpose of this discussion is twofold:

1. Provide an awareness of those security technologies most commonly used in modern IP-oriented networks, and
2. Identify the magnitude of issues associated with managing security mechanisms that are now common.

[5] As discussed in RFC 1035, "DOMAIN NAMES—IMPLEMENTATION AND SPECIFICATION," November 1987 as an absolute domain name.

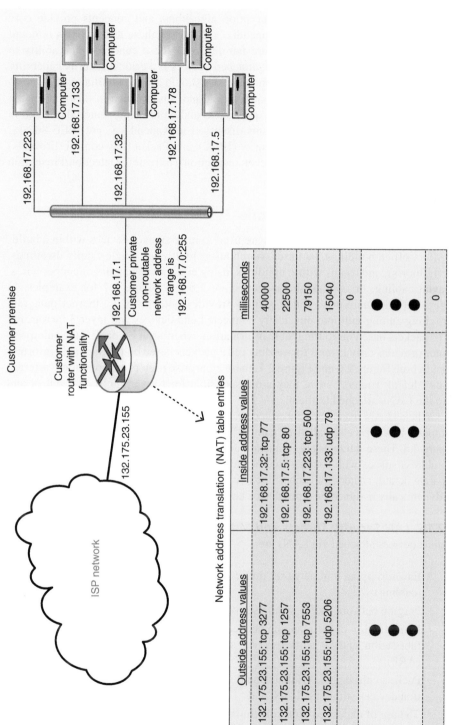

Figure 2.5. Basic NAT Operation.

A set of technologies based on encryption algorithms and concepts provide core capabilities for network security; Appendix A discusses these technologies in detail and the reader should ensure they are familiar with these concepts. The ability to authenticate the identities of network-attached devices is a critical security capability that is discussed in Appendix B which the reader should also be familiar with. A number of security mechanisms for use at layers 2 and 3 referenced in this chapter are discussed and described in detail in Appendix C and build on the material covered in Appendices A and B. The mechanisms discussed in Appendix C are IEEE 802.1x, IEEE 802.1ae, IEEE 802.11i, IP Security (IPsec), and Packet flow control (firewalls) inspection (gateways) and deep packet inspection (Intrusion Detection/Prevention Systems (IDS/IPS)).

2.2.1 Wired Local Area Networks

2.2.1.1 LAN Usage. Wired LANs are used to interconnect devices within a building (i.e., office buildings, factories, warehouses, multi- and single-family dwellings, etc.), floor(s), and rooms within buildings, using either twisted pairs of copper wires, coaxial cabling, or optical fibers; see Figure 2.6 and Figure 2.7 for examples. In Figure 2.6, the enterprise router switch provides both layer 2 Ethernet datagram switching among multiple physically connected end devices and layer 3 forwarding of IP packets based on routing table information; whereas in Figure 2.7 the enterprise router provides only layer 3 forwarding of IP packets based on routing table information. In both Figure 2.6 and Figure 2.7, these enterprise routers are commonly referred to as "default routers" since they are responsible for forwarding packet out of and into the LANs attached to them.

When a LAN spans multiple co-located buildings (i.e., school, college, or corporate campus), it is typically called a "campus" LAN or intranet, an example depicted in Figure 2.8. These intranets are frequently divided into subnets with related but separate IP address spaces with routers used at the points of interconnect. Figure 2.8 depicts separate default routers for each of the two LANs. IP addresses can be either statically or dynamically assigned on a per-device basis.

2.2.1.2 LAN Security Threats and Mitigation Technologies. The main attacks against devices attached via LANs are:

- Eavesdropping on network traffic via physical attachment to LAN media (cabling);
- Forging network traffic with false contents;
- Manipulation of the mapping between Medium Access Control (MAC) address fabrication and IP addresses via abuse of the Address Resolution Protocol (ARP);
- Packets entering a LAN that should not be allowed to be sent to specific destination devices within the LAN; and
- The use of undesired protocols flowing into a LAN or out of a LAN.

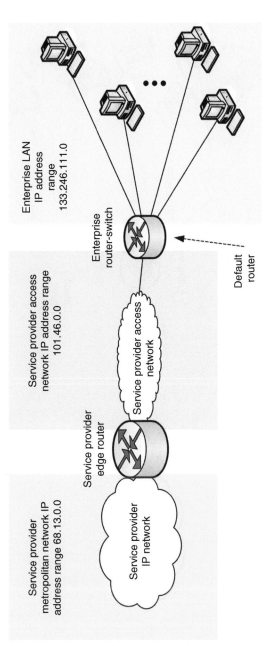

Service provider metropolitan network IP address range 68.13.0.0

Service provider IP network

Service provider edge router

Service provider access network IP address range 101.46.0.0

Service provider access network

Enterprise LAN IP address range 133.246.111.0

Enterprise router-switch

Default router

Figure 2.6. Enterprise Multi-port Router–Switch Address Space.

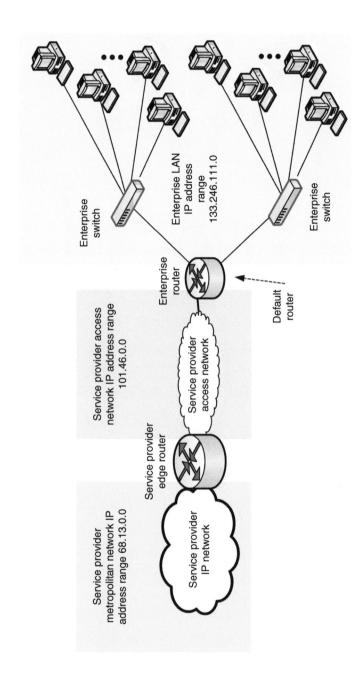

Figure 2.7. Enterprise Router and Multiple Switches Address Space.

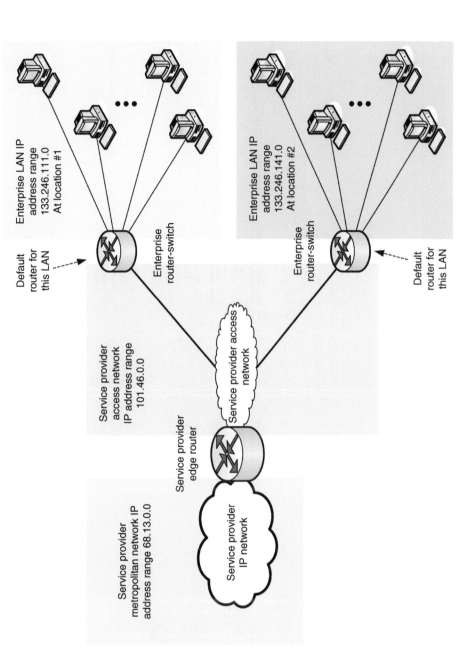

Figure 2.8. Enterprise Multi-location Intranet and Address Ranges.

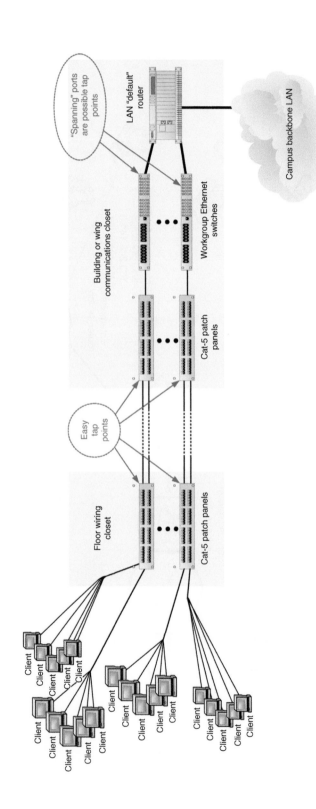

Figure 2.9. Typical Eavesdropping Locations Within Wired LANs.

2.2.1.2.1 LAN PHYSICAL ATTACHMENT EAVESDROPPING. In most businesses, and other large organizations, the Point-to-Point Switched LAN is more realistically shown in Figure 2.9. In this figure, each client workstation/computer/device directly connects to individual physical ports on a CAT-5 Patch Panel within a wiring closet. The Patch Panels in the closet are then interconnected to other Patch Panels and eventually to individual physical ports on layer 2 switches frequently allocated on a "workgroup" basis. The "workgroup" switches are then connected to a LAN "default" router either co-located or located elsewhere in the building. When there are multiple routers, these routers are interconnected into a campus backbone LAN (also called an intranet). Patch Panels represent locations where unauthorized access is possible for eavesdropping (also referred to as network sniffing and packet sniffing), highlighted in Figure 2.9. The primary defense against this type of eavesdropping is physical access control (locks) to the closet or room where the Patch Panels are located; these controls can be augmented by deploying networked intrusion sensors that alarm upon location entry. Layer 2 switches also present an eavesdropping opportunity via a switch's monitoring (spanning) port that allows for the capturing of traffic flowing into or from other ports on the switch, highlighted in Figure 2.9. Physical access to these switches should also be physically controlled and physical access monitoring used as with Patch Panel locations. One should ensure that access to "spanning" ports is limited to authorized personnel within the administrative functions of the switch for both local and remote administrative access.

2.2.1.2.2 ARP-SPECIFIC ATTACKS OR ABUSE. Some of the major forms of address mapping manipulation that can occur are:

- Interception attacks where a device's IP address becomes associated with a different device's MAC address (sometimes referred to as ARP cache poisoning);
- Man-in-the-Middle attacks where a device's IP address becomes associated with a different device's MAC address; and
- Denial of Service (DoS) attacks.

In all the three forms of attacks, the attacker either:

- replies to an ARP request for the MAC address, that should be associated with a specific IP address, with its own MAC address rather than the correct MAC address resulting in the device that had sent out the request then entering a wrong binding of IP address to MAC address in its ARP cache, or
- issues an unsolicited ARP message that directs other devices to modify their ARP caches to map a specific MAC address to a specified IP address.

With Interception attacks, the attacker's goal is to have any packets destined for another device to be sent to the attacker's MAC address for eavesdropping upon or attacker modification and retransmission. With Man-in-the-Middle attacks, the attacker's goal is to have all packets destined for the LAN's default router to be sent to the attacker's MAC address for eavesdropping upon or attacker modification followed by the attacker forwarding these packets to the actual LAN default router. With DoS attacks, the attacker's goal is to have any packets destined for another device to be sent to some MAC address that is not used by any device on the LAN. Another form of DoS attack occurs when an attacker simply transmits ARP request or reply messages at a sufficiently high rate so as to consume enough LAN bandwidth that legitimate LAN traffic is interfered with or actually cannot be transmitted in a timely manner.

Some of the commonly used defenses against attacks targeting wired LANs include:

- Manually configuring LAN-attached devices to use permanent (static) ARP cache entries for the mapping of other machine's MAC and IP addresses. This approach is not reasonable in any LAN to which many devices are attached, and some operating systems will still allow static ARP cache entries to be over-ridden by received ARP messages;
- Using switch port security where a layer 2 switch maintains tables of ARP bindings that note what MAC address is associated with the networked device attached to each of its physical ports and prevents the switching of ARP messages that would conflict with the switch's maintained bindings;
- Deploying an ARP monitoring tool, such as:
  - ARPwatch which is a program for Unix systems that listens for ARP replies on a network, sends a notification via email to a management system, and needs to be installed on every device that is to be protected;
  - Xarp which is a program for Windows and Linux systems that performs ARP packet inspection on a per-network interface basis and needs to be installed on every device that is to be protected;
  - arpON which detects and blocks all ARP poisoning and spoofing attacks and needs to be installed on every device that is to be protected;
  - Dynamic Host Configuration Protocol (DHCP) snooping within LAN routers that tracks IP address/MAC address associations but is limited to DHCP clients and can be easily circumvented;
- Deploying IEEE 802.1x to control the mapping of MAC addresses to specific switch ports based on authentication of devices and needs to be installed on every device that is to be protected (see Appendix C); Figure 2.10, Figure 2.11, and Figure 2.12 depict IEEE 802.1x control functionality within LAN default routers;
- Deploying IEEE 802.1ae to provide encryption-based confidentiality and needs to be installed on every device that is to be protected along with shared secret keys (see Appendix C).

2.2.1.2.3 PACKET FLOW AND PROTOCOL-SPECIFIC ATTACKS. In many commercial environments, only specific IP-based application protocols are allowed, nor are selected LAN-attached devices allowed to be the destination on packets entering the LAN via the LAN's default router. The most common mechanism used to enforce these types of

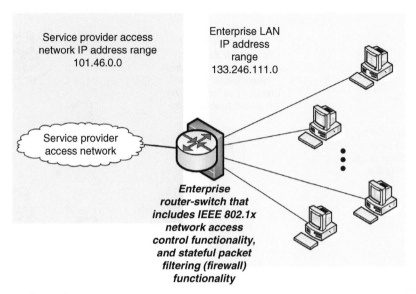

Figure 2.10. Enterprise Multi-port Router–Switch–Firewall with IEEE 802.1x.

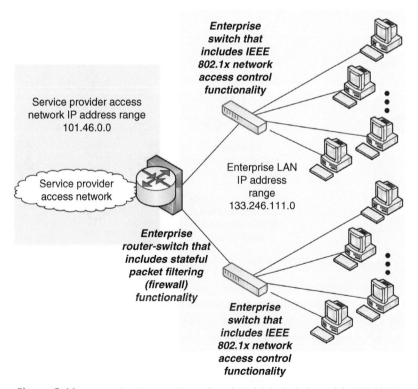

Figure 2.11. Enterprise Router–Firewall and Multiple Switches with IEEE 802.1x.

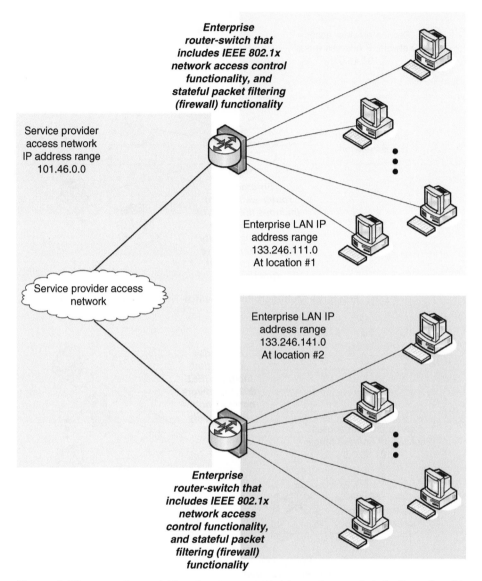

Figure 2.12. Enterprise Multi-location Intranet Multi-port Router–Switch–Firewalls with IEEE 802.1x.

control is packet filter functionality (also known as firewalls). This firewall functionality within a default router (see Appendix C) limits the forwarding of IP packets into and out of a LAN based on rules which specify what packets can be forwarded in either direction based on layer 3 and layer 4 protocol header information including source device (source IP address), destination device (destination IP address), transport protocol being used (TCP, UDP or SCTP), source application (TCP/UDP port number), and destination application (TCP/UDP port number). Figure 2.10 depicts a default router which includes layer 2 datagram switching, IEEE 802.1x port access control, and packet filtering. Figure 2.11 depicts a default router which includes packet filtering and two layer 2 datagram switches with IEEE 802.1x port access control functionality. Figure 2.12 depicts multiple default routers, for an enterprise intranet spanning multiple locations, which include layer 2 datagram switching, IEEE 802.1x port access control, and packet filtering.

2.2.2 Wireless Networks

The use of wireless networking has grown significantly over the last 10 years and fall into two primary groups: wireless communications over unlicensed radio frequencies (primarily for wireless LANs (WLANs), sensor, and ad hoc networks) versus over licensed radio frequencies (primarily for metropolitan access) as shown in Table 2.2.

2.2.2.1 Wireless LANs

2.2.2.1.1 WLAN USAGE. WLANs are used to interconnect devices in public outdoor spaces (i.e., city streets and parks, etc.), vehicles (i.e., airplanes, ships, busses, trains, etc.), and within both public (airports, coffee shops, WiFi "hotspots," etc.) and private buildings, using radio frequencies for transmission and reception.

These wireless networks can be thought of as wireless Ethernet LANs as a variant of IEEE 802.3 is frequently used, called Carrier Sense Multiple Access with Collision Avoidance (CSMA/CA) and adhere to the IEEE 802.11 link layer standard. These wireless LANs usually represent individual subnets with a separate IP address space and a router used at the point of interconnect to a wired LAN (as depicted in Figure 2.13). IP addresses are usually dynamically assigned on a per-device basis via a DHCP server located within the wireless LAN's default router.

2.2.2.1.2 WLAN SECURITY THREATS AND MITIGATION TECHNOLOGIES. Wireless LANs suffer from the same threats that any wired LAN can be exposed to, in addition to threats related to the wireless (lack of physical controls) nature of these networks and

TABLE 2.2. Types of Wireless Networking.

Wireless Network Type	Frequencies Used	Network Primary Usage
Wireless LANs	Unlicensed radio frequencies	Enterprise intranets, public Internet access
Sensor and Ad Hoc networks	Unlicensed radio frequencies	Telemetry and improvizational communications
Cellular networks	Licensed radio frequencies	Fixed and mobile telecommunications SP network access
IEEE 802.16 (WiMAX) networks	Licensed radio frequencies	Fixed and mobile telecommunications SP network access
Long-Term Evolution (LTE)	Licensed radio frequencies	Fixed and mobile telecommunications SP network access

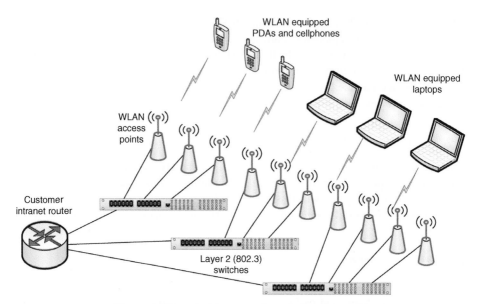

Figure 2.13. Example Enterprise Wireless Network.

the fact that communication can be disrupted via outright jamming of signals. By definition, wireless LAN signals are broadcasted everywhere within the range of an access point. Equipment for wireless eavesdropping ("tapping") is easily available, and the eavesdropping can be done without disruption of the service and without communicating parties being aware of it. Strong encryption is necessary to control LAN access and provide confidentiality of transmissions.

Since IEEE 802.11b and 802.11g use the 2.4 GHz band, equipment using these mechanisms can suffer interference from appliances (microwave ovens, cordless telephones, and amateur radio to name a few) that also use this band. This fact should be remembered as it identifies a possible DoS attack method against an IEEE 802.11b- or 802.11g-based WLAN by someone using a device that emits sufficient radio frequency energy in the 2.4 GHz band to render the WLAN unusable. The IEEE 802.11a standard uses the 5 GHz band, so 802.11a devices are not affected by products operating on the 2.4 GHz band. Equipment for IEEE 802.11a, 802.11b, and 802.11g are available that use the original IEEE-designed security mechanism called Wired Equivalent Privacy (WEP) based on a single shared secret key (for Data-origin authentication) and the RC4 symmetric encryption algorithm to control WLAN access and confidentiality. A paper (Newsham, 2001) was published in 2001 describing weaknesses in the WEP-based security design. By 2002, anyone could download attack software from websites that allowed a computer equipped with IEEE 802.11a, 802.11b, and 802.11g WLAN interface hardware to locate, identify, and calculate the shared secret key used for access authentication on these discovered WLANs in less than 15 seconds. This has led to the coining of a new activity called "war-driving" in which a person would drive around a town or neighborhood with a laptop computer, equipped with appropriate hardware and software, searching for WLANs in homes and offices that the war-driver could then connect to without the approval, or even knowledge, of the WLAN owner. Consequently, one is at risk operating a WEP-secured WLAN today. Fortunately, the IEEE developed a replacement for WEP called IEEE 802.11i that is discussed in Appendix C. IEEE 802.11i relies on use of shared secrets or deployment of RADIUS authentication servers.

2.2.2.2 Sensor and Ad Hoc Networks. Sensor and ad hoc networks utilize a decentralized approach for wireless networking as they do not rely on any pre-existing infrastructure of network access points that control network access or usage. In these networks, each device (node) participates in routing by forwarding data for other nodes as well as being senders and receivers of network traffic; so network connectivity is dynamic and some devices can become unreachable. There is no need for a pre-deployed infrastructure that makes these types of networks suitable for a variety of applications where a central infrastructure cannot be relied upon, such as:

- emergency situations e.g., natural disasters;
- military situation e.g., remote sensing/surveillance; and
- remote sensing/telemetry in geographic situations where fixed infrastructures would be difficult or time consuming to deploy.

These networks are comprised of multiple nodes/devices that are connected by broadcast radio frequency links between them. The capabilities (i.e., distance, bandwidth, connectivity, etc.) vary depending on each node's resources (e.g., available electrical power, transmitter power, computing power, and memory) by behavioral properties (e.g., reliability and trust-worthiness) and by link properties (e.g., line-of-sight interference, distance and signal loss, interference, and noise). Since existing links can be lost and new links become available at any time, these networks must be able to cope with dynamic changes and restructuring.

A mobile ad hoc network (MANET) is a self-configuring network of mobile devices connected by wireless links where each device in a MANET is free to move independently in any direction and will therefore change its links to other devices. Non-military MANET networks typically use IEEE 802.11g or 802.11n as their link layer configured in a non-infrastructure manner, thereby avoiding the use of access points. MANETs rely on the use of IP as their internetworking layer protocol, with each device providing packet forwarding (routing) between MANET devices and share routing information. The primary challenge for MANETs is the establishment and distribution of route information required to properly route traffic. There are a number of competing route calculation and distribution protocols[6] being developed within the IETF, yet none have been published as IETF standards track RFCs.

A wireless sensor network (WSN) consists of geographically distributed independent devices that cooperatively monitor physical or environmental conditions, such as

---

[6] RFC 3561, "Ad hoc On-Demand Distance Vector (AODV) Routing," 2003-07, status is Experimental; RFC 3626, "Optimized Link State Routing Protocol (OLSR)," 2003-10, status is Experimental; RFC 3684, "Topology Dissemination Based on Reverse-Path Forwarding (TBRPF)," 2004-02, status is Experimental; RFC 4728, "The Dynamic Source Routing Protocol (DSR) for Mobile Ad Hoc Networks for IPv4,"; 2007-02, status is Experimental.

temperature, sound, vibration, pressure, motion, or pollutants. There is research and development of WSNs using IEEE 802.11 wireless link layer technology, as well as additional work being done under the auspices of DARPA using non-802.11 wireless link layer technologies.

The sensor and ad hoc networks utilizing IEEE 802.11 link layer technologies face the same security issues as general WLANs, as discussed in Section 2.2.2.1 In addition, MANETs also have to contend with attacks targeting the falsification of distributed routing information which necessitates the use of cryptographic-based Peer-entity or Data-origin authentication relying on either shared secret keys or asymmetric encryption. Whenever shared secret keys or asymmetric encryption keys are involved, one has to provide key management capabilities, as discussed in Appendices A and B.

2.2.2.3 *Cellular Networks.* Commercial cellular networks have been developed by telephony/Internet service providers (ISPs) over the last few decades to initially support mobile telephony services and now data networking services. In almost all cases, these cellular networks actually provide mobile wireless access into existing wired networks, such as the existing PSTN and the Internet. The primary cellular technologies currently deployed are:

- Global System for Mobile Communications (GSM);
- Universal Mobile Telecommunications System (UMTS); and
- Code Division Multiple Access (CDMA), currently known as CDMA2000.

One of the key features of GSM is the Subscriber Identity Module which is a detachable smart card storing subscription and other user information. GSM was designed to authenticate the subscriber using a pre-shared secret key. GSM only authenticates the user to the network (and not vice versa). Communications between a subscriber handset and the network base station can be encrypted. The development of UMTS has introduced an optional Universal Subscriber Identity Module that uses a longer authentication key to give greater security, as well as mutually authenticating the network and the user—whereas the security model therefore offers confidentiality and authentication, but limited authorization capabilities, and no non-repudiation.

In 2009 and 2010, announcements were issued stating that a number of encryption algorithms used in GSM systems have been successfully attacked calling into question the confidentiality of GSM cellular systems. New attacks are continuously being explored to take advantage of poor security implementations of "smartphone" applications including a number of wiretapping and eavesdropping techniques based on malicious software (malware).

Both GSM and CDMA2000 networks rely on Home Location Register (HLR) central servers that contain details of each mobile phone subscriber that is authorized to use the GSM and or CDMA network to place calls. CDMA data networking relies on IP networked computers called Authentication, Authorization, and Accounting (AAA) servers. Current AAA servers communicate using the RADIUS protocol (discussed in Appendix B).

2.2.2.4 IEEE 802.16 Networks. The IEEE 802.16 wireless network standard is a telecommunications protocol for use in service provider (SP) access networks that supports fixed and fully mobile user devices. The name "WiMAX" was created by the WiMAX Forum and is based on the IEEE 802.16 standard which is also referred to as Broadband Wireless Access. As with cellular networks, WiMAX deployments make use of AAA servers located with what is called the Connectivity Service Network (CSN) to which are attached a number of Access Service Networks (ASNs) containing base stations that subscriber devices interact with. Another component of the CSN is a function called a "Home Agent" which keeps track of mobile subscriber devices that roam between ASNs. WiMAX relies on the IP protocol at layer 3 and the use of digital certificates and digital signatures for access authentication. As of 2011, the only U.S. SP deploying WiMAX is Sprint Nextel. Devices which communicate using WiMAX technology will not interoperate with devices which communicate using Long-Term Evolution (LTE) technology or vice versa.

2.2.2.5 Long-Term Evolution Networks. The LTE wireless network standard is a telecommunications protocol that provides fixed and fully mobile Internet access. LTE is based upon GSM/EDGE and UMTS/HSPA network technologies with the standard maintained by the 3rd Generation Partnership Project (3GPP) and the European Telecommunications Standards Institute (ETSI).

LTE is also referred to as Broadband Wireless Access. Similar to WiMAX, LTE deployments make use of AAA servers and base stations that subscriber devices interact with. Another component of the LTE is a function called a "Home Agent" which keeps track of mobile subscriber devices that roam within an LTE access network. LTE relies on IP at layer 3 and the use of digital certificates and digital signatures for access authentication. Sprint Nextel, MetroPCS, Verizon Wireless, and AT&T Wireless in the United States along with several worldwide carriers are deploying LTE-based access networks. Devices which communicate using LTE technology will not interoperate with devices which communicate using WiMAX technology or vice versa.

2.2.3 Metropolitan Area Networks

Metropolitan Area Networks (MANs) are used to interconnect LANs/intranets, WLANs, and campus LANs between multiple buildings located across a metropolitan geographic area, using either twisted pairs of copper wires, optical fibers, or even radio frequencies. Modern MANs are now structured into access and core/backbone components.

2.2.3.1 Access MANs. Access MAN components provide connectivity to customer intranets and primarily rely on a number of layered Data Link Layer protocols, such as: Digital Subscriber Line (DSL) (as shown in Figure 2.14), Passive Optical Network (PON) technologies (as shown in Figure 2.15), and Hybrid Fiber/Coax technologies (as shown in Figure 2.16).

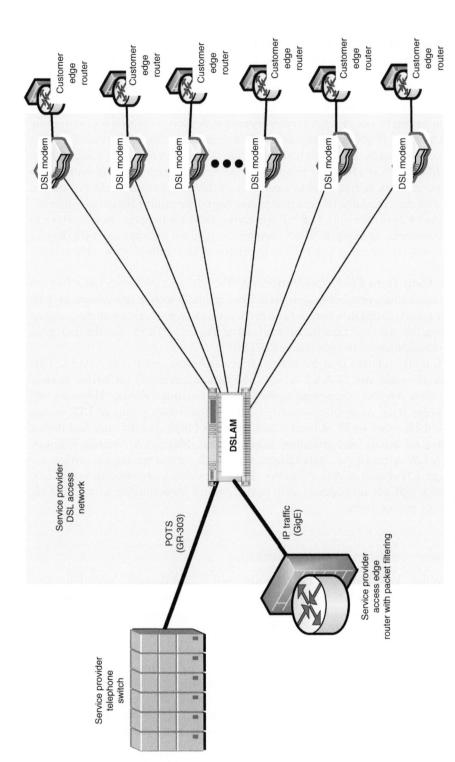

Figure 2.14. Service Provider DSL Access Network Example.

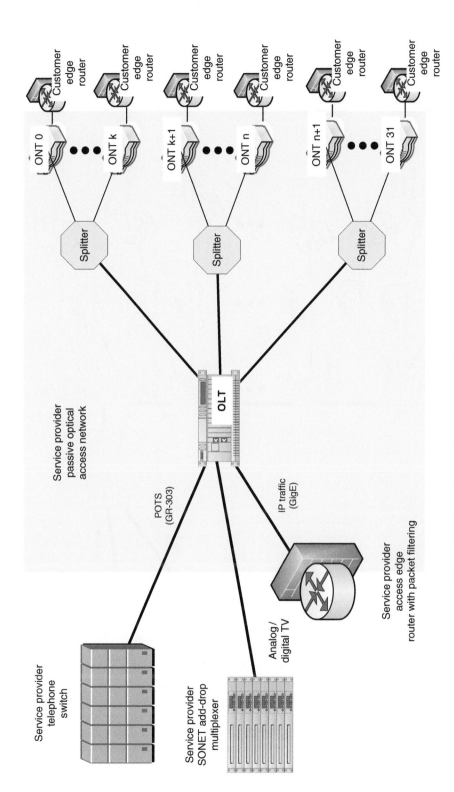

Figure 2.15. Service Provider Passive Optical Access Network Example.

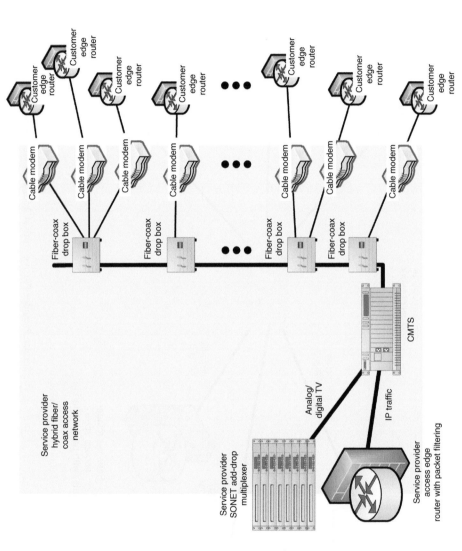

Figure 2.16. Service Provider Hybrid Fiber-Coax Access Network Example.

2.2.3.1.1 DSL ACCESS MANS. DSL access networks come in a number of configurations which differ in operating speed for up-link versus down-link traffic and distances supported between subscriber locations and the central DSL Access Modules (DSLAMs) located in a central location (the central office); Appendix F provides additional details. All DSL networks are organized in a "hub and spoke" configuration (as depicted in Figure 2.14) and utilize Asynchronous Transfer Mode (ATM) as the base Data Link Layer protocol to transport telephone traffic via ATM Application Adaption Layer 1 (AAL-1) and data traffic in the form of 802.3 Ethernet via Application Adaption Layer 5 (AAL-5). The DSLAM extracts telephony traffic from AAL-1 ATM cells for passing to a traditional PSTN telephone switch and extracts data traffic from AAL-5 ATM cells and forwards this traffic to a Service Provider Edge Router (SP-ER) via Gigabit Ethernet. SP-ERs act as the boundary between a Service Provider core/backbone MAN and the Service Provider Access MAN. It is at the SP-ER that packet filtering functions are deployed to control what protocols are allowed to flow between customer intranets/LANs and the core/backbone MAN. DSL access networks do not include any specific mechanisms for authentication or confidentiality so they basically rely on physical security controls and difficulty in accessing the metallic cable links.

2.2.3.1.2 PON ACCESS MANS. PON-based access networks come in two forms: the earlier version uses ATM over optical fibers (called BPON[7]) and the newer version uses Gigabit Ethernet over these optical fibers (called GPON[8]) and are organized in a "hub and spoke" configuration (as depicted in Figure 2.15); Appendix F provides additional details. BPON and GPON differ in operating speed for up-link versus down-link traffic, security mechanisms for authentication and confidentiality, along with base Data Link Layer technology used between subscriber locations and the central Optical Line Termination (OLT) equipment located in a central location (the central office). BPON supports 622 Mbps of downlink capacity shared by no more than 32 Optical Network Termination (ONT) subscriber devices and utilizes ATM as the base Data Link Layer protocol to transport telephone traffic via AAL-1 and data traffic in the form of 802.3 Ethernet via AAL-5. The BPON OLT extracts telephony traffic from AAL-1 ATM cells for passing to a traditional PSTN telephone switch and extracts data traffic from AAL-5 ATM cells and forwards this traffic to an SP-ER for packet filtering and forwarding into the core/backbone MAN. The security provided by BPON is a primitive form of transposing ATM cell contents, referred to as "churn," that is easily defeated. GPON supports 1 Gbps of downlink capacity shared by no more than 32 ONT subscriber devices and utilizes ATM as the base Data Link Layer protocol to transport telephone traffic via

[7] ITU-T Recommendation G.983.1, "SERIES G: TRANSMISSION SYSTEMS AND MEDIA, DIGITAL SYSTEMS AND NETWORKS, Digital transmission systems – Digital sections and digital line system – Optical line systems for local and access networks, Broadband optical access systems based on Passive Optical Networks (PON)", INTERNATIONAL TELECOMMUNICATION UNION, 10/1998

[8] ITU-T Recommendation G.984.1, "SERIES G: TRANSMISSION SYSTEMS AND MEDIA, DIGITAL SYSTEMS AND NETWORKS, Digital sections and digital line system – Optical line systems for local and access networks, General characteristics for Gigabit-capable Passive Optical Networks (GPON)", INTERNATIONAL TELECOMMUNICATION UNION, 03/2003

AAL-1 and Gigabit Ethernet to transport data traffic. The GPON OLT extracts telephony traffic from AAL-1 ATM cells for passing to a traditional PSTN telephone switch and forwards Gigabit Ethernet data traffic to an SP-ER for packet filtering and forwarding into the core/backbone MAN. The security provided by GPON is based upon the Advanced Encryption Standard (AES) symmetric encryption algorithm and shared secret keys which provide very robust Data-origin authentication and traffic confidentiality provided the shared secret keys are correctly managed. Both BPON and GPON Access MANs can, in addition to simultaneously transporting telephone and data traffic, distribute both analog and digital television program traffic.

2.2.3.1.3 HYBRID FIBER/COAX ACCESS MANs. Fiber to the curb (FTTC) is an access technology based on fiber-optic cables run to a platform that serves several customers. Each of these customers has a connection to this platform via coaxial cable or twisted pair. These access networks utilize technology that conforms to a set of specifications, defined by Cable Television Laboratories, Inc. (CableLabs), called Data Over Cable Service Interface Specification (DOCSIS[9]) that permits high-speed data transfer over Cable TV (CATV) system infrastructures. Common to all versions of DOCSIS is the use of cable modems, located at customer premises, and Cable Modem Termination System (CMTS) equipment, located at the CATV head-end location organized in a "multi-drop" configuration (as depicted in Figure 2.16). A typical CMTS is a device which controls downstream and upstream ports similar to a DSLAM. DOCSIS specifications include MAC layer security services defined in the Baseline Privacy Interface (BPI) specification recently enhanced as part of DOCSIS 3.0, and the specification was renamed "Security" (SEC). BPI/SEC provides confidentiality by encrypting data flows between the CMTS and customer site located cable modems using either the symmetric Digital Encryption Standard (DES) algorithm or AES symmetric encryption algorithm plus periodic re-keying. BPI+ strengthened the service protection feature by adding digital-certificate-based authentication with a Public Key Infrastructure (PKI) (see Appendix B) to its Key exchange protocol.

2.2.3.2 Backbone MAN Usage. MAN core/backbone components primarily utilize Synchronous Optical Networking (SONET) technology (see Appendix F) at layer 2 (see Figure 2.17) to transport IP-compliant packets between edge routers as well as edge routers to core routers and peering routers. Larger core/backbone MANs are now starting to use Wave Division Multiplexing (WDM) (see Appendix F) to increase the transport capacities on individual optical fibers.

Unlike LANs, this type of complex internetworking is provided by an SP for multiple customers, which poses additional security risks. The primary security capabilities are located with the SP-ERs and SP Peering Routers (PRs). These SP-ERs and SP-PRs will typically provide:

- Packer filtering (firewall), as discussed in Appendix C, allowing the SP to control the flow of packets and protocols between the SP access network and SP core/backbone network, and

[9] http://www.cablelabs.com/cablemodem/specifications/specifications20.html
http://www.cablelabs.com/cablemodem/specifications/specifications30.html

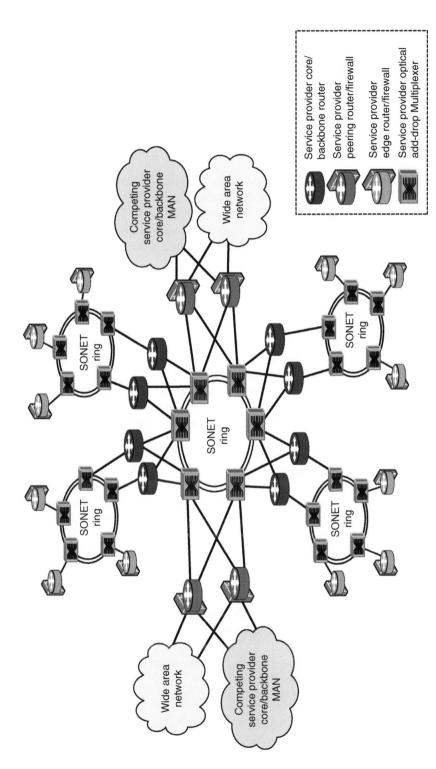

Figure 2.17. Typical Service Provider MAN Core/Backbone Components.

- Session Border Control (SBC), as discussed in Appendix C, allowing the SP to control the flow of RTP packets between the SP access network and SP core/ backbone network.

Over time, both SP-ERs and SP-PRs are likely to include deep packet inspection (either IDS or IPS) functionality, as discussed in Appendix C, as SP-ER and SP-PR hardware performance increases and IDS/IPS functionality decreases in cost. The SP-ERs will typically also provide:

- IEEE 802.1x functionality, as discussed in Appendix C, allowing the SP to enforce control over customer premise located access network attachment device (i.e., cable modems, DSL modems, and PON ONTs, etc.) usage of the SP access network, and
- SP-ERs frequently include DHCP servers that allocate temporary IPv4 addresses to customer edge routers (C-ERs) or directly connected customer devices/computers.

On the other hand, SP core/backbone routers (SP-CRs) and SP Optical Add-Drop Multiplexers (SP-ADMs) rarely include any security mechanisms applied to the traffic they forward as these devices are optimized to handle high (1 Gbps) to very high (up to 40+ Gbps) rates of customer traffic.

All SP-ERs, SP-PRs, SP-CRs, and SP-ADMs are capable of both local (via a physically local terminal/console) and remote (over a dedicated management network) management (administration and surveillance). The management of these devices must be strictly controlled and secured as any unauthorized changes to these devices could negatively affect many thousands of customers. Therefore, remote management should occur via a separate management-dedicated network interface. This management network interface would be either connected to a physically separate management network or a logically separate management network. A logically separate management network can be provided through the use of IPsec (as in an encrypted virtual private network). Remote management systems are commonly located in a Network Operation Center (NOC) that is established in a redundant manner to facilitate high availability management capabilities. In addition to general management capabilities, an NOC will also include security management capabilities although these security management capabilities are migrating into dedicated Security Operation Centers (SOCs).

2.2.4 Wide Area Networks

WANs are used to interconnect MANs with MANs in other geographic areas via either copper wires or optical fibers. WANs carry data over greater distances, typically spanning a whole city and especially between cities; see Figure 2.18. WANs provide communications traffic for a vastly increased number of users (from thousands to millions), which presents an additional security threat. WANs connect to SP MANs via SP-PRs. These SP-ERs and SP-PRs will typically provide:

- Packer filtering (firewall) functionality allowing the SP to control the flow of packets and protocols between MAN core/backbone networks and a WAN, and

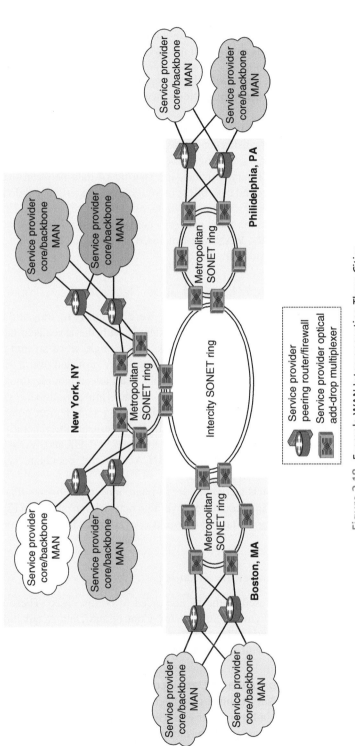

Figure 2.18. Example WAN Interconnecting Three Cities.

• SBC functionality allowing the SP to control the flow of RTP packets between MAN core/backbone networks and the WAN.

Over time, these SP-PRs are likely to include deep packet inspection (either IDS or IPS) functionality as ER and PR hardware performance increases and IDS/IPS functionality decreases in cost.

A common safeguard of WANs is partitioning of networks to provide isolated subnets where security mechanisms can be easily provisioned and controlled. Networks can be partitioned by physical or by logical separation. The first case is costly and not very flexible, and, although very efficient, the sharing of data between the network portions is very hard. The second case offers more flexible separation, and divides users in user groups, by creating many virtual networks out of a single network. The primary technology used to soft-partition these networks is MultiProtocol Label Switching (see Appendix F) between SP-PRs. WANs are structured similarly to core/backbone MANs with associated NOCs, and possibly SOCs.

2.2.5 Networks Are Now Layered upon Networks

As previously noted, the telephone networks were designed to transmit telephone conversations directly as analog or digitized signals with the associated call control signaling provided by a parallel network of links and a single set of layered protocols. Over the same period, data communications services were provided over a separate set of network of links and a set of layered protocols. With telecommunications SPs now merging their telephone and data communications services into a common, or converged, network infrastructure, the industry is now accommodating a much more complex set of Data Link Layer internetworking capabilities actually underneath the generally accepted internetworking layer. Figure 2.19 shows how multiple SONET and WDM links and rings are used as the foundation of both MAN Access and Backbone networks to construct a set of interconnected networks.

While Figure 2.20 depicts a complex set of interconnected networks that are over-layered, on top of the set of interconnected layer two networks are shown in Figure 2.19.

The deployment of complex layer 3 networks over complex layer 2 networks is now becoming quite common.

2.2.6 Additional Networking Developments

A number of terms being used in the IT area need to be discussed. These terms are SCADA, which is an acronym for Supervisory Control and Data Acquisition, sensor networks, and cloud computing. This section will briefly address these three subjects and discuss security issues with each concept.

2.2.6.1 Supervisory Control and Data Acquisition Systems. SCADA systems are comprised of supervisory control computer systems networked to sub-controller systems and frequently industrial sensors (for measuring humidity, temperature, pressure, liquid flow volumes, position, radiation, visible/non-visible light, etc.) and

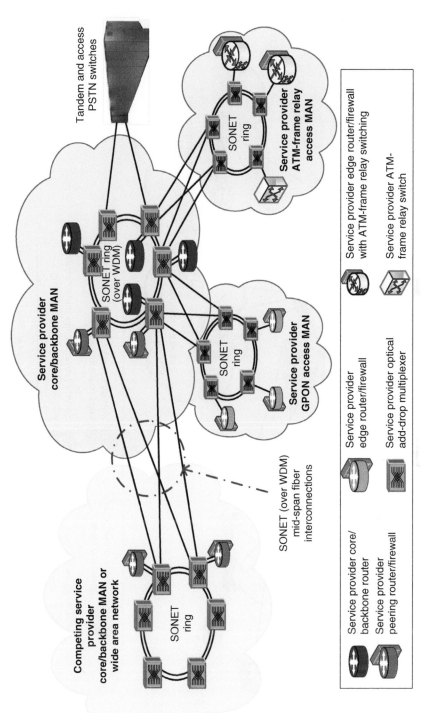

Tandem and access PSTN switches

Service provider core/backbone MAN

SONET ring (over WDM)

Service provider ATM-frame relay access MAN

SONET ring

Service provider GPON access MAN

SONET ring

Competing service provider core/backbone MAN or wide area network

SONET ring

SONET (over WDM) mid-span fiber interconnections

Service provider core/ backbone router

Service provider peering router/firewall

Service provider edge router/firewall

Service provider optical add-drop multiplexer

Service provider edge router/firewall with ATM-frame relay switching

Service provider ATM-frame relay switch

Figure 2.19. MAN Layer 2 Physical and Logical Interconnections.

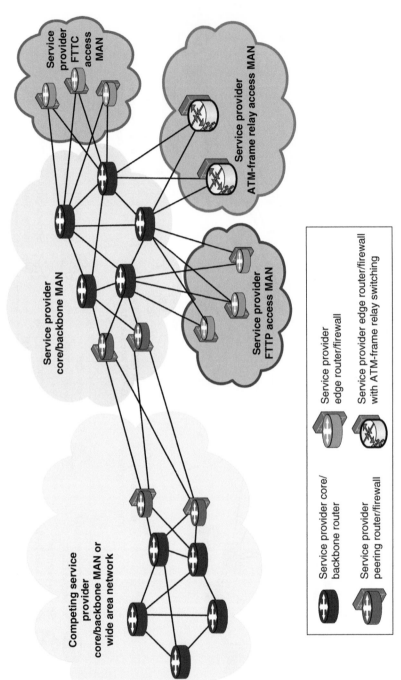

Service provider
FTTC
access
MAN

Service provider
ATM-frame relay access MAN

Service provider
core/backbone MAN

Service provider
FTTP access MAN

Competing service
provider
core/backbone MAN or
wide area network

Service provider
core/
backbone router

Service provider
edge router/firewall

Service provider
peering router/firewall

Service provider edge router/firewall
with ATM-frame relay switching

Figure 2.20. MAN Layer 3 Logical Interconnections.

electro-mechanical actuators (such as valves, motors, lights, alarms, etc.). SCADA systems are used to control many types of industrial processes, for example:

- product and chemical manufacturing production lines and systems;
- power plants (nuclear, fossil fueled, hydro-electric, and alternative energy based) and power distribution systems/grids;
- heating, ventilation, and air-conditioning systems; and
- telecommunications systems.

SCADA systems can be either closed or externally accessible. Closed SCADA systems do not have any external network connectivity, as they are self-contained and, therefore, primarily vulnerable to insider attacks. Given the lack of external/remote access, malicious software or malicious actions must be introduced or performed by an actor/person with direct access to SCADA control/supervisory computing devices or the network used to interconnect the SCADA components. The use of the Stuxnet malware to cause damage to the centrifuges used by the Iranian government for uranium purification is an example of an insider attack. Insider malicious activities can also be used to cause damage to, or cause erroneous operation by, SCADA systems. However, insider malicious activities can be mitigated through the use of robust authentication mechanisms, limiting "span of control" and "scope of commands" via role-based access controls or other mandatory access control mechanisms. Externally accessible SCADA systems possess the same vulnerabilities as closed SCADA systems. In addition, the external communications capabilities can be used for remotely performing malicious actions or remotely introducing malware. If the external communications utilize publically accessible networking resources, such as the "Internet," then the probability of remote attack or malicious activities increases unless rigorous security mechanisms are deployed to strictly control remote access. In 2011, a number of reports focusing on SCADA attacks have appeared, such as:

- An alleged attempt to damage a public water system in the state of Illinois; a later report stated that this event was not an actual attack but rather just a simple pump failure; a third report noted that remote access by a contractor from an international location (traveling) had nothing to do with the pump failure[10]; yet, a fourth report calls into question public explanations.[11] This sequence of reports raises the question of whether public officials would accurately report an actual SCADA attack as occurring;
- The security company Symantec released a survey claiming that the majority of critical infrastructure providers, many of whom completely rely on SCADA systems, do not participate in government critical infrastructure programs and may not be sufficiently prepared for an attack on their SCADA systems;

[10] http://www.washingtonpost.com/world/national-security/water-pump-failure-in-illinois-wasnt-cyberattack-after-all/2011/11/25/gIQACgTewN_story.html

[11] http://www.engadget.com/2011/11/23/feds-deny-hacking-caused-illinois-water-pump-failure/

- A report published by PikeResearch focuses on a nascent awareness by public utilities regarding "cyber security" and contends that this awareness will likely grow over the next few years, but we will have to wait and monitor whether this growing awareness results in increased SCADA system hardening against attacks;
- A report published by the security firm McAfee makes the point that critical infrastructure attacks are occurring now, and that most critical infrastructure operators/owners believe that foreign governments are involved.

Some question whether critical-infrastructure-related SCADA systems are under attack; yet in 2010, the world saw a SCADA attack using the Stuxnet worm. One must consider the probability of attacks as likely which should be considered a call to address SCADA security deficiencies that exist in the utilities, communications, and manufacturing sectors of society. A rapidly developing SCADA system for the power utilities is referred to as the "SmartGRID." The SmartGrid activity intends to insert intelligent devices throughout a nation's power generation and power distribution infrastructure and even include both commercial and retail power consumer facilities. Within the SmartGRID concept, power generation and distribution will be adjustable based on demand and allow more economical efficient consumption on a society-wide basis via the use of bidirectional interaction among components attached to the power grid(s). Unless security issues are addressed comprehensively from the start, a SmartGRID SCADA system represents a significant target for attack or abuse.

2.2.6.2 Sensor Networks.

Sensor networks are basically SCADA systems either based on fixed ("wired") network connectivity or wireless (radio-signal-based) network connectivity, and with a focus on sensors rather than process control capabilities. Fixed-connectivity-based sensor networks face the very same security issues that SCADA systems face. Wireless sensor networks (WSNs) are more vulnerable due to their use of wireless communications where wireless networking is potentially easier to eavesdrop upon, inject falsified communications traffic, or interfere with as in jamming (a DoS attack). Some sensor networks are centrally controlled while other sensor networks can be auto-affiliating as in MANETs. A MANET sensor network relies on all the component devices serving as both end nodes (source or sink of information) and intermediate nodes (forwarding information on behalf of other MANET nodes).

Generically, a MANET is defined as a self-configuring decentralized network of mobile devices connected by wireless links. Governments, for military and emergency/disaster situations, have expressed interest in MANETs due to perceived low deployment and administrative costs. Each device in a MANET is free to move independently in any direction, and will therefore change its links to other devices frequently. Each must forward traffic unrelated to its own use, and therefore be a router. The primary challenge in building a MANET is equipping each device to continuously maintain the information required to properly route traffic. Such networks may operate by themselves or may be connected to the larger Internet. Due to MANET devices serving as both end and intermediate nodes, MANET routing/packet forwarding mechanisms are likely targets for attack. In a MANET, one must also be concerned with a compromised device affiliating with the MANET and then serving as a launching point for attacks on other MANET-attached devices.

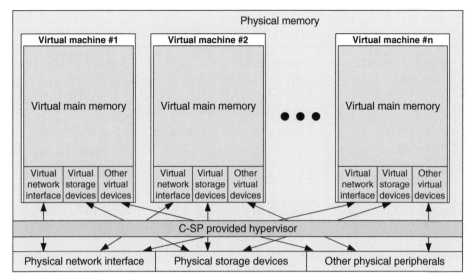

Figure 2.21. Basic Virtual Machine Context.

2.2.6.3 *Cloud Computing.* In recent years, a repackaging of past computing concepts has gained notice under the label of cloud computing as the three varieties of cloud computing reflect prior industry offerings but are now based on virtual machine (VM) techniques rather than dedicated hardware components. VM environments are created on a common computing platform as shown in Figure 2.21. The physical resources of this platform are under the control of a master operating system, called a hypervisor, which is responsible for controlling and mapping VM resources to the physical resources.

The three basic forms of cloud computing are as follows:

- "Hardware as a Service" is quite similar to past vendors offering to make available hardware configurable to customer specifications as either a backup to customer production systems or to provide overflow production processing demands;
- "Infrastructure as a Service" is quite similar to past vendors offering to make available hardware and operating system environment configurable to customer specifications as either a backup to customer production systems or to provide overflow production processing demands; and
- "Software as a Service" is quite similar to past vendors providing outsourced application level production data processing services to customers.

Let us explore each of these three forms in more detail.

2.2.6.3.1 HARDWARE AS A SERVICE. With "Hardware as a Service" offerings, the Cloud Service Provider (C-SP) makes available to customers a VM configuration that the customer can then use to increase production processing capabilities while

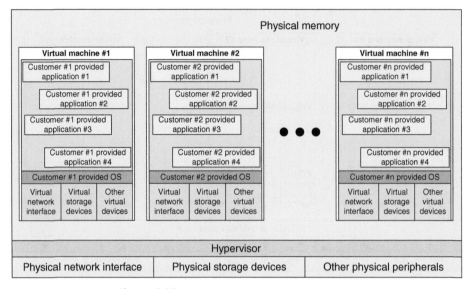

Figure 2.22. Hardware as a Service VM Context.

allowing the customer to avoid hardware-acquisition-, maintenance-, facility-, and utility-related costs. In this form of cloud computing, the SP provides the VM environment under the control of a master operating system (the hypervisor) which is responsible for managing multiple VMs within a common physical hardware platform, as shown in Figure 2.22.

In this form of cloud computing, the customer is responsible for providing an operating system for use within the VM allocated to that customer and applications the customer chooses to run within the allocated VM. The C-SP provides a VM for the customer to use under the control of the C-SP's hypervisor. From a security perspective, a number of issues need to be considered in a "Hardware as a Service" context, including:

- How is access to, and control over, the hypervisor managed by the C-SP? This is an issue as the hypervisor, as the master operating system of the physical computing system elements, has the ability to affect operation of every virtual machine and potentially interfere with VM behavior;
- Who is allowed to install the operating system and applications within a VM? Only the customer to whom the VM is allocated or can C-SP personnel perform these activities? To install software within a VM implies administrative access which could be used to interfere with the behavior of software executing with a VM;
- Who controls data processed within the VM environment? Typically, "Hardware as a Service" virtual services include availability of cloud-located virtual storage within a C-SP storage area network (SAN) facility. Is the customer the only party allowed to access the customer's information within the SAN? Can C-SP personnel access the customer's SAN-stored information? What happens if the C-SP is

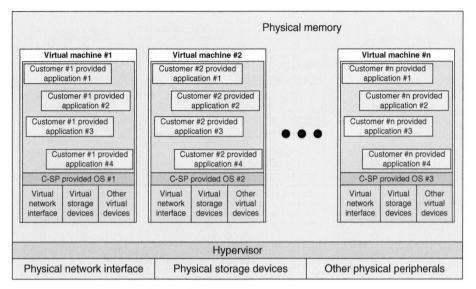

Figure 2.23. Infrastructure as a Service VM Context.

the subject of a court order to supply a customer's information to law enforcement? What happens to a customer's information should the C-SP file for bankruptcy?

To some extent, contract terms and conditions can be put into place regarding the afore-mentioned issues. But, can such terms and conditions be enforced, and who can ensure, via monitoring or auditing, that contract terms and conditions are not being violated?

2.2.6.3.2 INFRASTRUCTURE AS A SERVICE. As with "Hardware as a Service," "Infrastructure as a Service" customers are allocated a VM configuration. In this form of cloud computing, the C-SP provides the VM and an operating system for use within the allocated VM, as shown in Figure 2.23.

In this form of cloud computing, the customer is only responsible for providing applications the customer chooses to run within the allocated VM. From a security perspective, a number of issues need to be considered in an "Infrastructure as a Service" context, including:

- How is access to, and control over, the hypervisor managed by the C-SP?
- Who is allowed to install the operating system within a VM?
- Who is allowed to have administrative access to, and perform maintenance of, the operating system within a VM?
- Who is allowed to install applications within a VM?
- Who controls data processed within the VM environment? Typically, "Infrastructure as a Service" virtual services include availability of SAN-based virtual storage. Is the customer the only party allowed to access the customer's information within the SAN? Can C-SP personnel access the customer's

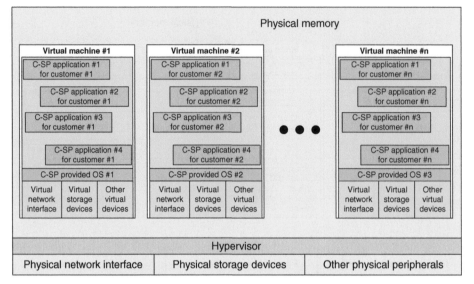

Figure 2.24. Application as a Service VM Context.

SAN-stored information? What happens if the C-SP is the subject of a court order to supply a customer's information to law enforcement? What happens to a customer's information should the C-SP file for bankruptcy?

To some extent, contract terms and conditions can be put into place regarding the afore-mentioned issues. But, will such terms and conditions be enforceable, and who can ensure, via monitoring or auditing, that contract terms and conditions are not being violated?

2.2.6.3.3 SOFTWARE (APPLICATIONS) AS A SERVICE. As with "Hardware as a Service" and "Infrastructure as a Service," "Software as a Service" customers are allocated a VM configuration. In this form of cloud computing, the SP provides the VM an operating system for use within the allocated VM and all applications that will be executed within the VM, as shown in Figure 2.24.

In this form of cloud computing, the customer is only responsible for providing the data the customer chooses to process using the C-SP provided applications within the allocated VM. From a security perspective, a number of issues need to be considered in an "Application as a Service" context, including:

- How is access to, and control over, the hypervisor managed by the C-SP?
- Who is allowed to install the operating system within a VM?
- Who is allowed to have administrative access to, and perform maintenance of, the operating system within a VM?
- Who is allowed to install applications within a VM?
- Who is allowed to have administrative access to, and perform maintenance of, the applications within a VM?

• Who controls data processed within the VM environment? Typically, "Application as a Service" virtual services include availability of SAN-based virtual storage. Is the customer the only party allowed to access the customer's information within the SAN? Can C-SP personnel access the customer's SAN-stored information? What happens if the C-SP is the subject of a court order to supply a customer's information to law enforcement? What happens to a customer's information should the C-SP file for bankruptcy?

To some extent, contract terms and conditions can be put into place regarding the aforementioned issues. However, will such terms and conditions be enforceable, and who can ensure, via monitoring or auditing, that contract terms and conditions are not being violated?

2.2.6.3.4 PUBLIC VERSUS PRIVATE CLOUDS. Whether one is discussing "Hardware as a Service," "Infrastructure as a Service," or "Applications as a Service" type clouds, access to, and control over customer data is a critical issue. Another issue for all three forms of cloud computing is network reachability to an allocated VM. There is a developing "third-party" market of C-SPs offering "Public Clouds," as well as some organizations developing internal cloud capabilities ("Private Clouds"). With "third-party" cloud services, customers typically connect to their allocated VM environments over public networks such as the Internet; whereas organization internal clouds rely on organization intranets for VM access. Public networks used to assess VMs pose increased risk of security events/breaches compared to organization intranet-based VM access, as, by their very nature, public networks must be accessible by the general public. Whenever the general public has access to a network, the probability that someone will attempt to use this access for malicious activities increases. Consequently, a "Private Cloud" is likely to be less vulnerable than a "Public Cloud." This reduced vulnerability is primarily due to the operator of the "Private Cloud" being part of the very customer organization utilizing a "Private Cloud," and therefore subject to the same security governance as the cloud clients.

2.2.7 Security Mechanisms in Modern Networks

Let us revisit the security mechanisms identified in the preceding section on network organizations. Table 2.3 maps the different security mechanisms to the network organizations discussed.

Whenever any of these types of networks requires the deployment of large numbers of networking devices (i.e., switches, router/firewalls, access points, PON/DSL/cable modems, DSLAMs, CMTSs, OLTs, ADMs, etc.), network management, especially security management, becomes critical for achieving unified and consistent control of security functions. How the security management occurs will have a major impact on the effectiveness of deployed security mechanisms.

Before moving onto Next Generation Networks (NGNs), it should be noted that in conventional networks, applications are responsible for providing their own security-related capabilities with little assistance from network resources. Few applications

TABLE 2.3. Security Mechanisms Used by Different Network Organizations.

Security Mechanism	LANs and Intranets	Wireless LANs	Sensor and Ad Hoc Networks	Cellular	WiMAX and LTE	Access MANs	Backbone MANs	WANs
IEEE 802.1x	Yes	Yes	Yes			Yes		
IEEE 802.11i		Yes						
IEEE 802.1ae	Yes							
IPsec	Yes	Yes	Yes			Yes (note 1)	Yes (note 1)	Yes (note 1)
Packet filtering	Yes	Yes				Yes	Yes	Yes
SBC	Yes (note 2)					Yes	Yes	Yes
Switch port security	Yes	Yes		Yes	Yes			
AAA servers	Yes (note 3)	Yes (note 4)		Yes (note 5)	Yes (note 5)	Yes (note 6)	Yes (note 6)	Yes (note 6)
ARP monitoring	Yes (note 7)							
Key management			Yes (note 8)	Yes	Yes	Yes (note 9)		
PKI	Yes (notes 10,12)	Yes (note 10)	Yes (notes 10,11)			Yes (note 13)	Yes (note 13)	Yes (note 13)
Networked intrusion sensors	Yes (note 11)		Yes (notes 10,11)			Yes (note 11)	Yes (note 11)	Yes (note 11)

Notes:

1. IPsec usage in Access MANs, Backbone MANs, and WANs should be used over SONET data communication channels (DCCs) and WDM Optical Supervisory Channels (OSCs) that make use of IP protocols to provide Peer-entity and Data-origin Authentication. When DCC and OSC use the OSI protocols, there is no protection against unauthorized receipt of messages sent by competitive provider equipment; see Appendix F.

2. SBC can be used in LANs but typically are found in Data Center LANs, not general intranets.

3. Wired LANs use AAA servers to support IEEE 802.1x network access controls.

4. Wireless LANs can use RADIUS AAA servers to support IEEE 802.11i and WPA security mechanisms.
5. Cellular and WiMAX networks use AAA servers for subscriber authentication and network access controls.
6. AAA servers are frequently used for authentication during remote administrative access.
7. As previously noted, there are a number of ARP monitoring mechanisms involving both clients and servers.
8. Sensor and Ad Hoc networks use a number of mechanisms for authentication, data integrity, and even confidentiality of distributed routing information where these mechanisms usually rely on use of shared secret keys that require generation, distribution, and replacement necessitating some form of key management.
9. GPON-based Access MANs rely on use of the AES symmetric encryption algorithm and shared secret keys that require generation, distribution, and replacement necessitating some form of key management.
10. LAN, Wireless, Sensor and Ad Hoc networks, MANs, and WANs can utilize asymmetric encryption for Peer-entity authentication requiring private keys and X.509v3 digital certificates in conjunction with AAA functions.
11. Sensor and Ad Hoc networks may use asymmetric encryption for Peer-entity authentication requiring private keys and X.509v3 digital certificates in conjunction with routing information distribution.
12. IPsec usage includes asymmetric encryption for Peer-entity authentication requiring private keys and X.509v3 digital certificates.
13. MAN and WAN equipment may rely on remote management activities protected via IPsec which includes asymmetric encryption for Peer-entity authentication requiring private keys and X.509v3 digital certificates.

expect network security capabilities beyond the availability of a PKI, RADIUS servers, or Kerberos authentication servers. Put another way, application security has been considered an end-to-end responsibility with little interaction with network security mechanisms. This approach is changing within the NGNs discussed next.

2.3 NEXT-GENERATION NETWORKS AND INTERFACES

SPs are rapidly evolving from the classic Time-Division-Multiplexed-based PSTNs to packet-based NGNs that rely on numerous access technologies and provide a wide array of customer/subscriber/user services. The technologies, protocols, and network organizations discussed earlier in this chapter are used within NGNs. However, the focus of the evolving NGN architecture work is to take a unified and organized view of all network technologies and mechanisms from a service perspective. The objective of this section is to provide a brief overview of the functional capabilities and architecture of standards-based NGNs (as described in ITU-T Y.2012[12] and ITU-T Y.2201[13]) and highlight the security concepts and mechanisms within NGNs. The ITU-T Y.2012 functional architecture recommendation provides a clear distinction between the definition and specification aspects of services provided by the NGN and the actual specification of the network technologies used to support those services. The following sections are based on these identified ITU-T recommendations (standards).

2.3.1 Framework and Topology of the NGN

The NGN increases the level of complexity over existing fixed networks as a result of its architecture and services. The addition of support for multiple access technologies and for mobility results in the need to support a wide variety of network configurations. Figure 2.25 shows an NGN core network with a set of example access networks.

In Figure 2.25, the NGN core/backbone network (likely an SP core/backbone MAN) is that part of the NGN that provides contracted-for services of the NGN to the user. It is different from SP MAN access network(s) in that it provides common functions shared across one or more access networks. MAN Access networks differ from the NGN core/backbone network in that they do not provide end-user services directly (other than transport). NGN access and core/backbone networks may be distinguished from each other based on aspects such as technology, ownership, or administrative needs. Different ownership implies that an NGN core/backbone network may very well be operated according to different security policies than those used within an attached NGN access network.

2.3.1.1 Functional Entities and Groups. A key component of the NGN architecture is the concept of Functional Entities (FEs) and Functional Groups (FGs). An FE is a cluster of sub-functions that is viewed as a single entity from the point of view of the

---

[12] ITU-T Recommendation Y.2012 (2006), Functional Requirements and Architecture of the NGN.

[13] ITU T Recommendation Y.2201 (2007), Next Generation Networks – Service aspects: Service capabilities and service architecture

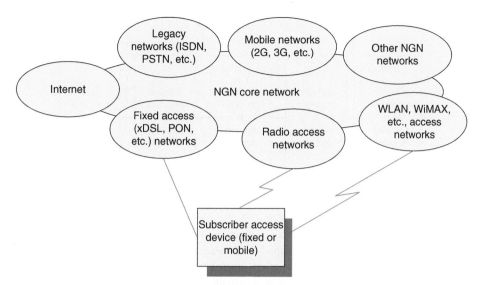

Figure 2.25. NGN Core and Access Networks. ISDN = Integrated Services Digital Networks; PSTN = Public Switched Telephone Networks; 2G = Second-Generation Cellular Networks; 3G = Third-Generation Cellular Networks; xDSL = Digital Subscriber Line Networks (Asymmetric, Symmetric, High Bit Rate, etc.); PON = Passive Optical Networks; WiMAX = Worldwide Interoperability for Microwave Access Networks.

end-to-end functional architecture. An FE may be localized at a single geographical location (e.g., a central office, a data center), or it may be implemented across several cooperating physical elements. An FE is typically a software process—or a portion of a software process—running on some network element. The correct granularity for an FE is based on the desired or required decomposition. If the functionality can be broken down into two or more processes that could advantageously be located at different geographical or physical locations, then it is better to define two or more separate, cooperating FEs with a relationship or association between them rather than considering the given functionality as a single FE.

It should be noted that it is the possibility (and potential desirability) of functional separation that matters here. Defining a set of sub-functions as a single, distinct FE (i.e., separately from some other set of sub-functions) does not constrain the mappings to a physical implementation. It simply allows for multiple physical scenarios for the same overall set of functionality. Of course it is always possible to combine two or more distinct FEs in a single physical implementation. This might be dictated by a particular vendor implementation or driven by performance requirements.

An FE Reference Model is an abstract description of a system architecture that provides a framework or structure for examining significant FEs and their key associations or relationships. The granularity of the reference model will vary with the use objectives for the model.

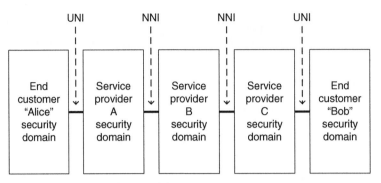

Figure 2.26. Example Domains.

Each FG, within the frameworks, contains an FE Reference Model.

An FG is a cluster of FEs grouped (and named) solely for convenience and architectural clarity. This concept is particularly useful in descriptions of functional reference models and functional architectures as it provides a means of organizing or clustering closely related FEs. FGs are less useful once FEs have been assigned or allocated to physical entities, as often there may not be a one-to-one mapping of FGs to physical entities.

However, FGs are not intended to constrain FE physical placement.

2.3.1.2 *Domains and Interfaces.* The concept of security domains has evolved over the preceding 20 years and now provides a generally accepted view of organizational ownership, control, and trust. These domain attributes may be tightly held by the domain owner or shared/entrusted to another party. Typically, all devices that are part of a domain can expect all other devices within the same domain to adhere to the same security policy. In Figure 2.26, five different security domains are shown: an Alice customer domain, a Bob customer domain, and three SP domains. Also shown here are the domain boundaries, referred to as interfaces, and named as follows:

- a domain interface between a customer and an SP is called a User–Network Interface (UNI), and
- a domain interface between two different SPs is called a Network–Network Interface (NNI).

The NGN architecture recognizes three major domains, namely:

- Customer (End-User) Domain;
- SP Access Domain; and
- SP Core/Services Domain.

The interface between the SP Access Domain and an SP Core/Services Domain can be an NNI or can be what is called an Internal NNI (INNI) when both domains belong to the same SP. The **Customer Domain** aggregates the various access methods for services, ranging from plain old telephones to IP phones and appliances, as well as applications that provide web access, messaging, and other non-verbal communication used by end users within a customer organization. The **SP Access Domain** has a number of technologies that implement layer 1 and layer 2 forwarding protocols in the access function. The access domain may also include distributed internetworking (layer 3) functions. Typically, the equipment deployed in the access domain has a relatively simple ring-based topology to distribute traffic between the end user and the Access (also called the Edge-Aggregation) Domain. The Access Domain may also implement a PON. The **SP Core/Services Domain** includes functions central to the delivery of suites of services to customers. FEs in this domain interact with FEs in all the other domains. The interfaces between the various FEs, as well as the boundary points between the domains, provide meeting points for integration and interoperability. The NGN architecture supports the notion that multiple NGN core/services networks may interoperate to provide an end-to-end service to the user. Restated, a single SP may deploy multiple core/services networks within and between metropolitan regions. In a simple case, an end-to-end session will have originating and terminating core/services networks. Depending on an SP's particular organization, one or more separate access networks might be involved. The specific division of functionality between core/services and access networks, and between the originating and terminating networks, is based on the, or multiple, SPs' business decisions, it is difficult to precisely define the attributes that make up each of these configuration elements. Rather than hard points of separation in the architecture, these aspects should be thought of as configurable topology elements that may be mixed and matched in many different ways.

The UNI interface represents a logical point of interconnection between a circuit switched (CS) network infrastructure element and an Access SP network infrastructure element. At the:

- Data Link Layer, two elements (serving as intermediate elements with one in the CS security domain and the other within the SP security domain) will be directly physically interconnected and will exchange signaling and control information for the purpose of information (as frames, cells, datagrams, packets) transfer of bearer (aka media or user) traffic from/to CS and SP network infrastructures;
- Internetworking Layer, two elements (serving as intermediate elements with one in the CS security domain and the other within the SP security domain) will rarely be directly physically interconnected but will exchange signaling and control information for the purpose of information (as packets) forwarding of bearer (aka media or user) traffic from/to CS and SP network infrastructures;
- Transport Layer, two elements (serving as end elements with one in the CS security domain and the other within the SP security domain) will not be directly physically interconnected but will exchange bearer (aka media or user) traffic and signaling and control information (as datagrams or byte streams) between specific

processes executing within each end element on an end-to-end basis within the CS and SP network infrastructures;

- Application Layer, two elements (serving as end elements either with one in the CS security domain and the other within the SP security domain or both in different CS security domains) will not be directly physically interconnected but will exchange bearer (aka media or user) messages, signaling and control messages, and possibly management messages between specified application functions executing within each end element on an end-to-end basis as defined within each application.

The INNI interface represents a logical point of interconnection between network infrastructure elements within the same security domain. At the:

- Data Link Layer, two elements (both within the same security domain) will be directly physically interconnected and will exchange signaling and control information for the purpose of information (as frames, cells, datagrams, packets) transfer of bearer (aka media or user) traffic within the network infrastructure;
- Internetworking Layer, two elements (both within the same security domain) will rarely be directly physically interconnected but will exchange signaling and control information for the purpose of information (as packets) forwarding of bearer (aka media or user) traffic within the network infrastructure;
- Transport Layer, two elements (serving as end elements both within the same security domain) will not be directly physically interconnected but will exchange bearer (aka media or user) traffic and signaling and control information (as datagrams or byte streams) between specific processes executing within each end element on an end-to-end basis within the network infrastructure;
- Application Layer, two elements (serving as end elements both within the same security domain) will not be directly physically interconnected but will exchange bearer (aka media or user) messages, signaling and control messages, and possibly management messages between specified application functions executing within each end element on an end-to-end basis as defined within each application.

The NNI (aka External NNI) represents a logical point of interconnection between two network infrastructure elements within two different SP security domains. At the:

- Data Link Layer, two elements (serving as intermediate elements with one in an SP security domain and the other within a different SP security domain) will be directly physically interconnected and will exchange signaling and control information for the purpose of information (as frames, cells, datagrams, packets) transfer of bearer (aka media or user) traffic from/to the two different SP network infrastructures;
- Internetworking Layer, two elements (serving as intermediate elements with one in an SP security domain and the other within a different SP security domain) will rarely be directly physically interconnected but will exchange signaling and

control information for the purpose of information (as packets) forwarding of bearer (aka media or user) traffic from/to the two different SP network infrastructures;

- Transport Layer, two elements (serving as end elements with one in an SP security domain and the other within a different SP security domain) will not be directly physically interconnected but will exchange bearer (aka media or user) traffic and signaling and control information (as datagrams or byte streams) between specific processes executing within each end element on an end-to-end basis within the two different SP network infrastructures;
- Application Layer, two elements (serving as end elements either with one in an SP security domain and the other within a different SP security domain) will not be directly physically interconnected but will exchange bearer (aka media or user) messages, signaling and control messages, and possibly management messages between specified application functions executing within each end element on an end-to-end basis as defined within each application.

The NGN network can be logically decomposed into different sub-networks, as shown in Figure 2.27. In this figure, four different SPs are depicted (SP #1 with core/services and access domains, SP #2 with only an access domain, SP #3 with core/services and access domains, and SP #4 with only a core/services domain). The emphasis on logical decomposition instead of physical decomposition is based on the fact that, in the future, physical equipment may have features of both the access and the core networks. A pure physical decomposition will encounter difficulties when such features are combined into a single network element.

The major NGN components depicted in the preceding discussion are:

- Customer network domain: A customer network can be a network within a home or an enterprise network. It is connected to an SP access network via a **UNI**. The UNI is the demarcation point between the SP and the customer. End users within a customer network may obtain content services from:
  - an SP providing access and core/services networking to the customer (as with Customer #1 and SP #1 in Figure 2.27);
  - an SP providing core/services networking to the customer (as with Customer #3 and either SP #1 or SP #3 in Figure 2.27);
  - FEs within the customer's network that provide public services; or
  - FEs within the customer's network that provide private services, possibly with a private addressing scheme.
- SP access network domain: An SP access network collects end-user traffic from customer networks and passes this traffic to an SP core/services network. The access network SP is responsible for the access network. The access network can be further partitioned into different sub-domains, with the intra-sub-domain interfaces called **INNIs** and the interfaces between access networks and core/services networks called **NNIs**. The access network resides within the Transport Stratum.

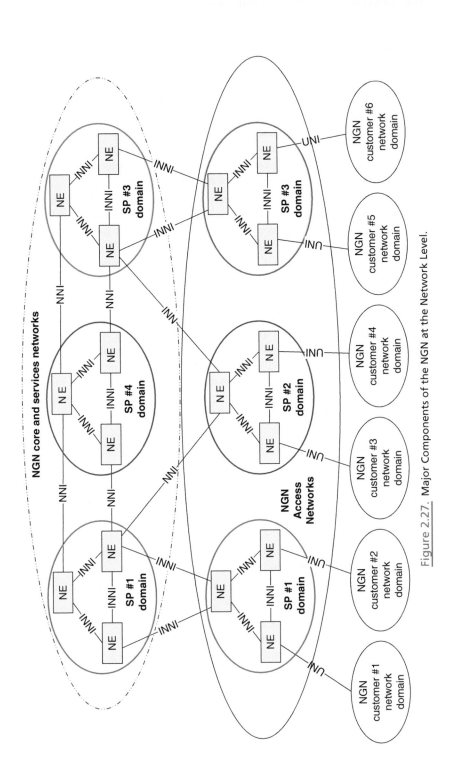

Figure 2.27. Major Components of the NGN at the Network Level.

- Core/services network domains: An SP core/services network interacts with end-user originated traffic and provides services the customer has contracted for. The core/services SP is responsible for its core/services network. The interface between a core/services network and an access network can be an INNI (in the case of partitioning as a single domain) or an NNI interconnecting access and core/services domains if both are provided by the same SP. Interconnection of core/services domains of different SPs are always over NNI interfaces. An SP core/services network contains functional capabilities that are part of both the Transport Stratum and the Service Stratum.

The concept of an NGN domain is introduced to outline the administrative boundaries. Detailed topology information may or may not be shared across the NNI, but may be shared, if available, for INNI links. As depicted in Figure 2.27, an access network and a core/services network may or may not belong to the same SP domain.

2.3.1.3 Protocol Layers Versus Functional Planes Versus Interfaces. Another concept introduced with the NGN, along with the concepts of UNI, NNI, and INNI, is the recognition that network traffic is not all the same, but represents activity that falls into the three areas of:

- User Plane activities (aka Data Plane or Media Plane) that serves as an abstraction of where user information is located, utilizes protocols such as RTP, HTML, and MIME, and responsible for traffic that carries information that users want, such as web pages, emails, messages, files, voice conversations, video streams/movies, etc.;
- Control Plane activities that serves as an abstraction of where signaling and control information is located, utilizes protocols such as SIP, BGP, OSPF, DHCP, ARP, and ICMP, and responsible for traffic that carries information used to control User Plane activities (referred to as signaling) or control network activities, such as packet routing, session control, etc.(referred to as control), which is called Signaling and Control Plane traffic; and
- Management Plane activities that serves as an abstraction of where management information is located, utilizes protocols such as SNMP, NTP, DNS, and LDAP, and responsible for traffic that carries information used to manage devices (as in Fault, Configuration, Accounting, Provisioning, and Security (FCAPS) messages).

Many legacy protocols, such as Telnet, FTP, tFTP, SMTP, and POP3, have historically combined control and user plane activity capabilities; yet, newer protocols, such as SIP and RTP, are now being developed that separate User Plane from Control Plane capabilities. Figure 2.28 shows the merger of protocols, interfaces, and the User Plane, Signaling and Control Plane, and Management Plane. All protocol layers may traverse the different types of interfaces (UNI, INNI, and NNI). Likewise, User Plane and Signaling Plane traffic may traverse these interfaces. However, Management Plane activities always occur as interactions between management functions and are regarded by transport, networking, Data Link, and physical protocol layers as simply the contents of application protocols.

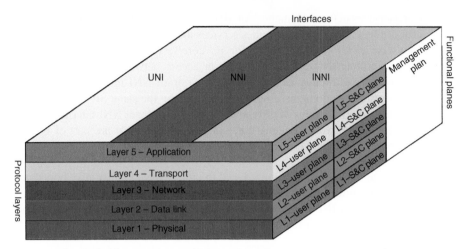

Figure 2.28. Protocol Layers Versus Functional Planes Versus Interfaces.

To help clarify the relationship between protocol layers, traffic (functional) planes, and interfaces, let us examine two examples. In the first example, a workstation within the "Alice" customer intranet is interacting with a server within the "Bob" customer intranet. Both the "Alice" customer intranet and the "Bob" customer intranet are attached to a common SP. This example is depicted in Figure 2.29, where one should notice that:

- Application (layer 5) and Transport (layer 4) User Plane and Signaling and Control Plane traffic extend end to end between the workstation and server only traversing UNIs. These traffic types are only transported by the SP infrastructure and do not interact directly with any SP devices beyond bytes to be forwarded with the exception that these traffic types may be inspected by SP-ERs for malicious content but otherwise would be viewed by these SP-ERs as bytes to be forwarded;

- Internetworking (layer 3) User Plane and Signaling and Control Plane traffic between C-ERs and SP-ERs traversing UNIs. These traffic types are only transported by the SP access networks and do not interact directly with any access network devices beyond bytes to be forwarded;

- Internetworking (layer 3) User Plane and Signaling and Control Plane traffic between SP-ERs and SP-CRs traversing INNIs. The Internetworking (layer 3) User Plane traffic may be inspected by SP-ERs for malicious content but otherwise would be viewed by these SP-ERs as bytes to be forwarded. On the other hand, the Internetworking (layer 3) Signaling and Control Plane will be processed by the SP ERs and SP-CRs to enable correct routing and forwarding of User Plane traffic;

- All Data Link Layer (layer 3) User Plane and Signaling and Control Plane traffic between the customer workstation and server will be processed by their associated C-ERs traversing INNIs. These two traffic types, from the C-ERs and SP

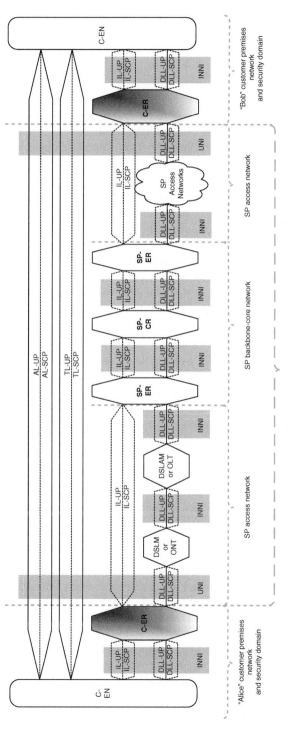

Figure 2.29. Example of two End Nodes and one SP.

Symbol key

C-EN	Customer end node (client or server)	DLL-SCP Data link layer signaling & control plane traffic
C-ER	Customer edge router	DLL-UP Data link layer user plane traffic
DSLM	DSL modem	IL-SCP Internetworking layer signaling & control plane traffic
ONT	Optical network terminator	IL-UP Internetworking layer user plane traffic
DSLAM	Digital subscriber line access module	TL-SCP Transport layer signaling & control plane traffic
SP-ER	Service provider edge router	TL-UP Transport layer user plane traffic
SP-CR	Service provider core router	AL-SCP Application layer signaling & control plane traffic
UNI	User network interface	AL-UP Application layer user plane traffic
INNI	Internal network–network interface	

access network devices (Digital Subscriber Line Modem (DSLM) or Optical Network Terminator (ONT)), will traverse UNIs. However, these two traffic types will traverse INNIs between devices within the SP access networks and the SP core/backbone network.

In the second example, a workstation within the "Alice" customer intranet is interacting with a server within the "Bob" customer intranet where the "Alice" customer intranet and the "Bob" customer intranet are attached to different SPs that are directly interconnected (the two SPs have a direct "peering" relationship). This example is depicted in Figure 2.30, where one should notice that:

- Application (layer 5) and Transport (layer 4) User Plane and Signaling and Control Plane traffic extend end to end between the workstation and server only traversing UNIs between the customers and their serving SPs but traverse NNIs when being forwarded between the core/backbone networks of the two different SPs. These traffic types are only transported by the two SP infrastructures and do not interact directly with any SP devices beyond bytes to be forwarded, with the exception that these traffic types may be inspected by the SP-ERs and SP-PRs for malicious content but otherwise would be viewed by these SP-ERs as bytes to be forwarded;
- Internetworking (layer 3) User Plane and Signaling and Control Plane traffic between C-ERs and either SP-ERs (SP "Alpha" or SP "Beta")) traverse UNIs. These traffic types are only transported by the SP access networks and do not interact directly with any access network devices beyond bytes to be forwarded;
- Internetworking (layer 3) User Plane and Signaling and Control Plane traffic between SP A ERs (SP-ERs) and SP A PRs (SP-PRs) traverse INNIs within the SP A core/backbone network and handled similarly between SP B ERs (SP-ERs) and SP B PRs (SP-PRs) over INNIs within the SP B core/backbone network. The Internetworking (layer 3) User Plane traffic may be inspected by the SP-ERs for malicious content but otherwise would be viewed by these SP-ERs as bytes to be forwarded. On the other hand, the Internetworking (layer 3) Signaling and Control Plane will be processed by the SP-ERs and SP-PRs to enable correct routing and forwarding of User Plane traffic. However, all Data Link Layer (layer 3) User Plane and Signaling and Control Plane traffic between the customer workstation and server will be processed by their associated C-ERs traversing INNIs. These two traffic types, from the C-ERs and either SP A or SP B, access network devices will traverse UNIs. However, these two traffic types will traverse INNIs between devices within the SP access networks and the SP core/backbone network but traverse an NNI between the SP core/backbone networks.

2.3.1.4 The NGN Functional Reference Model. Figure 2.31 depicts the high-level framework or structure that serves as the basis for the NGN Functional Reference Model. As described in ITU-T Y.2012, this framework is organized into two vertical "Strata" and a collection of applications in the vertical direction plus management functionality and three horizontal "Domains."

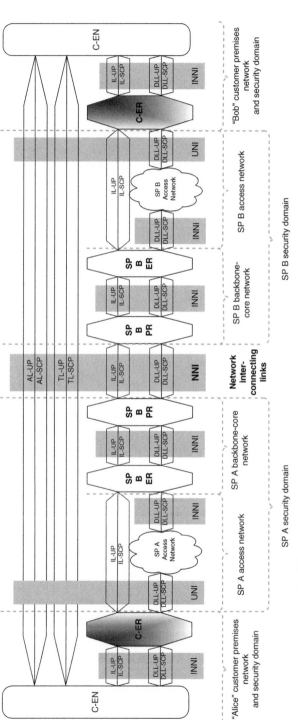

Figure 2.30. Example of two End Nodes and two SPs.

Symbol key

C-EN	Customer end node (client or server)
C-ER	Customer edge router
ER	Service provider edge router
PR	Service provider peering router
UNI	User network interface
INNI	Internal network–network interface
NNI	Network–network interface

DLL-SCP	Data link layer signaling & control plane traffic
DLL-UP	Data link layer user plane traffic
IL-SCP	Internetworking layer signaling & control plane traffic
IL-UP	Internetworking layer user plane traffic
TL-SCP	Transport layer signaling & control plane traffic
TL-UP	Transport layer user plane traffic
AL-SCP	Application layer signaling & control plane traffic
AL-UP	Application layer user plane traffic
SP A	Service provider "Alpha"
SP B	Service provider "Bravo"

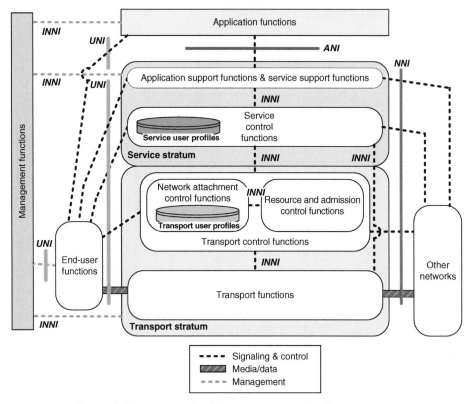

Figure 2.31. Framework of the NGN Functional Reference Model.

2.3.1.4.1 STRATA. The NGN architecture is divided into multiple interrelated, logical layers, two of which are called the Transport and Services Strata, along with Management and Applications FGs. The strata define logical subsets of the NGN's functions without regard to the technology used to implement those functions. Each functional layer provides capabilities to adjacent layers. This grouping is useful in understanding the functionality involved but does not imply any physical implementation.

2.3.1.4.2 MANAGEMENT FUNCTIONAL GROUP. The Management FG contains the management functionality relating to Quality of Service (QoS), Security, and System and Network Management. This FG is responsible for providing the FCAPS management functions to all FEs within all strata, for example, operational support functions such as provisioning, configuration management, accounting, and performance. This group will be discussed further when we get to NGN Management concepts.

2.3.1.4.3 APPLICATION FUNCTIONAL GROUP. The Application FG is responsible for:

1. defining and managing subscribers, including their subscriptions, their preferences, and their key data items;

2. defining and managing services, including the infrastructure to support services and the common data and media functions upon which they are built;

3. authenticating and authorizing users; and
4. providing the environment for the distinct service applications.

Unfortunately, ITU-T Y.2012 does not elaborate (provide any detailed discussion) on this FG.

2.3.1.5 The Transport Stratum.

The Transport Stratum includes the logical functions which provide the connectivity for all physically separated functions within an NGN. These functions support the transfer of media, signaling and control, and management information. Transport functions include access network functions, edge functions, core transport functions, and gateway functions. The Transport Stratum includes:

- Access network functions;
- Edge functions;
- Core transport functions;
- Gateway functions;
- Media handling functions; and
- Transport control functions.

The NGN architecture makes no assumptions about either the technologies to be used or the internal structure, for example, the core transport network and the access transport network. This is a key point in that multiple instantiations of Transport Stratum functions can be deployed in parallel logical networks which only intersect at layer 1 (via WDM) or layer 2 (via SONET, Generalized Framing Protocol, Generalized Multiprotocol Label Switching). Transport functionality, which focuses on layer 2 through 4 capabilities, will likely be replicated as the deploying organization physically, or logically, segregates or isolates signaling and control or management traffic to its own dedicated transport infrastructures. This will likely occur within SP infrastructures. Figure 2.32 shows an SP optical Metropolitan backbone network with subtending optical Metropolitan access networks and redundant interconnection to multiple SP WANs. Interconnection with the WAN of this SP would be optical and only involve protocol layers 1 and 2, but interconnections with the WANs of different SP would occur at layer 3 using the access control capabilities with a router specifically designed for inter-SP interconnection (known as peering).

Let us examine these types of networks further.

The **access network** functions handle end-user access to the network as well as collect and aggregate the traffic coming from these users toward the core network. These functions also perform QoS control mechanisms dealing directly with user traffic, including buffer management, queuing and scheduling, packet filtering, traffic classification, marking, policing, and shaping. Access networks include access-technology-dependent functions depending on the technology used for accessing NGN services, including:

- Cable (fiber/coaxial cables);
- xDSL (metallic twisted pair wires);
- wireless (e.g., IEEE 802.11, IEEE 802.16, LTE technologies); and
- optical fibers.

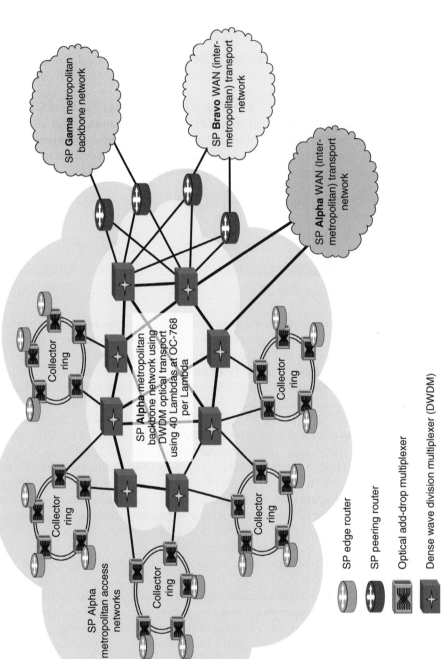

SP **Gama** metropolitan backbone network

SP **Bravo** WAN (inter-metropolitan) transport network

SP **Alpha** WAN (Inter-metropolitan) transport network

Collector ring

Collector ring

SP Alpha metropolitan backbone network using DWDM optical transport using 40 Lambdas at OC-768 per Lambda

Collector ring

Collector ring

Collector ring

SP Alpha metropolitan access networks

Collector ring

SP edge router

SP peering router

Optical add-drop multiplexer

Dense wave division multiplexer (DWDM)

Figure 2.32. Example SP Access and Backbone Metropolitan Optical Networks.

In Figure 2.33, we show an access network supporting PON and xDSL technologies. Access networks for cable and wireless technologies are very similar.

Edge functions provide media and traffic processing when aggregating traffic into the core transport network. Such functions include support for QoS and traffic control and are also used between core transport networks. Capabilities in this area additionally include stateful packet filtering, deep packet inspection, security tunnel termination, and SBC (mapping authorized signaling with corresponding media traffic). These capabilities may be provided by an SP-ER or by some device(s) co-located with the SP-ER.

Core transport functions are responsible for ensuring information transport throughout the core network and thus provide the means to differentiate the quality of transport in the core network. These functions provide QoS mechanisms dealing directly with user traffic, including buffer management, queuing and scheduling, packet filtering, traffic classification, marking, policing, shaping, gate control, and firewall capability. These capabilities may be provided by an SP Metropolitan backbone router, an SP Optical Add-Drop Multiplexer, or by some device(s) co-located with these elements.

Gateway functions provide capabilities to interwork with end-user functions and/ or other networks, including other types of NGN and many existing networks, such as the PSTN, Internet Service Providers, etc. These types of devices are not specified with the NGN standards, or shown in Figure 2.33, but are covered within the Internet Multimedia System (IMS) covered a little later.

Media handling functions provide media resource processing for service provision, such as generation of tone signals and recoding of digitized voice, and are specific to media resource handling.

Transport control functions include resource and admission control functions (RACFs) and network attachment control functions (NACFs). These types of devices are not specified with the NGN standards, or shown in Figure 2.33, but are covered within the IMS covered a little later.

The Resource and Admission Control Functions (**RACFs**) act as the arbitrator between service control functions (SCFs) and transport functions for QoS-related transport resource control within access and core networks. The RACFs provide an abstract view of transport network infrastructure to SCFs and make SPs agnostic to the details of transport facilities such as network topology, connectivity, resource utilization, and QoS mechanisms/technology, etc.

The RACFs perform the policy-based transport resource control upon the request of the SCF, determine the transport resource availability and admission, and apply controls to the transport functions to enforce the policy decision, including resource reservation, admission control and gate control, NAT and firewall control, and NAT traversal. The RACF interacts with transport functions for the purpose of controlling one or more of the following functions in the transport layer: bandwidth reservation and allocation, packet filtering; traffic classification, marking, policing, and priority handling; network address and port translation; and firewall. These types of devices are not specified with the NGN standards, or shown in Figure 2.33, but are covered within the IMS covered a little later.

The Network Attachment Control Functions (**NACFs**) provide registration at the access level and initialization of end-user functions for accessing NGN services,

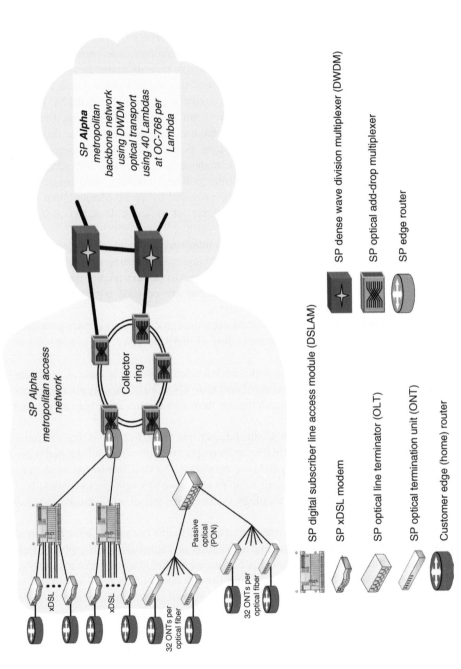

Figure 2.33. SP xDSL and PON Access Network Structures.

including Transport Stratum level identification/authentication, manage the IP address space of the access network, and authenticate access sessions. They also announce the contact point of NGN functions in the Service Stratum to the end user.

The NACF provides the following functionalities:

- Dynamic provisioning of IP addresses and other equipment configuration parameters;
- Endorsement of user, auto-discovery of user equipment capabilities, and other parameters;
- Authentication of user and network at the IP layer;
- Authorization of network access, based on user profiles;
- Access network configuration, based on user profiles; and
- Location management at the IP layer.

The NACFs include transport user profile which takes the form of a functional database representing the combination of a user's information and other control data into a single "user profile" function in the Transport Stratum. However, one needs to be careful regarding the term "user," as this can easily refer to service consuming users/subscribers, element administrators, or service administrations. These types of devices are not specified with the NGN standards, or shown in Figure 2.33, but are covered a little later.

2.3.1.6 The Service Stratum and the IP Multimedia Subsystem. The Service Stratum is responsible for handling the call processing and real-time routing of application layer traffic within the network. It manages the assignable resources of the Transport plane. Although ITU-T Y.2012 provides little detail for this area, the likely set of Service Stratum FEs are defined by the Internet Multimedia Subsystem (IMS) being specified by the ETSI in a large collection of interrelated standards. The IMS Service Stratum architecture will be covered in the next section.

2.3.2 IP Multimedia Subsystem

The IMS is:

- an architectural framework for delivering IP-based multimedia (voice, video, audio, messaging, etc.) to fixed location and mobile users, and
- a collection of different functions, linked by standardized interfaces, which when grouped together form one IMS administrative network, where an IMS administrative domain is the same as a security domain.

A function is not a node or element (hardware box); rather IMS functions are FEs and FGs just as in ITU-T Y.2012. Implementers can combine two, or more, functions in one element. Each element can also be present multiple times in a single network, for availability, load balancing, segregation, or other organizational needs.

The user can connect to an IMS network in various ways, all of which use the standard IP. Direct IMS terminals (such as mobile phones, personal digital assistants, and computers) can register directly on an IMS-enabled network, as well as roam into another IMS-enabled network (a visited network). The only requirement is that these IMS devices and networks use IPv6 (also IPv4 in early IMS versions) and run Session Initiation Protocol (SIP) user agents (UAs). Fixed access (e.g., DSL, cable modems, Ethernet), mobile access, and wireless access (e.g., WLAN, WiMAX) are all supported. Other phone systems like plain old telephone service (POTS—the old analog telephones), H.323, and non-IMS-compatible VoIP systems are supported through gateways.

The primary FGs within the Service Stratum of an IMS-enabled network include:

- Home Subscriber Servers
- Control Function Servers
- Application Servers
- Media Servers
- Breakout Gateways
- PSTN Gateways
- Media Resources

2.3.2.1 Home Subscriber Server. The **Home Subscriber Server (HSS)**, or User Profile Server Function (UPSF), is a master user database that supports the IMS network entities that actually handle calls. It contains subscription-related information (user profiles), performs authentication and authorization of the user, and can provide information about a user's physical location. It is similar to the GSM HLR and Authentication Center found in cellular phone systems. A Subscriber Location Function (SLF) is needed to map user addresses when multiple HSSs are used. As currently defined, an HSS only contains application-service-related subscriber information and is not used to support authentication and authorization for Transport Stratum functions such as access network attachment (i.e., IEEE 802.11i, IEEE 802.1x, GPON authentication, etc.). Both the HSS and the SLF communicate through the Diameter[14] protocol (see Appendix F for more detail on Diameter). The HSS user database contains the IP Multimedia Public Identity Uniform Resource Identifier (URI), IP Multimedia Private Identity URI, International Mobile Subscriber Identity, the telephone number of a user, and other information. The Diameter protocol is used by other IMS FEs to retrieve application service authentication and authorization information of IMS service subscribers only. Security (authentication, confidentiality, and data integrity) for Diameter protocol usage is provided by using IPsec (see Appendix C for details) as Diameter cannot provide these security services internally.

2.3.2.2 Call Session Control Functions. Several types of SIP servers or proxies, collectively called **Call Session Control Function (CSCF)**, are used to process SIP signaling packets in an IMS-enabled network. These server functions are:

- A **Proxy-CSCF (P-CSCF)** is a SIP proxy that is the first point of contact for the IMS terminal and can be located either in the visited network (in full IMS

---

[14] RFC 3588, "Diameter Base Protocol", Proposed Standard, IETF, 2003

networks) or in the home network. Some networks may use an SBC element for this function. A P-CSCF:

- is assigned to an IMS terminal during the SIP registration process and does not change for the duration of the registration;
- sits on the path of all signaling messages and can inspect every message;
- authenticates user devices, via IPsec IKE, containing SIP-UAs and establishes a set of IPsec associations with the user device. This prevents spoofing attacks and replay attacks and protects the privacy of the user. Other nodes rely on the P-CSCF authentication process and do not have to authenticate the subscriber device again at the network level;
- may include a Policy Decision Function (PDF), which authorizes media transfer resources (e.g., QoS, used for policy control, bandwidth management, etc.) where the PDF can also be a separate function; and
- generates charging records for service usage accounting.

- A **Serving-CSCF (S-CSCF)** is the central node of IMS signaling and is a SIP server, but performs session control too. The S-CSCF is always located in the home network and uses Diameter, over IPsec, to communicate with the HSS for the download and upload user profiles as it has no local storage of the user, and all necessary information is loaded from the HSS. The S-CSCF:
  - handles SIP registrations, which allows it to bind the user location (e.g., the IP address of the terminal) and the SIP address;
  - sits on the path of all signaling messages and can inspect every message SIP deep packet inspection;
  - decides to which application server(s) the SIP message will be forwarded, in order to provide its services;
  - provides routing services, typically using Electronic Numbering lookups; and
  - enforces the policy of the network operator.

  There can be multiple S-CSCFs in the network for load distribution and high availability reasons; thus, it is the HSS that assigns the S-CSCF to a user, when it is queried by the Interrogating-CSCF (I-CSCF). Communications between S-CSCFs and the HSS relies on the use of Diameter over IPsec.

- An **I-CSCF** is another SIP function located at the edge of an administrative domain. Its IP address is published in the DNS so that remote servers in other interconnected SP domains can find it, and use it as a forwarding point (e.g., registering) for SIP packets to this domain. The I-CSCF queries the HSS using Diameter, over IPsec, retrieve the user location, and then route the SIP request to its assigned S-CSCF.

2.3.2.3 Application Servers. **Application servers (ASs)** host and execute services, and interface with the S-CSCF using SIP. Depending on the actual service, the ASs can operate in SIP proxy mode, SIP-UA mode, or SIP Back-to-Back User Agent mode. An AS can be located in the home network or in a network of a different IMS SP. Communications between ASs and the HSS rely on the use of Diameter protected via IPsec.

2.3.2.4 Media Resource Functions. Media Servers, called **Media Resource Functions (MRFs)**, provide media-related functions such as media manipulation (e.g., conference bridging) and playing of tones and announcements. Each MRF has both a Media Resource Function Controller and a Media Resource Function Processor.

2.3.2.5 Gateway Control and Media Functions. A **Breakout Gateway Control Function (BGCF)** is a SIP server that includes routing functionality based on telephone numbers and is only used when calling from within IMS to a phone in a circuit switched (CS) network, such as the PSTN.

PSTN gateways interface with PSTN CS networks and include:

- **Signaling Gateway** which transforms protocols as Stream Control Transmission Protocol into Message Transfer Part protocols (Signaling System 7 protocols used by a PSTN);
- **Media Gateway Controller Function** controls the resources in a Media Gateway (MGW) with an H.248 interface; and
- **MGW** which interfaces with the Media Plane (voice circuits) of the PSTN.

ITU-T Y.2021 provides further details on the mapping of IMS into a Y.2012 NGN context. Figure 2.34 shows a likely positioning of IMS FEs within an NGN. Many of the Gateway-related FEs appear on the left of the figure supporting interconnection to other SP networks. Many of the media-handling-, control-, and infrastructure-support-related FEs appear at the top and right of the figure.

2.3.2.6 Border Control Functions. **Border Control Functions (BCFs)** provide a number of security capabilities within NGNs for the control of traffic between the NGN core/backbone network and the infrastructures that provide Access, Interconnect, Operations Support, Application Services, and SCFs, as shown in Figure 2.34. The border control capabilities for each of these attached infrastructures vary according to the roles of each infrastructure area. Two general capabilities of BCFs include:

- Stateful packet filtering (Firewall) primarily used to limit what application protocols may traverse between the NGN core/backbone infrastructure and a specific functional infrastructure and which destination systems are allowed to receive packets coming from the NGN core/backbone network;
- General deep packet inspection, as with IDS/IPS, used to inspect allowed application protocol messages to ensure that malware is not being transferred; and
- Network Address (/Port) Translation (NAT/P) may be present if the SP chooses to use a non-routable (private) address range within a specific functional infrastructure.

Looking more closely at BCFs by specific functional infrastructure, one is likely to find that the BCF functionality will be co-located with other functions within a single device that provides the capability to support multiple simultaneous virtual execution environments as currently available in commercial "carrier class" virtual router

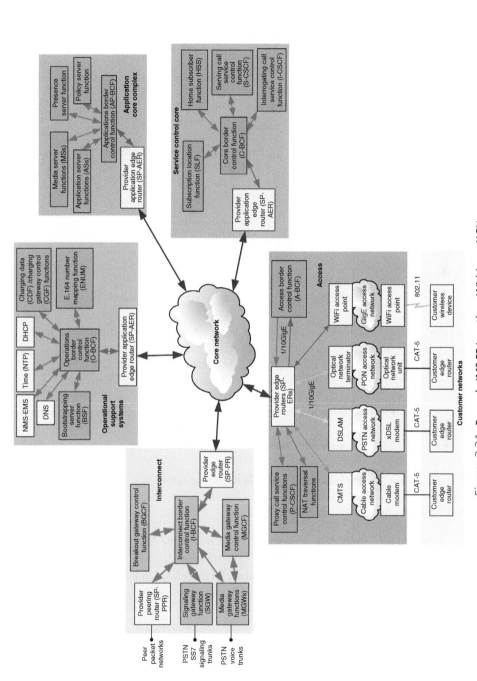

Figure 2.34. Example IMS FE Locations Within an NGN.

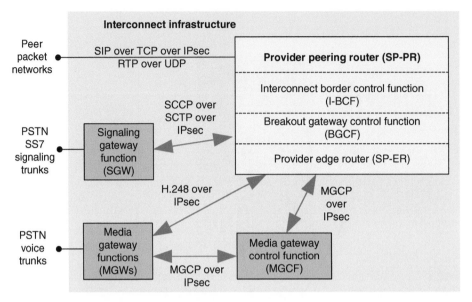

Figure 2.35. Interconnect Infrastructure Border Control Functions.

platforms. These virtual router products are designed to provide multiple individually configurable logical routers equivalent to physically independent router products.

Within the Interconnect infrastructure functional area, the Interconnect Border Control Function (I-BCF), depicted in Figure 2.35, will likely be co-located with:

- a virtual SP-ER function for routing packets to/from the NGN core/backbone network;
- a virtual SP-PR function for routing packets to the NGN infrastructures of other SPs; and
- BGCF for SIP URI mapping to PSTN telephone numbers.

The I-BCF function would support:

- tracking SIP application sessions established with the NGN infrastructures (SIP session eavesdropping) of other SPs (see Appendix C);
- blocking the flow of packets transporting RTP application media messages arriving from the NGN infrastructures (RTP "pin-hole" control, see Session Border Control in Appendix C) of other SPs;
- blocking the flow of packets based on source/destination IP addresses and transport/application protocols (see Firewalls in Appendix C) arriving from the NGN infrastructures of other SPs; and
- blocking the flow of packets based on complex application messages and other pattern and statistical criteria (see Deep Packet Inspection in Appendix C) arriving from the NGN infrastructures of other SPs.

Within the Operational Support Systems infrastructure functional area, the Operations Border Control Function (O-BCF) will likely be co-located with:

- a virtual Service Provider Application Edge Router (SP-AER) function for routing packets between Operational Support Systems and the SP's NGN core/ backbone network.

The O-BCF function would support:

- blocking the flow of packets based on source/destination IP addresses and transport/application protocols (see Firewalls in Appendix C) between Operational Support Systems and the NGN infrastructure, and
- blocking the flow of packets based on complex application messages and other pattern and statistical criteria (see Deep Packet Inspection in Appendix C) between Operational Support Systems and the NGN infrastructure.

Within the Application Core Complex infrastructure functional area, the Applications Border Control Function (AP-BCF) will likely be co-located with:

- a virtual SP-AER function for routing packets between ASs and the SP's NGN core/backbone network.

The AP-BCF would support:

- blocking the flow of packets based on source/destination IP addresses and transport/application protocols (see Firewalls in Appendix C) between ASs and the NGN infrastructure, and
- blocking the flow of packets based on complex application messages and other pattern and statistical criteria (see Deep Packet Inspection in Appendix C) between ASs and the NGN infrastructure.

Within the Service Control Core infrastructure functional area, the Core Border Control Function (C-BCF) will likely be co-located with:

- a virtual SP-AER function for routing packets between Service Control Servers and the SP's NGN core/backbone network.

The C-BCF would support:

- blocking the flow of packets based on source/destination IP addresses and transport/application protocols (see Firewalls in Appendix C) between Service Control Servers and the NGN infrastructure, and
- blocking the flow of packets based on complex application messages and other pattern and statistical criteria (see Deep Packet Inspection in Appendix C) between Service Control Servers and the NGN infrastructure.

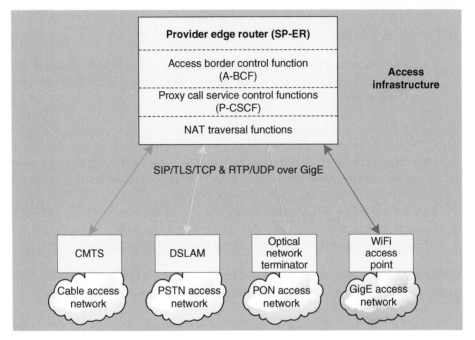

Figure 2.36. Access Infrastructure Border Control Functions.

Within the Access infrastructure functional area, the Access Border Control Function (A-BCF) will likely be co-located, as shown in Figure 2.36, with:

- A virtual SP-ER function for routing packets to/from the NGN core/backbone network;
- Proxy Call Service Control Function (P-CSCF); and
- A likely NAT traversal function and protocol (such as STUN,[15] ICE,[16] or TURN[17]).

The A-BCF (shown in Figure 2.32) would support:

- tracking SIP application sessions established with devices within NGN access infrastructures (SIP session eavesdropping, see Appendix C);
- blocking the flow of packets transporting RTP application media messages arriving from an NGN Access infrastructure (RTP "pin-hole" control, see Session Border Control in Appendix C);

---

[15] RFC 5389, "Session Traversal Utilities for NAT (STUN)", IETF Organization October 2008

[16] RFC 5245, "Interactive Connectivity Establishment (ICE): A Protocol for Network Address Translator (NAT) Traversal for Offer/Answer Protocols", IETF Organization, April 2010

[17] RFC 5766, "Traversal Using Relays around NAT (TURN): Relay Extensions to Session Traversal Utilities for NAT (STUN)", IETF Organization, April 2010

- blocking the flow of packets based on source/destination IP addresses and transport/application protocols (see Firewalls in Appendix C) arriving from an NGN access infrastructure; and
- blocking the flow of packets based on complex application messages and other pattern and statistical criteria (see Deep Packet Inspection in Appendix C) arriving from an NGN access infrastructure.

2.3.2.7 Relationship between NGN Transport and Service Domains. The NGN provides access to a wide variety of services. The specific services offered by any SP are determined by business needs and customer needs. Figure 2.37 shows an example that illustrates multiple domains within which services may be accessed.

In this example, SP #1 supports a two access network technology that provides access to three service domains via its core/services network, where:

1. One service domain is the Communications services bubble. These services may be completely within SP #1's domain or may support end-to-end services to other SPs. In this example, SP #1 supports end-to-end communication services interoperating with SP #2's communications services. They are interconnected through a transit network, which is nothing more than the core/services network of a different SP that only provided forwarding of SP traffic between different SPs. Network Access Control FEs are used to protect Service Domain FEs within a domain from FEs in other domains and the transit network. It should also be noted that the network on the other side of the transit network might be another type of external network, such as the PSTN.

2. A second service domain in this example is the Information services bubble of SP #1. This could provide services such as web hosting. These service FEs may be attached directly to SP #1's core network or may be provided by third parties through agreed upon security arrangements.

3. A third service domain shown here is access to Internet located services. These services are not part of SP #1's domain, nor are they provided by business arrangements with SP #1. These services are accessed via SP #1's transport connections between customers and the organizations that provide the contracted-for services via the Internet.

As mentioned earlier, this example shows only a small set of the possible configurations that might be supported by NGNs.

2.4 SUMMARY

As discussed in this chapter, the need for authentication, authorization/access controls, confidentiality, and data integrity exists in many functional areas of modern network infrastructures. Physical components need access controls that depend on authentication

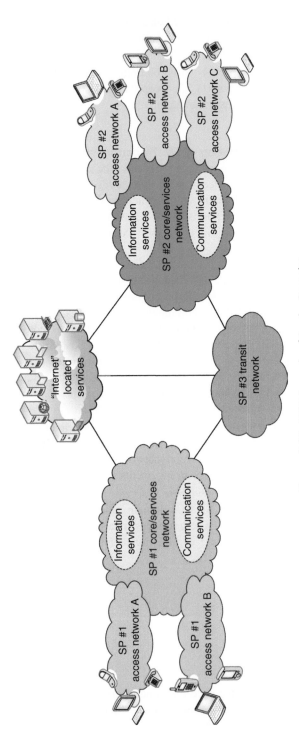

Figure 2.37. NGN Example of Service Domains.

of human identities prior to determining if physical access is allowed/authorized (i.e., doors unlocked via keys, access cards, PINs/passwords, fingerprints, etc.). Both wired and wireless communication links need access controls that depend on authentication of device identities prior to determining if logical access is allowed/authorized (i.e., IEEE 802.1x combined with PINs/passwords, shared secret keys, private-key-based digital signatures, security tokens, etc., either standalone or with RADIUS servers). Communication between different networks, or network segments/subnets, needs access controls that depend on either:

- access rules to determine if packets are allowed to flow within and between these networks, network segments/subnets, and even destination devices (i.e., stateful packet filtering, deep packet inspection, ARP monitoring agents, etc.), or
- authentication of device identities prior to determining if packets are allowed to flow between networks, network segments/subnets, and even destination devices (i.e., IPsec security associations based on private keys and digital certificates or shared secret keys).

In non-NGN–IMS infrastructures, transport of messages between applications within end devices is routinely protected using Transport Layer Security, Security Sockets Layer security, or Secure Shell (see Appendix C for more details on these mechanisms). All three of these transport level security mechanisms rely on identity authentication. In all these mechanisms, authentication is based on passwords, shared secret keys, private-key-based digital signatures, security tokens, etc.

The impact, of the wide use of security mechanism of various types and purposes, is that there are now numerous forms of credentials used for authentication of identities that require management in an efficient and secure manner. Likewise, authorization/access control mechanisms now take many forms which also require management in an efficient and secure manner. Historically, authentication and authorization within networked services were separately provided from network-oriented authentication and authorization, which is now becoming intertwined within NGN–IMS infrastructures.

In 2006, Basie von Solms authored a paper that contends that information security, and the management thereof, has progressed through three waves and is now into a fourth wave. Essentially, von Solms' proposition is that information security was initially considered as solely a technical issue, to be resolved by technical experts (first wave), and one can argue that the publication of ISO 7498-2/ITU-T X.800 represents this first wave of security and security management. von Solms considers the second wave as representing the "realization that Information Security has a strong management involvement" (von Solms, 2006, p. 165), and one can argue that the publication of ITU-T M.3000, M.3010, M.3020, M.3030, and M.3400 recommendations regarding the TMN represents this second wave of security and security management. von Solms' third wave goes on to say that the third wave is constituted by "the need to have some form of standardization of Information Security in a company, and aspects like best practices, certification, an Information Security culture and the measurement and monitoring of Information Security" (von Solms, 2006, p. 165). The publication of documents such as the ISO/IEC 27000 series can be considered as representing this evolution of how information security should be viewed. The fourth wave, von Solms contends, "relates to the development and crucial role of Information Security Governance" (von Solms, 2006, p. 165). This book agrees with von Solms' analysis. Therefore, Chapter 3 discusses the management of information security from a governance perspective, especially since the complexities discussed in this chapter highlight the fundamental need for a holistic view of managing security within the highly complex information environment within which twenty-first-century organizations exist.

FURTHER READING AND RESOURCES

At the present time, the primary sources for additional information on NGN architectures are approved standard and recommendation documents published by the ITU-T and the ETSI. As of 2010, ITU-T recommendations can be obtained at no cost from the ITU-T website.

ITU-T recommendations worth reading include:

- ITU-T Recommendation M.3010 (2000), Principles for a Telecommunications Management Network;
- ITU-T Recommendation M.3050.0 (2007), Enhanced Telecom Operations Map (eTOM)—Introduction;
- ITU-T Recommendation M.3050.1 (2004), Enhanced Telecommunications Operations Map—The Business Process Framework;
- ITU-T Recommendation M.3060/Y.2401 (2006), Principles for the Management of Next Generation Networks;
- ITU-T Recommendation M.3400 (2000), TMN Management Functions;
- ITU-T Recommendation Y.2001 (2004), General Overview of NGN;
- ITU-T Recommendation Y.2011 (2004), General Principles and General Reference Model for Next Generation Networks;
- ITU-T Recommendation Y.2012 (2006), Functional Requirements and Architecture of the NGN Release;
- ITU-T Recommendation Y.2012 (2006), Functional Requirements and Architecture of the NGN;
- ITU-T Recommendation Y.2021 (2006), IMS for Next Generation Networks;
- ITU-T Recommendation Y.2091 (2007), Terms and Definitions for Next Generation Networks;
- ITU-T Recommendation Y.2111 (2006), Resource and Admission Control Functions in Next Generation Networks;
- ITU-T Recommendation Y.2201 (2007), NGN Release 1 Requirements;
- ITU-T Recommendation Y.2601 (2006), Fundamental Characteristics and Requirements of Future Packet-Based Networks;
- ITU-T Recommendation Y.2701 (2007), Security Requirements for NGN Release 1;
- ITU-T Recommendation Y.2801 (2006), Mobility Management Requirements for NGN.

ETSI recommendations worth reading include:

- ETSI DTR/TISPAN-00001-NGN-R1, "Telecommunications and Internet Converged Services and Protocols for Advanced Networking (TISPAN); NGN Release 1; Release Definition NGN R1," 2006;
- ETSI DTR/TISPAN-00004-NGN, "Telecommunications and Internet Converged Services and Protocols for Advanced Networking (TISPAN); NGN Terminology NGN Terminology," 2006;
- ETSI DTS/TISPAN-01001-NGN-R1, "Telecommunications and Internet Converged Services and Protocols for Advanced Networking (TISPAN); Videotelephony over NGN; Stage 1 Service Description Videotelephony over NGN," 2006;
- ETSI DTS/TISPAN-01025-NGN-R1, "Telecommunications and Internet Converged Services and Protocols for Advanced Networking (TISPAN); Services and Capabilities Requirements NGN R1 Service and Capability," 2006;
- ETSI DES/TISPAN-02007-NGN-R1, "Telecommunications and Internet Converged Services and Protocols for Advanced Networking (TISPAN); NGN Functional Architecture Release 1 Overall Architecture," 2005;
- ETSI DES/TISPAN-02019-NGN-R1, "Telecommunications and Internet Converged Services and Protocols for Advanced Networking (TISPAN); PSTN/ISDN Emulation Sub-system (PES); Functional Architecture PES Architecture," 2006;
- ETSI DTS/TISPAN-02028-NGN-R1, "Telecommunications and Internet Converged Services and Protocols for Advanced Networking (TISPAN); IP Multimedia Subsystem (IMS); Stage 2 Description (3GPP TS 23.228 v7.2.0, Modified IMS stage 2 Endorsement)," 2006;
- ETSI DTS/TISPAN-02033-NGN-R1, "Telecommunications and Internet Converged Services and Protocols for Advanced Networking (TISPAN); XML Document Management; Architecture and Functional Description (OMA-AD-XDM-V1_0-20051006-C Modified) XML Management," 2006;
- ETSI DTS/TISPAN-03060-NGN-R1, "Telecommunications and Internet Converged Services and Protocols for Advanced Networking (TISPAN); IP Multimedia; Diameter Based Protocol for the Interfaces Between the Call Session Control Function and the User Profile Server Function/Subscription Locator Function; Signalling Flows and Protocol Details (3GPP TS 29.228 V6.8.0 and 3GPP TS 29.229 V6.6.0, Modified)," 2006;
- ETSI DTS/TISPAN-07014-NGN-R1, "Telecommunications and Internet Converged Services and Protocols for Advanced Networking (TISPAN); NGN SECurity (SEC); Requirements Security Requirements NGN-R1," 2006;
- ETSI DTR/TISPAN-07016-NGN-R1, "Telecommunications and Internet Converged Services and Protocols for Advanced Networking (TISPAN); TISPAN NGN Security (NGN_SEC); Threat and Risk Analysis Security Threat and Risk," 2006;
- ETSI DTS/TISPAN-07017-NGN-R1, "Telecommunications and Internet Converged Services and Protocols for Advanced Networking (TISPAN); NGN Security; Security Architecture Security architecture NGN R1," 2006.

Baran, P. (1964) On Distributed Communications Networks. IEEE Transactions on Communications Systems CS-12(1), pp. 1–9

CIO Website (2011), Symantec Survey Finds Global Critical Infrastructure Providers Less Aware and Engaged in Government Programs. Retrieved on November 28, 2011, from http://www.cio.com.au/mediareleases/13296/symantec-survey-finds-global-critical/

Huff Post CHICAGO—The Internet Newspaper (2011), Illinois Water Pump Failure: Feds Say Hacking Rumors Not True. Retrieved on November 28, 2011, from http://www.huffingtonpost.com/2011/11/23/illinois-water-pump-failu_0_n_1110096.html

MailOnline WebSite (2011), "Russian" hackers seize control of U.S. public water system by remotely destroying pump. Received on November 28, 2011, from http://www.dailymail.co.uk/sciencetech/article-2064283/Hackers-control-U-S-public-water-treatment-facilities.html

McAfee, (2009), In the Crossfire—Critical Infrastructure in the Age of Cyber War. Retrieved on November 28, 2011, from http://www.mcafee.com/us/resources/reports/rp-in-crossfire-critical-infrastructure-cyber-war.pdf

Newsham, T. (2001, July), Cracking WEP keys. In Black Hat USA 2001 conference. Las Vegas, USA, pp. 11–12

PikeResearch, (2011), Utility Cyber Security Seven Key Smart Grid Security Trends to Watch in 2012 and Beyond. Retrieved on November 28, 2011, from http://www.pikeresearch.com/wordpress/wp-content/uploads/2011/11/UCS-11-Pike-Research.pdf

von Solms, B. (2006), Information Security—The Fourth Wave, Computers & Security, 25(3), pp. 165–168. Retrieved from http://www.sciencedirect.com/science/article/pii/S01674048 0600054X

SECURITY MANAGEMENT IN CURRENT AND FUTURE NETWORKS

In Chapter 2, we examined how network architectures have evolved prior to, and since, the mid-1980s publication of ISO 7498-1 (ITU-T X.200). We have seen how modern network architectures have become far more complex than "simple hub-and-spoke" designs interconnecting dumb terminals to mainframe computers. Networks today have evolved into numerous public and private communications infrastructures interconnected in various ways with multiple components delivering a wide array of services to highly diverse business, retail, and governmental customers spanning numerous organizational security domains. We now have a network-based virtual "world" rapidly becoming as critical to modern societies as the physical world. The need for securing this virtual world continues to evolve and grow primarily along two dimensions: (i) the need to address increasing criminal use of this virtual environment (cybercrime) and (ii) the need to effectively and efficiently manage this virtual environment (governance).

Security Management of Next Generation Telecommunications Networks and Services,
First Edition. Stuart Jacobs.
© 2014 The Institute of Electrical and Electronics Engineers, Inc. Published 2014 by John Wiley & Sons, Inc.

3.1 CYBERCRIME AS A DRIVER FOR INFORMATION SECURITY MANAGEMENT

Let us consider cybercrime. Organized, and disorganized, criminals have discovered this virtual world and have transitioned many of their anti-social activities into this virtual world. Criminal activities have been occurring within societies for millennia and can be classified along a number of dimensions, such as:

- offences against a person or legal entity;
- offences involving physical or psychological violence; and
- offences against property.

Any of these types of offences can include acts of conspiracy or incitement to commit crimes. Table 3.1 provides examples of different criminal activities, where the victims can be either individual people or legal entities such as a nation, state, or other form of legally recognized organization.

Cybercrime is simply the use of this virtual world in the commission, or facilitation, of crimes that have plagued societies and individuals in the physical world. Cybercrime herein is being used to refer to cyber-terrorism and cyber-warfare as well since cyber-terrorism and cyber-warfare are nothing more that the mapping of acts of terrorism and warfare committed through the use, or assistance, of networked infrastructures. Networked services in the virtual environment are routinely used for:

- stalking, extortion, and blackmail targeting individuals via email, social networks, instant messaging, (Distributed)Denial of Service (DDoS) attacks, malware (Trojan horse, worms, viruses, key-loggers, etc.), spyware, etc.;
- theft of physical or intellectual property, forgery, impersonation, and cheating targeting individuals via email, social networks, instant messaging, DDoS attacks, malware (Trojan horse, worms, viruses, key-loggers, etc.), spyware, etc.;
- child sexual abuse, obscenity, exhibitionism, and sexual harassment targeting individuals via email, social networks, instant messaging, malware (Trojan horse, worms, viruses, key-loggers, etc.), spyware, etc.;
- murder and manslaughter targeting individuals via the potential usurpation (compromise) of critical machinery (i.e., networked medicine delivery equipment, SCADA systems, etc.);
- warfare, acts of terrorism, and espionage targeting societies via DDoS attacks, malware (Trojan horse, worms, viruses, key-loggers, etc.), usurpation (compromise) of critical systems (i.e., weapon command and control systems, SCADA systems, electronic financial systems, etc.); and
- acts of terrorism, extortion, espionage, and sabotage targeting legal entities via DDoS attacks, malware (Trojan horse, worms, viruses, key-loggers, etc.), usurpation (compromise) of critical systems (i.e., SCADA systems, electronic financial systems, etc.).

TABLE 3.1. Offences Against a Person or Legal Entity.

Offence	Individual People	Legal Entities
Fatal offences	Examples include: murder and manslaughter	Examples include: warfare, acts of terrorism, and sabotage
Sexual offences	Examples include: rape, child sexual abuse, obscenity, exhibitionism and voyeurism, telephone scatologia (making obscene telephone calls for the purpose of sexual arousal), and sexual harassment. Sexual offences could be considered a sub-category under assaults or battery	Some examples of sexual offences that can be considered as applying at the level of societies such as prostitution and/or pimping
Assaults causing a victim to fear physical or psychological violence	Examples include: stalking, robbery, extortion, and related offences such as blackmail	Examples include: extortion, acts of terrorism, sabotage, and espionage
Property offences	Examples include: theft of physical or intellectual property, burglary, vehicle theft, arson, forgery, impersonation, and cheating	Examples include: theft of physical or intellectual property, burglary, vehicle theft, arson, forgery, impersonation, cheating (as in tax fraud), and sabotage
Battery involving unlawful physical contact resulting in physical or psychological injury	Examples include: beatings and muggings	Do not apply
Behavioral offences	Behavioral offences against individuals tend to fall under the preceding categories	Some examples of behavioral offences that can be considered as applying at the level of societies include: trafficking or possession of harmful or dangerous drugs or material, public disorderliness or obstruction, attempts to disrupt commerce or financial markets and interrupt the flow of daily life and business according to societal standards, use of offensive weapons

This mapping of different criminal activities to specific services or mechanisms within the virtual context is not exhaustive; rather, it is simply a set of specific examples. A key point the reader should note is that many of the networked services and capabilities we take for granted can be used for malicious purposes just as easily as for honest purposes. The conference paper "Identities, anonymity and information warfare" (Jacobs et al., 2010) also makes this point by noting that many security mechanisms already exist that can mitigate malicious use of virtual services and mechanisms provided network administrators recognize the need for prompt deployment of these capabilities. Simply deploying such security mechanisms is insufficient unless coupled to appropriate management capabilities.

3.2 GOVERNANCE AS A DRIVER FOR INFORMATION SECURITY MANAGEMENT

3.2.1 What Is Governance?

According to the Oxford English Dictionary, governance can be considered as

> 1. b. Controlling, directing or regulating influence; control, sway, mastery (OED, 1971, p. 319).

> or

> 4. b. Conduct of life or business; mode of living, behavior, demeanour (OED, 1971, p. 319).

Since we are concerned with organizations/businesses, from these two definitions, the key points are: controlling, directing, and regulating conduct of business and behavior. Put another way, governance of a business or organization refers to how said business/organization is controlled, directed, and regulated regarding its conduct of business activities and the behavior of its personnel. From here on, we will use the generic term organization to refer to commercial organizations (businesses and corporations, etc.), governmental entities (national, state, and local governments and agencies, etc.), and non-governmental entities (charitable groups, political parties, etc.). Although the principles of governance apply to all organizations, the primary focus of our discussion is on governance of commercial organizations, which we will generically refer to as corporate governance regardless of the size (as measured by revenue, number of employees, magnitude, or types of customers), form of legal establishment (sole proprietor, LLC, corporation, etc.), or area of business activities (manufacturing, financial, utilities, services, etc.).

   At the highest level, corporate governance tends to be discussed relative to the principles raised in the Cadbury Report (Cadbury, 1992) which focused on the control and reporting functions of boards, the role of auditors, and a "Code of Best Practice" designed to set standards of corporate behavior. Within (Cadbury, 1992) corporate governance is presented as:

> Corporate governance is the system by which companies are directed and controlled. Boards of directors are responsible for the governance of their companies. The shareholders'

role in governance is to appoint the directors and the auditors and to satisfy themselves that an appropriate governance structure is in place. The responsibilities of the board include setting the company's strategic aims, providing the leadership to put them into effect, supervising the management of the business and reporting to shareholders on their steward-ship (Cadbury, 1992, Section 2.5).

The Principles on Corporate Governance as presented in (OECD, 2004) mirror (Cadbury, 1992), and both present general principals around which businesses are expected to operate to assure proper governance. The Sarbanes–Oxley Act (U.S. Congress, 2002), commonly referred to as SOX, is an attempt to legislate several of the principles recommended in the Cadbury and OECD reports by the federal government in the United States.

3.2.2 Information System Security Governance

In 2001, Carl Landwehr noted that "Commercial concerns naturally focus on the flow and protection of financial assets" (Landwehr, 2001, p. 4), which parallels the point that "The widespread recognition that information now constitutes a 'key corporate asset', which is of great commercial value" (Gerber et al., 2001, p. 32). Karyda et al. state

> Organisations nowadays depend largely on computer based Information Systems (IS) for a vital part of their operation. IS comprise the information that is being stored, or in any way processed by an organisation, the hardware and software that constitutes the configuration of computer systems, a social system that is formed by the actions and relations among the IS users, as well as a set of procedures that guide the users' actions (Karyda et al., 2005, p. 246).

While Gerber, von Solms, and Ocerbeek note that "in an information society, security emphasizes the protection of information and not only the infrastructure" (Gerber et al., 2001, p. 32), one can put forward a sound argument that information, and corresponding information processing infrastructure, constitutes significant financial value which needs to be properly managed from a corporate governance perspective which is consistent with the IT Governance Institute proposition:

> "While many organizations recognize the potential benefits that technology can yield, the successful ones also understand and manage the risks associated with implementing new technologies. Among the enterprise's challenges and concerns are:
>
> • Aligning IT strategy with the business strategy
> • Cascading strategy and goals down into the enterprise
> • Providing organizational structures that facilitate the implementation of strategy and goals
> • Insisting that an IT control framework be adopted and implemented
> • Measuring IT's performance
>
> Effective and timely measures aimed at addressing these top management concerns need to be promoted by the governance layer of an enterprise. Hence, boards and executive management need to extend governance, already exercised over the enterprise, to IT by way of an effective IT governance framework that addresses strategic alignment, performance

measurement, risk management, value delivery and resource management. Simply put, IT governance and the effective application of an IT governance framework are the responsibilities of the board of directors and executive management. IT governance is an integral part of enterprise governance and consists of the leadership and organizational structures and processes that ensure that the organization's IT sustains and extends the organization's strategies and objectives" (IGI, 2011).

Moulton and Coles have built upon the IT Governance Institute's view to say:

"In this context, governance focuses on managing the organization and making the best use of its resources. If we accept that security governance is a subset of corporate or enterprise governance, then by extending the definitions above, it could include:

- Security responsibilities and practices
- Strategies/objectives for security
- Risk assessment and management
- Resource management for security
- Compliance with legislation, regulations, security policies and rules
- Investor relations and communications activity (in relation to security)" (Moulton and Coles, 2003, p. 580).

and von Solms believes that "The reason for the lack of direct reference to information security in good corporate governance documents may be because when they were compiled, information security had not been such an important issue" (von Solms, 2001, p. 217). von Solms goes on to say that "information security should be addressed directly, and by name, in all documents describing good corporate governance. This will clearly indicate the role senior management and the Board have to play, and will greatly simplify the efforts of information security managers" (von Solms, 2001, p. 217). Consistent with these opinions, one is likely to see IT/IS security governance explicitly referenced in future corporate governance documents and related standards. In 2006, von Solms (von Solms, 2006) also makes the point that IS security governance is essentially a discipline for handling the mitigation of IT-related risks. Höne and Eloff note that

There are various controls and measures that can be—and indeed need to be—implemented within an organisation to ensure the effective working of information security. These controls and measures range from technical solutions and contractual regulations to organisational awareness of current risks, threats and vulnerabilities. Undoubtedly, the singularly most important of these controls is the information security policy (Höne and Eloff, 2002, p. 401).

Karyda et al. agree, stating that "The application of an IS security policy is one of the major mechanisms employed by IS security management" (Karyda et al., 2005, p. 247), and that

An IS security policy includes the intentions and priorities with regard to the protection of the IS, usually referred to as security objectives, together with a general description of the means and methods to achieve these objectives (Karyda et al., 2005, p. 247).

As an IS security management mechanism, an IS security policy should:

- explain the need for IS security;
- demonstrate senior management's dedication to IS security; and
- specify what behavior is acceptable and what behavior is unacceptable

to all of an organization's information resource users (Höne and Eloff, 2002, p. 401; Thomson and von Solms, 2005, p. 71). Some have described IS security management and IS security policies as no more than management exercising power over employees. However, Carl Landwehr contends that a

> Security policy provides the rules of the game in computer security ... A policy is simply a set of rules defined to meet a particular goal, in this case to secure a computer or the information it processes. A computer without a security policy is like a society without laws; there can be no illegal acts in the later and no security violations in the former (Landwehr, 2001, p. 4).

Although Landwehr talks about securing a computer, his point really applies to all aspects of an information system, namely, the computers, associated internetworking components, operational procedures and activities, personnel, planning, and the information processed. Landwehr's points are consistent with the point made by Cadbury, which noted that

> Raising standards of corporate governance cannot be achieved by structures and rules alone. They are important because they provide a framework which will encourage and support good governance, but what counts is the way in which they are put to use (Cadbury, 1992, Section 3.13).

So the next area that needs to be discussed are the Information Security Management frameworks commonly in use today.

3.3 INFORMATION SECURITY MANAGEMENT FRAMEWORKS

A number of information security (InfoSec) management frameworks have been developed over the years that support, and provide, an approach for realizing InfoSec governance. These frameworks include the:

- ISO/IEC 27000 series of international standards documents, especially:
  - The ISO/IEC Standard 27001 Standard for Information Security Management (ISO/IEC 27001, 2005);
  - The ISO/IEC Standard 27002 for Information Security Policies (ISO/IEC 27002, 2005);
- Service Management—Information Technology Infrastructure Library (ITIL);

- Control OBjectives for Information and related Technology (COBIT) Framework; and
- Federal Information Security Management Act (FISMA) Risk Management Framework (NIST, 2004; NIST, 2009; NIST, 2010).

In the following subsections we will discuss what each of these frameworks cover, how they relate to each other, and what each framework does not cover.

3.3.1 ISO/IEC 27000 Series

The international standardization effort for security management started after the publication of British Standard (BS) 7799 in 1995 by the UK Government's Department of Trade and Industry and consisted of several parts. The first part was revised in 1998 and adopted by ISO as ISO/IEC 27002, the second part to BS 7799 was first published in 1999 and was adopted by ISO as ISO/IEC 27001, and the third was published in 2005 and was adopted by ISO as ISO/IEC 27005. A key perspective within this series of international recommendations is the view that security management is a process instantiated as an Information Security Management System (ISMS) that spans people, policy, processes, and technology across an organization. ISO/IEC 27005 is discussed in Chapter 4 under risk management.

As a process, security management can be carried out within any size of organization from a home business to the largest of national and international organizations. A primary purpose of security management is to assure that the organization achieves its security goals and objectives while avoiding unnecessary risks to itself and to those it serves. Security management should:

- Identify what assets an organization considers of value and establish the asset sensitivity (e.g., public, proprietary, restricted, copyrighted, Attorney–Client–Privileged, etc.);
- Identify organizational groups (subgroups) and "need-to-know" groups;
- Identify asset ownership (custodial responsibilities);
- Specify form(s) of authorization required to access an asset; and
- Drive Security Model development/selection.

ISO/IEC 27001 (BS 7799-2) introduced the concepts of "Plan," "Do," "Check," and "Act" (PDCA) (see Table 3.2) derived from the work by Dr. W. Edwards Deming, who is generally considered as the father of modern quality control, aligning it with the ISO 9000 family of general quality standards.

3.3.1.1 The ISO/IEC 27001 Standard for Information Security Management. Within ISO/IEC 27001, the concept of an information security management program (ISMP) is discussed which represents management of security as a program/process that should be integrated into overall business management activities. This documents a set of specific functional requirements for establishing, implementing,

TABLE 3.2. Plan, Do, Check, and Act Phases.

Plan	Establish the objectives and processes necessary to deliver results in accordance with the expected output. By focusing on expected outputs, it differs from other techniques in that the completeness and accuracy of the specification is also part of the improvement
Do	Implement the new processes
Check	Measure the new processes and compare the results against the expected results to ascertain any differences
Act	Analyze the differences to determine their cause

operating, monitoring, reviewing, maintaining, and improving a documented ISMP against which an organization can be certified as compliant with. The requirements are defined in a structured, formal format suitable for compliance certification. It is intended to be used in conjunction with ISO/IEC 27002 which lists security control objectives and recommends a range of specific security controls (processes, organizational responsibilities, and mechanisms) and to capture said objectives and controls in the form of an organizational InfoSec policy document. Organizations that implement an ISMP in accordance with the best practice advice in ISO/IEC 27002 are likely to simultaneously meet the requirements of ISO/IEC 27001. Certification of an organization against the ISO/IEC 27001 requirements is entirely optional but should be viewed as providing a statement to customers, peers, and civil authorities that a certified organization has a sound approach toward the security of its infrastructure assets.

The ISO/IEC 27001 requirements for the implementation of security controls may be customized to the needs of individual organizations yet are designed to ensure the selection of adequate and proportionate security controls that protect information assets and give confidence to interested parties. It is intended to be suitable for several different types of uses, including:

- Formulating security requirements and objectives;
- Ensuring that security risks are cost-effectively managed;
- Ensuring compliance with laws and regulations;
- Specifying a process framework for implementation and management of controls that ensure specific security objectives of an organization are met;
- Defining new InfoSec management processes;
- Identifying and clarifying existing InfoSec management processes; and
- Use by
  - management to determine the status of InfoSec management activities;
  - internal and external auditors to determine degree of compliance with policies, directives, and standards; and
  - organizations to provide relevant information about InfoSec policies, directives, standards, and procedures to trading partners, customers, and other organizations.

TABLE 3.3. Mapping of PDCA to ISO/IEC 27001 Establish, Implement, Assess, and Improvement.

Plan (establish the ISMS)	Establish ISMS policy, objectives, processes, and procedures relevant to managing risk and improving information security to deliver results in accordance with an organization's overall policies and objectives
Do (implement and operate the ISMS)	Implement and operate the ISMS policy, controls, processes, and procedures
Check (monitor and review the ISMS)	Assess and, where applicable, measure process performance against ISMS policy, objectives, and practical experience and report the results to management for review
Act (maintain and improve the ISMS)	Take corrective and preventive actions, based on the results of the internal ISMS audit and management review or other relevant information, to achieve continual improvement of the ISMS

The five major sections of ISO/IEC 27001, shown in Table 3.3, contain over 153 explicit mandatory requirements based on the PDCA concept model discussed earlier; so many of these requirements use the words "establish, implement, operate, monitor, review, maintain, ensure, identify, address, and carry out" as depicted in Table 3.3 from ISO/IEC 27001 (page vi).

These requirements are identifiable through the use of the word "shall," even though not provided with unique identifiers, and stated at a moderate level of specificity yet can easily be further decomposed into finer grained (detailed) requirement statements against which an organization's security program can be verified for compliance. Table 3.4 highlights those ISO/IEC 27001 sections within which requirements appear.

A cornerstone set of requirements focus on the:

- definition of the scope of ISMS for the organization that spans "the characteristics of the business, the organization, its location, assets and technology, and including details of and justification for any exclusions from the scope" (ISO/IEC 27001, p. 4);
- development of an InfoSec policy that reflects "the characteristics of the business, the organization, its location, assets and technology" (ISO/IEC 27001, p. 4) of the organization; and
- definition of the organization's approach for risk identification, assessment, evaluation, and mitigation/control/treatment.

The next set of requirements focus on ISMS implementation and operation followed by requirements that focus on ISMS monitoring and review processes, and then requirements that deal with maintaining and improving the organization's ISMS. Another key set of requirements not only recognize but necessitate organization management involvement and active review of its ISMS. Consistent with the concepts expressed in ISO 9001 recommendation on quality systems, ISO/IEC 27001 includes requirements

TABLE 3.4. Major Requirements Containing ISO/IEC
27001 Sections.

4 Information security management system
    4.1 General requirements
    4.2 Establishing and managing the ISMS
        4.2.1 Establish the ISMS
        4.2.2 Implement and operate the ISMS
        4.2.3 Monitor and review the ISMS
        4.2.4 Maintain and improve the ISMS
    4.3 Documentation requirements
        4.3.1 General
        4.3.2 Control of documents
        4.3.3 Control of records
5 Management responsibility
    5.1 Management commitment
    5.2 Resource management
        5.2.1 Provision of resources
        5.2.2 Training, awareness, and competence
6 Internal ISMS audits
7 Management review of the ISMS
    7.1 General
    7.2 Review input
    7.3 Review output
8 ISMS improvement
    8.1 Continual improvement
    8.2 Corrective action
    8.3 Preventive action

for both preventing and correcting "nonconformities with the ISMS requirements" (ISO/IEC 27001, p. 11) to ensure that an organization's activities remain consistent with its ISMS, including the organization's InfoSec policy. Organizations are expected to conform to the guidelines provided in ISO/IEC 27002 for preparing an InfoSec policy document that captures how the organization complies with the requirements in ISO/IEC 27001.

3.3.1.2 The ISO/IEC 27002 Standard for Information Security Policies.

ISO/IEC 27002 provides guidelines and voluntary directions for InfoSec program management, but as guidelines this standard is subject to wide interpretation. However, organizations are expected to follow these guidelines as part of complying with ISO/IEC 27001. One should not consider the existence of an organization InfoSec policy as the sum of how an organization manages InfoSec-related activities, but rather the documenting of how an organization manages InfoSec-related activities. As a form of documentation, the policy should be shared with organization members so they become aware of their roles and responsibilities in maintaining the security of the organization's information and assets.

ISO/IEC 27002 contains the following major topics (clauses) which will be discussed in more detail later:

- Security Policy;
- Organization of Information Security;
- Asset Management;
- Human Resources Security;
- Physical and Environmental Security;
- Communications and Operations Management,
- Access Control;
- Information Systems Acquisition, Development, and Maintenance;
- Information Security Incident Management;
- Business Continuity Management; and
- Compliance.

This standard is meant to provide a high-level, general description of the areas currently considered important when initiating, implementing, or maintaining InfoSec in an organization and establishes guidelines and general principles. However, this standard does not currently cover all areas of importance but is a starting point. It primarily addresses topics in terms of policies and general good practices and identifies the need to manage the following, but does not provide specific technical guidance on the specific actions that need to be performed for:

- Establishing organizational security policy;
- Organizational security infrastructure;
- Asset classification and control;
- Personnel security;
- Physical and environmental security;
- Communications and operations management;
- Access control;
- Systems development and maintenance; and
- Business continuity management.

Let us explore the major suggestions within each of these sections.

3.3.1.2.1 ESTABLISHING ORGANIZATIONAL SECURITY POLICY (ISO/IEC 27002 SECTION 5). This section provides the rationale for why security policies are important and general guidelines for the intent and objectives of the security policy. It is noted that a security policy provides management direction and support for InfoSec. The InfoSec policy document should state management commitment and set out the organization's approach to managing InfoSec. The policy document should include at a minimum:

- a definition of InfoSec;
- a statement of management intent;
- a framework for setting objectives and controls;
- an explanation of the security policies, principles, standards, and compliance requirements important to the organization;
- an explanation of responsibilities for InfoSec management; and
- references to documentation which may support the policy (i.e., more detailed security policies and procedures for specific information systems or security rules).

Security policies should be disseminated to users so that it is relevant, accessible, and understandable to intended readers. The security policy should be assigned to an owner who has responsibility for the development, review, and evaluation of the security policy. Organizational security policies and documents routinely need to be tailored to the specific needs of an organization.

3.3.1.2.2 ORGANIZATIONAL SECURITY INFRASTRUCTURE (ISO/IEC 27002 SECTION 6). This section is structured as a number of sub-sections covering:

- Management commitment to InfoSec;
- InfoSec coordination;
- Allocation of InfoSec responsibilities;
- Authorization process for information processing facilities;
- Confidentiality agreements;
- Contact with authorities;
- Contact with special interest groups;
- Independent review of InfoSec;
- Identification of risks related to external parties;
- Addressing security when dealing with customers; and
- Addressing security in third-party agreements.

Guidance is provided on the necessary commitment by organization management at the highest levels to the security policy, and that a management framework should be established to initiate and control the implementation of InfoSec within the organization. The management framework should ensure that management approves the security policy, assures assignment of security roles, and coordinates and reviews the implementation of security across the organization. The sub-section also recognizes that depending on the size of the organization, responsibilities can be handled by a dedicated senior management forum/committee/group, especially in large organizations, or by an existing management body by smaller enterprises (perhaps members of a Board of Directors (BoD)).

The coordination of security activities should be done by representatives from different parts of the organization with relevant roles and job functions. Security coordination should involve the collaboration of managers, users, administrators, application designers, auditors, and security personnel, along with personnel from insurance, legal issues, human resources, IT, or risk management. Large organizations should consider forming a secondary management forum/committee/group that reports to the senior management forum/committee/group. If the size of the organization does not justify the establishment of a separate cross-functional group, then an existing management body or individual manager can provide necessary coordination.

The security policy should clearly identify the allocation and specific details of security responsibilities. The specification of these responsibilities will be frequently supplemented with more detailed guidance for specific sites and facilities. Individuals to whom security responsibilities are assigned may delegate security tasks to others; yet these individuals remain responsible and retain responsibility to determine that any delegated tasks have been correctly performed. The security policy should recognize and address the need for non-disclosure agreements that address the requirement to protect confidential information. Non-disclosure agreements need to comply with applicable laws and regulations to ensure they remain binding. Requirements for confidentiality and non-disclosure agreements should be reviewed periodically, and when changes occur that influence these requirements. These agreements should focus on protecting organizational information and ensure signatories are aware of their responsibility to protect, use, and disclose information in a responsible and authorized manner. Frequently an organization will use different forms of non-disclosure agreements in different circumstances.

Procedures should be in place that specify when, and by whom within the organization, authorities should be contacted. The types of authorities that may need to be contacted include law enforcement, fire department, and other organizations. In the event of possible criminal activities/actions, the policy should provide guidance on what should be reported, and to whom, which may include external third parties (such as an Internet Service Provider) to take action against the attack source, in addition to local, state, or federal agencies.

An organization's security management framework, and its implementation, should be reviewed independently at planned intervals, or following significant changes. An independent review ensures the continuing suitability, adequacy, and effectiveness of the approach to managing InfoSec and should include assessing opportunities for improvement and the need for changes to the security policy framework, delegation of responsibilities, and security controls. Individuals carrying out these reviews should have security skills and experience and should review results recorded and reported to the management group that initiated the review. Any results that identify inadequacy or not compliant with security policy should suggest that management consider corrective actions.

Risks to organizational assets involving access by external parties should be identified and appropriate controls implemented before granting access. Where there is a need to allow an external party access to assets, a risk assessment should be performed that identifies requirements for specific controls. Access by external parties should be covered by a signed contract that defines the terms and conditions for the connection or access and working arrangements. Customer access to organization assets should be allowed after addressing and complying with identified security requirements. Some of the areas that should be considered prior to giving customer access to any organization assets include:

- procedures to protect the organization's assets;
- procedures to determine whether any compromise of the assets has occurred;
- restrictions on copying and disclosing information;
- reasons, requirements, and benefits for customer access;
- permitted access methods and the control and use of user IDs and passwords;
- authorization process for user access and privileges;
- statement that all access that is not explicitly authorized is forbidden;
- process for revoking access rights or interrupting the connection between systems;
- arrangements for reporting, notification, and investigation of information inaccuracies, InfoSec incidents, and security breaches;
- description of each service to be made available;
- target and unacceptable levels of service;
- right to monitor, and revoke, any activity related to the organization's assets;
- respective liabilities of the organization and the customer; and
- legal responsibilities.

Agreements with third parties should include security requirements. Each agreement should ensure no misunderstanding between the organization and the third party. An agreement should possibly include:

- the security policy;
- procedures to protect assets;
- procedures to determine whether any compromise of the asset has occurred;
- controls to ensure return or destruction of information and assets;
- restrictions on copying and disclosing information;
- user and administrator training in methods and procedures; and
- clear reporting structure and agreed reporting formats.

3.3.1.2.3 ASSET CLASSIFICATION AND CONTROL (ISO/IEC 27002 SECTION 7). This section deals with the need that all assets should be inventoried, identified as to their importance, and have an identified owner or custodian. All assets should be identified and an inventory of important assets drawn up and maintained. The asset inventory should document information necessary in order to recover from a disaster (such as asset type, format, location, backup information, license information, and business value). Ownership and information classification should be established and documented for each asset. Based on the importance of the asset, its business value, and its security classification, levels of protection commensurate with the importance of the assets should be specified.

Asset owners should be responsible for ensuring that information and assets are appropriately classified and defining and periodically reviewing access restrictions and classifications. Internal and external users should follow rules for the acceptable use of information and assets, including rules for electronic mail and Internet usage and guidelines for use of mobile devices, especially outside the premises of the organization. Asset classifications should consider business needs for sharing or restricting information and the business impacts associated with such needs. Classification guidelines should include conventions for initial classification and reclassification over time. The asset owner should be responsible for defining the classification of an asset, periodically review it, and ensure it is kept up to date and at the appropriate level. Consideration should be given to the number of classification categories and the benefits to be gained from their use. Overly complex schemes are likely to be impractical.

Procedures for information labeling need to cover assets in physical and electronic formats. Output from systems containing information that is classified as being sensitive or critical should be marked with an appropriate classification label. The types of items include printed reports, screen displays, recorded media (such as tapes, disks, CDs, DVDs, "thumb drives"), electronic messages, and even file transfers. Each classification level should have identified handling procedures covering the processing, storage, transmission, declassification, and destruction. These procedures should also span chain of custody and logging of security relevant events.

3.3.1.2.4 Personnel Security (ISO/IEC 27002 Section 8). This section considers the most important aspect of securing assets, namely, the employees within the organization that have the greatest degree of access to assets. The security policy needs to ensure that employees, contractors, and third-party users understand their responsibilities, and are qualified for employment, so as to reduce the risk of theft, fraud, or misuse of assets.

Job/position descriptions should state security responsibilities and terms and conditions of employment. Screening, especially for sensitive jobs, should be performed on candidates for employment, contractors, and third-party users. An agreement on their security roles and responsibilities should be signed by employees, contractors, and third-party users of assets. Security roles and responsibilities should, at a minimum, include requirements to:

- comply with the organization's security policies;
- protect assets from unauthorized access;
- adhere to security processes and activities;
- hold an individual responsible for actions taken; and
- report security events or potential events or other security risks.

Security roles and responsibilities should be communicated to job candidates during the pre-employment process. Consistent with relevant privacy, protection of personal data, and/or employment-based legislation, verification checks should span the following:

- character references (both professional/business and personal);
- completeness and accuracy of an applicant's resume or curriculum vitae;
- confirmation of claimed qualifications;
- an identity check (passport or similar document); and
- possibly additional checks, such as credit checks, checks of criminal records, or even ability to obtain formal security clearances.

The terms and conditions of employment should reflect the organization's security policy regarding:

- legal responsibilities and rights, for example, regarding copyright laws or data protection legislation;
- responsibilities for the classification of information and management of organizational assets;
- responsibilities for the handling of information received from other companies or external parties;
- responsibilities for the handling of personal information;
- responsibilities that extend beyond the organization's premises and outside normal working hours, for example, in the case of home-working; and
- actions that may occur if the organization's security requirements are disregarded.

Execution of a non-disclosure agreement should be completed prior to being given access to assets.

Management responsibilities toward employees include ensuring that an adequate level of awareness, education, and training in security procedures and the correct use of assets should be provided to all employees, along with a formal disciplinary process for handling security breaches. Responsibilities of management should include ensuring that individuals:

- are properly briefed on security roles and responsibilities;
- are provided with guidelines stating security roles within the organization;
- are motivated to fulfill the security policies;
- demonstrate awareness on security relevant to their roles and responsibilities;
- conform to the terms and conditions of employment, including the security policy; and
- continue to have appropriate skills and qualifications.

Awareness training should begin with a formal induction process that introduces the organization's security policies and expectations. Ongoing training should be a part of normal business activities and include security requirements, legal responsibilities, and business controls, as well as training in the correct use of asset access.

An organization's disciplinary process should not begin prior to verification that a security breach has occurred. The disciplinary process should:

- ensure correct and fair treatment for employees who are suspected of committing breaches of security; and
- provide for a graduated response that takes into consideration the nature and gravity of the breach and its impact on business, if it is a first or repeat offence, if the violator had received training, etc.

The process should also support immediate suspension of duties, revocation of access rights and privileges, and immediate escorting out of the facility if necessary. In case of employment termination, management is responsible for ensuring individuals exit an organization or change employment in an orderly manner. This process should include the return of all equipment, software, credit cards, manuals/documentation, etc., and the removal of all access rights.

3.3.1.2.5 PHYSICAL AND ENVIRONMENTAL SECURITY (ISO/IEC 27002 SECTION 9). Organizational assets should be located in facilities that have defined security perimeters and include appropriate security barriers and entry controls to protect the assets from unauthorized access, damage, and interference. Security perimeters should be used to protect areas that contain information and information processing facilities. Following are some guidelines to consider:

- the date and time of entry and exit;
- access restricted to authorized persons only and sufficient authentication controls provided;
- wearing visible identification badges; and
- third-party support service personnel access allowed only when required, authorized, and monitored.

Consideration should be given to other events including a fire in a nearby building, roof water leaks, water pipe breaks, and even a street located utility explosion. Other considerations to avoid damage from fire, flood, earthquake, explosion, civil unrest, and other forms of natural or man-made disaster are as follows:

- Hazardous or combustible materials should be stored at a safe distance from a secure area. Bulk supplies such as stationery should not be stored within a secure area;
- Fallback equipment and back-up media should be sited at a safe distance to avoid damage from a disaster affecting the main site; and
  ○ Appropriate firefighting equipment should be provided and suitably placed.

To prevent loss, damage, theft, or compromise of assets and interruption to the organization's activities, equipment should be protected from physical and environmental threats.
    The protection of equipment is necessary to reduce the risk of unauthorized access to information and to protect against loss or damage. This should also consider equipment location. Special controls may be required to protect against physical threats and

TABLE 3.5. ISO/IEC 27002 Section 10 Covered Security Policy Areas.

Operational procedures and responsibilities	Documented operating procedures
	Change management
	Segregation of duties
	Separation of development, test, and operational facilities
Third-party service delivery management	Service delivery
	Monitoring and review of third-party services
	Managing changes to third-party services
System planning and acceptance	Capacity management
	System acceptance
Protection against malicious and Mobile Code	Controls against malicious code
	Controls against mobile code
Back-up	Information back-up
Network security management	Network controls
	Security of network services
Media handling	Management of removable media
	Disposal of media
	Information handling procedures
	Security of system documentation
Exchange of information	Information exchange policies and procedures
	Exchange agreements
	Physical media in transit
	Electronic messaging
	Business information systems
Electronic commerce service	Electronic commerce
	Online transactions
	Publicly available information
Monitoring	Audit logging
	Monitoring system use
	Protection of log information
	Administrator and operator logs
	Fault logging
	Clock synchronization

to safeguard supporting facilities, such as electrical power sources, heating–air conditioning, and cabling infrastructure.

3.3.1.2.6 COMMUNICATIONS AND OPERATIONS MANAGEMENT (ISO/IEC 27002 SECTION 10). This section focuses on ensuring the correct and secure operation of information processing assets. It goes into significant detail beyond what can be paraphrased here. Therefore, Table 3.5 is used to highlight the breadth of subjects covered in this section.

Responsibilities and procedures for the management and operation of all information processing facilities should be established. This includes the development of appropriate operating procedures.

Segregation of duties should be implemented, where appropriate, to reduce the risk of negligent or deliberate system misuse. Many of these subjects are further covered throughout the remaining chapters of this book.

3.3.1.2.7 ACCESS CONTROLS (ISO/IEC 27002 SECTION 11). This section deals with access to organizational assets which should be controlled on the basis of business and security requirements, and access control rules should take account of policies for information dissemination and authorization. An access control policy should be established, documented, and reviewed based on business and security requirements for access.

Access control rules and rights for each user or group of users should be clearly stated in an access control policy. Access controls are both logical and physical, and these should be considered together. Users and service providers should be given a clear statement of the business requirements to be met by access controls. A process for managing access controls should include, at a minimum, the following requirements:

- allocation of passwords;
- review of users' access rights at regular intervals;
- users should be made aware of their responsibilities for maintaining effective access controls, especially the use of passwords and the security of user equipment;
- use of screen "savers" to reduce the risk of unauthorized access;
- users should be required to follow good security practices in the selection and use of passwords;
- users should be made aware of the security requirements and procedures for protecting unattended equipment;
- access to networked services, both internal and external networked services, should be controlled;
- appropriate interface controls are in place between the organization's network and networks owned by other organizations, and public networks;
- appropriate authentication mechanisms are applied for users and equipment;
- control of user access to information services is enforced;
- physical and logical access to diagnostic and configuration ports should be controlled;
- groups of information services, users, and information systems should be segregated on networks;
- large networks should be divided into separate network domains;
- user connection to shared networks should be restricted or controlled through the use of network gateways and other devices that filter traffic by means of pre-defined tables or rules;
- limiting network access to certain times of day or dates should be considered;
- routing controls should consider source and destination address checking at internal and external network control points, especially when proxy and/or network address translation technologies are employed;

- security facilities should be used to restrict access to operating systems to authorized users;
- secure logon procedures should control access to operating systems;
- users should have a unique identifier (user ID) for their personal use only;
- suitable authentication techniques should be chosen to substantiate claimed user identities;
- interactive management of passwords should ensure quality passwords;
- tightly controlled or restricted access should be used for utility programs that could override system and application controls; and
- settable periods of inactivity should be used to shut down inactive sessions.

3.3.1.2.8 INFORMATION SYSTEMS ACQUISITION, DEVELOPMENT, AND MAINTENANCE (ISO/IEC 27002 SECTION 12). This section deals with security of information systems, including operating systems, infrastructure, business applications, off-the-shelf products, services, and user-developed applications.

Security requirements should be identified within the requirements phase of a project and justified, agreed, and documented prior to the development and/or implementation of information systems. The requirements for security controls for new systems, or enhancements to existing systems, should be specified and applied when evaluating software packages, developed or purchased, for business applications. Appropriate controls for the validation of input data, internal processing, and output data should be designed into application. A crucial aspect of these controls includes validation of data input to applications to ensure that this data is correct and appropriate to detect any corruption of information through processing errors or deliberate acts.

Requirements for ensuring authenticity and integrity of application messages should be identified and appropriate controls implemented. Cryptographic techniques can be used for message authentication and integrity, and the policy governing the use of cryptographic mechanisms should include key management. Key management should be established so that cryptographic keys can be protected against modification, loss, and destruction. Secret and private keys require protection against unauthorized disclosure, and equipment or software used to generate, store, and archive keys should be protected using multiple approaches.

Access to system files and program source code should be controlled in a secure manner with care given to avoid exposure of sensitive data in test environments. Access to program source code should be closely controlled. Change control procedures should be followed when implementing changes to operating systems and business critical applications, including reviews and tests to determine that there is no adverse impact on security. The leakage of information should be prevented with consideration given to exploitation of covert channels, including:

- scanning of outbound media and communications for hidden information;
- masking and modulating system and communications behavior;
- using high-integrity systems and software, such as using evaluated products;

- regular monitoring of personnel and system activities; and
- monitoring computer system resource usage.

Outsourced software development should be supervised and monitored and consideration given to:

- licensing arrangements, code ownership, and intellectual property rights;
- certification of quality and accuracy of the work carried out;
- escrow arrangements in the event of failure of the third-party developer;
- access rights to audit the quality and accuracy of the work done;
- contractual requirements for quality and security capabilities of code; and
- pre-installation testing to detect malicious functionality, let alone agreed to security capabilities.

Vulnerability management should be implemented to reduce risks resulting from exploitation of published vulnerabilities. The processes used for vulnerability management should be systematic and should result in repeatable measurements confirming effectiveness. Vulnerabilities in operating systems and applications should be considered. The gathering of timely information about vulnerabilities should occur and the degree of exposure to such vulnerabilities evaluated with appropriate measures taken to address the associated risk.

3.3.1.2.9 INFORMATION SECURITY INCIDENT MANAGEMENT (ISO/IEC 27002 SECTION 13). This section focuses on how to deal with the occurrence of security-related events. Event reporting and escalation procedures should be in place, with employees, contractors, and third-party users made aware of the procedures for reporting the different types of events and situations that might have an impact on the security of organizational assets. These individuals should be required to report any security events and weaknesses as quickly as possible. Incident response and escalation procedures should exist that describe the actions required on receipt of a report of a security event. Specific point of contact individuals should be identified for the reporting of InfoSec events with whom these "point of contacts" are disseminated throughout the organization.

Continual process improvement should be performed to security incident response, monitoring, and evaluation processes. Security event handling should be in compliance with legal requirements. Often, security event follow-up may include involvement of authorities as part of either civil actions (lawsuits) or criminal prosecution. Consequently, security event procedures should consider the collection and handling of evidence in conformance with rules of evidence. Failure to follow rules of evidence may directly impact whether or not the evidence can be used in court (admissibility) and the quality and completeness of the evidence (weight of evidence).

There should be mechanisms in place to enable the types, volumes, and costs of InfoSec incidents to be quantified and monitored. Part of the evaluation of security incidents should include identification of recurring or high-impact incidents. This activity may indicate the need for enhanced or additional controls to limit the frequency, damage, and cost of future occurrences, as well as the security policy review process.

3.3.1.2.10 BUSINESS CONTINUITY MANAGEMENT (ISO/IEC 27002 SECTION 14). This section is concerned with how to ensure the security aspects for continuation of business activities. Major failures of systems or disasters can cause interruptions to business activities that need to be counteracted in a timely manner. A business continuity management plan should be developed and processes implemented to minimize the impact on the organization and recover from loss of assets due to causes such as natural disasters, accidents, equipment failures, and deliberate actions. The plan and continuity processes should identify critical business processes and integrate security management requirements of business continuity with other continuity requirements for operations, staffing, materials, transport, and facilities. The plan and processes should integrate key elements of business continuity management, including:

- understanding the risks from a probability and an impact duration perspective;
- identifying and prioritizing critical business processes;
- identifying critical business processes and assets;
- recognizing the business interruptions likely to be caused by security incidents;
- considering the purchase of insurance as part of the overall business continuity process;
- implementing additional preventive and mitigating controls;
- identifying resources to address the identified InfoSec requirements;
- ensuring personnel safety; and
- protecting facilities and organizational property.

Business continuity planning should consider:

- identification of responsibilities, necessary business continuity procedures, and what constitutes acceptable loss of information and service;
- implementation of recovery and restoration of business operations and availability of information within specified time frames;
- completion of recovery and post-restoration operational procedures; and
- full, complete, and accessible documentation of the procedures and processes.

Business continuity plans are only as good as their testability. Tests should be conducted frequently to verify that the staff understands the recovery procedures, their responsibility for business continuity, and their role when a plan is invoked. The continuity plan should indicate how frequently each element of the plan should be tested.

3.3.1.2.11 COMPLIANCE (ISO/IEC 27002 SECTION 15). This section deals with compliance with adherence with laws, statutes, regulations and contractual obligations, and security requirements. The design, operation, use, and management of systems are likely to be subject to statutory, regulatory, and contractual security requirements.

Organization's legal advisers, or qualified legal practitioners, should be consulted on specific legal requirements. The specific security mechanisms and procedures to comply with these requirements should be defined and documented.

Procedures should ensure compliance with legislative, regulatory, and contractual requirements on the use of material where there may be intellectual property rights and how proprietary software products are deployed. Some of the following should be considered in regard to protecting material that may be considered intellectual property:

- publishing an intellectual property rights compliance policy that covers disciplinary action against personnel violating the policy;
- acquiring software only through known and reputable sources thereby not violating copyright;
- maintaining appropriate asset registers which identify assets with requirements to protect intellectual property rights along with proof and evidence of ownership of licenses, master disks, manuals, etc.;
- implementing controls to ensure that the maximum number of users permitted is not exceeded; and
- performing audits to ensure that only authorized software and licensed products are installed.

Organizational records constitute a significant asset and represent sensitive information that should be protected from loss, destruction, and falsification, in accordance with statutory, regulatory, contractual, and business requirements. Records should be categorized by record types, for example, accounting records, database records, transaction logs, audit logs, and operational procedures. Each type of record should have details of retention periods and type of storage media, for example, paper, microfiche, magnetic, and optical, established and documented in an asset inventory. Cryptographic keys and software used with encrypted archives or digital signatures should be retained to enable decryption of the records for as long as the records are retained. All forms of media used for records storage will deteriorate over time, so storage and handling procedures should reflect likely media life spans.

Organizations should deter users from using processing and communications assets for unauthorized purposes. Use of these assets for non-business purposes or unauthorized purposes should be regarded as improper use. Should unauthorized activity be identified by monitoring, or other means, this activity should result in consideration of appropriate disciplinary and/or legal action.

Compliance with organizational security policies and standards should be regularly reviewed to ensure security of system assets. These reviews should be performed against the security policies with systems audited for compliance with security standards. Managers should regularly review the systems under their control and responsibility for compliance with security policies, standards, and security requirements. If any non-compliance is found as a result of the review, managers should determine the causes of the non-compliance, evaluate the need for actions to ensure that non-compliance does not recur, determine and implement corrective changes, and review corrective actions taken. Systems should be regularly audited for compliance with security standards. These compliance audits should utilize only authorized experienced and trained personnel and appropriate software tools, resulting in the generation of reports for subsequent analysis. Penetration tests and vulnerability assessments should be performed with caution to avoid compromise of system security. Audit requirements and activities of operational systems should be carefully planned to minimize the risk of disruption to business processes. Guidelines for audits should include agreement on audit requirements, scope of audits, what software and data are included, and resources for performing the audit. Audit tools should be separated from development and operational systems and given an appropriate level of additional protection to safeguard their integrity and prevent misuse of these tools.

3.3.1.3 What Is Lacking in the ISO/IEC 27000 Series? The ISO/IEC 27001/27002 documents provide an excellent starting point for integrating InfoSec management into core business processes and activities. However, there are a number of ISO/IEC 27001 and 27002 issues worth considering, namely:

- The level of specificity in ISO/IEC 27001 requirements is relatively low in their actual wording and, as such, vulnerable to interpretation unless accompanied by elaboration within an accompanying ISO/IEC 27002 conforming InfoSec policy;
- ISO/IEC 27001 does not specifically reference ISO/IEC 27005 for risk management; it references an older technical report (ISO/IEC TR 13335-3, Information technology—Guidelines for the management of IT Security—Techniques for the management of IT Security). A revision of ISO/IEC 27001 should be published that not only references ISO/IEC 27005 but also explains how ISO/IEC 27005 risk management integrates into the ISO/IEC 27001 ISMS;
- ISO/IEC 27002 discusses an ISMS as applying to a whole enterprise, which is reasonable for most organizations but not necessarily valid for large to very large enterprises comprised of multiple relatively independent divisions or autonomous subsidiaries. In the case of large to very large enterprises, it is reasonable for each division or autonomous subsidiary to implement their own ISMS with all these ISMSs linked to a master InfoSec management policy;
- Both ISO/IEC 27001 and 27002 envision that an ISMS is documented in a single InfoSec management policy document. The problem with this view is that the security policy specifics that apply to different enterprise groups can be quite large, resulting in a single InfoSec policy document becoming larger than employees want, or perhaps need, to read and follow. A more effective InfoSec policy approach is to have the over-arching enterprise InfoSec policy document reference, and leverage, policy statements in a number of secondary, department-specific InfoSec policy documents. It is quite reasonable to see department-specific InfoSec policy documents for the Human Resources, Finance, Research and Development, Sales-Marketing, Operations, and Manufacturing organizations within a large enterprise. With this approach, the members of a department would

need to be familiar, and comply, with the over-arching enterprise and group-specific InfoSec policy documents, thereby making the dissemination of InfoSec policy responsibilities and requirements more manageable;

- Neither ISO/IEC 27001 nor 27002 takes the next step, that of linking InfoSec policy to specific types of InfoSec-related processes and procedures. It is these very InfoSec-related processes and procedures that actually instantiate much of an ISMS. Without elaboration on InfoSec-related processes and procedures, it becomes difficult to ensure that the "Do," "Check," and "Act" aspects of ISO/IEC 27001 objectives are being achieved; and

- Although ISO/IEC 27001 discusses enterprise management responsibilities, it does not elaborate on, or provide guidance relating to, where, when, and how management should be actually engaged in ISMS activities. A number of questions should be addressed in this area, specifically:

  ○ Should there be an Executive level InfoSec policy approval process?

  ○ Who should be responsible for developing InfoSec policies, middle management or executive level management?

  ○ What role should a BoD have relative to InfoSec policy and ISMS compliance?

  ○ Are there advantages to an enterprise integrating ISMS operational responsibilities into line organizations versus establishing a separate InfoSec organization?

  ○ If an enterprise does establish a separate InfoSec organization, who should this organization's leader, such as a Chief Security Officer (CSO), report to (i.e., a member of the BoD or the Chief Executive Officer (CEO))?

  ○ If an enterprise integrates ISMS operational responsibilities into line organizations, then how will ISMS non-compliance be handled so as to avoid conflicts of management goals?

The aforementioned questions are far from trivial, and for ISO/IEC 27001 and 27002 to not address these points reduces the usability of these standards. Another issue with the ISO/IEC standards is that they are silent regarding the derivation of security requirements tied to InfoSec policy statements. These security requirements provide an unambiguous baseline set of capabilities against which enterprise activities and systems security can be evaluated. When the security requirements are directly derived from InfoSec policy, then a system or activity that complies with the security requirements can be stated as complying with the InfoSec policy.

3.3.2 The Information Technology Infrastructure Library Framework

The ITIL is a set of practices for IT service management that focuses on aligning IT services with business needs. ITIL describes procedures, tasks, and checklists that are not organization-specific and allows an organization to establish a baseline from which it can plan, implement, and measure. Five volumes comprise ITIL v3, published in May 2007 and updated in July 2011. These volumes are:

1. ITIL Service Strategy;
2. ITIL Service Design;
3. ITIL Service Transition;
4. ITIL Service Operation; and
5. ITIL Continual Service Improvement

available from the following URL:

http://www.best-management-practice.com/Portfolio-Library/IT-Service-Management-ITIL/

The ITIL Service Design provides good, practical guidance on the design of IT services, processes, and other service management activities. Design within ITIL spans all aspects relevant to technology service delivery, not just the design of the technology itself. Consequently, service design addresses:

* how a planned service solution interacts with business and technical environments;
* service management systems required to support the service;
* processes which interact with the service, technology, and architecture required to support the service; and
* the supply chain required to support the planned service.

The ITIL processes covered under service design are:

* Design Coordination;
* Service Catalogue;
* Service Level Management;
* Availability Management;
* Capacity Management;
* IT Service Continuity Management;
* Information Security Management System; and
* Supplier Management.

Of interest to us is ITIL security management. The ITIL security management process deals with fitting the management of security into the overall management organization or the organization and is based on the ISO/IEC 27001 standard. A basic concept of InfoSec management is to ensure the appropriate selection, implementation, and operation of InfoSec control, whereas the primary goal of InfoSec controls is to ensure the safety and availability of information and other assets. The goal of ITIL security management is the realization of the security requirements derived from an organization's InfoSec policies along with external requirements from contracts, legislation, and regulations. Compliance with these requirements measures the degree to which an organization's activities conform to the organization's InfoSec policies. The security requirements are translated into security services (security quality) that need to be

TABLE 3.6. **ITIL Sub-processes.**

Sub-activities	Descriptions
Classifying and managing of IT applications	Process of formally grouping configuration items by type, for example, software, hardware, documentation, environment, application.
	Process of formally identifying changes by type, for example, project scope change request, validation change request, infrastructure change request. This process leads to asset classification and control documents
Implement personnel security	Here, measures are adopted in order to give personnel safety and confidence and measures to prevent a crime/fraud
Implement security management	In this process, specific security requirements and/or security rules that must be met are outlined and documented
Implement access control	In this process, specific access security requirements and/or access security rules that must be met are outlined and documented
Reporting	In this process, the whole "implement as planned" process is documented in a specific way

provided by security controls/mechanisms. Security plans are developed which identify those aspects of security policies addressed and the security services to be provided. These security plans are then implemented and the implementation is then evaluated.

The first activity in the ITIL security management process is the "Control" sub-process. This sub-process includes organizing and managing the security management process itself. The Control sub-process defines the processes and the allocation of responsibility for policy statements.

The ITIL security management framework defines the Control sub-processes for:

- the development of security plans;
- the implementation of security plans;
- the evaluation of security plans; and
- how the results of the evaluations are translated into action plans.

The second activity in the ITIL security management process is the "Plan" sub-process. This sub-process includes activities that are related to procedures and contracts which are specific to InfoSec. In the Plan sub-process, the goals of InfoSec are specified in the form of operational procedures for a specific internal organization entity.

The third activity in the ITIL security management process is the "Implementation" sub-process. This sub-process makes sure that all measures, as specified in the plans, are properly implemented. The activities that take place within the implementation sub-process are summed up in Table 3.6.

The forth activity in the ITIL security management process is the "Evaluation" sub-process. The Evaluation of the implementation and the plans is very important as it measures the success of the implementation and the security plans. The results of the

Evaluation sub-process are used to verify how completely the chosen security mechanisms, their implementation, and administration satisfy the organization's security policies and security requirements. Evaluation results can lead to new requirements. ITIL identifies three types of Evaluation: self-assessment, internal audit, and external audit. Self-assessment is mainly carried out by organizations responsible for following the processes and procedures. Internal audits are carried out by internal IT auditors, and external audits are carried out by external, independent IT auditors. Additionally, evaluations based on security incidents should also take place.

The fifth activity in the ITIL security management process is the "Maintenance" sub-process. Due to changes in an IT infrastructure, and changes in the organization itself, security-related risks will change over time. Maintenance is based on the results of the Evaluation sub-process and insight into changing risks. Maintenance results in proposed changes to policies, requirements, plans, and/or procedures as inputs for the Plan sub-process and goes through the whole cycle.

3.3.2.1 What Is Lacking in ITIL?. The main problem with ITIL in the author's opinion is that ITIL takes solely a process perspective on managing InfoSec rather than taking a governance perspective. Regarding InfoSec security requirements, ITIL is just as silent as the ISO/IEC standards. As noted earlier, these security requirements provide an unambiguous baseline set of capabilities against which enterprise activities and systems security can be evaluated. When the security requirements are directly derived from InfoSec policy, then a system or activity that complies with the security requirements can be stated as complying with the InfoSec policy. While ITIL, in many respects, picks up where the ISO/IEC standards stop, ITIL's process perspective lacks any linkage to an enterprise's security policies, or derived InfoSec requirements, which makes any form of compliance verification difficult. A major addition to ITIL would be a discussion regarding how ITIL processes map to the InfoSec governance subjects covered by the ISO/IEC standards. Additionally, the cost of ITIL documentation is a problem; if the ITIL documentation is easily available for in-depth analysis and peer review, then its adoption would more likely increase. Furthermore, there are currently no accreditation and certification mechanisms for ITIL, whereas such mechanisms exist for the ISO/IEC standards.

3.3.3 COBIT Framework

Initially an acronym for "Control OBjectives for Information and Related Technology," COBIT is a framework for enterprise information technology (IT) governance, developed by the Information Systems Audit and Control Association (ISACA), that provides a toolset for managers to deal with control requirements, technical issues, and business risks. The current version of COBIT is 4.1 which provides a framework for 34 IT management processes, where each process is defined together with:

- process inputs and outputs;
- key process activities; and
- process objectives and performance measures.

ISACA considers COBIT to be an "integrator of existing guidance materials from other sources that will summarize key objectives under one umbrella framework that link to good practice models with governance and business requirements." COBIT version 5 is planned for release in 2012 and incorporate ISACA's Risk IT framework. ISACA published the Risk IT framework in 2009 to provide an end-to-end view of risks related to the use of IT and how to manage said risks at all levels within an organization. ISACA has published three documents:

- *The Risk IT Framework*, ISACA, ISBN 978-1-60420-111-6, can be downloaded from http://www.isaca.org/Knowledge-Center/Risk-IT-IT-Risk-Management/Pages/Risk-IT1.aspx;
- *The Risk IT Practitioner Guide*, ISACA, ISBN 978-1-60420-116-1, is available to ISACA members only; and
- *IT Standards, Guidelines, and Tools and Techniques for Audit and Assurance and Control Professionals* can be downloaded from http://www.isaca.org/Knowledge-Center/Risk-IT-IT-Risk-Management/Pages/Risk-IT1.aspx.

The Risk IT Framework document defines three domains of risk-related areas, along with the processes and process activities: Risk Governance, Risk Evaluation, and Risk Response. The Risk Governance Domain focuses on ensuring that IT risk management practices are embedded within the enterprise so that enterprises secure optimal risk-adjusted returns. This domain spans the following activities:

- Establish and Maintain a Common Risk View:
  - Perform enterprise IT risk assessment;
  - Propose IT risk tolerance thresholds;
  - Approve IT risk tolerance;
  - Align IT risk policy;
  - Promote IT risk-aware culture; and
  - Encourage effective communication of IT risk;
- Integrate With General Enterprise Risk Management Activities:
  - Establish and maintain accountability for IT risk management;
  - Coordinate IT risk strategy and business risk strategy;
  - Adapt IT risk practices to enterprise risk practices;
  - Provide adequate resources for IT risk management; and
  - Provide independent assurance over IT risk management;
- Make Risk-Aware Business Decisions:
  - Gain management buy-in for the IT risk analysis approach;
  - Approve IT risk analysis;
  - Embed IT risk consideration in strategic business decision making;
  - Accept IT risk; and
  - Prioritize IT risk response activities.

The Risk Evaluation Domain focuses on ensuring that enterprise IT-related risks and opportunities are identified, analyzed, and presented in business terms. This domain spans the following activities:

- Collect Data:
  - Establish and maintain a model for data collection;
  - Collect data on the operating environment;
  - Collect data on risk events; and
  - Identify risk factors;
- Analyze Risk:
  - Define IT risk analysis scope;
  - Estimate IT risk;
  - Identify risk response options; and
  - Perform a peer review of IT risk analysis;
- Maintain Risk Profile:
  - Map IT resources to business processes;
  - Determine business criticality of IT resources;
  - Understand IT capabilities;
  - Update risk scenario components;
  - Maintain the IT risk register and IT risk map; and
  - Develop IT risk indicators.

The Risk Response Domain focuses on ensuring that enterprise IT-related risk issues, opportunities, and events are addressed in a cost-effective manner and in line with business priorities. This domain spans the following activities:

- Articulate Risk:
  - Communicate IT risk analysis results;
  - Report IT risk management activities and state of compliance;
  - Interpret independent IT assessment findings; and
  - Identify IT-related opportunities;
- Manage Risk:
  - Inventory controls;
  - Monitor operational alignment with risk tolerance thresholds;
  - Respond to discovered risk exposure and opportunity;
  - Implement controls; and
  - Report IT risk action plan progress;
- React to Events:
  - Maintain incident response plans;
  - Monitor IT risk;

- ○ Initiate incident response; and
- ○ Communicate lessons learned from risk events.

For each of these processes, each process should have documented:

- Process components;
- Management practice;
- Inputs and outputs;
- RACI charts; and
- Goals and metrics.

The Risk IT Practitioner Guide is made up of the following eight sections:

1. Defining a Risk Universe and Scoping Risk Management;
2. Risk Appetite and Risk Tolerance;
3. Risk Awareness, Communication, and Reporting;
4. Expressing and Describing Risk;
5. Risk Scenarios;
6. Risk Response and Prioritization;
7. A Risk Analysis Workflow; and
8. Mitigation of IT Risk Using COBIT.

The IT Standards, Guidelines, and Tools and Techniques for Audit and Assurance and Control Professionals document is organized into the following three sections:

- Standards which specify mandatory requirements for IT audit and assurance necessary to achieve the minimum level of acceptable performance required to meet the professional responsibilities set out in the ISACA Code of Professional Ethics;
- Guidelines for applying the IT Audit and Assurance Standards; and
- Example Tools and Techniques which provide information on how to meet the standards.

Both the Standards and Guidelines sections include discussions of Audit Charters, Audit Reporting, Audit Planning, and IT Governance. The IT Audit and Assurance Standards section discusses additional audit-related topics on:

- Independence of Auditing;
- Professional Ethics and Standards for Auditing;
- Competence;
- Performance of Audit Work;
- Follow-up Activities;

- Irregularities and Illegal Acts;
- Use of Risk Assessment in Audit Planning;
- Using the Work of Other Experts;
- Audit Evidence; and
- IT Controls.

The IT Audit and Assurance Guidelines section also discusses:

- Guidelines that focus on Auditing spanning:
  - Using the Work of Other Auditors;
  - Audit Evidence Requirement;
  - Using Computer-Assisted Audit Techniques;
  - Outsourcing of IS Activities to Other Organizations;
  - Materiality Concepts for Auditing Information Systems;
  - Due Professional Care;
  - Audit Documentation;
  - Audit Considerations for Irregularities and Illegal Acts;
  - Effect of Non-audit Role on the IT Audit and Assurance Professional's Independence;
  - Irregularities and Illegal Acts, July 1, 2002;
  - Audit Sampling; and
  - Use of Risk Assessment in Audit Planning;
- Guidelines that focus on Controls spanning:
  - Effect of Pervasive IS Controls;
  - Effect of Third Parties on an Organization's IT Controls;
  - Biometric Controls;
  - Access Controls;
  - Post-implementation Review; and
  - Organizational Relationship and Independence;
- Guidelines that focus on Applications and Technology areas spanning:
  - Application Systems Review;
  - Enterprise Resource Planning Systems Review;
  - Business-to-Consumer E-commerce Review;
  - System Development Life Cycle Reviews;
  - Internet Banking;
  - Review of Virtual Private Networks;
  - Business Process Reengineering Project Reviews;
  - Mobile Computing;
  - General Considerations on the Use of Internet; and
  - Electronic Funds Transfer;

- Guidelines that focus on Business Processes spanning:
  - ○ Computer Forensics;
  - ○ Competence;
  - ○ Privacy;
  - ○ Business Continuity Plan;
  - ○ Responsibility, Authority, and Accountability;
  - ○ Follow-up Activities;
  - ○ Configuration Management Process;
  - ○ IT Organization;
  - ○ Security Management Practices;
  - ○ Return on Security Investment; and
  - ○ Continuous Assurance.

The IT Audit and Assurance Tools and Techniques section also discusses use of:
- IS Risk Assessment;
- Digital Signatures;
- Intrusion Detection;
- Viruses and Other Malicious Code Detection/Elimination;
- Control Risk Self-assessment;
- Firewalls;
- Security Assessment—Penetration Testing and Vulnerability Analysis;
- Evaluation of Management Controls over Encryption Methodologies; and
- Business Application Change Controls.

3.3.3.1 *What Is Lacking in COBIT?* The main problem with COBIT in the author's opinion is that COBIT primarily takes a process perspective on managing InfoSec rather than taking a governance perspective. Regarding InfoSec security requirements, COBIT is just as silent as the ISO/IEC standards. As noted earlier, these security requirements provide an unambiguous baseline set of capabilities against which enterprise activities and systems security can be evaluated. When the security requirements are directly derived from InfoSec policy, then a system or activity that complies with the security requirements can be stated as complying with the InfoSec policy. While COBIT in many ways picks up where ISO/IEC 27001 and 27001 stop, COBIT's process perspective lacks any linkage to an enterprise's security policies, or derived InfoSec requirements, which makes any form of compliance verification difficult. A major addition to COBIT would be a discussion regarding how COBIT processes map to the InfoSec governance subjects covered by the ISO/IEC standards. Additionally, the cost of COBIT documentation is a problem; if the COBIT documentation is easily available for in-depth analysis and peer review, then its adoption would more likely increase. Furthermore, there are currently no accreditation and certification mechanisms for COBIT, whereas such mechanisms exist for the ISO/IEC standards.

3.3.4 FISMA Framework

In 2002, FISMA was added to U.S. Federal law as Title III of the E-Government Act of 2002 (Public Law 107-347, 116 Stat. 2899). Although this law requires the development, documentation, and implementation of programs addressing InfoSec by federal agencies, including any organization providing information processing services to an agency, there are non-governmental organizations that have adopted FISMA as their InfoSec governance framework. NIST established a FISMA Implementation Project to produce security standards and guidelines which include:

- Federal Information Processing Standard (FIPS) Publication 199 "Standards for Security Categorization of Federal Information and Information Systems";
- FIPS Publication 200 "Minimum Security Requirements for Federal Information and Information Systems";
- NIST Special Publication (SP) 800-53 "Recommended Security Controls for Federal Information Systems";
- SP 800-59 "Guideline for Identifying an Information System as a National Security System"; and
- SP 800-60 "Guide for Mapping Types of Information and Information Systems to Security Categories."

In support of the project, NIST has also developed additional documents, including:

- SP 800-37 "Guide for Applying the Risk Management Framework to Federal Information Systems—A Security Life Cycle Approach";
- SP 800-39 "Managing Risk from Information Systems—An Organizational Perspective"; and
- SP 800-53A "Guide for Assessing the Security Controls in Federal Information Systems and Organizations—Building Effective Security Assessment Plans"

while continuing to produce other security standards and guidelines. All of these NIST publications can be downloaded from: http://csrc.nist.gov/publications/. FISMA takes a risk-based approach for achieving InfoSec. The selection and specification of security controls should be specified as part of an organization-wide InfoSec program that involves the management of organizational risk.

In the view of FISMA, the management of organizational risk is a key element in the organization's InfoSec program and provides a framework for selecting the appropriate security controls for an information system. A risk-oriented approach is promoted for selecting and specifying security controls and advocates considering a control's effectiveness, efficiency, and constraints due to laws, directives, policies, standards, and regulations. Six related activity steps are presented (Categorize, Select, Implement, Assess, Authorize, and Monitor) for managing organizational risk that FISMA considers paramount to an effective InfoSec governance that should be applicable to both new

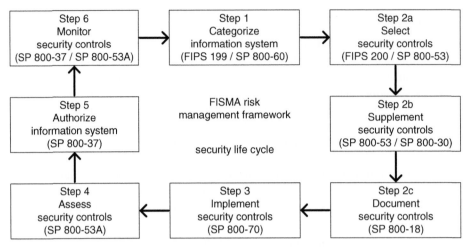

Figure 3.1. FISMA risk management framework.

and legacy information systems. Figure 3.1 highlights the six steps and identifies applicable FIPS and NIST SP guidance documents.

In Step 1 (**Categorize**), the organizations should perform an impact analysis on each system, and the information it processes, stores, or communicates with other systems. Based on this analysis, categorize the organizational impact due to system or information loss as Low, Moderate, or High along the three dimensions of confidentiality, integrity, and availability according to FIPS 199 and NIST SP 800-60 guidance. In Step 2 (**Select**), an initial set of baseline security controls for the information system based on the security categorization should be chosen (Step 2a). This baseline of security controls, as discussed in NIST SPs 800-53 and 800-60, should be tailored and supplemented based on an organization's assessment of risk and local conditions (Step 2b) and documented (Step 2c). In Step 3 (**Implement**), the organization implements the security controls documented in Step 2c. Unfortunately, the Step 3 guidance document (SP 800-70) discusses implementation solely from the perspective of using "checklists" to identify what security controls should be applied. The checklists available should be those developed by the NIST and the Defense Information Systems Agency. FISMA expects these checklists to not only identify required security controls but also include specific controls installation instructions. Currently, there are 233 available checklists that can be retrieved from: http://web.nvd.nist.gov/view/ncp/repository spanning the 28 product categories listed in Table 3.7.

The NIST checklists are based on commonly accepted technical security principles and practices, as well as SP 800-27 "Engineering Principles for Information Technology Security (A Baseline for Achieving Security)" and the NSA Information Assurance Technical Framework, available at: http://oai.dtic.mil/oai/oai?verb=getRecord&metadataPrefix=html&identifier=ADA393328

TABLE 3.7. NIST Available Checklist Categories.

• Anti-virus software	• Applications servers	• Configuration management software
• Malware	• Desktop applications	• Desktop clients
• Directory services	• DNS servers	• Email servers
• Encryption software	• Enterprise applications	• General-purpose servers
• Handheld devices	• Identity management	• Database management systems
• Network switches	• Network routers	• Multi-functional peripherals
• Office application suites	• Operating systems	• Peripheral devices
• Security servers	• Firewalls	• Virtualization software
• Web browsers	• Web servers	• Wireless email
• Wireless networks		

In Step 4 (**Assess**), the organization is expected to routinely assess the security controls. The purpose of these assessments is to determine the extent to which:

- the controls are implemented correctly;
- operating as intended;
- mitigating likely security threats; and
- reducing exposure of vulnerabilities

in respect to complying with security requirements and organizational InfoSec policies. Organizations are expected to follow the security control assessment procedures defined in NIST Special Publication 800-53. In Step 5 (**Authorize**), federal government systems require a priori authorization for information system operation based upon a determination of the risks that operation of the information system represent and determination that said risk is acceptable. Step 6 (**Monitor**) focuses on continued assessment, and more specifically, the monitoring and reporting the security state of the system to appropriate management personnel within the organization. This ongoing assessment and monitoring is expected to include not just regular assessment activities but also documenting changes to the system, operational environment, and conducting security impact analyses of changes. Guidance on monitoring the security controls and ongoing risk determination, acceptance, and authorization for operation is provided in NIST Special Publication 800-37.

NIST is in the process of developing a series of Frequently Asked Questions (FAQs), Roles & Responsibilities and Quick Start Guide documents and considers the supporting materials for Steps 3 through 6 to be a "work in progress" with continued development expected.

3.3.4.1 What Is Lacking in FISMA?

A foundation document for FISMA is SP 800-53 which documents many aspects of what an enterprise security policy document would address in its Appendix F. However, unlike an ISO/IEC 27001-compliant security policy, SP 800-53 is not organized in any manner that reflects enterprise organizational structure; it does not address security policy responsibilities by organization groups, nor does it specify responsibilities for complying with enterprise security obligations or objectives. The complete body of documents upon which FISMA relies represents many thousands of pages, all focusing on government entities. Any commercial enterprise attempting to use FISMA as the basis for information security governance should be prepared to invest significantly in studying the FISMA foundation documents, developing tailored versions of said material, and will still have to develop appropriate security policy statements that provide the basis for deploying appropriate security controls.

3.4 A HOLISTIC APPROACH FOR SECURITY MANAGEMENT

A thorough enterprise InfoSec governance program needs to address a number of areas, including:

- security governance organization;
- security governance policies;
- security functional requirements;
- security risk identification, analysis, and mitigation;
- security technical controls; and
- security operational controls and procedures,

in an integrated manner. The following sections address these areas with the exception that:

- Chapter 4 discusses security risk identification, analysis, and mitigation; and
- Chapter 5 discusses security operational controls and procedures.

3.4.1 Organizational Aspects of Security Governance and Management

All organizations should have an individual who holds final responsibility for the security governance of the organization. Frequently, this person is assigned the title of CSO or Chief Information Security Officer. In some typically smaller enterprises, the CSO role is part of the responsibilities assigned to the individual with the title of Chief Technology Officer or Chief Information Officer (CIO). Very large enterprises sometimes segregate out responsibility for privacy issues to a Chief Privacy Officer (CPO); however, the convention used here is to assume the CSO role includes CPO responsibilities. Given that an enterprise's BoD has ultimate legal responsibility for the activities and behavior of an enterprise, including security-related activities, the individual holding CSO responsibilities should be directly accountable to the BoD and be able to provide independent input to the BoD. A second concern is maintaining consistency of security governance activities across all business units, divisions, and subsidiaries. Therefore, the more independent the CSO position is from the other organization's groups requiring oversight, the more objective and consistent the security governance

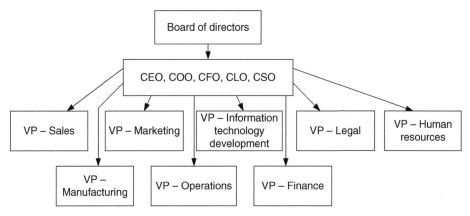

Figure 3.2. Typical large corporate organization structure.

results will be in ensuring consistent policy compliance. A further advantage, when the CSO reports into the management hierarchy at a sufficiently high level, is that the CSO will have the authority to enforce security policy compliance upon development and operations groups, as well as other enterprise units. It is advisable for CSO responsibilities to be located at a level of authority and responsibility equal to the CEO, Chief Operations Officer, Chief Legal Officer (CLO), and Chief Financial Officer (CFO). Figure 3.2 depicts the CSO as a direct report into the BoD providing the CSO with significant authority over the enterprise governance of its security program.

In most organizations, the:

- CIO holds the position of Vice-President (VP) of the IT Development organization;
- CFO holds the position of VP of the Finance organization;
- CLO holds the position of VP of the Legal and Regulatory organization; and

the enterprise should establish an independent security organization headed by the CSO, possibly with the title of VP for Information Security Governance. Senior managers, either the VP or a delegate, from each of the aforementioned enterprise groups should belong to a Senior Management Security Governance Steering Committee (see Figure 3.3), chaired by the CSO, and be responsible for:

- directing the development of all enterprise InfoSec governance policy documents;
- the approval of all enterprise InfoSec governance policy documents; and
- resolving conflicts between enterprise groups regarding InfoSec governance policy applicability and interpretation.

The Senior Management Security Governance Steering Committee should have the responsibility to grant/withhold official organization approval of security policy

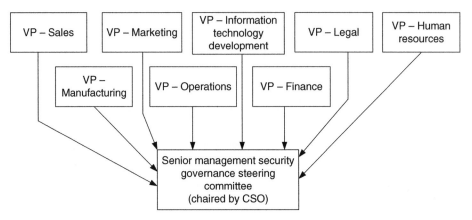

Figure 3.3. Senior Management relationship with steering committee.

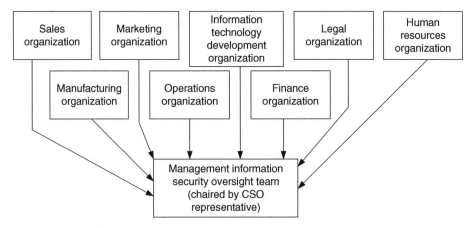

Figure 3.4. Organization relationship with oversight team.

statements, guidelines, and procedures. Inability to reach agreement within this committee would be escalated to the CSO and potentially to the BoD for resolution.

The actual preparation of the enterprise's InfoSec governance policy documents would be delegated to a "Management Information Security Oversight Team" usually chaired by a senior manager from within the CSO organization, with managers representing other enterprise groups as shown in Figure 3.4.

The Management Information Security Oversight Team should have delegated to it the responsibility for developing security policy statements, guidelines, and procedures subject to Senior Management Security Governance Steering Committee approval. This team should also function as a security discussion forum wherein security issues and potential solutions may be shared and leveraged across the enterprise. Inability to reach agreement within this team would be escalated to the Senior Management Security Governance Steering Committee for resolution. The relationship of the Steering Committee and the Oversight Team is shown in Figure 3.5.

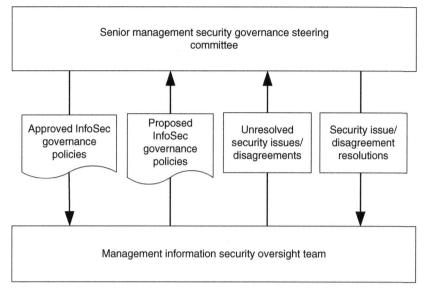

Figure 3.5. Committee and team relationship.

The enterprise should establish a Computer Event Response Team (CERT) coordination capability within the CSO's organization. The CSO's organization's CERT coordination capability would be responsible for developing the plans and procedures for the a priori planning and training required to assemble specific CERTs where the personnel assigned to a CERT would be drawn from existing groups with operational responsibilities. Some enterprises colocate business continuity/disaster recovery responsibilities within the CSO's organization as there are considerable similarities between business continuity due to disasters versus information security events.

Another CSO organization's responsibility is the conducting of InfoSec audits and reviews on a regular basis. Performing audits by enterprise personnel allows the enterprise to monitor how well its InfoSec governance program/processes are complying with the enterprise InfoSec policies. As these internally performed audits/reviews identify security problems (policy non-compliance situations), each security problem can be prioritized (once analyzed, mitigation actions identified, mitigation schedules established, and costs determined). Enterprises that are subject to legislative/regulatory mandates are often required to be audited by third-party personnel on an annual basis. The results of internal audits allow the enterprise to better prepare for external audits as many security issues can be found in advance of an external audit and remediation plans established. This pro-active internal auditing not only helps with getting through external audits without many "surprises" but even more importantly serves as a cornerstone for the ongoing monitoring of enterprise security activities. The CSO organization would also serve as the primary point of contact for external auditing agencies/personnel. The major groups within the CSO organization are shown in Figure 3.6.

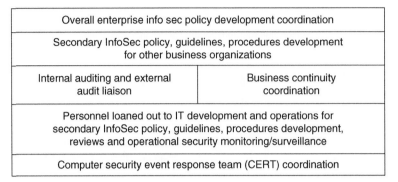

Figure 3.6. Major CSO organization groups.

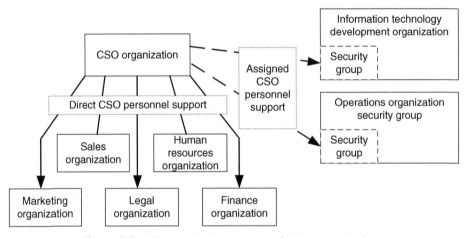

Figure 3.7. CSO organization support of other organizations.

Quite often, the IT Development and Operations organizations will either possess internal security groups or have personnel assigned on a semi-permanent basis from the CSO organization to support the development of InfoSec policies, procedures, and guidelines, as well as assist with security reviews and monitoring/surveillance activities. However, CSO group personnel would provide direct assistance to the remaining enterprise organizations on an "as-needed" basis, as shown in Figure 3.7.

3.4.2 Policies and Policy Hierarchies

The size of an organization will dictate whether there is a single organizational InfoSec governance policy document or multiple policy documents. Most organizations develop, use, and maintain a set of InfoSec governance policy documents that form a foundation for enterprise governance. "Tier 1" policy documents (Table 3.8) would be used, and applied to, all parts of an organization.

TABLE 3.8. Tier 1 Policy Areas.

Employment
Employee Standards of Conduct
Conflict of Interest
Procurement and Contracts
Performance Management
Employee Discipline
Information Security
Corporate Communications
Workplace Security
Business Continuity Planning
Records Management

TABLE 3.9. Tier 2 Policy Areas.

Security Organization
Personnel Security
Asset Classification and Control
Physical and Environmental Security
Computer and Network Management
System Access Control
Systems Development and Maintenance
Business Continuity Planning
Compliance
E-mail Security
Anti-virus/Malware Policy
Acceptable Use of the Internet

There will likely exist a second set of policy documents that are topic/area specific. The most common set of "Tier 2" policies with organizations are listed in Table 3.9.

Some organization may also use additional topic-specific policy documents, such as shown in Table 3.10.

As currently written, ISO/IEC 27001 and 27002 discuss an enterprise's InfoSec governance policy as a single document that spans all the Tier 1 and Tier 2 policy areas just presented. There is a tendency to use a single policy document in many enterprises; however, this approach typically results in a large document that few employees look forward to working with. Appendix D provides an example of such a single Information Security Policy document. It is advisable to constrain the number of InfoSec policy documents within an enterprise and organize these documents around related activity areas, for example:

Human Resources and Personnel InfoSec policy document spanning:

* Employment;
* Employee Standards of Conduct;
* Conflict of Interest;

TABLE 3.10. **Topic-Specific Policy Areas.**

Likely Additional Policies
Electronic Communications
Internet Security
Information Protection
Information Classification
Mobile and Tele-computing/commuting
Application Access Control
Data and Software Exchange
Network Access Control
Information System Operations
User Access
Customer Access
Passwords and Authentication
Public Key Infrastructure and Digital Certificates
Internet Accessible System Security
Firewalls and Intrusion Detection–Prevention
Workstation and Laptop Security
PDA and "Smartphone" Security

- Employee Discipline;
- Personnel Security; and
- Employee Security Training;

Legal and Financial InfoSec policy document spanning:

- Procurement and Contracts;
- Performance Management;
- Information Security;
- Corporate Communications;
- Workplace Security; and
- Records Management;

General InfoSec Governance Policy document spanning:

- Asset Classification and Control;
- Physical and Environmental Security;
- Workstation and Laptop Security;
- PDA and "Smartphone" Security;
- Business Continuity Planning;
- Compliance;
- Information Protection;

- Information Classification;
- Business Continuity Planning; and
- Internal and External Auditing;

Information Technology and Operations InfoSec policy document spanning:

- Computer and Network Management;
- System Access Control;
- Systems Development and Maintenance;
- E-mail Security;
- Anti-virus/Malware Policy;
- Acceptable Use of the Internet;
- Electronic Communications;
- Internet Security;
- Mobile and Tele-computing/commuting;
- Application Access Control;
- Data and Software Exchange;
- Network Access Control;
- Information System Operations;
- User Access;
- Customer Access;
- Passwords and Authentication;
- Public Key Infrastructure and Digital Certificates;
- Internet Accessible System Security; and
- Firewalls and Intrusion Detection–Prevention.

These recommended policy documents should generally follow the structure presented in the ISO/IEC 27002 recommendation but be tailored appropriately to cover those sections to which each policy document applies. Not to be forgotten, all employees should have access to enterprise InfoSec governance policy documents as these documents state how InfoSec governance within the enterprise is to be accomplished and allocate responsibilities to specific groups and sub-organizations. All enterprise employees should be briefed on the enterprise InfoSec governance policies on an annual basis.

3.4.3 Functional and Operational Security Requirements

The organization's security policy includes numerous statements regarding what and how the organization will focus on information security. However, these statements are often stated at too high a level to actually control specific activities, processes, and information and communications components. Thus, the policy statements need to be broken down into specific detailed statements called requirements. The value of these detailed requirement statements is threefold, in that the detailed requirements can be:

1. included in a Request for Quote/Request for Proposal when the enterprise is purchasing new equipment, systems, subsystems, or services;
2. used in a development specification to specify necessary capabilities of a planned new system or application being developed in-house; and
3. used in the development of quality assurance or acceptance testing procedures to ensure the developed, or purchased, equipment, systems, subsystems, or services will comply with the enterprise's InfoSec policy.

Detailed requirements are intended to be verifiable (through inspection, testing, analysis, or documentation), and they should be composed of simple statements, for example, "X" shall perform "Y." When a policy statement identifies alternative actions from a specified set of choices, a number of detailed requirements should be written where each requirement identifies a single one of the policy statement alternatives. It is strongly advised that requirements use the key words "MUST," "MUST NOT," "REQUIRED," "SHALL," "SHALL NOT," "SHOULD," "SHOULD NOT," "RECOMMENDED," "NOT RECOMMENDED," "MAY," and "OPTIONAL" as described in RFC-2119 (Bradner, 1997). Those charged with detailed requirements development should always consider how a proposed requirement can be verified. Among other attributes, each resulting requirement should have a unique identifier, or tag, that allows explicit reference to the requirement.

The process of requirements decomposition begins with an analysis of the enterprise InfoSec policy and what it requires from a functional perspective. The text extract in Figure 3.8 comes from the example Company InfoSec Policy in Appendix D.

Table 3.11 demonstrates appropriate detailed security-related requirements for each of the aforementioned example InfoSec policy statements.

It is quickly apparent that there is not always a one-to-one match between policy statements and detailed requirements. This occurs due to a number of reasons. InfoSec policy documents, and the statements contained therein, are intended to be read and understood by the general enterprise employee population. Consequently, policy statements will utilize commonly found language sentence structuring, such as comma-separated lists. However, such structure, although easily read, results in compound sentences that include multiple requirements. Another reason is a failure of policy developers to recognize derived and implied requirements; for example, refer to requirements SR-34 and SR-35 described earlier. For these two requirements, there are two additional requirements that are necessary, namely, requirements SR-36 and SR-37, both of which are implied requirements.

By following a well-managed process, derived and implied requirements are less likely to be overlooked. Since the detailed security requirements flow from the policy statements, not establishing a mapping between requirements and policies will weaken a claim of "due diligence" in court or even result in fines or penalties depending on the type of enterprise affected. Therefore, the team(s) responsible for security require-

10.5.2 Logon Procedures

It is the responsibility of service providers, system administrators, and application developers to implement logon procedures that minimize opportunities for unauthorized access. Thresholds and time periods are to be defined by the trustee.

Logon procedures should be enabled that disclose the minimum of information about the system, application, or service in order to avoid providing an unauthorized user with unnecessary assistance.

Logon procedures should:

- Not display system or application identifiers until the logon process has been successfully completed.
- Not disclose/display on the screen the password entered during login.
- Display a company-specific warning that the computer and/or application should only be accessed by authorized users (see Section 10.5.2.1).
- Not provide Help messages during the logon procedure that would aid an unauthorized user.
- Validate the logon information only on completion of all input data. If an error condition arises, the system should not indicate which part of the data is correct or incorrect.
- Limit the number of unsuccessful logon attempts allowed before an access denial action is taken. Three attempts are recommended and in no circumstance should more than six be allowed.
- Support thresholds for the maximum number of denial actions within a given period before further unsuccessful logon attempts are considered a security relevant event. Six attempts by the same logon ID or requesting device in a 24-hour period should be set as an upper threshold.
- Limit the maximum time period allowed for the logon procedure. Twenty (20) seconds is recommended; however, thirty to forty seconds may be required for two factor authentication.
- Disconnect and give no assistance after a rejected attempt to logon.
- Display the following information on completion of a successful logon:
  ○ Date and time of the previous successful logon
  ○ Details of any unsuccessful logon attempts since the last successful logon

Exceeding established thresholds should cause one or more of the following:

- The authentication device is suspended or rendered inoperable until reset.
- The authentication device's effectiveness is suspended for a specified period of time.
- Logging of the invalid attempts and/or a real-time alert is generated.
- A time delay is forced before further access attempts are allowed.

Figure 3.8. Example InfoSec policy statements.

TABLE 3.11. Decomposition of Policy into Requirements.

Security Policy Document Statements	Appropriate Detailed Security Requirements
It is the responsibility of service providers, system administrators, and application developers to implement logon procedures that minimize opportunities for unauthorized access	SR-1. Service providers SHALL implement logon procedures that minimize opportunities for unauthorized access SR-2. System administrators SHALL implement logon procedures that minimize opportunities for unauthorized access SR-3. Application developers SHALL implement logon procedures that minimize opportunities for unauthorized access
Thresholds and time periods are to be defined by the Trustee	SR-4. Information Trustees SHALL define Logon Thresholds SR-5. Information Trustees SHALL define Logon Time periods
Logon procedures should be enabled that disclose the minimum of information about the system, application, or service in order to avoid providing an unauthorized user with unnecessary assistance	SR-6. System Logon procedures SHOULD be enabled that disclose the minimum of information about the system in order to avoid providing an unauthorized user with unnecessary assistance SR-7. Application Logon procedures SHOULD be enabled that disclose the minimum of information about the application in order to avoid providing an unauthorized user with unnecessary assistance SR-8. Service Logon procedures SHOULD be enabled that disclose the minimum of information about the service in order to avoid providing an unauthorized user with unnecessary assistance
(Logon procedures should) Not display system or application identifiers until the logon process has been successfully completed	SR-9. Logon procedures SHOULD not display system identifiers until the logon process has been successfully completed SR-10. Logon procedures SHOULD not display application identifiers until the logon process has been successfully completed
(Logon procedures should) Not disclose/display on the screen the password entered during login	SR-11. Logon procedures SHOULD not disclose/ display on the screen the password entered during login
(Logon procedures should) Display a company-specific warning that the computer and/or application should only be accessed by authorized users (see Section 10.5.2.1)	SR-12. Logon procedures SHOULD display a company-specific warning that the computer SHOULD only be accessed by authorized users (see Section 10.5.2.1) SR-13. Logon procedures SHOULD display a company-specific warning that the application SHOULD only be accessed by authorized users (see Section 10.5.2.1)
(Logon procedures should) Not provide help messages during the logon procedure that would aid an unauthorized user	SR-14. Logon procedures SHOULD not provide help messages during the logon procedure that would aid an unauthorized user

Security Policy Document Statements	Appropriate Detailed Security Requirements
(Logon procedures should) Validate the logon information only on completion of all input data. If an error condition arises, the system should not indicate which part of the data is correct or incorrect	SR-15. Logon procedures SHOULD validate the logon information only on completion of all input data SR-16. If an error condition arises, the Logon procedure SHOULD not indicate which part of the data is correct or incorrect
(Logon procedures should) Limit the number of unsuccessful logon attempts allowed before an access denial action is taken. Three attempts are recommended and in no circumstance should more than six be allowed	SR-17. Logon procedures SHOULD limit the number of unsuccessful logon attempts allowed before an access denial action is taken SR-18. Logon procedures SHALL limit the number of unsuccessful logon attempts allowed to no more than six unsuccessful attempts
(Logon procedures should) Support thresholds for the maximum number of denial actions within a given period before further unsuccessful logon attempts are considered a security relevant event. Six attempts by the same logon ID or requesting device in a 24-hour period should be set as an upper threshold	SR-19. Logon procedures SHOULD support thresholds for the maximum number of unsuccessful logon attempts within a given period before further unsuccessful logon attempts are considered a security relevant event SR-20. Six unsuccessful logon attempts by the same logon ID in a 24-hour period SHOULD be set as an upper threshold SR-21. Six unsuccessful logon attempts by the same device in a 24-hour period SHOULD be set as an upper threshold
(Logon procedures should) Limit the maximum time period allowed for the logon procedure. Twenty seconds is recommended; however 30–40 seconds may be required for two-factor authentication	SR-22. Logon procedures SHOULD be able to limit the maximum time period allowed for the logon procedure SR-23. Logon procedures SHOULD use a default time period of 20 seconds for the logon procedure SR-24. Logon procedures SHOULD use a default time period of 40 seconds for the logon procedure for two-factor authentication
(Logon procedures should) Disconnect and give no assistance after a rejected attempt to logon	SR-25. Logon procedures SHOULD disconnect a device after a rejected attempt to logon SR-26. Logon procedures SHOULD give no assistance after a rejected attempt to logon
(Logon procedures should) (Display the following information on completion of a successful logon) Date and time of the previous successful logon	SR-27. Logon procedures SHOULD display the date and time of the previous successful logon on completion of a successful logon
(Logon procedures should) (Display the following information on completion of a successful logon) Details of any unsuccessful logon attempts since the last successful logon	SR-28. Logon procedures SHOULD display on completion of a successful logon the dates and times of any unsuccessful logon attempts since the last successful logon SR-29. Logon procedures SHOULD display on completion of a successful logon the device used for any unsuccessful logon attempts since the last successful logon

(continued)

TABLE 3.11. *(cont'd)*

Security Policy Document Statements	Appropriate Detailed Security Requirements
(Exceeding established thresholds should cause one or more of the following) The authentication device is suspended or rendered inoperable until reset	SR-30. Exceeding the configured threshold for unsuccessful logon attempts SHOULD cause the keyboard being used for login to be rendered inoperable until reset SR-31. Exceeding the configured threshold for unsuccessful logon attempts SHOULD cause the device being used for login to be prevented from further logon attempts until reset SR-32. A reset capability SHALL be provided for re-enabling the use of a disabled keyboard for login attempts SR-33. A reset capability SHALL be provided for re-enabling the use of a disabled device for login attempts
(Exceeding established thresholds should cause one or more of the following) The authentication device's effectiveness is suspended for a specified period of time	SR-34. Exceeding the configured threshold for unsuccessful logon attempts SHOULD cause the keyboard being used for login to be rendered inoperable for a specified period of time SR-35. Exceeding the configured threshold for unsuccessful logon attempts SHOULD cause the device being used for login to be prevented from further logon attempts for a specified period of time SR-36. The capability to configure a time period for re-enabling the use of a disabled keyboard for login attempts SHALL be provided SR-37. The capability to configure a time period for re-enabling the use of a disabled device for login attempts SHALL be provided
(Exceeding established thresholds should cause one or more of the following) Logging of the invalid attempts and/or a real-time alert is generated	SR-38. Exceeding established threshold for unsuccessful logon attempts SHOULD cause the logging of the invalid attempts to a system log file SR-39. Exceeding established threshold for unsuccessful logon attempts SHOULD cause the generation and transmission of a real-time alert message to a management system SR-40. The capability to configure the identity and IP address of a management system to receive unsuccessful logon attempt threshold exceeding real-time messages SHALL be provided
(Exceeding established thresholds should cause one or more of the following) A time delay is forced before further access attempts are allowed	SR-41. Exceeding configured unsuccessful logon attempt thresholds SHOULD cause a time delay before further access attempts are allowed

ments analysis (and documenting said requirements) should include CSO organization's security engineering staff working closely with personnel from other affected departments/organizations. Through the use of cross-functional teams, detailed security requirements can be crafted that not only reflect technical or operational capabilities, limitations, or acceptability but also facilitate security knowledge transfer to the non-security team members.

3.5 SUMMARY

This chapter began with consideration to the drivers for information security management and how this has evolved into information security governance. The four primary framework approaches for information security governance were then reviewed and deficiencies in each discussed. We then proceeded to consider what a comprehensive (holistic) approach for information security governance needed to cover; organization, policies and requirements with risk identification and analysis, technical controls, and operational controls are to be covered in succeeding chapters.

FURTHER READING AND RESOURCES

Bradner, S. (1997) RFC 2119, Key words for use in RFCs to Indicate Requirement Levels, Best Current Practice, Internet Engineering Task Force

Cadbury, A. (1992) Report of the Committee on the Financial Aspects of Corporate Governance. London: Gee, December

Gerber, M., von Solms, R., Overbeek, P. (2001) Formalizing information security requirements, Information Management & Computer Security, 9(1), pp. 32–37

Höne, K., Eloff, J.H.P. (2002) Information security policy—what do international information security standards say?, Computers & Security, 2(5), pp. 402–409

IGI (2011) About IT Governance, IT Governance Institute. Retrieved from http://www.itgi.org/template_ITGIa166.html?Section=About_IT_Governance1&Template=/ContentManagement/HTMLDisplay.cfm&ContentID=19657

ISO/IEC7498-1:1984, Information Technology—Open Systems Interconnection—Basic Reference Model: The Basic Model, International Standards Organization (ISO), 1984

ISO/IEC 27001 (2005) Information Technology—Security Techniques—Information Security Management Systems—Requirements, International Organization for Standardization and International Electrotechnical Commission

ISO/IEC 27002 (2005) Information Technology—Security Techniques—Code of Practice for Information Security Management, International Organization for Standardization and International Electrotechnical Commission

Jacobs, S., Chitkushev, L.T., Zlateva, T. (2010, July) Identities, anonymity and information warfare, 9th European Conference on Information Warfare and Security (ECIW 2010), University of Macedonia, Thessaloniki, Greece

Karyda, M., Kiountouzis, E., Kokolakis, S. (2005) Information systems security policies: a contextual perspective, Computers & Security, 24(3), pp. 246–260

Landwehr, C.E. (2001) Computer security, International Journal of Information Security, 1(1), pp. 3–13

Moulton, R., Coles, R.S. (2003) Applying information security governance, Computers & Security, 22(7), pp. 580–584

NIST (2004) Federal Information Processing Standard (FIPS) 199 standards for security categorization of federal information and information systems, National Institute of Science and Technology (NIST), U.S. Department of Commerce

NIST (2009) Special Publication 800-53 Recommended Security Controls for Federal Information Systems and Organizations, National Institute of Science and Technology (NIST), U.S. Department of Commerce

NIST (2010) Special Publication 800-37 Guide for Applying the Risk Management Framework to Federal Information Systems—A Security Life Cycle Approach, National Institute of Science and Technology (NIST), U.S. Department of Commerce

OECD (2004) OECD Principles of Corporate Governance, Organization for Economic Co-operation and Development (OECD)

OED (1971) Oxford English Dictionary Compact Edition, Oxford University Press, Vol. 1

Thomson, K.L., von Solms, R. (2005) Information security obedience: a definition, Computers & Security, 24(1), pp. 69–75

U.S. Congress (2002) Sarbanes–Oxley Act of 2002

von Solms, B. (2001) Corporate governance and information security, Computers & Security, 20(2001), pp. 215–218

von Solms, B. (2006) Information security—The Fourth Wave, Computers & Security, 25(3), pp. 165–168

X.200, 1994-07 (1994) Information Technology—Open Systems Interconnection—Basic Reference Model: The Basic Model, International Telecommunications Union—Telecommunications Sector

4

RISK MANAGEMENT IN CURRENT AND FUTURE NETWORKS

As noted in Chapter 3, this chapter addresses security risk identification, analysis, and mitigation, typically referred to as risk management. *Risk Management* is the methodological process of identifying risks, analyzing the extent of damage that can be caused by these risks, and determining how to mitigate (reduce) risks. The term *Threat-Vulnerability Analysis* (TVA) is often used to refer to activities that are part of Risk Management. There are two contexts within which Risk Management needs to be performed:

- As part of the system development life cycle; and
- As part of the ongoing production system operational usage.

Figure 4.1 depicts both contexts where the Requirements Gathering and Analysis Phase through the Deployment Phase are typically considered under system development and the Operations/Maintenance Phase considered under ongoing production system operational usage.

Security Management of Next Generation Telecommunications Networks and Services,
First Edition. Stuart Jacobs.
© 2014 The Institute of Electrical and Electronics Engineers, Inc. Published 2014 by John Wiley & Sons, Inc.

The key steps within Risk Management are:

- Asset Identification
- Impact Analysis
  - Existing System Impact Analysis
  - New System Impact Analysis
  - Risk Mitigation Analysis
- Malicious Security Events and Threats Assessment Risk Assessment Analysis
- Risk Mitigation Controls Acquisition or Development
  - Procedures Development
  - Controls Implementation
  - Integration Testing
- Risk Mitigation Controls Deployment
  - Field Testing
  - Operational Readiness Testing
- Risk Mitigation Operations and Maintenance
  - Operations, Administration, Maintenance, and Provisioning (OAM&P)
  - Effectiveness Reviews
  - Compliance Verification Reviews

The remainder of this chapter discusses each of these steps in detail.

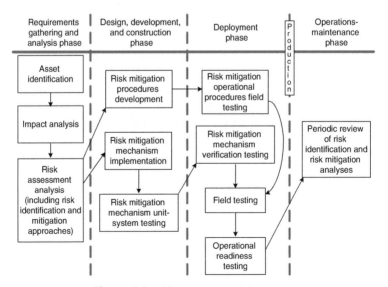

Figure 4.1. Risk Management Contexts.

4.1 ASSET IDENTIFICATION: DEFINITION AND INVENTORYING

Risk Management begins with the identification and compiling of an inventory of enterprise assets. Assets fall into two categories: (i) tangible and (ii) intangible. Tangible assets are physical things that an enterprise considers valuable and are used, or relied upon, for an enterprise's operations. Obvious tangible assets include physical facilities (i.e., buildings/offices and their contents, vehicles, personnel, outside communications components, and utilities). Tangible assets within the building/office contents category include:

- necessary furniture and fittings;
- printed (hard copy) documentation of many types (i.e., phone directories, organizational charts, source code printouts, reports, plans, procedures, policies, and physical data files/records to name a few);
- communications infrastructure components (i.e., data and other communications cabling and associated devices);
- information processing components (i.e., workstations, mobile devices, server systems, storage systems, printing systems, and multi-function devices);
- heating, ventilation, and air-conditioning (HVAC) components (i.e., furnaces/boilers, air chillers/conditioners, fans/blowers);
- power-related components (i.e., power generation systems and power distribution systems/wiring); and
- fire and security components (i.e., water sprinkler systems, non-water fire suppression systems, video surveillance systems, physical intrusion detection/alarm systems, and electronic and physical access control systems).

Loss of, or damage to, physical assets can degrade, or even prevent, an organization's ability to conduct business and deliver the products and services that provide revenue. Intangible assets are either logical or abstract. Logical intangible assets include:

- operations software (i.e., operating systems, applications, utility, and management programs);
- operational records (i.e., system and transaction log files, soft-copy reports, data files, databases, and message/electronic mail archives to name a few); and
- developmental software (i.e., program source code archives, utilities, and tools).

Loss or damage to logical intangible assets can degrade, or even prevent, an organization's ability to conduct business and deliver the products and services that provide revenue. Abstract intangible assets include:

- public trust in organization (i.e., ability to retain or acquire new customers or suppliers);
- organizational financial position (i.e., to maintain market equity positions or to obtain financing at optimal rates); and
- prevention of litigation liabilities (i.e., minimization of legal defense expenses and avoidance of liability expenses and civil fines).

Loss or damage to abstract intangible assets should not be ignored for reasons such as follows:

- When an organization's reputation for protecting customer- or supplier-associated information is called into question, the organization may see customers switch to competitors, rate of acquiring new customers diminish, current suppliers less willing to provide favorable contract terms, or increased difficulty or expense in acquiring alternative supplier products and services;
- damage to an organization's reputation (especially due to a security-related incident/breach) has been seen to directly and indirectly affect an organization's equity and capital situation; and
- Forty-six U.S. states have enacted Personally Identifiable Information (PII) breach-related laws (see Appendix H), many of which not only allow affected customers the ability to pursue civil actions but also allow for class action torts. The legal defense costs to an organization, especially in class action torts, can become significant (Gaudin, 2007).
- Significant research exists that considers how security issues/breaches result in organizations experiencing negative financial impacts (Fama, 1969; Hovav and D'Arcy, 2003; Campbell et al., 2003a; Garg et al., 2003a; Campbell et al., 2003b; Garg et al., 2003b; Cavusoglu et al., 2004; Hovav and D'Arcy, 2004; Hovav and D'Arcy, 2005; Acquisti et al., 2006; Ko and Dorantes, 2006; Kannan et al., 2007; Telang and Wattel, 2007; Goel and Shawky, 2009).

As noted earlier, an organization should assemble an inventory of its assets as a starting point to determining what assets it possesses, the relative value of these assets, who is responsible for each asset, and how critical each asset is for business continuity.

The first step in asset definition is to define the scope of the effort. In this step, the boundaries of the assets to be analyzed are specified since one needs to determine if:

- all assets of the organization are being considered;
- the assets of a business unit/division;
- the assets of a separate facility/remote facility;
- the assets of a work group; or
- the assets of a specific system or subsystem.

The boundaries of the organization, business unit, group, system, application, platform, or business process are established and agreed to. This activity needs to include all related information (hardware, software, interfaces, data, persons, processes, and information). The purpose (mission) of these assets should be recorded along with their criticality to the organization's primary business activities. There are a number of tools available to gather the relevant information, such as:

- Questionnaires;
- On-site interviews;
- Document review (policy statement, legislation, requirements, directives, etc.); and
- Scanning tools (network mapping).

When identifying, defining, and constructing an inventory of assets, a number of per-asset-related questions that should be asked, and answered, include:

1. Who are the valid users?
2. What is the mission of the user organization?
3. What is the purpose of the asset to the organization?
4. How important is the asset to the user organization's mission?
5. What are the availability requirements? (Recovery Time Objectives)
6. What information is required by the organization?
7. What information is generated, consumed, processed, or stored–retrieved by the asset?
8. Importance of the information to the organization's mission?
9. Paths of information flow?
10. Type of information stored (personnel, sales, marketing, PII, financial, research and development (R&D), manufacturing (such as Enterprise Resource Planning (ERP) data), command and control)?
11. Classification level of the information (i.e., Confidential, Internal Use Only, Proprietary, Client–Attorney Privileged, Trade Secret, Public, etc.)?
12. Where is the information processed and stored?
13. Types of information storage?
14. Potential impact to the organization if the information is disclosed?
15. Effect on the mission of the organization if the information is not reliable?

One inventory approach is to construct a database of assets along the lines of the partial examples shown in Table 4.1, Table 4.2, Table 4.3, Table 4.4, Table 4.5, Table 4.6, Table 4.7, Table 4.8, Table 4.9 and Table 4.10. These tables are structured as a set of relational database tables. The asset description column in every table, except Table 4.1, is included for human readability only. Table 4.1 provides the starting point for inventorying enterprise assets, and the suggested column headings are:

- **Asset Name**—Names a specific asset item type.
- **Asset ID**—Uniquely identifies a specific asset item.
- **Asset Type**—Identifies if the asset is physical or logical in nature.
- **Asset Description**—Description of a specific asset item.

In Table 4.2, the column headings are:

- **Asset ID**—Uniquely identifies a specific asset item.
- **Asset Description**—Description of a specific asset item. The Asset Description column is included for human readability only.
- **Asset Owning Organization**—Identifies the organization unit or group which has primary responsibility for the asset. One can simply identify the general group or a discrete sub-group such as, but not limited to:
  ○ IT Desktop-User Operations, Administration, Maintenance, and Provisioning (OAM&P);

TABLE 4.1. **Asset Inventory Partial Listing Example.**

Asset Name	Asset ID	Asset Type	Asset Description
Employee Data	HR000001	Logical	Employee Data
Accounts Receivables Data	FN000100	Logical	Accounts Receivables Data
Accounts Payables Data	FN000200	Logical	Accounts Payables Data
General Ledger Data	FN000300	Logical	General Ledger Data
Supplier Contracts Data	FN000400	Logical	Supplier Contracts Data
Management Data	FN000500	Logical	Miscellaneous Data
Sales Data	SA000001	Logical	Sales Data
Marketing Data	SA000100	Logical	Marketing Data
Sales Literature	SA000200	Logical	Publicly available Sales Data
Business Customer Data	SA000300	Logical	Business Customer Data
Retail Customer Data	SA000400	Logical	Retail Customer Data
Government Customer Data	SA000500	Logical	Government Customer Data
DMZ outside CER	IT000001	Physical	CER between DMZ and ISP
DMZ inside Router	IT000002	Physical	Router-firewall between DMZ and enterprise intranet
Finance edge router	IT000003	Physical	Router-firewall between Finance subnet and enterprise intranet
Sales edge router	IT000004	Physical	Router-firewall between Sales subnet and enterprise intranet
Marketing edge router	IT000005	Physical	Router-firewall between Marketing subnet and enterprise intranet
Support edge router	IT000006	Physical	Router-firewall between Customer Support & Call Center subnet and enterprise intranet
R&D edge router	IT000007	Physical	Router-firewall between R&D subnet and enterprise intranet
Manufacturing edge router	IT000008	Physical	Router-firewall between Manufacturing subnet and enterprise intranet
Facilities edge router	IT000009	Physical	Router-firewall between Facilities subnet and enterprise intranet
OAM&P edge router	IT000010	Physical	Router-firewall between IT OAM&P subnet and enterprise intranet
Sr. Managment edge router	IT000011	Physical	Router-firewall between Sr. Management subnet and enterprise intranet
FE edge router	IT000012	Physical	Router-firewall between Field Support subnet and enterprise intranet
IT Workstation	IT001001	Physical	HR VP Workstation

Asset Name	Asset ID	Asset Type	Asset Description
IT Workstation	IT001002	Physical	HR Manager Workstation
IT Workstation	IT001004	Physical	HR Administrator Workstation
IT Workstation	IT001006	Physical	HR Representative Workstation
IT Workstation	IT001101	Physical	CFO Workstation
IT Workstation	IT001102	Physical	Finance GL Manager Workstation
IT Workstation	IT001103	Physical	Finance AR Manager Workstation
IT Workstation	IT001104	Physical	Finance AP Manager Workstation
IT Workstation	IT001105	Physical	Finance Audit Manager Workstation
IT Workstation	IT001106	Physical	Finance Clerk Workstation
IT Workstation	IT001201	Physical	CTO Workstation (R&D)
IT Workstation	IT001202	Physical	R&D Administrator Workstation
IT Workstation	IT001203	Physical	R&D Dev. Manager Workstation
IT Workstation	IT001204	Physical	R&D QA Manager Workstation
IT Workstation	IT001205	Physical	R&D Purchasing Manager Workstation
IT Workstation	IT001206	Physical	R&D Clerk Workstations
IT Workstation	IT001207	Physical	R&D Records Mgt. Workstations
IT Workstation	IT001301	Physical	CLO Workstation
IT Workstation	IT001302	Physical	Lawyer Workstation
IT Workstation	IT001303	Physical	Para-Legal Assistant Workstation
IT Workstation	IT001304	Physical	Legal Administrator Workstation
IT Workstation	IT001305	Physical	Legal Audit Manager Workstation
IT Workstation	IT001306	Physical	Legal Clerk Workstation
R&D Workstation	RD001501	Physical	R&D Workstation
R&D Workstation	RD001502	Physical	R&D Workstation
R&D Workstation	RD001503	Physical	R&D Workstation
R&D Workstation	RD001504	Physical	R&D Workstation
IT Workstation	IT001601	Physical	CIO Workstation
IT Workstation	IT001602	Physical	Desktop Manager Workstation
IT Workstation	IT001604	Physical	Server Manager Workstation
IT Workstation	IT001606	Physical	Network Manager Workstation
IT Workstation	IT001607	Physical	Network Administration Workstation
IT Workstation	IT001701	Physical	Operations/Manufacturing VP Workstation
IT Workstation	IT001702	Physical	Operations/Manufacturing Manager Workstation
IT Workstation	IT001704	Physical	Operations/Manufacturing Administrator Workstation
IT Workstation	IT001706	Physical	Operations/Manufacturing Technician Workstation
IT Workstation	IT001801	Physical	Sales/Marketing VP Workstation
IT Workstation	IT001802	Physical	Sales Manager Workstation
IT Workstation	IT001804	Physical	Sales Administrator Workstation
IT Workstation	IT001806	Physical	Sales Representative Workstation

(continued)

TABLE 4.1. *(cont'd)*

Asset Name	Asset ID	Asset Type	Asset Description
IT Workstation	IT001807	Physical	Sales Representative Workstation
IT Workstation	IT001808	Physical	Marketing Manager Workstation
IT Workstation	IT001809	Physical	Marketing Administrator Workstation
IT Workstation	IT001810	Physical	Marketing Representative Workstation
IT Workstation	IT001811	Physical	Marketing Representative Workstation
IT Workstation	IT001901	Physical	Sales Terminal Device
IT Workstation	IT001902	Physical	Sales Terminal Device
IT Workstation	IT001903	Physical	Sales Terminal Device
IT Workstation	IT001904	Physical	Sales Terminal Device #31
Security Workstation	SC002001	Physical	CSO Workstation
Security Workstation	SC002001	Physical	Physical Security Manager Workstation
Security Workstation	SC002001	Physical	Audit Manager Workstation
Security Workstation	SC002001	Physical	Surveillance Manager Workstation
Security Workstation	SC002001	Physical	Security Technician Workstation
Administration server	IT010001	Physical	General Administration server system
Administration server	IT010010	Physical	Finance server system
Administration server	IT010020	Physical	HR Employee Web server system
Administration server	IT010030	Physical	Sales e-commerce web server system
Administration server	IT010040	Physical	Marketing server system
Administration server	IT010050	Physical	Contracts server system
Administration server	IT010060	Physical	Legal server system
Administration server	IT010070	Physical	Customer support Web server system
Administration server	IT010071	Physical	Customer server system
Administration server	IT010090	Physical	Operations server system
Administration server	IT010100	Physical	Manufacturing server system
Administration server	IT010300	Physical	Network Management server system
Administration server	IT010301	Physical	Desktop Management server system
Administration server	IT010302	Physical	IT Administration server system
Administration server	IT010303	Physical	DNS server system
Administration server	IT010310	Physical	NTP server system
Administration server	IT010320	Physical	Radius server system
Security server	SC010001	Physical	Security video surveillance server system
Security server	SC010010	Physical	Security perimeter surveillance server system
Security server	SC010020	Physical	Security central Syslog server system
Security server	SC010030	Physical	Security Firewall-IPS management server system

Asset Name	Asset ID	Asset Type	Asset Description
Security server	SC010040	Physical	Security Physical access control server system
Security server	SC010050	Physical	Security administration server system
R&D server	RD020001	Physical	R&D administration server system
Administration server	IT010330	Physical	S/W release and patch management server system
R&D server	RD020020	Physical	R&D source code archive server system
R&D server	RD020030	Physical	R&D administration server system
R&D server	RD020040	Physical	R&D test management server system
Enterprise SAN component	IT030001	Physical	SAN edge router-firewall
Enterprise SAN component	IT030010	Physical	SAN disk array #1
Enterprise SAN component	IT030020	Physical	SAN disk array #2
Enterprise SAN component	IT030030	Physical	SAN tape library #1
Enterprise SAN component	IT030040	Physical	SAN tape library #2
Printing system	IT040101	Physical	Administration printing system
Printing system	IT040201	Physical	Operations printing system
Printing system	RD040301	Physical	R&D printing system
Printing system	SC040401	Physical	Security printing system
HVAC component	FC090101	Physical	Roof HVAC Chiller-Condenser #1
HVAC component	FC090102	Physical	Roof HVAC Chiller-Condenser #2
HVAC component	FC090201	Physical	Data Center HVAC Chiller-Condenser #1
HVAC component	FC090202	Physical	Data Center HVAC Chiller-Condenser #2
Power system component	FC090302	Physical	Power service entrance-distribution panel
Power system component	FC090302	Physical	Backup Power generator #1
Power system component	FC090302	Physical	Backup Power generator #2
Fire suppression—water	FC090401	Physical	Water fire control-alarm system
Fire suppression—chemical	IT090501	Physical	Data Center & SAN non-water fire control system
Fire suppression—chemical	RD090501	Physical	R&D non-water fire suppression system
Fire suppression—chemical	SC090501	Physical	Security non-water fire suppression system

(*continued*)

TABLE 4.1. *(cont'd)*

Asset Name	Asset ID	Asset Type	Asset Description
Video surveillance	SC050001	Physical	Video surveillance control system
Video surveillance	SC050101	Physical	Video surveillance main entrance camera #1
Video surveillance	SC050205	Physical	Video surveillance loading dock camera #5
Video surveillance	SC050434	Physical	Video surveillance hall camera #34
Physical intrusion detection	SC051001	Physical	Physical intrusion detection/alarm control system
Physical intrusion detection	SC051104	Physical	Loading dock IR sensor #4
Physical intrusion detection	SC051208	Physical	Cafeteria IR sensor #8
Physical intrusion detection	SC051303	Physical	Elevator IR sensor #3
Physical intrusion detection	SC051422	Physical	Hall IR sensor #22
Physical intrusion detection	SC051512	Physical	Data Center IR sensor #12

...

- ○ IT Network OAM&P;
- ○ IT Server OAM&P;
- ○ IT Management OAM&P;
- ○ IT Manufacturing OAM&P;
- ○ IT Sales/Field Personnel Support OAM&P;
- ○ IT Customer Support OAM&P;
- ○ R&D Workstation OAM&P;
- ○ R&D Network OAM&P; and
- ○ R&D Server OAM&P.
- • **Asset Custodian**—Identifies the specific individual by title or by name within the organization unit who is responsible for defining and specifying the level of protection provided for an asset consistent with organizational information security governance policy documents. The level of protection provided to each asset should be specified in terms of identification, authentication, authorization, access controls, information and data integrity, availability, and non-repudiation security services and controls. This individual also has responsibility to the asset owning organization unit or group for verifying that specified levels of asset protection controls have been deployed and remain effective. One can simply identify the individual by title (such as CFO, CIO, CTO, CSO) or identify a specific employee by name. The individual identified can be limited to the individual who heads the group or an employee to whom responsibility has been delegated to by the head employee of the organizational group.

TABLE 4.2. **Asset Inventory Owner and Location Partial Example.**

Asset ID	Asset Description	Asset Owning Unit-Group	Asset Custodian	Asset Location
HR000001	Employee Data	HR	HR VP	HR server system— IT010020
FN000100	Accounts Receivables Data	Finance	CFO	Finance server system— IT010010
FN000400	Supplier Contracts Data	Finance	CFO	Finance server system— IT010010
SA000100	Marketing Data	Sales	Sales VP	Marketing server system— IT010040
SA000200	Publicly available Sales Data	Sales	Sales VP	Sales server system— IT010030
IT000001	CER between DMZ and ISP	IT	CIO	Room 21070
IT000002	Router-firewall between DMZ and enterprise intranet	IT	CIO	Room 21070
IT000006	Router-firewall between Customer Support & Call Center subnet and enterprise intranet	IT	CIO	Room 21100
IT000007	Router-firewall between R&D subnet and enterprise intranet	IT	CIO	Room 21070
IT000010	Router-firewall between IT OAM&P subnet and enterprise intranet	IT	CIO	Room 21070
IT000012	Router-firewall between Field Support subnet and enterprise intranet	IT	CIO	Room 21070
IT001001	HR VP Workstation	IT	CIO	Room 13105
IT001006	HR Representative Workstation	IT	CIO	Room 12110
IT001101	CFO Workstation	IT	CIO	Room 13106
IT001106	Finance Clerk Workstation	IT	CIO	Room 12130
IT001203	R&D Manager Workstation	IT	CIO	Room 23110
IT001204	R&D QA Manager Workstation	IT	CIO	Room 23120
IT001206	R&D Clerk Workstations	IT	CIO	Room 23130

(continued)

TABLE 4.2. *(cont'd)*

Asset ID	Asset Description	Asset Owning Unit-Group	Asset Custodian	Asset Location
IT001302	Lawyer Workstation	Legal	CLO	Room 13201
IT001305	Legal Audit Manager Workstation	Legal	CLO	Room 13217
IT001306	Legal Clerk Workstation	Legal	CLO	Room 13235
RD001504	R&D Workstation	R&D	CTO	Room 23010
IT001607	Network Admin. Workstation	IT	CIO	Room 22001
IT001702	Ops/Manuf. Manager Workstation	IT	CIO	Room 33010
IT001706	Ops/Manuf Tech. Workstation	IT	CIO	Room 33020
IT001806	Sales Representative Workstation	IT	CIO	Room 11101
IT001808	Marketing Manager Workstation	IT	CIO	Room 12220
IT001809	Marketing Admin. Workstation	IT	CIO	Room 12230
IT001904	Sales Terminal Device #31	IT	CIO	Room 11005
SC002001	CSO Workstation	Security	CSO	Room 13107
SC002001	Surveillance Manager Workstation	Security	CSO	Room 22101
SC002001	Security Technician Workstation	Security	CSO	Room 22106
IT010010	Finance server system	IT	CIO	Room 21010
IT010020	HR employee web server	IT	CIO	Room 21010
IT010030	Sales e-commerce web server	IT	CIO	Room 21010
IT010040	Marketing server system	IT	CIO	Room 21010
IT010050	Contracts server system	IT	CIO	Room 21010
IT010060	Legal server system	IT	CIO	Room 21010
IT010100	Manufacturing server system	IT	CIO	Room 21010
IT010300	Network Mgt. server system	IT	CIO	Room 21010
IT010303	DNS server system	IT	CIO	Room 21010
IT010310	NTP server system	IT	CIO	Room 21010
IT010320	Radius server system	IT	CIO	Room 21010
SC010020	Security central Syslog server	Security	CSO	Room 22201
SC010030	Security Firewall-IPS mgt. server	Security	CSO	Room 22201

Asset ID	Asset Description	Asset Owning Unit-Group	Asset Custodian	Asset Location
IT010330	S/W release and patch management server system	IT	CIO	Room 21010
RD020020	Dev. source code archive server	R&D	CTO	Room 23201
IT030001	SAN edge router-firewall	IT	CIO	Room 21010
IT030010	SAN disk array #1	IT	CIO	Room 21010
IT030030	SAN tape library #1	IT	CIO	Room 21010
RD040301	R&D printing system	IT	CIO	Room 23110
SC040401	Security printing system	Security	CSO	Room 22110
FC090101	Roof HVAC Chiller-Condenser #1	Facilities	VP	Building roof
FC090202	Data Center HVAC Chiller-Condenser #2	Facilities	VP Facilities	Building roof
FC090302	Backup Power generator #1	Facilities	VP Facilities	Building roof
SC090501	Security non-water fire suppression system	Facilities	VP Facilities	Building Area 4
SC050001	Video surveillance control system	Security	CSO	Room 22101
SC050101	Main entrance camera #1	Security	CSO	West wall
SC050434	Video surveillance hall camera #34	Security	CSO	Hall 1
SC051001	Physical intrusion detection/ alarm control system	Security	CSO	Room 22101
SC051422	Hall IR sensor #22	Security	CSO	Hall 4
SC051512	Data Center IR sensor #12	Security	CSO	Room 21101
...				

- **Asset Location**—The location of physical assets should be specified in terms of building, floor, room, or possibly even wall. Logical asset location should be specified in terms of the physical asset wherein the logical asset resides (is stored).

In Table 4.3, the column headings are:

- **Asset ID**—Uniquely identifies a specific asset item.
- **Asset Description**—Description of a specific asset item. The Asset Description column is included for human readability only.
- **Asset Valid Enterprise Users**—Identifies those enterprise employees who are allowed to access an asset either for administration purposes (OAM&P) or to interact with applications or information stored or processed by the asset. Employees include, but are not limited to, personnel, sales, marketing, PII, finance, R&D, manufacturing (such as ERP data), and command and control.
- **Purpose of Enterprise User Access to Asset**—Identifies purposes for employee access to interact with applications or information stored or processed by the asset.

In Table 4.4, the column headings are:

- **Asset ID**—Uniquely identifies a specific asset item.
- **Asset Description**—Description of a specific asset item. The Asset Description column is included for human readability only.
- **Customer Access to Asset**—Identifies customer types that may access the applications or information stored or processed within the asset. Customer types include, but are not limited to, general public (Public), retail customers (Retail), wholesale customers (Wholesale), business customers (Business), and government agency customers (Government). If no type of customer is allowed access, then not applicable (NA) is entered.
- **Purpose of User Access to Asset**—Identifies the general purpose for customer access to the applications or information stored or processed by the asset. If no type of customer is allowed access, then not applicable (NA) is entered.

In Table 4.5, the column headings are:

- **Asset ID**—Uniquely identifies a specific asset item.
- **Asset Description**—Description of a specific asset item. The Asset Description column is included for human readability only.
- **Third-Party Personnel Allowed Asset Access**—Identifies third-party personnel types (equipment or application supplier field support) that may access the applications or information stored or processed within the asset. If no type of third-party personnel is allowed access, then not applicable (NA) is entered.
- **Purpose of Third-Party Personnel Access to Asset**—Identifies the general purpose for third-party personnel access to the applications or information stored or processed by the asset. If no type of third-party personnel is allowed access, then not applicable (NA) is entered.

In Table 4.6, the column headings are:

- **Asset ID**—Uniquely identifies a specific asset item.
- **Asset Description**—Description of a specific asset item. The Asset Description column is included for human readability only.
- **Other Assets That Interact with This Asset**—Identifies assets that this asset interacts with. If no other enterprise assets interact with this asset, then it is marked as not applicable (NA).
- **Purpose of Other Asset Access to Asset**—Identifies the purpose of the inter-asset interaction.

TABLE 4.3. Asset Inventory User Access Partial Example.

Asset ID	Asset Description	Asset Valid Enterprise Users	Purpose of Enterprise User Access to Asset
HR000001	Employee Data	All employees and HR staff	To review and manage employee HR information such as benefits
FN000100	Accounts Receivables Data	Finance staff	To review and manage enterprise accounts receivables information
FN000400	Supplier Contracts Data	Finance, Legal, IT, Operations, and Manufacturing staff	To review and manage enterprise supplier contracts information
SA000100	Marketing Data	Sales and Marketing staff	To review and manage enterprise marketing information
SA000200	Publicly available Sales Data	Sales and Marketing staff	To review and manage enterprise publicly accessible sales and marketing information
IT000001	CER between DMZ and ISP	IT OAM&P and Security staff	Network and security OAM&P
IT000002	Router-firewall between DMZ and enterprise intranet	IT OAM&P and Security staff	Network and security OAM&P
IT000006	Router-firewall between Customer Support & Call Center subnet and enterprise intranet	IT OAM&P and Security staff	Network and security OAM&P
IT000007	Router-firewall between R&D subnet and enterprise intranet	IT OAM&P and Security staff	Network and security OAM&P
IT000010	Router-firewall between IT OAM&P subnet and enterprise intranet	IT OAM&P and Security staff	Network and security OAM&P
IT000012	Router-firewall between Field Support subnet and enterprise intranet	IT OAM&P and Security staff	Network and security OAM&P
IT001001	HR VP Workstation	HR VP and IT OAM&P staff	Application usage and workstation OAM&P
IT001006	HR Representative Workstation	HR and IT OAM&P staff	Application usage and workstation OAM&P

(continued)

TABLE 4.3. (cont'd)

Asset ID	Asset Description	Asset Valid Enterprise Users	Purpose of Enterprise User Access to Asset
IT001101	CFO Workstation	CFO and IT OAM&P staff	Application usage and workstation OAM&P
IT001106	Finance Clerk Workstation	Finance and IT OAM&P staff	Application usage and workstation OAM&P
IT001203	R&D Manager Workstation	R&D and IT OAM&P staff	Application usage and workstation OAM&P
IT001204	R&D QA Manager Workstation	R&D and IT OAM&P staff	Application usage and workstation OAM&P
IT001206	R&D Clerk Workstations	R&D and IT OAM&P staff	Application usage and workstation OAM&P
IT001302	Lawyer Workstation	Legal and IT OAM&P staff	Application usage and workstation OAM&P
IT001305	Legal Audit Manager Workstation	Legal and IT OAM&P staff	Application usage and workstation OAM&P
IT001306	Legal Clerk Workstation	Legal and IT OAM&P staff	Application usage and workstation OAM&P
RD001504	R&D Workstation	R&D staff	R&D application usage and workstation OAM&P
IT001607	Network Admin. Workstation	IT OAM&P staff	Network OAM&P
IT001702	Ops/Manuf. Manager Workstation	Operations and IT OAM&P staff	Application usage and workstation OAM&P
IT001706	Ops/Manuf Tech. Workstation	Operations and IT OAM&P staff	Application usage and workstation OAM&P
IT001806	Sales Representative Workstation	Sales and IT OAM&P staff	Application usage and workstation OAM&P
IT001808	Marketing Manager Workstation	Marketing and IT OAM&P staff	Application usage and workstation OAM&P

ID	Name	Description
IT001809	Marketing Admin. Workstation	Marketing and IT OAM&P staff	Application usage and workstation OAM&P
IT001904	Sales Terminal Device #31	Sales and IT OAM&P staff	Process customer purchases performed locally and device OAM&P
SC002001	CSO Workstation	CSO, IT OAM&P staff	Application usage and workstation OAM&P
SC002001	Surveillance Manager Workstation	Security staff	Application usage and workstation OAM&P
SC002001	Security Technician Workstation	Security staff	Application usage and workstation OAM&P
IT010010	Finance server system	Finance and IT OAM&P staff	Server OAM&P and access to financial information
IT010020	HR employee web server	HR and IT OAM&P staff	Server OAM&P and web page management
IT010030	Sales e-commerce web server	Sales and IT OAM&P staff	Server OAM&P and web page management
IT010040	Marketing server system	Marketing and IT OAM&P staff	Server OAM&P and access to marketing information
IT010050	Contracts server system	Legal, Finance, and IT OAM&P staff	Server OAM&P and access to contracts information
IT010060	Legal server system	Legal and IT OAM&P staff	Server OAM&P and access to legal information
IT010100	Manufacturing server system	Operations and IT OAM&P staff	Server OAM&P and interaction with manufacturing applications (i.e., ERP) and information
IT010300	Network Mgt. server system	IT OAM&P staff	Server OAM&P and OAM&P of intranet infrastructure devices
IT010303	DNS server system	IT OAM&P staff	Server OAM&P
IT010310	NTP server system	IT OAM&P staff	Server OAM&P
IT010320	Radius server system	IT OAM&P and Security staff	Server OAM&P

(continued)

TABLE 4.3. (cont'd)

Asset ID	Asset Description	Asset Valid Enterprise Users	Purpose of Enterprise User Access to Asset
SC010020	Security central Syslog server	Security staff	Server OAM&P and log analysis-report generation
SC010030	Security Firewall-IPS mgt. server	Security staff	Server OAM&P and OAM&P of enterprise firewall and IPS network and host functions
IT010330	S/W release and patch management server system	IT OAM&P staff	Server OAM&P and OAM&P of production OS and application S/W release and patch management
RD020020	Dev. source code archive server	R&D staff	Server OAM&P and OAM&P of source code libraries and archives for S/W under development
IT030001	SAN edge router-firewall	IT OAM&P and Security staff	Network and security OAM&P
IT030010	SAN disk array #1	IT OAM&P staff	Device OAM&P
FC090101	Roof HVAC Chiller-Condenser #1	Facilities—maintenance staff	Device OAM&P
FC090202	Data Center HVAC Chiller-Condenser #2	Facilities—maintenance staff	Device OAM&P
FC090302	Backup Power generator #1	Facilities—maintenance staff	Device OAM&P
SC090501	Security non-water fire suppression system	Facilities—maintenance staff	Device OAM&P
SC050001	Video surveillance control system	Security staff	OAM&P of Video surveillance control system and cameras
SC050101	Main entrance camera #1	Security staff	Device OAM&P
SC050434	Video surveillance hall camera #34	Security staff	Device OAM&P
SC051001	Physical intrusion detection/alarm control system	Security staff	OAM&P of Intrusion detection/alarm system and sensors
SC051422	Hall IR sensor #22	Security staff	Device OAM&P
SC051512	Data Center IR sensor #12	Security staff	Device OAM&P
...			

TABLE 4.4. **Asset Inventory Customer Access Partial Example.**

Asset ID	Asset Description	Customer Access to Asset	Purpose of Customer Access to Asset
HR000001	Employee Data	NA	NA
FN000100	Accounts Receivables Data	NA	NA
FN000400	Supplier Contracts Data	NA	NA
SA000100	Marketing Data	NA	NA
SA000200	Publicly available Sales Data	Public, Retail, Wholesale, Business, Government	To access publically available information regarding enterprise provided products and services
IT000001	CER between DMZ and ISP	NA	NA
IT000002	Router-firewall between DMZ and enterprise intranet	NA	NA
IT000006	Router-firewall between Customer Support & Call Center subnet and enterprise intranet	NA	NA
IT000007	Router-firewall between R&D subnet and enterprise intranet	NA	NA
IT000010	Router-firewall between IT OAM&P subnet and enterprise intranet	NA	NA
IT000012	Router-firewall between Field Support subnet and enterprise intranet	NA	NA
IT001001	HR VP Workstation	NA	NA
IT001006	HR Representative Workstation	NA	NA
IT001101	CFO Workstation	NA	NA
IT001106	Finance Clerk Workstation	NA	NA
IT001203	R&D Manager Workstation	NA	NA
IT001204	R&D QA Manager Workstation	NA	NA
IT001206	R&D Clerk Workstation	NA	NA
IT001302	Lawyer Workstation	NA	NA
IT001305	Legal Audit Manager Workstation	NA	NA
IT001306	Legal Clerk Workstation	NA	NA
RD001504	R&D Workstation	NA	NA
IT001607	Network Admin. Workstation	NA	NA
IT001702	Ops/Manuf. Manager Workstation	NA	NA
IT001706	Ops/Manuf Tech. Workstation	NA	NA
IT001806	Sales Representative Workstation	NA	NA
IT001808	Marketing Manager Workstation	NA	NA
IT001809	Marketing Admin. Workstation	NA	NA
IT001904	Sales Terminal Device #31	NA	NA

(*continued*)

TABLE 4.4. *(cont'd)*

Asset ID	Asset Description	Customer Access to Asset	Purpose of Customer Access to Asset
SC002001	CSO Workstation	NA	NA
SC002001	Surveillance Manager Workstation	NA	NA
SC002001	Security Technician Workstation	NA	NA
IT010010	Finance server system	NA	NA
IT010020	HR employee web server	NA	NA
IT010030	Sales e-commerce web server	Public, Retail, Wholesale, Business, Government	To access publically available information regarding enterprise provided products and services. To purchase enterprise provided products and services
IT010040	Marketing server system	NA	NA
IT010050	Contracts server system	NA	NA
IT010060	Legal server system	NA	NA
IT010100	Manufacturing server system	NA	NA
IT010300	Network Mgt. server system	NA	NA
IT010303	DNS server system	NA	NA
IT010310	NTP server system	NA	NA
IT010320	Radius server system	NA	NA
SC010020	Security central Syslog server	NA	NA
SC010030	Security Firewall-IPS mgt. server	NA	NA
IT010330	S/W release and patch management server system	NA	NA
RD020020	Dev. source code archive server	NA	NA
IT030001	SAN edge router-firewall	NA	NA
IT030010	SAN disk array #1	NA	NA
FC090101	Roof HVAC Chiller-Condenser #1	NA	NA
FC090202	Data Center HVAC Chiller-Condenser #2	NA	NA
FC090302	Backup Power generator #1	NA	NA
SC090501	Security non-water fire suppression system	NA	NA
SC050001	Video surveillance control system	NA	NA
SC050101	Main entrance camera #1	NA	NA
SC050434	Video surveillance hall camera #34	NA	NA
SC051001	Physical intrusion detection/ alarm control system	NA	NA
SC051422	Hall IR sensor #22	NA	NA
SC051512	Data Center IR sensor #12	NA	NA

...

TABLE 4.5. Asset Inventory Third-Party Access Partial Example.

Asset ID	Asset Description	Third-party Personnel Allowed Asset Access	Purpose of Third-party Personnel Access to Asset
HR000001	Employee Data	NA	NA
FN000100	Accounts Receivables Data	NA	NA
FN000400	Supplier Contracts Data	NA	NA
SA000100	Marketing Data	NA	NA
SA000200	Publicly available Sales Data	NA	NA
IT000001	CER between DMZ and ISP	Supplier field support personnel	On-site repair with direct OAM&P personnel supervision
IT000002	Router-firewall between DMZ and enterprise intranet	Supplier field support personnel	On-site repair with direct OAM&P personnel supervision
IT000006	Router-firewall between Customer Support & Call Center subnet and enterprise intranet	Supplier field support personnel	On-site repair with direct OAM&P personnel supervision
IT000007	Router-firewall between R&D subnet and enterprise intranet	Supplier field support personnel	On-site repair with direct OAM&P personnel supervision
IT000010	Router-firewall between IT OAM&P subnet and enterprise intranet	Supplier field support personnel	On-site repair with direct OAM&P personnel supervision
IT000012	Router-firewall between Field Support subnet and enterprise intranet	Supplier field support personnel	On-site repair with direct OAM&P personnel supervision
IT001001	HR VP Workstation	NA	NA
IT001006	HR Representative Workstation	NA	NA
IT001702	Ops/Manuf. Manager Workstation	NA	NA
IT001706	Ops/Manuf. Tech. Workstation	NA	NA
IT001806	Sales Representative Workstation	NA	NA
IT001808	Marketing Manager Workstation	NA	NA
IT001809	Marketing Admin. Workstation	NA	NA
IT001904	Sales Terminal Device #31	Supplier field support personnel	On-site repair with direct OAM&P personnel supervision

TABLE 4.5. (cont'd)

Asset ID	Asset Description	Third-party Personnel Allowed Asset Access	Purpose of Third-party Personnel Access to Asset
SC002001	CSO Workstation	NA	NA
SC002001	Surveillance Manager Workstation	NA	NA
SC002001	Security Technician Workstation	NA	NA
IT010010	Finance server system	Supplier field support personnel	On-site repair with direct OAM&P personnel supervision
IT010020	HR employee web server	Supplier field support personnel	On-site repair with direct OAM&P personnel supervision
IT010030	Sales e-commerce web server	Supplier field support personnel	On-site repair with direct OAM&P personnel supervision
IT010040	Marketing server system	Supplier field support personnel	On-site repair with direct OAM&P personnel supervision
IT010050	Contracts server system	Supplier field support personnel	On-site repair with direct OAM&P personnel supervision
IT010060	Legal server system	Supplier field support personnel	On-site repair with direct OAM&P personnel supervision
IT010100	Manufacturing server system	Supplier field support personnel	On-site repair with direct OAM&P personnel supervision
IT010300	Network Mgt. server system	Supplier field support personnel	On-site repair with direct OAM&P personnel supervision
IT010303	DNS server system	Supplier field support personnel	On-site repair with direct OAM&P personnel supervision
IT010310	NTP server system	Supplier field support personnel	On-site repair with direct OAM&P personnel supervision
IT010320	Radius server system	Supplier field support personnel	On-site repair with direct OAM&P personnel supervision
SC010020	Security central Syslog server	Supplier field support personnel	On-site repair with direct OAM&P personnel supervision

ID	Description		
SC010030	Security Firewall-IPS mgt. server	Supplier field support personnel	On-site repair with direct OAM&P personnel supervision
IT010330	S/W release and patch management server system	Supplier field support personnel	On-site repair with direct OAM&P personnel supervision
RD020020	Dev. source code archive server	Supplier field support personnel	On-site repair with direct OAM&P personnel supervision
IT030001	SAN edge router-firewall	Supplier field support personnel	On-site repair with direct OAM&P personnel supervision
IT030010	SAN disk array #1	Supplier field support personnel	On-site repair with direct OAM&P personnel supervision
FC090101	Roof HVAC Chiller-Condenser #1	Supplier field support personnel	On-site repair and periodic vendor maintenance
FC090202	Data Center HVAC Chiller-Condenser #2	Supplier field support personnel	On-site repair and periodic vendor maintenance
FC090302	Backup Power generator #1	Supplier field support personnel	On-site repair and periodic vendor maintenance
SC090501	Security non-water fire suppression system	Supplier field support personnel, Fire Dept. personnel	On-site repair and periodic vendor maintenance and Fire Dept. Inspection
SC050001	Video surveillance control system	Supplier field support personnel	On-site repair with direct OAM&P personnel supervision
SC050101	Main entrance camera #1	Supplier field support personnel	On-site repair with direct OAM&P personnel supervision
SC050434	Video surveillance hall camera #34	Supplier field support personnel	On-site repair with direct OAM&P personnel supervision
SC051001	Physical intrusion detection/alarm control system	Supplier field support personnel	On-site repair with direct OAM&P personnel supervision
SC051422	Hall IR sensor #22	Supplier field support personnel	On-site repair with direct OAM&P personnel supervision
SC051512	Data Center IR sensor #12	Supplier field support personnel	On-site repair with direct OAM&P personnel supervision

...

TABLE 4.6. Asset Inventory Inter-asset Access Partial Example.

Asset ID	Asset Description	Other Assets That Interact with This Asset	Purpose of Other Asset Access to This Asset
IT000001	CER between DMZ and ISP	ISP access network devices on one side and both enterprise DMZ devices and IT000002 on other side	Forwarding and filtering packets between DMZ attached devices and ISP access network
IT000002	Router-firewall between DMZ and enterprise intranet	Enterprise DMZ attached devices and CER IT000001 on one side and enterprise intranet attached devices on other side	Forwarding and filtering packets between DMZ attached devices and enterprise intranet attached devices
IT000006	Router-firewall between Customer Support & Call Center subnet and enterprise intranet	Enterprise intranet attached devices and IT000002 on one side and enterprise Customer Support & Call Center subnet attached devices on other side	Forwarding and filtering packets between enterprise intranet attached devices and Customer Support & Call Center subnet attached devices
IT000007	Router-firewall between R&D subnet and enterprise intranet	Enterprise intranet attached devices and IT000002 on one side and enterprise R&D subnet attached devices on other side	Forwarding and filtering packets between enterprise intranet attached devices and R&D subnet attached devices
IT000010	Router-firewall between IT OAM&P subnet and enterprise intranet	Enterprise intranet attached devices and IT000002 on one side and enterprise IT OAM&P subnet attached devices on other side	Forwarding and filtering packets between enterprise intranet attached devices and IT OAM&P subnet attached devices
IT000012	Router-firewall between Field Support subnet and enterprise intranet	Enterprise intranet attached devices and IT000002 on one side and enterprise Field Support subnet attached devices on other side	Forwarding and filtering packets between enterprise intranet attached devices and Field Support subnet attached devices
IT001001	HR VP Workstation	HR subnet attached devices, Enterprise intranet devices, and HR employee web server IT010020	Access to HR and enterprise servers, IT OAM&P operations
IT001006	HR Representative Workstation	HR subnet attached devices, Enterprise intranet devices, and HR employee web server IT010020	Access to HR and enterprise servers, IT OAM&P operations
IT001101	CFO Workstation	Finance subnet attached devices, Enterprise intranet devices, and Finance server IT010010	Access to Finance and enterprise servers, IT OAM&P operations
IT001106	Finance Clerk Workstation	Finance subnet attached devices, Enterprise intranet devices, and Finance server IT010010	Access to Finance and enterprise servers, IT OAM&P operations
IT001203	R&D Manager Workstation	R&D subnet attached devices, Enterprise intranet devices, and Dev. source code archive server RD020020	Access to R&D and enterprise servers, IT OAM&P operations

IT001204	R&D QA Manager Workstation	R&D subnet attached devices, Enterprise intranet devices, and Dev. source code archive server RD020020	Access to R&D and enterprise servers, IT OAM&P operations
IT001302	Lawyer Workstation	Legal subnet attached devices, Enterprise intranet devices, and Legal server IT010060	Access to Legal and enterprise servers, IT OAM&P operations
RD001504	R&D Workstation	R&D subnet attached devices, Enterprise intranet devices, and Dev. source code archive server RD020020	Access to R&D and enterprise servers, IT OAM&P operations
IT001607	Network Admin. Workstation	IT OAM&P subnet attached devices, Enterprise intranet devices, and Network Mgt. server IT010300	Access to IT OAM&P and enterprise servers, IT OAM&P operations
IT001706	Ops./Manuf Tech. Workstation	Operations/Manufacturing subnet attached devices, Enterprise intranet devices, and Manufacturing server IT010100	Access to Operations/Manufacturing and enterprise servers, IT OAM&P operations
IT001806	Sales Representative Workstation	Sales–Marketing subnet attached devices, Enterprise intranet devices, and Sales e-commerce web server IT010030	Access to Sales–Marketing and enterprise servers, IT OAM&P operations
IT001808	Marketing Manager Workstation	Sales–Marketing subnet attached devices, Enterprise intranet devices, and Marketing server IT010040	Access to Sales–Marketing and enterprise servers, IT OAM&P operations
IT001904	Sales Terminal Device #31	Sales e-commerce web server IT010030	Access to Sales e-commerce web server IT010030 for retail sales, IT OAM&P operations
SC002001	CSO Workstation	Security subnet attached devices, Enterprise intranet devices, and Security central Syslog server SC010020, Security Firewall-IPS mgt. server SC010030	Access to Security and enterprise servers
SC002001	Security Technician Workstation	Security subnet attached devices, Enterprise intranet devices, and Security central Syslog server SC010020, Security Firewall-IPS mgt. server SC010030	Access to Security and enterprise servers

(*continued*)

TABLE 4.6. (cont'd)

Asset ID	Asset Description	Other Assets That Interact with This Asset	Purpose of Other Asset Access to This Asset
IT010020	HR employee web server	Enterprise intranet servers (IT010303, IT010310, IT010320, IT010320, SC010020) and HR workstations	Accessed by enterprise employee workstations for data processing and IT010330 for S/W updates; assesses IT010303 for DNS address–host resolution, IT010310 for Network time updates, IT010320 for centralized authentication, and SC010020 for Central log file updates
IT010030	Sales e-commerce web server	Enterprise intranet servers (IT010303, IT010310, IT010320, IT010320, SC010020) and Sales workstations	Accessed by HR workstations for data processing, customer workstations for purchasing products and services, and IT010330 for S/W updates; assesses IT010303 for DNS address–host resolution, IT010310 for Network time updates, IT010320 for centralized authentication, and SC010020 for Central log file updates
IT010100	Manufacturing server system	Enterprise intranet servers (IT010303, IT010310, IT010320, IT010320, SC010020) and Finance workstations	Accessed by operations/manufacturing workstations for data processing and IT010330 for S/W updates; assesses manufacturing control devices, IT010303 for DNS address–host resolution, IT010310 for Network time updates, IT010320 for centralized authentication, and SC010020 for Central log file updates
IT010300	Network Mgt. server system	Enterprise intranet attached network infrastructure devices and IT OAM&P workstations, including enterprise intranet servers (IT010303, IT010310, IT010320, IT010320, SC010020)	Accessed by IT OAM&P workstations for data processing and IT010330 for S/W updates; assesses all enterprise devices for OAM&P activities, IT010303 for DNS address–host resolution, IT010310 for Network time updates, IT010320 for centralized authentication, and SC010020 for Central log file updates

ID	System	Devices	Description
IT010303	DNS server system	Enterprise intranet attached devices	Accessed by IT010330 for S/W updates, IT010300 for OAM&P activities; assesses IT010310 for Network time updates, IT010320 for centralized authentication, and SC010020 for Central log file updates; provides for address–host resolution requests by enterprise devices
IT010310	NTP server system	Enterprise intranet attached devices	Accessed by IT010330 for S/W updates, IT010300 for OAM&P activities; assesses IT010303 for DNS address–host resolution, IT010320 for centralized authentication, and SC010020 for Central log file updates; provides common system time source to all enterprise devices
IT010320	Radius server system	Enterprise intranet, DMZ and SAN attached devices	Accessed by IT010330 for S/W updates, IT010300 for OAM&P activities; assesses IT010303 for DNS address–host resolution, IT010310 for Network time updates, and SC010020 for Central log file updates; provides centralized login authentication and authorization service to all enterprise devices
SC010020	Security central Syslog server	Enterprise intranet, DMZ and SAN attached devices	Accessed by IT010330 for S/W updates, IT010300 for OAM&P activities; assesses IT010303 for DNS address–host resolution, IT010310 for Network time updates, and SC010020 for Central log file updates; provides centralized system log collection, analysis, archiving, and reporting service for all enterprise devices

(*continued*)

TABLE 4.6. (cont'd)

Asset ID	Asset Description	Other Assets That Interact with This Asset	Purpose of Other Asset Access to This Asset
SC010030	Security Firewall-IPS mgt. server	Enterprise intranet servers (IT010303, IT010310, IT010320, SC010020), Enterprise Router-Firewalls (IT000001, IT000002, IT000006, IT000007, IT000010, IT000012, IT030001), and network IPSs (IT000020, IT000021, IT000022, IT000023, IT000025, IT000025, IT000026, IT000026)	Accessed by Security OAM&P workstations for data processing, IT010330 for S/W updates; assesses all enterprise devices for OAM&P activities, IT010303 for DNS address–host resolution, IT010310 for Network time updates, IT010320 for centralized authent ication, and SC010020 for Central log file updates
IT010330	S/W release and patch management server system	Enterprise intranet attached servers and workstations	Accesses all enterprise devices to provide S/W updates
RD020020	Dev. source code archive server	Enterprise intranet servers (IT010303, IT010310, IT010320, IT010320, SC010020) and R&D workstations	Accessed by IT010330 for S/W updates, IT010300 for OAM&P activities; assesses IT010303 for DNS address–host resolution, IT010310 for Network time updates, and SC010020 for Central log file updates; provides centralized access to R&D workstations for source code archiving and development
IT030001	SAN edge router-firewall	Enterprise intranet devices and IT000002 on one side and enterprise SAN attached devices on other side	Forwarding and filtering packets between enterprise intranet attached devices and SAN attached devices; accessed by Security OAM&P workstations for data processing, IT010330 for S/W updates; assesses IT010303 for DNS address–host resolution, IT010310 for Network time updates, IT010320 for centralized authentication, and SC010020 for Central log file updates

ID	Description	Access
IT030010	SAN disk array #1	SAN edge router-firewall IT030001, other SAN attached devices, enterprise intranet devices	Accessed by IT010330 for S/W updates, IT010300 for OAM&P activities; assesses IT010303 for DNS address–host resolution, IT010310 for Network time updates, and SC010020 for Central log file updates; provides centralized enterprise disk storage
FC090101	Roof HVAC Chiller-Condenser #1	Enterprise facilities status monitoring system FC091020	Accessed by FC091020 for OAM&P activities
FC090302	Backup Power generator #1	Enterprise facilities status monitoring system FC091020	Accessed by FC091020 for OAM&P activities
SC090501	Security non-water fire suppression system	Enterprise facilities status monitoring system FC091020	Accessed by FC091020 for OAM&P activities
SC050001	Video surveillance control system	Video surveillance cameras	Accessed by SC050001 for video data retrieval
SC050434	Video surveillance hall camera #34	Video surveillance control system SC050001	Accessed by SC050001 for video data retrieval
SC051001	Physical intrusion detection/alarm control system	Physical intrusion detection/alarm sensors	Accessed by Security OAM&P workstations for data processing, IT010330 for S/W updates; assesses IT010303 for DNS address–host resolution, IT010310 for Network time updates, IT010320 for centralized authentication, and SC010020 for Central log file updates; accesses enterprise alarm sensors
SC051512	Data Center IR sensor #12	Physical intrusion detection/alarm control system SC051001	Accessed by SC051001 for alarm processing
...			

In Table 4.7, the column headings are:

- **Asset ID**—Uniquely identifies a specific asset item.
- **Asset Description**—Description of a specific asset item. The Asset Description column is included for human readability only.
- **Operating System (OS) Used Within Asset**—Identifies what OS and current version is used within the asset.
- **Date When OS Was Most Recently Patched or Updated**—Identifies date of last OS patch or new version installed within asset.

In Table 4.8, the column headings are:

- **Asset ID**—Uniquely identifies a specific asset item.
- **Asset Description**—Description of a specific asset item. The Asset Description column is included for human readability only.
- **Email Application S/W Used Within Asset**—Name of user electronic mail client application and associated version number.
- **Date When Email Application Client Most Recently Patched or Updated**.

In Table 4.9, the column headings are:

- **Asset ID**—Uniquely identifies a specific asset item.
- **Asset Description**—Description of a specific asset item. The Asset Description column is included for human readability only.
- **Web Browser Application S/W Used Within Asset**—Name of user web browser application and associated version number.
- **Date When Web Browser Application Most Recently Patched or Updated**.

In Table 4.10, the column headings are:

- **Asset ID**—Uniquely identifies a specific asset item.
- **Asset Description**—Description of a specific asset item. The Asset Description column is included for human readability only.
- **Anti-malware Application S/W Used Within Asset**—Name of anti-malware application and associated version number.
- **Date When Anti-malware Application Most Recently Patched or Updated**.

TABLE 4.7. Asset Inventory Operation System Partial Example.

Asset ID	Asset Description	OS and Applications Used Within Asset	Dates of Last Patching or Update
IT000001	CER between DMZ and ISP	Cisco IOS Rel. 22	May 22, 2012
IT000002	Router-firewall between DMZ and enterprise intranet	Cisco IOS Rel. 22	May 22, 2012
IT000006	Router-firewall between Customer Support & Call Center subnet and enterprise intranet	Cisco IOS Rel. 22	May 22, 2012
IT000007	Router-firewall between R&D subnet and enterprise intranet	Cisco IOS Rel. 22	May 22, 2012
IT000010	Router-firewall between IT OAM&P subnet and enterprise intranet	Cisco IOS Rel. 22	May 22, 2012
IT000012	Router-firewall between Field Support subnet and enterprise intranet	Cisco IOS Rel. 22	May 22, 2012
IT001101	CFO Workstation	Windows 7 Business SP1	Every Tuesday at 19:30
IT001106	Finance Clerk Workstation	Windows 7 Business SP1	Every Tuesday at 19:30
IT001806	Sales Representative Workstation	Windows 7 Business SP1	Every Tuesday at 19:30
SC002001	CSO Workstation	Windows 7 Business SP1	Every Tuesday at 19:30
SC002001	Security Technician Workstation	Windows 7 Business SP1	Every Tuesday at 19:30
IT010010	Finance server system	Trusted Solaris, patch 31	Mar 3, 2011
IT010020	HR employee web server	Trusted Solaris, patch 31	Mar 3, 2011
IT010030	Sales E-commerce web server	Trusted Solaris, patch 31	Mar 3, 2011
IT010303	DNS server system	Trusted Solaris, patch 31	Mar 5, 2011
IT010310	NTP server system	Trusted Solaris, patch 31	Mar 5, 2011
IT010320	Radius server system	Trusted Solaris, patch 31	Mar 5, 2011
SC010020	Security central Syslog server	Trusted Solaris, patch 31	Mar 6, 2011
SC010030	Security Firewall-IPS mgt. server	Trusted Solaris, patch 31	Mar 6, 2011
RD020020	Dev. source code archive server	Trusted Solaris, patch 31	Mar 6, 2011
IT030001	SAN edge router-firewall	Cisco IOS Rel. 22	May 22, 2012
IT030010	SAN disk array #1	HPUX 103, patch 3	May 1, 2012
FC090101	Roof HVAC Chiller-Condenser #1	Honeywell R44361-5	Jan 22, 2012
FC090302	Backup Power generator #1	Generac R102.34.66	Jan 2, 2012
SC050001	Video surveillance control system	ConVideo	Feb 1, 2012
SC050101	Main entrance camera #1	ConVideo R33.523.81	Feb 1, 2012
SC051001	Physical intrusion detection/ alarm control system	ADT R01003	Feb 2, 2012
SC051422	Hall IR sensor #22	ADT R01101	Feb 2, 2012
...			

TABLE 4.8. Asset Inventory Email Client Application Software Partial Example.

Asset ID	Asset Description	Email Client Applications Used Within Asset	Date of Last Patching or Update
IT001001	HR VP Workstation	Thunderbird 12.0.1	May 10, 2012
IT001006	HR Representative Workstation	Thunderbird 12.0.1	May 10, 2012
IT001101	CFO Workstation	Thunderbird 12.0.1	May 10, 2012
IT001106	Finance Clerk Workstation	Thunderbird 12.0.1	May 10, 2012
IT001203	R&D Manager Workstation	Thunderbird 12.0.1	May 10, 2012
IT001204	R&D QA Manager Workstation	Thunderbird 12.0.1	May 10, 2012
IT001206	R&D Clerk Workstations	Thunderbird 12.0.1	May 10, 2012
IT001302	Lawyer Workstation	Thunderbird 12.0.1	May 10, 2012
IT001305	Legal Audit Manager Workstation	Thunderbird 12.0.1	May 10, 2012
IT001306	Legal Clerk Workstation	Thunderbird 12.0.1	May 10, 2012
RD001504	R&D Workstation	Thunderbird 12.0.1	May 10, 2012
IT001607	Network Admin. Workstation	Thunderbird 12.0.1	May 10, 2012
IT001702	Ops/Manuf. Manager Workstation	Thunderbird 12.0.1	May 10, 2012
IT001706	Ops/Manuf. Tech. Workstation	Thunderbird 12.0.1	May 10, 2012
IT001806	Sales Representative Workstation	Thunderbird 12.0.1	May 10, 2012
IT001808	Marketing Manager Workstation	Thunderbird 12.0.1	May 10, 2012
IT001809	Marketing Admin. Workstation	Thunderbird 12.0.1	May 10, 2012
SC002001	CSO Workstation	Thunderbird 12.0.1	May 10, 2012
SC002001	Surveillance Manager Workstation	Thunderbird 12.0.1	May 10, 2012
SC002001	Security Technician Workstation	Thunderbird 12.0.1	May 10, 2012

...

TABLE 4.9. Asset Inventory Web Browser Application Software Partial Example.

Asset ID	Asset Description	Web Browser Application Used Within Asset	Dates of Last Patching or Update
IT001001	HR VP Workstation	Firefox 11.0	May 12, 2012
IT001006	HR Representative Workstation	Firefox 11.0	May 12, 2012
IT001101	CFO Workstation	Firefox 11.0	May 12, 2012
IT001106	Finance Clerk Workstation	Firefox 11.0	May 12, 2012
IT001203	R&D Manager Workstation	Firefox 11.0	May 12, 2012
IT001204	R&D QA Manager Workstation	Firefox 11.0	May 12, 2012
IT001206	R&D Clerk Workstations	Firefox 11.0	May 12, 2012
IT001302	Lawyer Workstation	Firefox 11.0	May 12, 2012
IT001305	Legal Audit Manager Workstation	Firefox 11.0	May 12, 2012
IT001306	Legal Clerk Workstation	Firefox 11.0	May 12, 2012
RD001504	R&D Workstation	Firefox 11.0	May 12, 2012
IT001607	Network Admin. Workstation	Firefox 11.0	May 12, 2012
IT001702	Ops./Manuf. Manager Workstation	Firefox 11.0	May 12, 2012
IT001706	Ops./Manuf. Tech. Workstation	Firefox 11.0	May 12, 2012
IT001806	Sales Representative Workstation	Firefox 11.0	May 12, 2012
IT001808	Marketing Manager Workstation	Firefox 11.0	May 12, 2012
IT001809	Marketing Admin. Workstation	Firefox 11.0	May 12, 2012
SC002001	CSO Workstation	Firefox 11.0	May 12, 2012
SC002001	Surveillance Manager Workstation	Firefox 11.0	May 12, 2012
SC002001	Security Technician Workstation	Firefox 11.0	May 12, 2012
...			

TABLE 4.10. Anti-malware Application Software Partial Example.

Asset ID	Asset Description	Anti-malware Application Used Within Asset	Dates of Last Patching or Update
IT001001	HR VP Workstation	Symantec Enterprise Security 10	Hourly
IT001006	HR Representative Workstation	Symantec Enterprise Security 10	Hourly
IT001101	CFO Workstation	Symantec Enterprise Security 10	Hourly
IT001106	Finance Clerk Workstation	Symantec Enterprise Security 10	Hourly
IT001203	R&D Manager Workstation	Symantec Enterprise Security 10	Hourly
IT001204	R&D QA Manager Workstation	Symantec Enterprise Security 10	Hourly
IT001206	R&D Clerk Workstations	Symantec Enterprise Security 10	Hourly
IT001302	Lawyer Workstation	Symantec Enterprise Security 10	Hourly

(continued)

TABLE 4.10. (*cont'd*)

Asset ID	Asset Description	Anti-malware Application Used Within Asset	Dates of Last Patching or Update
IT001305	Legal Audit Manager Workstation	Symantec Enterprise Security 10	Hourly
IT001306	Legal Clerk Workstation	Symantec Enterprise Security 10	Hourly
RD001504	R&D Workstation	Symantec Enterprise Security 10	Hourly
IT001607	Network Admin. Workstation	Symantec Enterprise Security 10	Hourly
IT001702	Ops./Manuf. Manager Workstation	Symantec Enterprise Security 10	Hourly
IT001706	Ops./Manuf. Tech. Workstation	Symantec Enterprise Security 10	Hourly
IT001806	Sales Representative Workstation	Symantec Enterprise Security 10	Hourly
IT001808	Marketing Manager Workstation	Symantec Enterprise Security 10	Hourly
IT001809	Marketing Admin. Workstation	Symantec Enterprise Security 10	Hourly
SC002001	CSO Workstation	Symantec Enterprise Security 10	Hourly
SC002001	Surveillance Manager Workstation	Symantec Enterprise Security 10	Hourly
SC002001	Security Technician Workstation	Symantec Enterprise Security 10	Hourly
...			

The aforementioned tables are only partial examples of the types of information that should be collected during an asset inventory activity.

4.2 IMPACT ANALYSIS

Risk impact analysis is the process of identifying asset criticality for new systems or sub-systems as well as for existing systems. The process of evaluating impact of existing and new systems differs so each is discussed individually as follows.

4.2.1 Existing System Impact Analysis

The impact of risks to existing systems (assets) would occur during the asset inventory process. A key source of impact information is the owning organization relative to existing asset criticality to ongoing business activities and operations. Asset custodians should always be involved in the asset inventory process. Table 4.11 could be used to capture sensitivity attributes of the information of, or within, the asset where the column headings are:

- **Asset ID**—Uniquely identifies a specific asset item.
- **Asset Description**—Description of a specific asset item. The Asset Description column is included for human readability only.
- **Asset Purpose to Organization**—Identifies the service or function a physical asset provides to the enterprise, or for logical assets, the type and use of information stored or processed within/by a physical asset.
- **Asset Availability Requirements**—Identifies the:
  - required Availability (A^o) of the asset as a percentage of time on an annual basis;
  - required worst case mean time to repair/restore (MTTR) for asset in terms of minutes; and
  - required worst case mean time between failures (MTBF) for asset in terms of days; MTBF is not applicable (NA) for logical assets.

There are 31,536,000 seconds in a year (365 days × 24 hours × 3600 seconds), and the availability value (A^o) represents the percentage of seconds the asset must be available and able to provide normal service functionality, and the inverse of the A^o value represents the amount of unplanned/unscheduled non-availability considered acceptable on an yearly basis. Table 4.12 provides conversion of common A^o values into the corresponding amounts of time per year that the asset is not available.

When MTTR is measured in terms of minute, one can compare the inverse of the A^o value to the MTTR to determine if availability controls are required. For example, asset IT000001, the Customer edge router-firewall (CER) between demilitarized zone (DMZ) and Internet service provider (ISP) has:

- an A^o value of 99.999, meaning that it cannot be non-functional for more than 5.256 minutes per year; and
- an MTTR of 0.5 minutes

which means that the MTTR falls well within the value, and no availability controls are required due to the average time for repairing the asset. The MTBF for this asset is 2555 days (= approximately 7 years), and the asset is likely to be replaced/upgraded well before it is likely to fail, meaning that no availability controls are required due to the average frequency of asset failures.

One MUST remember that MTTR and MTBF values provided by manufacturers refer to hardware- and operating-system-based failures and NOT failures due to being the target of a cyber attack. In theory, one could develop statistics that reflect attack versions of the MTTR and MTBF values; however; using the following is likely to be more effective in real-world situations:

- Five-point Impact scale, as shown in Table 4.17;
- Five-point Probability scale, as shown in Table 4.18; and
- Probability Versus Impact Composite Values, as shown in Table 4.19.

TABLE 4.11. **Asset Inventory Availability Partial Example.**

Asset ID	Asset Description	Asset Purpose to Organization	Asset Availability Requirements		
			A^O	MTTR	MTBF
HR000001	Employee Data	Enterprise employee electronic records	99.9	30	NA
FN000100	Accounts Receivables Data	Primary enterprise financial electronic records	99.9	30	NA
FN000400	Supplier Contracts Data	Primary enterprise financial electronic records	99.9	30	NA
SA000200	Publicly available Sales Data	Product/services catalog, data sheets, etc.	99.99	30	NA
IT000001	CER between DMZ and ISP	Provides first line of enterprise network defense	99.999	0.5	2555
IT000002	Router-firewall between DMZ and enterprise intranet	Provides second line of enterprise network defense	99.999	0.5	2555
IT000006	Router-firewall between Customer Support & Call Center subnet and enterprise intranet	Controls access between work group from enterprise intranet	99.999	0.5	2555
IT000007	Router-firewall between R&D subnet and enterprise intranet	Controls access between work group from enterprise intranet	99.999	0.5	2555
IT000010	Router-firewall between IT OAM&P subnet and enterprise intranet	Controls access between work group from enterprise intranet	99.999	0.5	2555
IT000012	Router-firewall between Field Support subnet and enterprise intranet	Controls access between work group from enterprise intranet	99.999	0.5	2555
IT001001	HR VP Workstation	Employee desktop system	99.9	156	1095
IT001006	HR Representative Workstation	Employee desktop system	99.9	156	1095
IT001101	CFO Workstation	Employee desktop system	99.9	156	1095
IT001106	Finance Clerk Workstation	Employee desktop system	99.9	156	1095
IT001203	R&D Manager Workstation	Employee desktop system	99.9	156	1095
IT001204	R&D QA Manager Workstation	Employee desktop system	99.9	156	1095
IT001206	R&D Clerk Workstations	Employee desktop system	99.9	156	1095
IT001302	Lawyer Workstation	Employee desktop system	99.9	156	1095
IT001305	Legal Audit Manager Workstation	Employee desktop system	99.9	156	1095

ID	Device	Description			
IT001306	Legal Clerk Workstation	Employee desktop system	99.9	156	1095
RD001504	R&D Workstation	Employee S/W dev. desktop	99.9	156	1095
IT001607	Network Admin. Workstation	Employee desktop system	99.99	52	1095
IT001702	Ops./Manuf. Manager Workstation	Employee desktop system	99.9	156	1095
IT001706	Ops./Manuf. Tech. Workstation	Employee desktop system	99.99	52	1095
IT001806	Sales Representative Workstation	Employee desktop system	99.9	156	1095
IT001808	Marketing Manager Workstation	Employee desktop system	99.9	156	1095
IT001809	Marketing Admin. Workstation	Employee desktop system	99.9	156	1095
IT001904	Sales Terminal Device #31	Retail sales terminal	99.99	52	1095
SC002001	CSO Workstation	Employee desktop system	99.99	52	1095
SC002001	Surveillance Manager Workstation	Employee desktop system	99.99	52	1095
SC002001	Security Technician Workstation	Employee desktop system	99.99	52	1095
IT010010	Finance server system	Stores and processes financial data	99.99	52	1825
IT010020	HR employee web server	Provides employees with web access to employee records and HR services	99.99	52	1825
IT010030	Sales e-commerce web server	Provides general public web access to B-to-B and B-to-C products and services	99.999	5	1825
IT010040	Marketing server system	Stores and processes marketing data	99.99	52	1825
IT010050	Contracts server system	Stores and processes supplier contracts data	99.99	52	1825
IT010060	Legal server system	Stores and processes legal data	99.99	52	1825
IT010100	Manufacturing server system	Stores and processes manufacturing data and controls manufacturing equipment	99.999	5.2	1825
IT010300	Network Mgt. server system	Provides General OAM&P functionality	99.999	5.2	1825
IT010303	DNS server system	Provides intranet DNS services	99.999	5.2	1825
IT010310	NTP server system	Provides intranet central time services	99.999	5.2	1825
IT010320	Radius server system	Provides intranet authentication and authorization services	99.999	5.2	1825
SC010020	Security central Syslog server	Manages and controls central collection, analysis, and reporting of system logs	99.999	5.2	1825
SC010030	Security Firewall-IPS mgt. server	Provides Firewall-IPS OAM&P functionality	99.999	5.2	1825

(*continued*)

TABLE 4.11. (cont'd)

Asset ID	Asset Description	Asset Purpose to Organization	Asset Availability Requirements		
			A°	MTTR	MTBF
IT010330	S/W release and patch management server system	Repository and management of versions and patches to operational S/W	99.99	52	1825
RD020020	Dev. source code archive server	Repository and management of source code for versions of S/W under development	99.99	52	1825
IT030001	SAN edge router-firewall	Controls access between SAN from enterprise intranet	99.999	5.2	2555
IT030010	SAN disk array #1	Provides high availability storage of enterprise files and databases	99.999	5.2	1825
FC090101	Roof HVAC Chiller-Condenser #1	Provides general facility HVAC	99.999	5.2	2555
FC090202	Data Center HVAC Chiller-Condenser #2	Provides data center HVAC	99.999	5.2	2555
FC090302	Backup Power generator #1	Provides standby electrical power	99.999	5.2	2555
SC090501	Security non-water fire suppression system	Non-water-based fire suppression for SOC	99.999	5.2	2555
SC050001	Video surveillance control system	Controls enterprise surveillance cameras and archives video files	99.999	5.2	2555
SC050101	Main entrance camera #1	Provides video surveillance	99.999	5.2	2555
SC050434	Video surveillance hall camera #34	Provides video surveillance	99.999	5.2	2555
SC051001	Physical intrusion detection/alarm control system	Controls enterprise intrusion sensors	99.999	5.2	2555
SC051422	Hall IR sensor #22	Enterprise intrusion sensor	99.999	5.2	2555
SC051512	Data Center IR sensor #12	Enterprise intrusion sensor	99.999	5.2	2555

...

TABLE 4.12. Mapping A° Values into Non-available Time per Year.

Percentage of Time Available (A°)	No. of Seconds of Required Availability per Year	Acceptable No. of Seconds of Non-availability per Year	Acceptable No. of Minutes of Non-availability per Year	Acceptable No. of Hours of Non-availability per Year	Acceptable No. of Days of Non-availability per Year
99.999	31535684.64	315.36	5.256	0.0876	0.00365
99.99	31532846.4	3153.6	52.56	0.876	0.0365
99.9	31504464	31536	525.6	8.76	0.365
99	31220640	315360	5256	87.6	3.65

Table 4.13 could be used to capture this information where the column headings are:

- **Asset ID**—Uniquely identifies a specific asset item.
- **Asset Description**—Description of a specific asset item. The Asset Description column is included for human readability only.
- **Type of Attack Against Asset**—Identifies the type of attack being considered, such as:
  - Unauthorized access (including logging into asset, reading data within asset, remote access to asset) which can be mitigated via identification, authentication, authorization/access, and confidentiality controls;
  - Unauthorized modification (including alteration and deletion of data or software within asset, changing information which controls asset operation) which can be mitigated via identification, authentication, authorization/access, data integrity, information integrity, and non-repudiation controls;
  - Malware (spanning viruses, worms, Trojan horses, keystroke logging, root-kit malicious software which seek to copy, alter, or delete data or software within asset or changing information which controls asset operation) which can be mitigated via anti-malware utilities, intrusion protection systems (IPS), authorization/access controls, and data integrity controls;
  - Flooding (Denial of Service (DoS)) (spanning TCP SYN floods, ICMP message misuse (i.e., ping), ARP floods, UDP ping floods, and real-time transfer protocol (RTP) misuse which seek to disrupt or interfere with asset operation) which can be mitigated via packet filtering (firewalls), IPS, network access controls (IEEE 802.1x), and packet flow monitoring controls;
  - Phishing (which attempts to socially engineer user into divulging login identification and authentication information) which can be mitigated via anti-malware utilities, IPS, user education, and URL blocking controls (white/black listing);
  - Spear-phishing (which attempts to socially engineer user into divulging login identification and authentication information) which can be mitigated via anti-malware utilities, IPS, user education, URL blocking controls (white/black listing);

- Spyware (spanning viruses, worms, Trojan horses, keystroke logging, root-kit malicious software which seek to copy, alter, or delete data or software within asset or changing information which controls asset operation) which can be mitigated via anti-malware utilities, IPS, authorization/access controls, and data integrity controls; and

- Removable media (spanning viruses, worms, Trojan horses, keystroke logging, root-kit malicious software which seek to copy, alter, or delete data or software within asset or changing information which controls asset operation and unauthorized exporting of information) which can be mitigated via anti-malware utilities, IPS, authorization/access controls, and hardware usage controls.

- **Probability of Attack Occurring**—Identifies the probability of the attack occurring as: Low (1), Low to Medium (2), Medium (3), Medium to High (4), High (5).

- **Likely Impact of Attack Against Asset**—Identifies the impact magnitude of the attack occurring successfully as: Low (1), Low to Medium (2), Medium (3), Medium to High (4), High (5).

- **Asset Vulnerability Lever**—Identifies the vulnerability of the asset to attack as probability times impact.

TABLE 4.13. Asset Inventory Attack Vulnerability.

Asset ID	Asset Description	Type of Attack	Probability of Attack Occurring	Impact of Attack	Vulnerability Level
HR000001	Employee Data	Unauthorized access	2	4	8
HR000001	Employee Data	Unauthorized modification	2	4	8
FN000100	Accounts Receivables Data	Unauthorized access	3	5	15
FN000100	Accounts Receivables Data	Unauthorized modification	3	5	15
FN000400	Supplier Contracts Data	Unauthorized access	3	5	15
FN000400	Supplier Contracts Data	Unauthorized modification	3	5	15
IT000001	CER between DMZ and ISP	Unauthorized access	5	5	25
IT000001	CER between DMZ and ISP	Unauthorized modification	5	5	25
IT000001	CER between DMZ and ISP	Malware	2	5	10
IT000001	CER between DMZ and ISP	Flooding (DoS)	5	5	25
IT000002	Router-firewall between DMZ and enterprise intranet	Unauthorized access	4	5	20

Asset ID	Asset Description	Type of Attack	Probability of Attack Occurring	Impact of Attack	Vulnerability Level
IT000002	Router-firewall between DMZ and enterprise intranet	Unauthorized modification	4	5	20
IT000002	Router-firewall between DMZ and enterprise intranet	Flooding (DoS)	4	5	20
IT000002	Router-firewall between DMZ and enterprise intranet	Malware	2	5	10
IT000006	Router-firewall between Customer Support & Call Center subnet and enterprise intranet	Unauthorized access	3	5	15
IT000006	Router-firewall between Customer Support & Call Center subnet and enterprise intranet	Unauthorized modification	3	5	15
IT000006	Router-firewall between Customer Support & Call Center subnet and enterprise intranet	Flooding (DoS)	3	5	15
IT001001	HR VP Workstation	Unauthorized access	4	3	12
IT001001	HR VP Workstation	Unauthorized modification	4	3	12
IT001001	HR VP Workstation	Malware	5	4	20
IT001001	HR VP Workstation	Phishing	5	2	10
IT001001	HR VP Workstation	Spear-phishing	5	3	15
IT001001	HR VP Workstation	Spyware	5	3	15
IT001001	HR VP Workstation	Removable media	5	3	15
IT001203	R&D Manager Workstation	Unauthorized access	4	3	12
IT001203	R&D Manager Workstation	Unauthorized modification	4	3	12
IT001203	R&D Manager Workstation	Malware	5	4	20
IT001203	R&D Manager Workstation	Phishing	5	2	10
IT001203	R&D Manager Workstation	Spear-phishing	5	3	15
IT001203	R&D Manager Workstation	Spyware	5	3	15
IT001203	R&D Manager Workstation	Removable media	5	3	15

(*continued*)

TABLE 4.13. (*cont'd*)

Asset ID	Asset Description	Type of Attack	Probability of Attack Occurring	Impact of Attack	Vulnerability Level
IT010010	Finance server system	Unauthorized access	3	5	15
IT010010	Finance server system	Unauthorized modification	3	5	15
IT010010	Finance server system	Malware	5	4	20
IT010010	Finance server system	Removable media	5	3	15
IT010010	Finance server system	Flooding (DoS)	3	5	15
IT010030	Sales e-commerce web server	Unauthorized access	5	5	25
IT010030	Sales e-commerce web server	Unauthorized modification	5	5	25
IT010030	Sales e-commerce web server	Malware	5	4	20
IT010030	Sales e-commerce web server	Removable media	5	3	15
IT010030	Sales e-commerce web server	Flooding (DoS)	5	5	25
IT010040	Marketing server system	Unauthorized access	3	5	15
IT010040	Marketing server system	Unauthorized modification	3	5	15
IT010040	Marketing server system	Malware	5	4	20
IT010040	Marketing server system	Removable media	5	3	15
IT010040	Marketing server system	Flooding (DoS)	3	5	15
SC010020	Security central Syslog server	Unauthorized access	4	5	20
SC010020	Security central Syslog server	Unauthorized modification	4	5	20
SC010020	Security central Syslog server	Malware	5	4	20
SC010020	Security central Syslog server	Removable media	5	3	15
SC010020	Security central Syslog server	Flooding (DoS)	4	5	20
RD020020	Dev. source code archive server	Unauthorized access	4	3	12
RD020020	Dev. source code archive server	Unauthorized modification	4	3	12
RD020020	Dev. source code archive server	Malware	5	4	20
RD020020	Dev. source code archive server	Removable media	5	3	15

Asset ID	Asset Description	Type of Attack	Probability of Attack Occurring	Impact of Attack	Vulnerability Level
RD020020	Dev. source code archive server	Flooding (DoS)	3	5	15
SC050001	Video surveillance control system	Unauthorized access	4	3	12
SC050001	Video surveillance control system	Unauthorized modification	4	3	12
SC050001	Video surveillance control system	Malware	5	4	20
SC050001	Video surveillance control system	Removable media	5	3	15
SC050001	Video surveillance control system	Flooding (DoS)	3	5	15
...					

Table 4.14 can be used to capture this information where the column headings are:

- **Asset ID**—Uniquely identifies a specific asset item.
- **Asset Description**—Description of a specific asset item. The Asset Description column is included for human readability only.
- **Type of Information Stored Within Asset**—Identifies the type of information the asset represents, stores, or processes such as, but not limited to, personnel, sales, customer, contracts, marketing, PII, financial, R&D, administrative, manufacturing (such as ERP data), OAM&P, and security.
- **Classification Level of the Information Stored Within Asset**—Identifies the classification level of the information the asset represents, stores, or processes, such as, but not limited to:
  - **4**=Assets classified as **Client-Attorney Privileged** or **Trade Secret** are information that, if disclosed, would likely result in extremely significant financial damage to the organization including probable criminal or civil actions or loss of competitive advantage over other enterprises/businesses;
  - **3**=Assets classified as **Confidential** or **Proprietary** are information that, if disclosed, would likely result in very significant financial damage to the organization including probable criminal or civil actions or loss of competitive advantage over other enterprises/businesses;
  - **2**=Assets classified as **Internal Use Only** are information that, if disclosed, would likely result in financial damage to the organization including possible criminal or civil actions or loss of competitive advantage over other enterprises/businesses;
  - **1**=Assets classified as **Public** are information that is freely available to the general public.

- **Asset Sensitivity**—Identifies the degree of concern regarding the level of protection necessary for information about the asset or the information processed, stored, or produced by the asset:
  - ○ **4** = Extremely sensitive assets require extremely strong authentication, authorization access, confidentiality, data integrity, and non-repudiation controls;
  - ○ **3** = Highly sensitive assets require very strong authentication, authorization access, confidentiality, data integrity, and non-repudiation controls;
  - ○ **2** = Moderately sensitive assets require strong authentication, authorization access, confidentiality, data integrity, and non-repudiation controls;
  - ○ **1** = Non-sensitive assets require authentication, authorization access, confidentiality, and data integrity controls.
- **Asset Criticality**—Identifies the degree of criticality of the asset to the organization's ability to conduct business activities:
  - ○ **12 or 16** = Extremely Critical assets provide capabilities that, if damaged or destroyed, would prevent or jeopardize the continuation of normal, or even degraded, organizational activities;
  - ○ **4, 6, or 9** = Highly Critical assets provide capabilities that, if damaged or destroyed, would degrade or jeopardize organizational activities to levels, or capabilities, below normal levels;
  - ○ **2 to 3** = Moderately Critical assets provide capabilities that support, or supplement, normal organizational activities and, if such assets were damaged or destroyed, would cause long-term problems with normal activities;
  - ○ **1** = Non-Critical assets provide capabilities that enhance normal organizational activities and, if such assets were damaged or destroyed, would not cause long-term problems with normal activities.
- **Asset Risk Level**—Represents Asset Criticality multiplied by an asset's Vulnerability Level and quantifies the degree of risk that the asset, or the information within the asset, is no longer available for supporting the organization's normal activities or the magnitude of damage to the organization due to a security-related attack or breach, where a value of:
  - ○ **340 to 400** = Extremely High risk to asset capabilities or financial value of information within asset;
  - ○ **270 to 339** = High risk to asset capabilities or financial value of information within asset;
  - ○ **200 to 269** = Moderate-High risk to asset capabilities or financial value of information within asset;
  - ○ **120 to 189** = Moderate risk to asset capabilities or financial value of information within asset;
  - ○ **61 to 119** = Moderate-Low risk to asset capabilities or financial value of information within asset;
  - ○ **1 to 60** = Low risk to asset capabilities or financial value of information within asset.

TABLE 4.14. **Asset Inventory Information Criticality Partial Example.**

Asset ID	Asset Description	Type of Information	Info. Classif. level	Asset Sensitivity Level	Asset Criticality	Asset Risk Level
HR000001	Employee Data	Personnel, PII	3	3	9	72
FN000100	Accounts Receivables Data	Financial, PII	3	3	9	72
FN000400	Supplier Contracts Data	PII	3	3	9	135
IT000001	CER between DMZ and ISP	Security, Operations	3	4	12	300
IT000002	Router-firewall between DMZ and enterprise intranet	Security, Operations	3	4	12	240
IT000006	Router-firewall between Customer Support & Call Center subnet and enterprise intranet	Security, Operations	3	4	12	180
IT001001	HR VP Workstation	Personnel, PII	4	3	12	240
IT001203	R&D Manager Workstation	R&D	3	2	6	240
IT010010	Finance server system	Financial	4	3	12	240
IT010030	Sales e-commerce web server	Sales, PII	3	3	9	225
IT010040	Marketing server system	Marketing	3	2	6	120
SC010020	Security central Syslog server	Security, Operations	4	4	16	320
RD020020	Dev. source code archive server	R&D	3	2	6	120
SC050001	Video surveillance control system	Security	3	3	9	180
...						

When an asset has multiple Vulnerability Levels associated with it, the highest Vulnerability Level value should be used in this calculation.

The Asset Risk Level would be used to establish priorities for allocating organizational funds for selection and deployment of appropriate security controls sufficient to reduce the Asset Risk Level to an acceptable level. More will be said about risk mitigation analysis in Section 4.2.3.

4.2.2 New System Impact Analysis

For new systems/sub-systems, one should begin by performing a Risk Impact Analysis during the Requirements Gathering and Analysis Phase. The Risk Impact Analysis is a technique used to identify and assess risks that may jeopardize project or system development success or the ability of a proposed project or system to provide specified functions or capabilities. A Risk Impact Analysis should include a cost–benefit analysis that covers:

- Features and benefits of the security capabilities and controls within the system or process being analyzed; namely, how said security capabilities and controls will mitigate the likelihood of the system or process being compromised (successfully attacked/breached or authorized access abused);
- Costs of the security capabilities and controls within the system or process; both the acquisition (procurement and/or development) along with the operation and maintenance costs (documentation development, user and infrastructure support training, and possible upgrades);
- Costs should be examined in terms of dollars and staffing implications;
- Consideration of the impact if proposed security capabilities and controls are not approved; namely, how would not moving forward impact:
  - the competitive advantage of the organization?
  - the organization's ability to meet the mission of the organization?
  - strategic business partners, suppliers, vendors, and other stakeholders?
  - the organization's ability to meet legal or regulatory compliance issues?

TABLE 4.15. Project Risk Impact Analysis Questionnaire Example.

Issue	Applicable Y/N	Comments
Will the proposed security capabilities and controls place unacceptable demands on any computer resources required for the development, test, or operating environments?		
Must any tools be acquired to implement and test the proposed security capabilities and controls?		
How will the proposed security capabilities and controls affect the sequence, dependencies, effort, or duration of any tasks currently in the project plan?		
Will prototyping or other user input be required to verify the proposed security capabilities and controls?		
How much effort that has already been invested in the project will be lost if the proposed security capabilities and controls are accepted?		
Will the proposed security capabilities and controls cause an increase in product unit cost, such as by increasing third-party product licensing fees?		
Will the proposed security capabilities and controls affect any marketing, manufacturing, training, or customer support plans?		

Table 4.15 shows an example Risk Impact Analysis Questionnaire that can help to record and organize Risk Impact Analysis–related information. The reader should NOT consider this example questionnaire as covering all risk impact areas; rather the example provides a starting point only.

Table 4.16 shows a possible risk impact analysis weighting scheme to help quantify the magnitude of different risk impacts to the organization.

In the weighting scheme shown in Table 4.16, one would use the numeric values to record the magnitude of impact for each of the listed criteria. If one then summed the Risk Impact Magnitude Values obtained, one will get a snapshot of the aggregate risk impact of the project ranging from a bottom-end aggregate score of five (very low risk impact) to a top-end aggregate score of 25 (very high risk impact). For example, if the analysis determined that:

- Project Development Cost impact would be recorded as a 4 if the cost was estimated to be in the range of $2 to $4 million;
- Technology Usage impact would be recorded as a 1 if "The project will use off-the-shelf third-party-supplied security capabilities and controls that do not require customization";
- Development Process impact would be recorded as a 3 if "There are significant changes needed to existing documentation, procedures, or training for development staff";
- Operational impact would be recorded as a 4 if "Documentation must be developed and training required for end-users and operations staff"; and
- Decommissioning Cost impact would be recorded as a 1 if the cost to remove and discard the proposed system was estimated to be less than $500 K

then the aggregate risk impact score would be 12 representing a moderate risk impact level.

An Impact Analysis report should be produced that captures business reasons that justify the decision to move forward with the project or system regardless of the aggregate risk impact level calculated. This report will be used twice:

- Once when the decision is made whether to proceed with the project or system, and
- Then again when a third party (such as external auditors or attorneys) asks the management to show its decision-making process.

A Risk Analysis Report should, at a minimum, cover the following areas:

1. Name of project and brief description;
2. Project champion/owner;
3. Business reason or need for project;
4. Estimated risk level of project in terms of:
   - Money
   - Time
   - Resources

TABLE 4.16. Risk Impact Analysis Weighting Example.

Risk Area	Risk Impact Magnitude Value	Risk Impact Magnitude Range or Criteria
Development or Acquisition Cost Impact of proposed security capabilities and controls	1 2 3 4 5	Less than $500 K $500 K–$1 M $1 M–$2 M $2 M–$4 M $4 M or greater
Technology Used Impact by proposed security capabilities and controls	1	The project will use off-the-shelf third-party-supplied security capabilities and controls that do not require customization
	2	The project will use in-house developed security capabilities and controls based on standard methodologies and technology
	3	The project will use in-house developed security capabilities and controls that are not proven or in wide use
	4	The project will use security capabilities and controls developed with third-party resources outside of organizational control with technology that is proven and in wide use
	5	The project will use security capabilities and controls developed with third-party resources outside of organizational control with technology that is not proven or in wide use
Development Process Impact for proposed security capabilities and controls	1	There are no significant changes needed to existing documentation, procedures, or training for development staff
	2	
	3	There are significant changes needed to existing documentation, procedures, or training for development staff
	4	
	5	Documentation, procedure, and training requirements for development staff are not known
Operational Impact of proposed security capabilities and controls	1	There is no significant new documentation, procedures, or training required
	2	Documentation is provided by the vendor. End-users of the system are the only group for which training is required
	3	There is significant new documentation, procedures, or training required for end-users
	4	Documentation must be developed and training is required for end-users and operations staff
	5	Documentation and training requirements are not known
Decommissioning Impact of proposed security capabilities and controls	1 2 3 4 5	Less than $500 K $500 K to $1 M $1 M to $2 M $2 M to $4 M $4 M or greater

TABLE 4.17. Example 5-Point Impact Scale.

Impact Factor	Definition
Low (1)	Single work group or department affected. Little or no impact on the business processes
Low to Medium (2)	One or more departments affected. Slight delay in meeting mission objectives
Medium (3)	Two or more departments or a business unit is affected. Four to six hour delay in meeting mission objectives
Medium to High (4)	Two or more departments or a business unit is affected. One to two day delay in meeting mission objectives
High (5)	Entire mission of the enterprise is affected. Significant delay in meeting mission objectives

TABLE 4.18. Example 5-Point Probability Scale.

Probability Factor	Definition
Low (1)	Extremely unlikely that an impact causing event will occur during the next 12 months
Low to Medium (2)	Unlikely that an impact causing event will occur during the next 12 months
Medium (3)	Possible that an impact causing event will occur during the next 12 months
Medium to High (4)	Likely that an impact causing event will occur during the next 12 months
High (5)	Highly likely that an impact causing event will occur during the next 12 months

TABLE 4.19. Probability Versus Impact Composite Values.

		Event Impact Level				
		Low	Low to Medium	Medium	Medium to High	High
Event Probability Occuring	Low	Low	Low	Low	Moderate Low	Moderate Low
	Low to Medium	Low	Moderate Low	Medium	Moderate High	Moderate High
	Medium	Low	Moderate Low	Medium	Moderate High	High
	Medium to High	Moderate Low	Medium	Moderate High	High	High
	High	Moderate Low	Medium	Moderate High	High	High

5. Regulatory impact;
6. Infrastructure impact;
7. Maintenance cost; and
8. Time line (schedule).

In Table 4.17 and Table 4.18 are proposed semi-quantitative approaches for capturing impact and probability of occurrence using 5-point scales which also use colors to highlight impact level and probability of occurrence.

Table 4.19 demonstrates how event probability and likely impact can be related to arrive at a composite value.

4.2.3 Risk Mitigation Analysis

During the Risk Assessment Analysis, one identifies:

- the assets at risk (part of the asset inventory development process);
- the unintentional events that could render these assets inoperative (unavailable); and
- the intentional events (attacks) that could render these assets either inoperative (unavailable), degrade asset usefulness, alter asset behavior, or compromise (damage, delete, change, steal) information within assets.

Unintentional events can be of non-human origin (i.e., natural events like forest fires, flooding, wind, earthquakes, hurricanes, tornadoes) or of human origin (i.e., non-malicious operational errors or other non-malicious events such as nearby firefighter activities, utility personnel activities, vehicle accidents, etc.). Intentional events constitute direct threats to assets, and available or appropriate threat (event, threat agent, and attack activity/vector) mitigation techniques (both procedural and technical mechanisms) are necessary to reduce or eliminate the magnitude of damage that such an event occurrence can produce. This analysis is used to determine what events exist that can affect an asset, the risk level associated with occurrence of the event, and the recommended approach to reducing (mitigating) the probability of an identified event. Table 4.20 highlights a number of example natural and human unintentional events that can affect assets.

Unintentional events such as power loss (blackouts) can be caused by human activities or by natural events and can, therefore, be classified under either the natural or human categories. Even though the aforementioned unintentional events are not malicious, such events need to be considered as part of an organization's risk analysis. There is also a group of unintentional (non-malicious) human events that can leave an organization's assets exposed to intentional events (i.e., attacks) and should be considered as malicious security events. More specifically, these unintentional (non-malicious) human events represent erroneous operational (configuration-, setup-, or use-related) activities by organizational personnel which make organizational assets vulnerable to attacks by insider or outsider groups or individuals.

TABLE 4.20. Example Unintentional (Non-malicious) Events.

Security Event	Should Be Considered?	Probability of Occurrence	Asset Impact	Existing Control?	Residual Risk Level	Residual Risk Acceptable?
Unintended natural events						
High winds (30–60 mph)	Yes	Twice per year	Low	None	Low	Yes
Hurricane (70 to 100 mph)	Yes	Once in 10 years	Moderate	None	Low	Yes
Hurricane (100 to 130 mph)	Yes	Once in 20 years	High	Backup site	Low	Yes
Hurricane (130 to 150 mph)	Yes	Once in 30 years	High	Backup site	Low	Yes
Lightning strikes	Yes	Once per month	High	Lightning arrestors	Low	Yes
High water flooding	Yes	Once per year	High	Backup site	Low	Yes
Earthquake	No					
Tornado	Yes	Once in 50 years	High	Backup site	Low	Yes
Forest fire	No					
Asteroid/comet impact	No					
Roof collapse due to snow	Yes	Once in 10 years	High	Annual structural inspections	Low	Yes
...						
Unintentional human caused events						
Power surge—high voltage conditions	Yes	6 times per month	Moderate	UPS	Low	Yes
Power sag—low voltage conditions	Yes	6 times per month	Moderate	UPS	Low	Yes
Minor blackout—brownout or loss of power for less that 30 minutes	Yes	Once per 3 months	Moderate	UPS	Low	Yes
Moderate blackout—loss of power for less that 36 hours	Yes	Once per year	Moderate to High	Backup generator	Low	Yes

(continued)

TABLE 4.20. (*cont'd*)

Security Event	Should Be Considered?	Probability of Occurrence	Asset Impact	Existing Control?	Residual Risk Level	Residual Risk Acceptable?
Major blackout—loss of power for more than 36 hours	Yes	Once in 10 years	Moderate to High	Backup site	Low	Yes
Flooding—plumbing related	Yes	Once in 5 years	High	Regular monitoring and isolation	Low	Yes
Flooding—fire sprinkler system failures	Yes	Once in 10 years	High	Annual inspections	Low	Yes
Flooding—firefighting related	Yes	Once in 20 years	High	None	High	Yes
Fire related	Yes	Once per year	High	Fire sprinkler system	Low	Yes
...						

Note: UPS, Uninterruptible Power Supply.

4.2.4 Malicious Security Events and Threat Assessment

As noted earlier, intentional events represent direct security threats to assets and require that appropriate threat mitigation controls are necessary to reduce, or eliminate, the occurrence of the malicious event or the magnitude of damage that such an event occurrence can produce. These direct security threats are typically malicious activities specifically attempting to:

- steal organizational information assets;
- alter organizational information assets;
- falsify organizational information assets;
- destroy organizational information assets;
- alter the behavior of organizational networking and computing assets;
- misuse organizational networking and computing assets;
- interfere with organizational networking and computing asset functionality;
- prevent or interfere with legitimate access to organizational information, networking, and computing assets;
- steal login/account information of an organization's employees; and
- gather intelligence about organizational information, networking, and computing assets.

One should also consider erroneous operational activities by organizational personnel as a form of threats to organizational assets.

Threat assessment (establishing the risk level) provides the organization with the information needed to make decisions regarding the selection of appropriate controls, measures, safeguards, or countermeasures to lower the risk of a threat causing damage to an acceptable level. A security risk is a function of the probability that an identified threat (event, threat agent, and attack activity/vector) will occur and the magnitude of the impact on the ability of the organization to provide products or services. Security risk assessment is commonly referred to as risk management and encompasses seven primary steps:

- Asset definition, identification, and inventorying (which are covered as part of the asset inventory);
- Security threat identification;
- Probability of security threat event occurrence;
- Security threat event impact analysis;
- Residual security threat risk level determination;
- Security control(s) recommendations; and
- Security threat assessment results documentation.

Following asset definition, identification, and inventory assembly, the types of events that could cause damage to, or render inoperative, assets need to be examined. A threat is the potential for a particular event to successfully steal, alter, damage, or make unavailable an asset. Put another way, an identified threat can be considered as the potential for a particular event to successfully exercise a particular vulnerability of an asset based on the following definitions:

- **Threat**—an undesirable event that could impact the business objectives, value, or mission of the organization's asset;
- **Vulnerability**—a weakness in a system or control that can be exploited to violate the system's intended behavior;
- **Threat Impact**—the effect or result of an event occurring that affects the business objective or mission of the enterprise;
- **Threat Probability**—the likelihood that an event will occur.

A complete list of threats should be constructed, and the following techniques can assist in this activity:

- Brainstorming;
- Checklist;
- Historical data; and
- Annual rates of occurrence.

Also consider contacting Law enforcement, Insurance underwriters, and other centers for information regarding the types of events likely to occur in the area where the asset(s) are located or to be deployed alone with the probability of a specific event occurrence. Some excellent sources of security-related vulnerability and threat information are:

- U.S. Computer Emergency Readiness Team (http://www.us-cert.gov/);
- The MITRE Common Vulnerabilities and Exposures (CVE) website (http://cve.mitre.org/);
- The MITRE Common Weakness Enumeration (CWE) website (http://cwe.mitre.org/); and
- The Carnegie Mellon University (CMU) CERT Coordination Center (CERT/CC) (http://www.cert.org/certcc.html).

Table 4.21 shows a partial sample list of human-initiated malicious threats.
Following are some definitions and explanations included in Table 4.21:

- Table column headings are:
  - **Threat**—Refers to some form of activity by an individual or a group which the organization considers a threat to the assets of the organization;

TABLE 4.21. Example Threats, Associated Attributes, Controls, and Residual Risks.

Threat	Should Be Considered?	Probability of Occurrence	Threat Impact	Existing Control?	Residual Risk Level	Residual Risk Acceptable?
Outsider—system hacking	Yes	1 per month	High	Centralized authentication	Moderate	No
Outsider—social engineering	Yes	2 per year	Moderate	Every 6 months user training	Low	Yes
Outsider—dumpster diving	Yes	1 per month	Moderate	Locked dumpsters	Low	Yes
Outsider—phishing	Yes	10 per month	Moderate	Every 6 months user training	Low	Yes
Outsider—spear-phishing	Yes	1 per month	High	Every 6 months user training	Low	Yes
Outsider—DDoS attack	Yes	5 per month	High	Network firewall	Moderate	No
Outsider—worm	Yes	10 per month	High	Host anti-malware	Moderate	No
Outsider—rootkit	Yes	5 per month	High	Host anti-malware	Moderate	No
Outsider—virus	Yes	20 per month	High	Host anti-malware	Moderate	No
Outsider—invalid access to internal WiFi subnets	Yes	1 per month	High	802.11 WEP	High	No
Outsider—SAINT, SATAN, ISS-based intel. gathering	Yes	1 per month	High	Network firewall	High	No
...						
Employee—system hacking	Yes	1 per month	High	Centralized authentication	Moderate	No
Employee—worm	Yes	10 per month	High	Host anti-malware	Moderate	No
Employee—Trojan horse	Yes	5 per month	High	Host anti-malware	Moderate	No
Employee—virus	Yes	20 per month	High	Host anti-malware	Moderate	No
Employee—security-related programming errors	Yes	1 per 1000 lines of code	Moderate	Peer code reviews	Moderate	No
Employee—administrative operational errors	Yes	5 per month	High	Every 6 months user training	Moderate	No
Employee—unauthorized access	Yes	5 per month	High	Every 6 months user training	Moderate	No
Employee—unauthorized copying files	Yes	10 per month	High	Every 6 months user training	Moderate	No
Employee—use of social networks or IM	Yes	10 per day	High	Every 6 months user training	Moderate	No
Employee—browsing gambling websites	Yes	10 per day	High	Every 6 months user training	Moderate	No

(continued)

TABLE 4.21. (cont'd)

Threat	Should Be Considered?	Probability of Occurrence	Threat Impact	Existing Control?	Residual Risk Level	Residual Risk Acceptable?
Employee—invalid access to internal WiFi subnets	Yes	1 per month	Moderate	802.11 WEP	Moderate	No
Employee—invalid access to internal wired subnets	Yes	1 per month	Moderate	None	Moderate	No
Employee—SAINT, SATAN, ISS-based intel. gathering	Yes	1 per month	High	Intranet network firewalls	High	No
...						
MtoM peering—malicious incoming SIP messages	Yes	5 per month	High	Network firewall	Moderate	No
MtoM peering—invalid RTP messages	Yes	5 per month	High	Network firewall	Moderate	No
MtoM peering—invalid DNS interaction with outside DNS servers	Yes	10 per day	High	None	High	No
MtoM peering—false OSPF route updates	Yes	10 per day	High	None	High	No
...						
Inside 3rd Party—system hacking	Yes	1 per year	High	Centralized authentication	Moderate	No
Inside 3rd Party—worm	Yes	10 per month	High	Host anti-malware	Moderate	No
Inside 3rd Party—Trojan horse	Yes	5 per month	High	Host anti-malware	Moderate	No
Inside 3rd Party—virus	Yes	20 per month	High	Host anti-malware	Moderate	No
Inside 3rd Party—unauthorized access	Yes	5 per month	High	Per host access controls	Moderate	No
Inside 3rd Party—unauthorized copying files	Yes	10 per month	High	Per host access controls	Moderate	No
Inside 3rd Party—invalid access to internal WiFi subnets	Yes	1 per month	Moderate	802.11 WEP	Moderate	No
Inside 3rd Party—invalid access to internal wired subnets	Yes	1 per month	Moderate	None	Moderate	No
Inside 3rd Party—SAINT, SATAN, ISS-based intel. gathering	Yes	1 per month	High	Intranet network firewalls	High	No
...						

- ○ **Should Be Considered?**—Refers to whether the organization considers the threat one that needs to be mitigated;
- ○ **Probability of Occurrence**—Refers to the likelihood of the threat occurring;
- ○ **Threat Impact**—Refers to the degree of damage the threat could inflict on the organizational asset if the threat occurred;
- ○ **Existing Control?**—Refers to some form of technical control or procedural mechanism that has been deployed by the organization to mitigate the impact, or likely occurrence, of the threat damaging an organizational asset;
- ○ **Residual Risk Level**—Refers to the level of risk remaining following the deployment of existing risk mitigation/control mechanisms; and
- ○ **Residual Risk Acceptable?**—Refers to whether the organization considers the Residual Risk level acceptable from a "cost of doing business" perspective.

- An Outsider is some person or organization attempting to access organizational assets for malicious purposes;
- System hacking includes most or all forms of unauthorized login into, modification of, or access to organizational system or informational assets;
- Centralized authentication refers to the use of RADIUS or equivalent form of centralized Authentication, Authorization, and Accounting (AAA) protocol and associated server(s);
- Spear-phishing is specially crafted phishing messages targeting specific organizational employees;
- DDoS refers to Distributed Denial of Service (DDoS) attacks against an organization's networking and computing assets;
- Network firewall refers to a stateful packet filtering function within the organization's edge router that provides the organization with Internet access;
- Host anti-malware refers to some form of anti-virus/worm/spyware utility installed on an individual's organization-owned computer (server, workstation, laptop, PC, etc.);
- WiFi refers to an organization's use of wireless networking based on the IEEE 802.11 standard (either 802.11a, 802.11b, or 802.11g);
- WEP refers to the Wired Equivalent Privacy security mechanism used by 802.11a, 802.11b, or 802.11g wireless network devices;
- SAINT, SATAN, Nmap, Nessus, Metasploit, and ISS are examples of available utilities that can be used for scanning networks, identifying network addresses in use, devices attached to networks, device network applications enabled, and other data that facilitate network-based attacks on an organization's networking and computing assets;
- Employee refers to any individual that is employed by the organization;

- Security-related programming errors refers to deficiencies in in-house developed software and "shell" scripts that create exploitable vulnerabilities;
- Administrative operational errors refers to deficiencies in operational procedures or activities that create exploitable vulnerabilities;
- Unauthorized access refers to attempts to access organizational assets where access has not been authorized;
- Unauthorized copying files refers to attempts to copy organizational information assets to removable media or sending said information to remote locations where such copying or transmission has not been authorized;
- Use of social networks or instant messaging (IM) refers to the use of social networking applications/websites, peer-to-peer sharing networks, or IM applications where such use has not been authorized and is prohibited by the organization's information security policies;
- Browsing gambling websites refers to connecting to websites, be they for gambling, sex, or other activities, or subjects where such activity has not been authorized and is prohibited by the organization's information security policies;
- Machine to machine (MtoM) peering refers to forms of computer to computer communication;
- Malicious incoming Session Initiation Protocol (SIP) messages refers to the use of the SIP to steal organizational services or engage in any other malicious activities;
- Invalid RTP messages refers to the use of the Time Protocol to steal organizational services or engage in any other malicious activities;
- Invalid Domain Name System (DNS) interaction with outside DNS servers refers to situations where:
  ○ organizational systems are redirected to false/invalid DNS servers;
  ○ organizational systems receive DNS replies from false/invalid DNS servers; or
  ○ organizational DNS server information is modified/changed/deleted due to attacker activities.
- False Open Shortest Path First (OSPF) routing protocol route updates refers to either an attacker interfering with the valid distribution of OSPF route update messages or the attacker fabricating such messages for the purpose of disrupting normal organizational network packet forwarding behavior; and
- Inside 3rd Party refers to any individual who is not an organization employee but is granted in-house (physical) access to organizational, physical, information, computing, or networking assets; examples of such individuals include janitorial personnel, vendor service personnel, visitors, guests, etc.

Table 4.22 represents a second iteration of Table 4.21, which highlights consideration of additional new controls to further mitigate risks associated with these human-initiated malicious threats not acceptably mitigated as shown in Table 4.21.

TABLE 4.22. Example Reduction of Residual Risks via Additional Controls.

Threat	Existing Control?	Residual Risk Level	Residual Risk Acceptable?	Proposed New Additional Controls	New Residual Risk Level	New Residual Risk Acceptable?
Outsider—system hacking	Centralized authentication	Moderate	No	RBAC	Low	Yes
Outsider—social engineering	Every 6 months user training	Low	Yes	None needed	–	–
Outsider—dumpster diving	Locked dumpsters	Low	Yes	None needed	–	–
Outsider—phishing	Every 6 months user training	Low	Yes	None needed	–	–
Outsider—spear-phishing	Every 6 months user training	Low	Yes	None needed	–	–
Outsider—D(SoS) attack	Network firewall	Moderate	No	Network IPS	Low	Yes
Outsider—worm	Host anti-malware	Moderate	No	Network IPS	Low	Yes
Outsider—rootkit	Host anti-malware	Moderate	No	Network IPS	Low	Yes
Outsider—virus	Host anti-malware	Moderate	No	Network IPS	Low	Yes
Outsider—invalid access to internal WiFi subnets	802.11 WEP	High	No	IEEE 802.11i	Low	Yes
Outsider—SAINT, SATAN, ISS-based intel. gathering	Network firewall	High	No	Network IPS	Low	Yes
...						
Employee—system hacking	Centralized authentication	Moderate	No	RBAC	Low	Yes
Employee—worm	Host anti-malware	Moderate	No	Host IPS	Low	Yes
Employee—Trojan horse	Host anti-malware	Moderate	No	Host IPS	Low	Yes
Employee—virus	Host anti-malware	Moderate	No	Host IPS	Low	Yes
Employee—security-related programming errors	Peer code reviews	Moderate	No	Source code scanning	Low	Yes
Employee—administrative operational errors	Every 6 months user training	Moderate	No	RBAC	Low	Yes

(continued)

TABLE 4.22. *(cont'd)*

Threat	Existing Control?	Residual Risk Level	Residual Risk Acceptable?	Proposed New Additional Controls	New Residual Risk Level	New Residual Risk Acceptable?
Employee—unauthorized access	Every 6 months user training	Moderate	No	RBAC	Low	Yes
Employee—unauthorized copying files	Every 6 months user training	Moderate	No	ACLs	Low	Yes
Employee—use of social networks or IM	Every 6 months user training	Moderate	No	Network IPS	Low	Yes
Employee—browsing gambling websites	Every 6 months user training	Moderate	No	Host IPS	Low	Yes
Employee—invalid access to internal WiFi subnets	802.11 WEP	Moderate	No	IEEE 802.11i	Low	Yes
Employee—invalid access to internal wired subnets	None	Moderate	No	IEEE 802.1x	Low	Yes
Employee—SAINT, SATAN, ISS-based intel. gathering	Intranet network firewalls	High	No	Network IPS	Low	Yes
...						
MtoM peering—malicious incoming SIP messages	Network firewall	Moderate	No	SBC	Low	Yes
MtoM peering—invalid RTP messages	Network firewall	Moderate	No	SBC	Low	Yes
MtoM peering—invalid DNS replies from outside DNS servers	None	High	No	DNSSEC, IPsec/PKI	Low	Yes
MtoM peering—false OSPF route updates	None	High	No	IPsec/PKI	Low	Yes
...						
Inside 3rd Party—system hacking	Centralized authentication	Moderate	No	RBAC	Low	Yes

Inside 3rd Party—worm	Host anti-malware	Moderate	No	Host IPS	Low	Yes
Inside 3rd Party—Trojan horse	Host anti-malware	Moderate	No	Host IPS	Low	Yes
Inside 3rd Party—virus	Host anti-malware	Moderate	No	Host IPS	Low	Yes
Inside 3rd Party—unauthorized access	Per host access controls	Moderate	No	RBAC	Low	Yes
Inside 3rd Party—unauthorized copying files	Per host access controls	Moderate	No	ACLs	Low	Yes
Inside 3rd Party—invalid access to internal WiFi subnets	802.11 WEP	Moderate	No	IEEE 802.11i	Low	Yes
Inside 3rd Party—invalid access to internal wired subnets	None	Moderate	No	IEEE 802.1x	Low	Yes
Inside 3rd Party—SAINT, SATAN, ISS-based intel. gathering	Intranet network firewalls	High	No	Network IPS	Low	Yes

...

Following are some definitions and explanations included in Table 4.22.

- New table column headings are:
  - **Proposed New Additional Controls**—Refers to proposed technical or procedural controls that could/should be deployed in addition to technical or procedural controls already deployed;
  - **New Residual Risk Level**—Refers to the level of risk that would result from deploying the proposed new technical or procedural controls;
  - **New Residual Risk Acceptable?**—Refers to whether the new Residual Risk level can be considered an acceptable "cost of doing business."
- RBAC refers to Role-Based Access Controls within server and workstation operating systems;
- Network IPS refers to Intrusion Protection functionality deployed within a router or a standalone network device;
- IEEE 802.11i refers to the IEEE-specified replacement mechanism for 802.11g- and 802.11n-based wireless network devices which relies on IEEE 802.1x, RADIUS authentication servers, and symmetric Advanced Encryption Standard;
- Host IPS refers to Intrusion Protection functionality deployed within a server, workstation, laptop, or PC device;
- Source code scanning refers to any one of a number of commercial utilities designed to scan and analyze application source code looking for coding errors and program logic that result in software logic vulnerabilities that can be exploited;
- Access Control Lists (ACLs) refers to an access enforcement within server and workstation operating systems by which use of removable media can be tightly controlled;
- IEEE 802.1x refers to the IEEE specified layer two network access control mechanism which provides the equivalent of an "electronic lock" to prevent usage of an organization's intranet prior to successful authentication and authorization;
- Session Boarder Control (SBC) refers to a function typically deployed in routers that provides monitoring, inspection, and analysis of SIP signaling messages so as to provide the ability to accept or block SIP messages entering into, or departing from, an organization's intranet;
- DNSSEC refers to the use of DNS Security extensions that enforce verification of DNS system data updates and allow DNS replies to queries to be verified as coming from an authentic DNS server;
- IPsec refers to IP Security which provides authentication, data integrity, and data confidentiality services for gateway-to-gateway, gateway-to-end device, and end-device-to-end-device communications activities;
- PKI refers to Public Key Infrastructures which are a collection of digital certificate issuing systems organized in a verifiable hierarchy that ensure that a user of system has the correct asymmetric public key that is associated with a specific identity.

TABLE 4.23. Threat Mitigation Priority by Probability Versus Impact.

		Threat Impact Level				
		Low	Low to Medium	Medium	Medium to High	High
Threat Probability	**Low**	Low	Low	Low	Moderate Low	Moderate Low
	Low to Medium	Low	Moderate Low	Moderate	Moderate High	Moderate High
	Medium	Low	Moderate Low	Moderate	Moderate High	High
	Medium to High	Moderate Low	Moderate	Moderate High	High	High
	High	Moderate Low	Moderate	Moderate High	High	High

TABLE 4.24. New Risk Mitigation Priority.

Color	Action
High	Immediate action should be considered to further mitigate the impact or occurrence likelihood of the threat
Moderate High	Near-term action should be considered to further mitigate the impact or occurrence likelihood of the threat (within the next 4–6 months)
Moderate	Action should be considered in the near future to further mitigate the impact or occurrence likelihood of the threat (within the next 6–12 months)
Moderate Low	Continue to monitor situation
Low	No action required at this time

In Table 4.21 and Table 4.22, the columns titled "Residual Risk Level" and "New Residual Risk Level" could be specified using a 3-point scale (High, Medium, Low) or a 5-point scale (High, Medium-High, Medium, Medium-Low, and Low).

Once the threats have been identified, recorded, and quantified, the next question is whether a specific risk needs to be dealt with (further mitigated) immediately or some time later. The color coding approach of Probability Versus Impact Composite Values (shown in Table 4.23 and Table 4.24) can be used in conjunction with the following scheme when determining the priority (actionable) of implementing additional threat mitigation controls.

TABLE 4.25. Risk Acceptance Decision Maker.

Residual Risk Level	Level of Management Responsible for Residual Risk Acceptance Decision
High	Residual Risk acceptance decision should be made at the Board of Directors (BoD) or Chief Executive Officer (CEO) level depending on the magnitude of potential impact. Further risk mitigation mandatory through application/deployment of additional controls. All levels of management hierarchy should be involved
Moderate High	Residual Risk acceptance decision should be made at the Chief Information Officer (CiO), Director or Chief Information Security Officer (CISO) level depending on the magnitude of potential impact. Further risk mitigation strongly recommended through application/ deployment of additional controls. Subordinate levels of management hierarchy should be involved
Moderate	Residual Risk acceptance decision should be made at the Chief Information Officer (CiO), Director or Chief Information Security Officer (CISO) level depending on the magnitude of potential impact. Further risk mitigation strongly recommended through application/ deployment of additional controls. Subordinate levels of management hierarchy should be involved
Moderate Low	Residual Risk acceptance decision should be made at the local management level depending on the magnitude of potential impact. Further risk mitigation advised through application/deployment of additional controls. Subordinate levels of management hierarchy should be involved
Low	Residual Risk acceptance decision should be made at the local management level depending on the magnitude of potential impact. Further risk mitigation may be achievable through application/deployment of additional controls

Table 4.25 can be used to identify who should be the responsible individual within the organization for making the decisions regarding implementation of additional controls and acceptability of new residual risk levels.

Table 4.26 represents a second iteration of Table 4.22 which now captures priority of additional new controls to further mitigate risks associated with these human-initiated malicious threats not acceptably mitigated as shown in Table 4.22, and who within the organization is responsible for making the decisions regarding implementation of additional controls, and whether the new residual risk level, based on new controls, is acceptable.

In Table 4.26, additional table column headings have been added:

- **New Control Priority**—Refers to the priority (time frame) for deploying the proposed new technical or procedural controls;
- **Approved By**—Refers to who within the organization "signed off" on deploying the proposed new control and the new residual risk level acceptability once the control has been deployed.

TABLE 4.26. Example Additional Controls Priority Tracking.

Threat	Residual Risk Level	Proposed New Additional Controls	New Residual Risk Level	New Residual Risk Acceptable?	New Control Priority	Approved by
Outsider—system hacking	Moderate	RBAC	Low	Yes	Moderate High	
Outsider—social engineering	Low	None needed	–	–	–	
Outsider—dumpster diving	Low	None needed	–	–	–	
Outsider—phishing	Low	None needed	–	–	–	
Outsider—spear-phishing	Low	None needed	–	–	–	
Outsider—D(SoS) attack	Moderate	Network IPS	Low	Yes	Moderate High	
Outsider—worm	Moderate	Network IPS	Low	Yes	Moderate High	
Outsider—rootkit	Moderate	Network IPS	Low	Yes	Moderate High	
Outsider—virus	Moderate	Network IPS	Low	Yes	Moderate High	
Outsider—invalid access to internal WiFi subnets	High	IEEE 802.11i	Low	Yes	High	
Outsider—SAINT, SATAN, ISS-based intel. gathering	High	Network IPS	Low	Yes	High	
...						
Employee—system hacking	Moderate	RBAC	Low	Yes	Moderate High	
Employee—worm	Moderate	Host IPS	Low	Yes	Moderate High	
Employee—Trojan horse	Moderate	Host IPS	Low	Yes	Moderate High	
Employee—virus	Moderate	Host IPS	Low	Yes	Moderate High	
Employee—security-related programming errors	Moderate	Source code scanning	Low	Yes	Moderate	
Employee—administrative operational errors	Moderate	RBAC	Low	Yes	Moderate High	
Employee—unauthorized access	Moderate	RBAC	Low	Yes	Moderate High	
Employee—unauthorized copying files	Moderate	ACLs	Low	Yes	Moderate High	
Employee—use of social networks or IM	Moderate	Network IPS	Low	Yes	Moderate High	
Employee—browsing gambling websites	Moderate	Host IPS	Low	Yes	Moderate High	
Employee—invalid access to internal WiFi subnets	Moderate	IEEE 802.11i	Low	Yes	Moderate High	

(continued)

TABLE 4.26. (cont'd)

Threat	Residual Risk Level	Proposed New Additional Controls	New Residual Risk Level	New Residual Risk Acceptable?	New Control Priority	Approved by
Employee—invalid access to internal wired subnets	Moderate	IEEE 802.1x	Low	Yes	Moderate High	
Employee—SAINT, SATAN, ISS-based intel. gathering	High	Network IPS	Low	Yes	High	
...						
MtoM peering—malicious incoming SIP messages	Moderate	SBC	Low	Yes	Moderate	
MtoM peering—invalid RTP messages	Moderate	SBC	Low	Yes	Moderate	
MtoM peering—invalid DNS replies from outside DNS servers	High	DNSSEC, IPsec/PKI	Low	Yes	Moderate High	
MtoM peering—false OSPF route updates	High	IPsec/PKI	Low	Yes	Moderate High	
...						
Inside 3rd Party—system hacking	Moderate	RBAC	Low	Yes	Moderate High	
Inside 3rd Party—worm	Moderate	Host IPS	Low	Yes	Moderate High	
Inside 3rd Party—Trojan horse	Moderate	Host IPS	Low	Yes	Moderate-High	
Inside 3rd Party—virus	Moderate	Host IPS	Low	Yes	Moderate-High	
Inside 3rd Party—unauthorized access	Moderate	RBAC	Low	Yes	Moderate-High	
Inside 3rd Party—unauthorized copying files	Moderate	ACLs	Low	Yes	Moderate-High	
Inside 3rd Party—invalid access to internal WiFi subnets	Moderate	IEEE 802.11i	Low	Yes	Moderate High	
Inside 3rd Party—invalid access to internal wired subnets	Moderate	IEEE 802.1x	Low	Yes	Moderate High	
Inside 3rd Party—SAINT, SATAN, ISS-based intel. gathering	High	Network IPS	Low	Yes	Moderate High	
...						

Once the priorities have been established, and recorded, for deploying/implementing additional threat mitigation controls, budget decisions can be made and funds allocated according to the approved priorities. It is important to record the priorities for additional controls as this, and the other steps in the risk management process, provides evidence that the organization has taken a sound approach to risk management and has made decisions regarding the deployment of security controls from a sound business perspective. Such a process will be critical if the organization becomes a defendant in a civil action (i.e., tort, lawsuit). The next steps in the risk management process are the acquisition/implementation, deployment, and testing of the new control(s), which are addressed next.

4.3 RISK MITIGATION CONTROLS ACQUISITION OR DEVELOPMENT

Once the decision has been made to deploy new security controls, a project plan should be established and a deployment team assembled. The majority of Risk Mitigation Controls are either technical or procedural in nature. We first discuss the development and deployment of procedural risk mitigation controls.

4.3.1 Procedural Risk Mitigation Controls

One of the most effective approaches is the use of procedural risk mitigation controls. The need for these procedures continues to grow as the complexity of capabilities, especially security capabilities, grows. Enterprises are increasingly deploying:

- Stateful firewalls driven by filtering rules that, if not configured correctly, will unintentionally allow malicious network traffic to pass;
- IPS deep-packet-inspection rules and algorithms that, if not configured correctly, will unintentionally allow malicious network traffic to pass;
- Remote log collection (as in Syslog mechanisms) and audit trail recording;
- IPsec remote access gateways (remote client to intermediate gateway) requiring definition of security association parameters (i.e., IKE timers, session re-key frequencies, acceptable transforms, and credentials);
- More types of authentication and authorization controls (including RADIUS, TACACS+, Diameter, PKI CAs and RAs, DCE/Kerberos server/client software, single sign-on applications), some of which will interoperate and others are closed/siloed approaches;
- Anti-malware applications driven by signatures and other data that become obsolete unless updated regularly.

All of the aforementioned mechanisms require correct and timely configuration and surveillance to accomplish their objectives effectively. Today's operations environments are experiencing increased personnel turnover rates. Many employees also seek re-assignments to new duties periodically to further career progress. The results of these two forces are:

- New personnel having to be integrated into the operations staff;
- A likely increase in operational errors as staff struggle with immediate issues and activities; and
- Higher levels of stress as staff struggle with the "learning curve" each new mechanism represents.

A comprehensive set of guidelines and procedures will serve as productivity enhancers over the life cycle of infrastructure elements and capabilities.

4.3.2 New Technical Risk Mitigation Controls

4.3.2.1 Controls Implementation. Whether an organization builds, buys, or uses outside integrators to produce the equipment, sub-systems, and service servers it relies upon, the organization still has to comply with its security policies and, as we have seen, the requirements derived from the policy. Thus, communicating these security requirements to those organizations developing the product or service needs to be clear and effective. This communication process will differ if the development group is part of the organization versus procurement/purchase from an outside supplier/manufacturer or integrator.

When development occurs "in-house" by an IT organization, communication of security requirements should include:

- Joint meetings between operations, IT, security, and planning staff to finalize functional, performance, and operational requirements and the planned verification methods of requirement compliance. One of the greatest threats to meeting schedule and introducing vulnerabilities is "requirements creep" which occurs when new requirements are added without necessary review and engineering analysis;
- Regularly held status, coding, integration, and testing reviews. The earlier a security problem is recognized and resolved in the design cycle, the less costly and more integrated into the whole architecture the solution will be. Fixes/ patches to security problems after deployment are usually incomplete, often create new security vulnerabilities, and routinely affect customers and operations staff.

In the case of product purchase or integration by a 3rd party, communication of security requirements should include:

- Only requirements that are functional and performance related. An enterprise cannot hold a supplier or integrator responsible for operational security requirements strictly from an engineering perspective. However, product operational support, maintenance, and improvement security requirements are typically found in contracts. This will be discussed further;

- It is helpful for large organizations, especially communications service providers and major e-commerce businesses, to have periodic meetings with manufacturers that present an organization's information/service infrastructure direction and priorities for availability of security capabilities, for example:
  - ○ support of PKI;
  - ○ authenticated patch management;
  - ○ multiple management network interfaces;
  - ○ packet filtering;
  - ○ software configuration monitoring;
  - ○ IPsec, TLSv1, DTLSv1 security protocols; and
  - ○ use of PKCS #10, #11, and #12 data formats for credentials management.
- All product manufacturers/suppliers operate around multi-year product development life cycles that necessitate product capability finalization likely two to three years prior to availability. Consequently, the sooner security capability needs are shared with industry, the sooner these capabilities will be included in product planning and thereby available to the marketplace.

4.3.2.2 Acquisition. Most commercial, non-defense governmental enterprises and non-governmental organizations rely on commercial hardware, operating systems/utilities, and applications; so they do little in-house development yet frequently rely on complex internal information infrastructures. Consequently, these types of enterprises use their systems engineering staff to support the purchase/procurement of hardware, software, outsourced services, and even integration projects. Procurement typically follows from issuance of a Request for Information (RFI), to Request for Proposal (RFP), and may proceed to a Request for Quote (RFQ). A frequent shortcut used in many RFIs and RFPs is to site compliance with standards (either national or international) which can be a problem we will discuss further. The third major security consideration with procurement is testing what is being purchased and are all security requirements being complied with as per the contract/sales agreement. So let us look at these areas in more detail and consider things to do or avoid.

4.3.2.2.1 REQUEST FOR INFORMATION AND REQUEST FOR PROPOSAL. When an organization wants/needs to learn what products are available with capabilities deemed needed, they will usually prepare and issue a Request for Information (RFI) that identifies what the requester is interested in doing and asking about the capabilities of different manufacturer's products. From a security systems engineering perspective, the discussion of security capabilities and specified security requirements should not dictate any specifics of capability implementation unless these implementation specifics have a direct impact on the integrity, availability, functionality, or manageability of security mechanisms. The requirements should simply identify those security capabilities that the requester considers critical, necessary, or desired. Following are two example sets of typical RFI security requirements:

Example 1

- Please describe how your platform provides Human–Element identification and authentication, including Login Identifiers, Login Passwords, and Element Login Functions.
- Please describe how your platform provides Authorization and Access Controls, including Security Levels, User Activity Timers, Access Control Lists, and Access Control Mediation.
- Please describe how your platform provides Security Audit Trail Logging.
- Please describe how your platform provides security for software, including Software Installation and Upgrading, Operating Systems, and Applications.
- Does your platform implementation rely on unsecured protocols such as Telnet, TFTP, and SNMPv1? If so, how does it provide authentication, confidentiality, and integrity?
- Please list the protocols/standards used in your solution to secure the platform.
- Does your platform support the use of customer network private address spaces where NAT is used? If NAT is not currently supported, what are your plans to support it? What mechanisms have been implemented in your architecture for handling private IP address spaces to interwork with the signaling protocols such as H.323 and SIP?
- Does your platform support the use of encrypted virtual private networks (VPNs)? If so:
  - what symmetric and/or asymmetric algorithms and key lengths are supported?
  - how is your VPN capability compliant with IETF IPsec, ISAKMP, and IKE RFCs?
  - do you support X.509-compliant digital certificates, and what certificate authorities do you interwork with?
- Please describe how your platform supports encrypted VPN and NAT Interworking.
- Please describe how your platform supports Ingress–Egress Packet Filtering.
- Please describe the impact on the performance of the platform when the proposed security measures are implemented (e.g., when using encryption or packet filters).
- Please describe how your solution will detect intrusion attempts.
- Please describe how your platform supports Network Element (NE) Local Management Console Security, including Identification/Authentication, Authorization/Access Control Levels, Data Integrity, and Security Audit Trail Logs.
- Please describe how your platform supports EMS Management Console Security, including Identification/Authentication, Authorization/Access Control Levels, Data Integrity, and Security Audit Trail Logs.
- Please describe how your platform supports EMS Security Management, including Login Account Management, Encryption Key Management and Distribution, Security Alarm Processing, and Security Reports.
- Please describe how your platform supports NE–EMS Interface Security, including Identification/Authentication, Authorization/Access Control Levels, Data Integrity, and Security Audit Trail Logs.

- Please describe how your platform supports NE–OSS Interface Security, including Identification/Authentication, Authorization/Access Control Levels, Data Integrity, and Security Audit Trail Logs.

Example 2

1. What Identification, Authentication, System Access Control, Resource Access Control, Confidentiality, and Security Auditing/Logging capabilities exist or are planned for secure "open" interconnection with systems of Requester's external business partners?

2. What Identification, Authentication, System Access Control, Resource Access Control, Confidentiality, and Security Auditing/Logging capabilities exist for securing Requester employee access to product functionality, especially remote access?

3. What capabilities exist for using common standards-based identification, authentication, and confidentiality techniques such as PKI, X.509 certificates, smart cards, and lightweight directory access protocol?

4. Please describe the extranet security model you employ to maintain authenticity, integrity, and confidentiality for access to OSS information from wireless external handheld devices.

5. Please describe the security strategy of your product. Specifically, describe how your product can be used across different trust domains and can maintain authenticity, integrity, and confidentiality while accommodating various security environments, such as links over open, unsecured networks.

6. Please describe how your product performs identification and authentication of Requester employees.

7. Please describe the System and Resource Access Controls of your product, including how they are set up, managed, and executed within your product.

8. Please describe all auditable processes, events, alarms, outcomes, and audit trail logging.

9. Please describe any mechanisms provided by your product to ensure data confidentiality when communicating with other applications and systems.

10. Please describe how your product handles data that must be passed through or processed in encrypted form.

11. Please describe any mechanisms provided by your product to ensure data integrity when communicating with other applications and systems.

12. Please describe how a security policy can be implemented by the product. Indicate how and when (development, installation, or configurable) various aspects of this are implemented.

13. Please describe how your platform supports direct Login Security to a management server, at the EML/NML/SML/BML layers, including Identification/Authentication, Authorization/Access Control Level, Data Integrity, Confidentiality, and Security Audit Trail Logging.

14. Please describe how your platform supports remote (over a network) Login Security to a management server, at the EML/NML/SML/BML layers, including

Identification/Authentication, Authorization/ Access Control Level, Data Integrity, Confidentiality, and Security Audit Trail Logging.

15. Please describe how your platform supports EML/NML/SML/BML management application security, including Login Account Management, Encryption Key Management and Distribution, Security Alarm Processing, Security Audit Trail Log Analysis, and Security Reports.

16. Please describe how your platform supports NE–EML/NML/SML/BML interface security to managed elements, including Identification/Authentication, Authorization/Access Control Levels, Data Integrity and Security Audit Trail Logs, and Log Analysis.

17. If your solution provides End User Domain Administration capabilities, please describe how your platform provides security for these capabilities, including Identification/Authentication, Authorization/Access Control Levels, Data Integrity and Security Audit Trail Logs, and Log Analysis.

18. If your solution provides remote access for customer teleworker/remote applications, please describe what are the protocols used and how your platform provides security for these capabilities, including Identification/Authentication, Authorization/Access Control Levels, Data Integrity and Security Audit Trail Logs, and Log Analysis.

19. Please describe how your platform provides Human–Element identification and authentication, including Login Identifiers, Login Passwords, and Element Login Functions.

20. Please describe how your platform provides Authorization and Access Controls, including Security Levels, User Activity Timers, Access Control Lists, and Access Control Mediation.

21. Please describe how your platform provides Security Audit Trail Logging.

22. Please describe how your platform provides security for software, including Software Installation and Upgrading, Operating Systems, and Applications.

23. Does your platform implementation rely on unsecured protocols such as Telnet, TFTP, or SNMPv1/v2? If so, please describe how it provides authentication, confidentiality, and integrity?

24. Please list the protocols/standards used in your solution to secure the platform and describe their usage.

25. Does your platform support the use of encrypted VPNs? If so:
    • what symmetric and/or asymmetric algorithms and key lengths are supported?
    • how is your VPN capability compliant with IETF IPsec, ISAKMP, and IKE RFCs?
    • do you support X.509-compliant digital certificates, and what certificate authorities do you interwork with?

26. Please describe how your solution will detect intrusion attempts.

27. Do you ensure that programmers, designers, and testers are knowledgeable about common flaws (such as buffer overflows) in the design and implementation of products?

28. Have you established a Security Response Capability that consists of one or more individuals or groups that are responsible for responding to vulnerability reports, verifying vulnerabilities, patching vulnerabilities, and releasing bulletins and patches?

29. Do you have a publicly published process for notifying customers of vulnerabilities within your products within 24 hours and potential impact within 72 hours of first vulnerability report?

30. Do you provide alternative security measures, within 72 hours of first vulnerability report, which can be implemented while waiting for a patch to the vulnerability?

Neither of these examples is intended to be exhaustive; they are a starting point only and should be revised to fit each specific RFI.

Following review and analysis of RFI responses from industry, the requesting organization's team will, as part of the engineering process, assist with preparing an RFP. At this point the organization has progressed through detailed system requirements analysis and can now document specific security requirements. The security requirements within an RFP, like those of an RFI, should not dictate implementation details for the same reasons noted earlier. Following are some sample RFP requirements likely used.

In the example RFP requirements, the term GA date represents the point in time that a product or service becomes generally available in the marketplace. This term is frequently included in RFP requirements to specify when requirements compliance is required by the purchasing organization. This sample can be found in Appendix I—RFP Security Appendix Example, which, as its name implies, provides a sample baseline set of generic RFP security requirements. An organization issuing an RFP should expect to receive a very large amount of data back in the form of proposals.

The more effective the requester/purchaser is at mandating that proposals provide explicit responses to requirements, the more productive the proposal analysis will be. Analysis productivity is important to make manageable the reduction of proposal responses into decision-oriented information. Following is an excerpt of a proposal security section extracted from Appendix J—RFP Security Analysis of ABC Proposal. The author has seen situations from RFPs where you get 10 proposals, with each proposal security response covering 2000 security requirements, resulting in the analysis of over 20,000 requirement responses. Mandating proposals to include a security requirements response by spreadsheet, as shown in Figure 4.2, allows the preparation of spreadsheet equations/formulas/macros to be developed in advance of proposal receipt. This approach can significantly speed up analysis and proposal comparisons. Such an example spreadsheet is contained in Appendix J—RFP Security Analysis of ABC Proposal.xls.

Larger organizations will often issue either a revised RFP or an RFQ. With the revised RFP, the requester may modify requirements from the RFP or add additional requirements and will almost always require price/cost information. The RFQ is typically limited to requests for pricing on already selected products. Once the organization

Section or Requirement Num.	Requirement Text	FC = Comply 100% by 1/1/2009	PC = Partially Comply by 1/1/2009	WFC = Will Comply 100% by (enter date)	WCX = Will Comply w / Exception by (enter date)	WNC = Will Not Comply	NA = Not Applic.	Note Product Release Level(s) Associated with Responses in Columns C-F
7. Security 7.1 Response Instructions 7.2 Security Terminology 7.3 Security Requirements 7.3.1 General								
R [7.1]	Communications security (specifically authentication, authorization, and confidentiality) between network elements (NEs), management systems (MSs), and operations support systems (OSSs) shall NOT be based on availability and use of a "trusted network segment"							
R [7.2]	NE and MS direct login security (specifically authentication and authorization) shall NOT be based on physical security (e.g., where physical access to these components is limited) is sufficient. Required by RFP GA date.							
R [7.3]	If the proposed solution requires the deployment of an authentication server (such as Radius server, Diameter server, Kerberos server, public key infrastructure (including certificate and registration authorities), key management center/server), then the proposal, and cost model, shall include such a server. Required by RFP GA date.							
R [7.4]	The proposed solution shall NOT assume the existence of an authentication server. Required by RFP GA date.							
R [7.5]	The proposed solution shall NOT state that any specific requirement can be complied with if an authentication server is present but not proposed. Required by RFP GA date.							
R [7.6]	Membership with the Forum of Incident Response and Security Teams (FIRST) shall be required. Required by RFP GA date.							
R [7.7]	Programmers, designers, and testers shall have received training and be knowledgeable about common flaws (such as buffer overflows) in the design and implementation of products. Required by RFP GA date.							

Figure 4.2. Sample RFP Evaluation Spreadsheet.

has chosen which products and services will be purchased, a contract is prepared including a Statement of Work (SOW).

4.3.2.2.2 CONTRACTS AND STATEMENTS OF WORK. The contract negotiated between the purchasing organization and the supplier/manufacturer/vendor will clearly state the terms and conditions for product/service purchase. Security-related contract terms should:

- require the vendor to comply with the terms found in a security SOW;
- require the vendor to comply with the detailed security requirements in the RFP as committed to by the vendor in their proposal; and
- specify financial penalties for non-compliance.

The SOW usually captures both non-technical and technical security obligations by the supplier. Appendix K includes a Sample Security SOW.

4.3.2.2.3 STANDARDS COMPLIANCE. Many enterprises, rather than specifying individual requirements, will specify compliance with industry standards in the RFP. This practice should not be ignored provided it is done correctly. Given that the purchaser will need to test the product or service before taking final delivery, the more explicit and objective the testing, the purchaser is more likely to get what they requested/bought. For the testing to be as accurate as necessary, the requirements being tested against should be uniquely identifiable and testable. Unfortunately there are many security-related standards that do not provide uniquely identifiable and testable requirements; two examples of this situation are ITU-T recommendations X.805 and X.2702. Neither of these two documents includes any unique requirement identification, nor do they utilize complex sentence structures; they only provide very high level guidance. On the other hand, standards, such as ISO 27001, ANSI Standard T1.276, and ITU-T recommendation M.3410, provide requirements that RFPs can, and should, reference as part of the RFP by reference.

4.3.2.2.4 ACCEPTANCE TESTING. When a product or service is acquired via a well engineered set of requirements, especially security requirements, then both acceptance testing and regression testing of deficiencies identified can proceed in a planned and thorough fashion. Once a sufficient number of acceptance testing deficiencies are resolved, the organization can proceed to field and operational readiness activities with a higher likelihood of success. The purpose of these tests is to confirm that the services, products, and infrastructure elements to be deployed comply with requirements derived from the enterprise's security policies and programs.

These functional, performance, and operational security requirements should, by this point, have been decomposed to simple statements that (by their use of the words "shall," "should," "may," "shall not," "should not," and "may not") identify if each requirement is mandatory, wanted, or simply desirable. Requirements will naturally group by what security service is involved (authentication, authorization, integrity, confidentiality, or non-repudiation) and by computing or communications functional groupings. For every set of security requirements, a test plan should be developed that identifies what requirements are to be verified, necessary minimum review criteria, and the specific tests used to verify requirement compliance. Each test in a test plan is described in a corresponding test procedure. The specific details of test plans and procedures will vary across organizations. The critical point here is that the verification of requirements compliance is the "keystone" of any sound security program.

Acceptance testing should occur whenever a new product, service, modification, or component is acquired, irrespective of development, integration, or purchase. The acceptance tests should not be performed by the supplier (i.e., manufacturer, developer, or integrator); rather these tests should be conducted and the results reviewed by an independent group, with oversight by the Management Security Oversight Team or representatives of the CSO.

4.3.2.3 In-House Development.

The development of infrastructure elements, servers, and applications performed in-house should follow a process that ensures all necessary engineering activities are identified and accounted for. Two development process approaches worth following are the Capability Maturity Model—Integrated (CMMI) and the ISO-9001 quality framework. The ISO-9001 approach does not dictate any specific process details yet spells out what any process should span. This approach is deployable across many types of business activities. For complex systems development, CMMI is more applicable as it focuses on development results being predictable and achieves specific measurable levels of quality and performance. One of the most critical areas for security, and most overlooked, is software development, not just in design but in coding and testing.

4.3.2.3.1 CODING. Since many attacks are designed explicitly to cause unexpected exception conditions for which there is no, or inadequate, logic to safely and correctly recover from, exception handling cannot be overlooked during design and coding. Any inputs to an application, regardless of source (i.e., networked peer systems, user input, and data files), should be verified for correct format and valid field values. Whenever inputs to an application internal data structure exceed the data structure capacity (as in length checking and field **bounds checks**), **exception handling** logic should be invoked to either truncate the input or signal the input as invalid and rejected. When covert channels or residual data disclosure are of concern, then the use of **shared libraries** of functions/subroutine should be avoided and **static libraries** used instead.

Over 10 years ago, two Microsoft employees, as part of a Microsoft "Trustworthy Computing" initiative, formulated a model for threat analysis, called STRIDE (Howard and LeBlanc, 2001), which can assist software developers build security controls into software. STRIDE is named after the following six identified categories of threats:

- **S**poofing identity;
- **T**ampering with data;
- **R**epudiation;
- **I**nformation disclosure;
- **D**enial of service; and
- **E**levation of privilege.

The primary value to the STRIDE view of threats is as a model to categorize attacks that should be considered when developing software. Table 4.27 maps STRIDE threat categories to threats.

TABLE 4.27. Mapping STRIDE Threat Categories to Threats.

STRIDE Threat Category	Threats from
Spoofing identity	Disclosure, illicit use, modification, damage
Tampering with data	Modification, damage
Repudiation	Illicit use, modification
Information disclosure	Disclosure
Denial of service	Denial of Service
Elevation of privilege	Disclosure, illicit use, modification, damage

4.3.2.3.2 CODE REVIEWS. Another technique for improving the quality and security of developed software is the peer code review. With peer code reviews, members of the development team are tasked to review the source code produced by other team members. This form of review provides a "second set of eyes" examination for source code logic errors, missing exception handling logic, lack of bounds checking, and use of dangerous language constructs, such as the C function "strcpy." An ancillary benefit is an increase in the maintainability of in-house developed applications.

4.3.2.3.3 SOURCE CODE SCANNING TOOLS. Well over ten years ago, people started looking into automated approaches for finding and identifying security flaws and problems within the vast area of software development. Academic work on this subject is typified by Viega et al. (2002), wherein the authors discuss a token-based approach to scanning C and C++ source codes for security problems and compare their approach results against alternative approaches. Trade journals also have reported on the value of security scanning of source code with Nazario (2002) being just one such article. In this article, the author makes the point that source code scanners "are not a replacement for manual checks and edits," but these tools can provide valuable guidance when looking to develop a secure code.

The National Institute of Standards and Technology (NIST) has also considered the use and value of source code scanning tools, or as they put it "a source code security analyzer examines source code to detect and report weaknesses that can lead to security vulnerabilities."[1] NIST considers such tools as "the last lines of defense to eliminate software vulnerabilities during development or after deployment."[2] NIST has developed the following two documents to assist organizations in the use of source code scanning tools:

- Source Code Security Analysis Tool Functional Specification Version 1.1, NIST Special Publication 500-268, February 2011, http://samate.nist.gov/docs/source_code_security_analysis_spec_SP500-268_v1.1.pdf
- Source Code Security Analysis Tool Test Plan Version 1.1, NIST Special Publication 500-270, July 2011, http://samate.nist.gov/docs/source_code_security_analysis_tool_test_plan_SP500-270.pdf

both of which are freely available from NIST's website. Another useful NIST resource is Table 4.28 which identifies a number of available scanning tools. The NIST table is copied here to ensure availability.

[1] http://samate.nist.gov/index.php/Source_Code_Security_Analyzers.html

[2] http://samate.nist.gov/index.php/Source_Code_Security_Analyzers.html

TABLE 4.28. NIST Identified Source Code Scanning Tools.

Tool	Language(s)	Available from	Finds or Checks for	As of
ABASH	Bash	Free	String expansion errors, option insertion errors, and other weaknesses that may lead to security vulnerabilities	Mar 2012
ApexSec Security Console	PL/SQL (Oracle Apex)	Recx	SQL Injection, Cross-Site Scripting, Access Control, and Configuration issues within an Apex application	Mar 2010
Astrée	C	AbsInt	Undefined code constructs and run-time errors, e.g., out-of-bounds array indexing or arithmetic overflow	Jun 2009
BOON	C	Free	Integer range analysis determines if an array can be indexed outside its bounds	Feb 2005
bugScout	Java, C#, Visual Basic, ASP, php	Buguroo	Multiple security failures, such as deprecated libraries errors, vulnerable functions, sensitive information within the source code comments, etc.	March 2012
C Code Analyzer (CCA)	C	free	Out-of-bounds array indexing or arithmetic overflow aims for no false positives	Apr 2006
C++test	C, C++	Parasoft	Defects such as memory leaks, buffer issues, security issues, and arithmetic issues, plus SQL injection, cross-site scripting, exposure of sensitive data, and other potential issues	Apr 2006
cadvise	C, C++	HP	Many lint-like checks plus memory leak, potential null pointer dereference, tainted data for file paths, and many others	Mar 2009
Checkmarx	Java, C#, C, C++, VB, ASP, Apex, Visualforce	Checkmarx	Covers all known OWASP and SANS vulnerabilities and complies with PCI and other standards. Includes a query language that enables infinite customization and detection accuracy with virtually zero false positives.	Apr 2010
Clang Static Analyzer	C, Objective-C	Free	Reports dead stores, memory leaks, null pointer deref, and more. Uses source annotations like "nonnull"	Aug 2010
CodeCenter	C	ICS	Incorrect pointer values, illegal array indices, bad function arguments, type mismatches, and uninitialized variables	Apr 2011
CodePeer	Ada	AdaCore	Detects uninitialized data, pointer misuse, buffer overflow, numeric overflow, division by zero, dead code, concurrency faults (race conditions), unused variables, etc.	Apr 2010

Name	Language	Company	Description	Date
CodeScan	ASP Classic, PHP, ASP.Net	CodeScan Labs	Specialize in inspecting web source code for security holes and source code issues	Jul 2008
CodeSecure	PHP, Java (ASP. NET soon)	Armorize Technologies	XSS, SQL Injection, Command Injection, tainted data flow, etc.	Mar 2007
CodeSonar	C, C++	GrammaTech	Null-pointer dereferences, divide-by-zeros, buffer over- and under-runs	Mar 2005
Coverity Static Analysis	C, C++, Java, C#	Coverity	Flaws and security vulnerabilities—reduces false positives while minimizing the likelihood of false negatives	Apr 2011
Cppcheck	C, C++	Free	Pointer to a variable that goes out of scope, bounds, classes (missing constructors, unused private functions, etc.), exception safety, memory leaks, invalid STL usage, overlapping data in sprintf, division by zero, null pointer dereference, unused struct member, passing parameter by value, etc. Aims for no false positives	Feb 2010
CQual	C	Free	Uses type qualifiers to perform a taint analysis, which detects format string vulnerabilities	Feb 2005
Csur	C	Free	Cryptographic protocol-related vulnerabilities	Apr 2006
DevPartner SecurityChecker	C#, Visual Basic	Compuware	Known and potential security vulnerabilities	Oct 2006
DoubleCheck	C, C++	Green Hills Software	Like buffer overflows, resource leaks, invalid pointer references, and violations of MISRA	Jul 2007
Flawfinder	C/C++	Free	Uses of risky functions, buffer overflow (strcpy()), format string ([v][f]printf()), race conditions (access(), chown(), and mktemp()), shell metacharacters (exec()), and poor random numbers (random())	2005
Fluid	Java	Call	"Analysis-based verification" for attributes such as race conditions, thread policy, and object access with no false negatives	Oct 2005
Goanna	C, C++	Red Lizard Software	Memory corruptions, resource leaks, buffer overruns, null pointer dereferences, C++ hazards	Aug 2009

(continued)

TABLE 4.28. (cont'd)

Tool	Language(s)	Available from	Finds or Checks for	As of
HP QAInspect	C#, Visual Basic, JavaScript, VB Script	Fortify	Application vulnerabilities	Apr 2011
Insight	C, C++, Java, and C#	Klocwork	Buffer overflow, unvalidated user input, SQL injection, path injection, file injection, cross-site scripting, information leakage, weak encryption, and vulnerable coding practices, as well as quality, reliability, and maintainability issues	May 2011
ITS4	C, C++	Free for non-competing uses	Potentially dangerous function calls, with risk analysis of some	Feb 2005
Jlint	Java	Free	Bugs, inconsistencies, and synchronization problems	Feb 2006
LAPSE	Java	Free	Helps audit Java J2EE applications for common types of security vulnerabilities found in Web applications.	Sep 2006
ObjectCenter	C/C++	ICS	"Runtime and static error detection—more than 250 types of errors, including more than 80 run-time errors—inter-module inconsistencies"	Apr 2011
PLSQLScanner 2008	PLSQL	Red-Database-Security	SQL Injection, hardcoded passwords, cross-site scripting (XSS), etc.	Jun 2008
PHP-Sat	PHP	Free	Static analysis tool, XSS, etc. description	Sep 2006
Pixy	PHP	Free	Static analysis tool; only detects XSS and SQL Injection	Jun 2007
PMD	Java	Free	Questionable constructs, dead code, duplicate code	Feb 2006
PolySpace	Ada, C, C++	MathWorks	Runtime errors, unreachable code	Feb 2005
PREfix and PREfast	C, C++	Microsoft proprietary		Feb 2006
QA-C, QA-C++, QA-J	C, C++, Java	Programming Research	A suite of static analysis tools, with over 1400 messages; detects a variety of problems from undefined language features to redundant or unreachable code	May 2009

Name	Languages	Vendor	Description	Date
Quality checker	VB6, Java, C#	Qualitychecker	Static analysis tool	Sep 2007
Rational AppScan Source Edition	C, C++, Java, JSP, ASP.NET, VB.NET, C#	IBM (formerly Ounce Labs)	Coding errors, security vulnerabilities, design flaws, policy violations, and offers remediation	Aug 2010
RATS (Rough Auditing Tool for Security)	C	Free	Potential security risks	2005
Resource Standard Metrics (RSM)	C, C++, C#, and Java	M Squared Technologies	Scan for 50 readability or portability problems or questionable constructs, e.g. different number of "new" and "delete" key words or an assignment operator (=) in a conditional (if)	Apr 2011
Sentry	C, C++	Vigilant Software	Critical software defects, such as memory access errors, resource leaks, and potential crashes, with a low false positive rate	Dec 2009
Smatch	C	Free	Simple scripts look for problems in simplified representation of code, primarily for Linux kernel code	Apr 2006
SCA	ASP.NET, C, C++, C# and other .NET languages, Java, JSP, PL/SQL, T-SQL, VB.NET, XML	Fortify Software	Security vulnerabilities, tainted data flow, etc.	Apr 2006
SPADE	Translators are available for a Pascal subset and for the following assemblers: 68020, 8096, and Z8002	Praxis	The SPADE tools provide flow analysis and verification facilities based on a model of the program being analyzed. The model is generated by automatic translators which operate on the original source code	Dec 2008

(continued)

TABLE 4.28. (cont'd)

Tool	Language(s)	Available from	Finds or Checks for	As of
SPARK tool set	SPARK (Ada subset)	Praxis	Ambiguous constructs, data- and information-flow errors, any property expressible in first-order logic (Examiner, Simplifier, and SPADE)	Aug 2006
Splint	C	Free	Security vulnerabilities and coding mistakes; with annotations, it performs stronger checks	2005
TBsecure	C, C++	LDRA Software Technology	The TBsecure plug-in to TBvision comes complete with the Carnegie Mellon Software Engineering Institute (SEI) CERT C secure coding standard. TBsecure identifies security vulnerabilities and enables implementation of the just released CERT C Secure Coding Standard version 1.0	Dec 2008
UNO	C	Free	Uninitialized variables, null-pointers, and out-of-bounds array indexing and "allows for the specification and checking of a broad range of user-defined properties"; aims for a very low false alarm rate	Feb 2006
PVS-Studio	C++	OOO "Program Verification Systems" (Co LTD)	PVS-Studio is a static analyzer that detects errors in source code of C/C++/C++0x applications. There are three sets of rules included in PVS-Studio: (1) diagnosis of 64-bit errors (Viva64), (2) diagnosis of parallel errors (VivaMP), (3) general-purpose diagnosis	Jan 2010
xg++	C	unk	Kernel and device driver vulnerabilities in Linux and OpenBSD through range checking, etc.	Feb 2005
Yasca	Java, C/C++, JavaScript, ASP, ColdFusion, PHP, COBOL, .NET, etc.	Free	A "glorified grep" and aggregator of other tools, including FindBugs, PMD, JLint, JavaScript Lint, PHPLint, CppCheck, ClamAV, RATS, and Pixy. "It is designed to be very flexible and easy to extend; writing a new rule is as easy as coming up with a regular expression"	Mar 2010

The U.S. Department of Homeland Security (DHS) has also weighed in on this subject and has developed a "business case" for using source code scanning tools; see:https://buildsecurityin.us-cert.gov/bsi/articles/tools/code/262-BSI.html

Not only does DHS present the potential benefits of such tools, also presented are a number of tool limitations, namely:

* not designed to find architecture- or design-level flaws;
* not well suited for finding integration bugs;
* somewhat limited when it comes to analyzing large systems; and
* not able to find all vulnerabilities in a software system.

So DHS recommends that organizations should not rely solely on security scanners as the sole means of securing software source code. Another well respected source on the subject of source code security scanning tools is the Open Web Application Security Project (OWASP). Check out their website at:https://www.owasp.org/index.php/Source_Code_Analysis_Tools

This website provides advice on what these tools are good at and questions an organization should explore when considering use of such tools along with tool selection criteria.

4.3.2.3.4 CONTROLS TESTING. Testing of security mechanism's correct functionality should occur throughout the implementation process as part of the basic unit testing, systems testing, and integration testing. Penetration testing and attack simulation are additional forms of useful approaches up through system integration. Planned attack activities during field testing are also valuable, provided appropriate safeguards are in place to prevent damage or injury to customers or other parties.

4.4 RISK MITIGATION CONTROLS DEPLOYMENT TESTING

Regardless of how services, products, and infrastructure elements are acquired (e.g., internal development, external integration/development, or purchase), there are a series of verification tests that need to be performed, namely:

* Acceptance Testing;
* Field Testing; and
* Operational Readiness Testing.

The purpose of these verification tests is to confirm that the services, products, and infrastructure elements to be deployed comply with requirements derived from the enterprise's security policies and programs, as discussed under "Security Process Management and Standards" in Document 4.

These functional, performance, and operational security requirements should, by this point, have been decomposed to simple statements that identify if each requirement is mandatory, wanted, or simply desirable. This approach relies on the definitions found in Bradner (1997) for the use of the words "shall," "should," "may," "shall not," "should not," and "may not." Requirements will naturally group by what security service is involved (authentication, authorization, integrity, confidentiality, or non-repudiation) and by computing or communications functional groupings. For every set of security requirements, a test plan should be developed that identifies what requirements are to be verified, necessary minimum review criteria, and the specific tests used to verify requirement compliance. Each test in a test plan is described in a corresponding test procedure. The specific details of test plans and procedures will vary across organizations. The critical point here is that the verification of requirement compliance is the "keystone" of any sound security program.

Acceptance testing should occur whenever a new product, service, modification, or component is acquired, irrespective of development, integration, or purchase. The acceptance tests should not be performed by the supplier (i.e., manufacturer, developer, or integrator); rather these tests should be conducted and the results reviewed by an independent group, with oversight by the Management Security Oversight Team or representatives of the CSO.

Field testing focuses on whether the new product, service, modification, or component is able to continue meeting all requirements while being deployed in a constrained field context with moderate service traffic volumes. The increased size of the testing environment allows the enterprise to evaluate scalability, field deployment, and logistics issues. All enterprise operational, logistical, and maintenance personnel affected are involved. The results of these tests allow development and refinement of the production operational procedures necessary.

In many cases, operational readiness testing is combined with the latter part of field testing. The readiness testing provides assurance that all organizational resources are prepared to support wide-scale deployment.

4.5 SUMMARY

As this chapter has noted, risk management is a cornerstone component of a sound security governance program. The foundation of risk management is determining what needs protection, which is why establishing an asset inventory is fundamental. This chapter has provided detailed guidance on constructing such an inventory and how to capture vulnerabilities, availability needs, and risk attributes for assets. The captured vulnerabilities, availability needs, and risk attribute information can then be used to establish the need for additional security controls, both procedural and technical. Also addressed at this point is the prioritizing of risks and the decision-making process as to which new controls should be deployed/implemented over time. The chapter then moved to consider how new controls are acquired, that is, built in-house or purchased. Also discussed are procurement issues and finally consideration of new controls testing. In Chapter 5, we discuss operations security (OPSEC) and management of OPSEC.

FURTHER READING AND RESOURCES

Acquisti, A., Friedman, A., Telang, R. (2006) Is There a Cost to Privacy Breaches?, 27th International Conference on Information Systems and Fifth Workshop on the Economics of Information Security (WEIS). Retrieved from http://citeseerx.ist.psu.edu/viewdoc/download? doi=10.1.1.73.2942&rep=rep1&type=pdf

Bradner, S. (1997) RFC 2119, Key words for use in RFCs to Indicate Requirement Levels, Best Current Practice, Internet Engineering Task Force (IETF)

Campbell, K., Gordon, L., Loeb, M., Zhou, L. (2003a) The economic cost of publicly announced information security breaches: empirical evidence from the stock market, Journal of Computer Security, 11(3), pp. 431–448. Retrieved from http://iospress.metapress. com/content/5nkxhffc775tuel9/

Campbell, K., Gordon, L.A., Loeb, M.P., Zhou, L. (2003b) The economic cost of publicly announced information security breaches: empirical evidence from the stock market, Journal of Computer Security 11(3), pp. 431–448

Cavusoglu, H., Mishra, B., Raghunathan, S. (2004) The effect of Internet security breach announcements on market value: capital market reactions for breached firms and Internet security developers. International Journal of Electronic Commerce, 9(1), pp. 70–104. Retrieved from http://www.jstor.org/stable/27751132

Fama, E.F. (1969) Efficient capital markets: a review of theory and empirical work, The Journal of Finance, 25(2), pp. 383–417. Retrieved from http://www.jstor.org/stable/2325486

Garg, A., Curtis, J. Halper, H. (2003a) The financial impact of IT security breaches: what do investors think?, Information Systems Security, 12(1), pp. 22–33

Garg, A., Curtis, J., Halper, H. (2003b) Quantifying the financial impact of IT security breaches, Information Management & Computer Security, 11(2), pp. 74–83

Gaudin, S. (2007) Estimates Put T.J. Maxx Security Fiasco At $4.5 Billion, InformationWeek, United Business Media LLC. Retrieved from http://www.informationweek.com/news/ 199203277

Goel, S., Shawky, H.A. (2009) Estimating the market impact of security breach announcements on firm values, Information & Management, 46(7), pp. 404–410

Hovav, A., D'Arcy, J. (2003) The impact of denial-of-service attack announcements on the market value of firms, Risk Management and Insurance Review, 6(2), pp. 97–121

Hovav, A., D'Arcy, J. (2004) The impact of virus attack announcements on the market value of firms, Information Systems Security, 13(3), pp. 32–40

Hovav, A., D'Arcy, J. (2005) Capital market reaction to defective IT products: the case of computer viruses, Computers & Security, 24(5), pp. 409–424. Retrieved from http://www.science direct.com/science/article/pii/S0167404805000374

Howard, M., LeBlanc, D. (2001) Writing Secure Code, Microsoft Press

Kannan, K., Rees, J., Sridhar, S. (2007) Market reactions to information security breach announcements: an empirical analysis, International Journal of Electronic Commerce, 12(1), pp. 69–91. Retrieved from http://dx.doi.org/10.2753/JEC1086-4415120103

Ko, M, Dorantes, C. (2006) The impact of information security breaches on financial performance of the breached firms: an empirical investigation, Journal of Information Technology Management, XVII(2). Retrieved from http://jitm.ubalt.edu/XVII-2/ article2.pdf

Nazario, J. (2002) Source code scanners for better code, Linux Journal. Retrieved from http://www.linuxjournal.com/article/5673

Telang, R., Wattel, S. (2007) An empirical analysis of the impact of software vulnerability announcements on firm stock price, IEEE Transactions on Software Engineering, 33(8), pp. 544–557

Viega, J., Bloch, J. T., Kohno, T., McGraw, G. 2002 Token-based scanning of source code for security problems, ACM Transactions on Information and Systems Security (TISSEC), 5(3), pp. 238–261. Retrieved from http://doi.acm.org/10.1145/545186.545188

5

OPERATIONAL MANAGEMENT OF SECURITY

We conclude with a discussion of management and more specifically the operational management of security. No matter how many security mechanisms we deploy, nor where we deploy them, security mechanisms will not protect us unless we have a way to manage, administer, and observe the mechanisms.

Operational security management relies on both technological and procedural security management mechanisms. This chapter focuses on both of these areas. We begin our discussion with the technological mechanisms known as management applications, commonly referred to as Element Management Systems (EMSs), Network Management Systems (NMSs), and Services Management Systems, and the communication between these systems and the devices being managed. All the three types of management systems (MS) are involved in managing security either as a primary Fault, Configuration, Accounting, Performance, and Security (FCAPS) responsibility or in support of other management functionality. Additionally, from a security perspective, these MS have to be recognized as managed devices incorporating security mechanisms securing their internal activities and interdevice management communications. We conclude with the consideration of procedural and supporting technological mechanisms for operational security management. These mechanisms include security-specific tools and procedures that an operations security staff should rely upon.

Security Management of Next Generation Telecommunications Networks and Services,
First Edition. Stuart Jacobs.

5.1 SECURING MANAGEMENT APPLICATIONS AND COMMUNICATIONS

Before we can dive into the issues surrounding management of security mechanisms, we need to consider how network infrastructures are now managed.

5.1.1 Security within Element and Network Management Systems

The concepts of Element and Network Management Systems were introduced in Chapter 1. EMSs are responsible for the management of elements in the network that are the same or from the same manufacturer. EMSs typically support the FCAPS model, and an EMS provides for interfaces to all the elements under its control. At the same time, the EMS must support interfaces to NMSs and Operations Support Systems (OSSs). The security needs of EMSs and NMSs include:

- System authentication;
- System and application access controls;
- Confidentiality of any customer-specific information within such systems;
- Reliable log file creation (preferably stored remotely via syslog mechanisms); and
- Use of communications protocols that include robust authentication and data integrity.

EMS/NMS operating system (OS) login authentication should not rely on simple login passwords. Rather, stronger EMS/NMS login authentication mechanisms should be used. Some examples of stronger authentication mechanisms include "pluggable authentication modules" (PAMs) utilizing Kerberos, security tokens (i.e., RSA Secure ID) or "smartcards," all of which offer significant protection against the use of simple/short passwords, passwords being written down, password dictionary attacks, password snooping, and password sharing issues. EMS and NMS OSs should utilize Role-Based Access Control (RBAC) so as to ensure only authorized users are able to access element and network management applications. RBAC also eliminates the need for logging in as "root" and any need to share the "root" login password. The access control bits used on Unix/Linux-based systems only provide course-grained controls that can be easily bypassed by someone with "super-user" privileges. To provide confidentiality for any stored customer information, EMS/NMS applications should employ a database management system (DBMS) that supports selective field encryption so that sensitive customer information can only be accessed by authorized DBMS users. If a sophisticated attacker is able to gain administrative/ privileged access to an EMS/NMS OS, the attacker will want to modify system log files so as to hide his/her unauthorized activities. To protect these OS log files, centralized log file management, such as remote syslog, should be used to prevent such log file modifications. EMS/NMS OSs should provide security functions, such as packet filtering (host firewalls), deep-packet inspection (host intrusion protection), and malware scanning. For communications with other MS and managed elements, EMSs/NMSs should conform to the communications security capabilities specified in ITU-T recommendations M.3016.0 through M.3016.4, which are also captured in ANSI/ATIS T1.276-2003. The ability to reasonably secure EMS/NMS northbound interfaces is not a major effort as most EMS/NMS products have been, or can be, standardized on technologies such as IPsec, TLSv1, SSH, and Secured XML. In most cases, the EMS/NMS applications run on OSs that allow for the ability to use IPsec so that the EMS/NMS requires no code change to support authenticated communication channels, which is the primary need. The only caveat is that an EMS/NMS application be capable of being hosted on an OS that supports this feature. The major issue is securing EMS/NMS southbound interfaces. There are a myriad of remote management protocols used by manufacturers, and each has its own issues. Secure management communication to elements adds cost to the device as well as complexity.

5.1.2 Telecommunications Management Network Security

The Telecommunications Management Network (TMN) was introduced in Chapter 1. Management networking security issues between TMN elements at all layers are covered in the ITU-T M.3016 series of recommendations. The M.3016 documents consider the security of management directives, monitoring and control communication used to protect assets (i.e., computers, networks, data, or other resources) from unauthorized access, use, or activity. Loss of data, denial of service (DoS), and theft of service are only some of the results of security incidents, and Table 5.1 depicts such common threat categories and examples. System and network administrators need to protect systems and their component elements from internal and external users and from attackers. Although security is multifaceted (spanning operations, physical, communications, processing, and personnel), of concern here are security problems resulting from weaknesses inherent in commonly employed configurations and technology. A threat consists of, but is not limited to, disclosure, unauthorized use, information element modifications, and DoS.

TABLE 5.1. **TMN Threats.**

Threat Category	Examples of Threats
Unauthorized Access	Hacking
	Unauthorized system access to carry out attacks
	Theft of service
Masquerade	Session replay
	Session hijacking
	Man-in-the-middle attacks
Threats to System Integrity	Unauthorized manipulation of system configuration files
	Unauthorized manipulation of system data
Threats to Integrity	Unauthorized manipulation of data
Threats to Confidentiality	Eavesdropping
	Session recording and disclosure
	Authorization violations
Denial of Service	TCP SYN flood
	ICMP "ping attacks"
	Malformed packet attacks
	Distributed DoS

The M.3016 documents address security for application management plane activities, security features to ensure that the network can be administered and managed in a secure manner. The following risks are among those with the capability to compromise the management plane:

- Inappropriate actions by authorized users or attackers that can be either malevolent or accidental,
- Bypassing or disabling control plane security (e.g., signaling, routing, naming, and discovery protocols),
- The effects of vulnerabilities in specific management utilized protocols, and
- Malware (e.g., viruses, Trojan horses, worms, or other embedded code). Once malware successfully compromises any network elements/management systems (NE/MS), the malware may use the secure network communication links to transmit attacks to other NE/MS components. These attacks may continue until network managers detect the attack and take action to eliminate it.

Basic tenets (guidelines) of M.3016 are listed in Table 5.2.

TABLE 5.2. **Design Guidelines Considered.**

Guideline	Description
Isolation	Insulation of management traffic from customer traffic
Effective Security Policies	Requirements and supporting architectures must allow for policies that are definable, flexible, enforceable, auditable, verifiable, reliable, and usable
Strong Authentication, Authorization, and Accounting (AAA)	Reliable accounting of properly authorized sessions between authenticated entities
Highest Benefit for a Given Cost	Improve security by implementing security mechanisms that are standardized, have widely available implementations, and widespread deployment, so that use histories allow security mechanisms to be evaluated
Path for Improvement	Consider next steps for enhancing and improving network management security to further satisfy given requirements with evolving technology and mechanisms or to satisfy newly defined security requirements
Technical Feasibility	Requirements must be satisfied with products, solutions, and/or technologies available today
Housekeeping	Requirements should be consistent with standard operating procedures of well-run network management operations
Open Standards	Use ideas and concepts that are already standardized or are being standardized by the standards organizations (e.g., IP security (IPsec), digital signatures). All aspects of the open standards should be considered, including system, protocols, modes, algorithm, option, key size, and encoding

5.1.3 Operations Support System Security Needs

As introduced in Chapter 1, OSSs are the computerized and automated systems that help enable Service Providers (SPs) to manage their services, share information, process orders and billing, handle maintenance, and report requests of new customers. OSS is a generic name provided to any software system that is used to manage these services, but the term was originally coined for voice line entities. Since then, OSS applications have evolved to support voice, data, and application/presentation level functionality.

As an OSS is nothing more than a software-based system (with its own security complexities), it would include its own way of providing policy and privilege management, as well as its own approach to dealing with integrity and confidentiality issues. More importantly, each OSS would include its own model of securing provided capabilities, such as:

- User level access and authentication;
- Access controls; and
- Security and user action logging.

OSS systems also have been implemented in a number of ways using many different hardware and software services and methodologies. The first OSSs were proprietary mainframe system based with tightly integrated presentation and application functionality, while newer OSS products make use of open systems, and client–server models, where the presentation of information is completely separate from application functionality, and each requires its own level of security management based upon the services it offers. For example:

- The OSS application software maintains the actual management information and implements OSS activity functionality for administrator/user actions and application layer northbound (toward other MS) and southbound (toward NMS, EMS, and elements) interfaces; and
- The Human–System interface functionality can be another piece of software (such as a web server application) also executing on the same OSS system communicating with a user agent application (such as a web browser) running on a completely different machine that allows the user to interact with the application functions through a communications channel across potentially an unsecured network.

By using a myriad of different architectural designs and system components, the management of security within, and between, OSSs becomes ever more complex, purely due to the total number of different platforms and how services can be, and are, exhibited on each.

5.1.3.1 Order Entry and Business Workflow. The starting point for any customer-driven work performed at an SP is to take an order via a service representative within the call center and enter the order into the system that initiates the activities to provide services for the customer. The order can appear through a few different input portals (entry mechanisms). One method is for the representative to enter the order information manually via a graphical user interface, such as a web browser, or a text-based terminal interface. The second method is via a wholesale gateway, which is simply a message broker that bridges the traffic from Competitive Local Exchange Carrier (CLEC)/Data Local Exchange Carrier (DLEC) companies and SPs. A number of transport mechanisms are used, including CORBA, XML Web Services, and batch files, to transfer data once authenticated.

From a security perspective, these message brokers should utilize asymmetric key pairs to provide for endpoint authentication. The public keys should be secured by encapsulation within IEEE X.509 digital certificates issued by enterprise Public Key Infrastructures (PKIs) with the corresponding private keys stored locally in the message broker systems in order to ensure the identity of the requester and the provider of each request. The use of PKIs provides a single point of access for public key requests and ensures key authenticity. One must remember that a PKI is only responsible for binding public keys with subject identities, not for directly authenticating subjects. A single trust model does not always fit when dealing with external companies, so various trust models need to be supported, such as cross-CA certification and single rooted hierarchical CA trees. This approach allows the authorities that signed the certificates provided by the remote partner to control the level of security required in dealing with other SPs. This will differ from interface to interface and the sensitivity of the data that is carried over it. It should also be noted that for wholesale gateways, requests may not always be transported over private networks, and, therefore, as there is confidential customer information contained in the requests, the underlying network transport mechanisms (protocols) should be authenticated, verified, and confidentially protected.

Once the order has been entered into the OSS, a business workflow takes over the responsibility to flow the order to all the necessary systems. There are many different ways of communicating these orders from order entry system to other OSSs. Each OSS usually provides for its own method of secured communications, or lack thereof.

Finally, the ordering system and its supporting workflow maintain all of the customer details, network information, and any billing details taken on the original order in a local database of information. This information should be considered highly sensitive and therefore undergo a level of backup and security commiserate with the level of sensitivity. Both local and external orders are stored in a long-term storage system along with security audit information and security logging which must be stored in such a way as to ensure non-repudiation and data integrity of the logs.

5.1.3.2 Provisioning and Activation Services. Once an order has been taken, the next major step is to ensure the necessary network resources exist to provide the requested level of service to the customer. If those resources do in fact exist, then the necessary changes are made to the network to support that new service. It is the provisioning and activation OSSs that provide this level of functionality. If the provisioning OSS determines there are sufficient resources, then those resources are allocated (locked) and a request is sent to the activation modules for real-time processing support the requested services. As the provisioning OSS maintains the holistic view of the network from end to end, it is also responsible for providing these details to test and fault management OSS systems to initiate the monitoring of the new service and to enter the proper work tickets where applicable.

It should be noted at this point that this level of provisioning is considered service level provisioning. There is yet another layer called infrastructure provisioning that is performed prior to services turn-up. This is when new equipment is acquired, placed in the proper central offices, and then the necessary physical interconnects established, as well as the resources within the device to support auto-flow provisioning.

Once the provisioning OSS has fully allocated and locked down the resources, the activation OSS takes over and communicates either to EMSs, NMSs, or network/service elements directly through a number of different protocol types and stacks. Each protocol and stack has its own security requirements and needs. Another area of security control is the information that represents the global view of the network. This data is a corporate asset that must be secured: who is able to alter that view must also be controlled as well, and whether that request appears from a machine-to-machine interface or a user-to-machine interface. Changes to the network, all actions, and requests should be audited and stored for long-term retrieval. This raises concerns for repudiation and both information and data integrity for those audits and as well generalized security logging.

5.1.3.3 Testing Services.
Once a new service has been turned up by the activation and provisioning OSSs, all of the necessary customer service information is sent to the test OSS, and a request to verify the integrity of the new service is specified. The test OSS will then issue various tests that can be either disruptive or non-disruptive to ensure that the service is in fact working as it should be. Another mode of request is when the SP operations organization is provided a work/trouble ticket specifying that a customer indicated service is in a non-working state. The test OSS will be used to determine where the fault, if any, may lie. The requests to the test OSS should be submitted over a secured communications channel (aka northbound interface). To perform these services, the test OSS is provided a complete services view of the new customer. As these tests can, in some cases, be service-affecting, it is important that policy and privilege management be managed to ensure that the request is legitimate before service disruption occurs.

5.1.3.4 Fault Management Services.
After a service has been turned up and has undergone test to ensure it is working, it is then turned over to the fault management OSS to monitor the service to ensure it is always working. If at any time a disruption occurs for the service, it is the responsibility of the fault management OSS to alert the necessary operations personnel to investigate the problem and fix it if necessary.

Once the service has been turned up and tested, the entire service order and the entire layout of the underlying infrastructure required to support that service are transmitted to the fault management OSS. The incoming information should be authenticated and then stored for monitoring. This data should be considered sensitive so the necessary controls should be used to ensure this data is not corrupted by accident or maliciously.

Now the fault management OSS monitors the resources supporting all services. In most cases, the fault management OSS communicates with an EMS, NMS, or directly to elements. All of these interfaces must undergo authentication and authorization to ensure access is allowed to authorized entities.

There is no one single OSS that supports fault management for all services, so responsibilities for different service infrastructure elements are covered by a number of different OSSs. There are a number of places where services are layered on top of other services. When a problem occurs, the monitoring OSSs must coordinate to ensure a single work trouble ticket is issued to the proper Network Operations Center (NOC) based upon where in the layering of resources the problem has occurred. Because of this, it means the fault management OSSs must all intercommunicate and share data. As such, all those communication channels used for data sharing should be authenticated and protected for confidentially.

5.1.3.5 Billing. Once the order has been completed, information about it is sent to the billing OSS so that the necessary charges can be sent to the customer. The data transferred requires the proper levels of authentication and authorization since financial information is involved. The data contained in the request for billing will also contain customer information that is highly confidential and, if subverted, could lead to customer identity theft, fraud, or other loss.

5.1.3.6 Engineering/Inventory. To support any customer service, a number of elements must be installed and managed. The engineering/inventory OSSs store the details about each new equipment/element, the exact instance of each equipment type (i.e., number of cards, type, etc.), and where it is located. This information is transmitted to the provisioning OSSs. This is done so that the equipment can be used immediately for customer services. It is also done to ensure proper synchronization with the provisioning OSSs and the actual NE. The provisioning OSSs need to know that the information about assets is, in fact, from an authenticated source, and that the requesting engineer is authorized to make the request. Coordinated authentication and access control mechanisms need to exist between the OSSs.

5.1.3.7 Work/Trouble Ticketing Systems. When a customer calls the SP to report a problem, a report (a ticket) is initiated which is then tracked though the various support organizations that will fix and monitor the problem until resolution. This ticket is opened for the lifetime of that trouble. For SPs, the number of troubles reported and the duration of each is tracked daily for reports to management and, more importantly, the Federal Communications Commission and Public Utilities Commission which could result in fines due to outages. As with any OSS, authentication and access controls are important to prevent spoofed tickets, which could result in lost dollars due to wasted deployment of trucks or workforce. More importantly, the tickets must also be verified as to their information validity. The long-term storage as well as the reporting must ensure proper authenticity of the ticket, it was time-stamped with a secured source of time to ensure proper duration, and non-repudiation.

5.1.3.8 Outside Plant Management. Outside plant (OSP) management includes not only systems (work/trouble ticketing OSSs) to manage the workforce outside of the central offices but also any supporting system that assists them in the roles they perform. As such, work requests will arrive into OSP management OSSs, need to be authenticated, and then processed. These work requests can arrive either from the work/ trouble ticketing OSS or the provisioning OSS. There are a number of supporting services that assist the OSP workforce. For example, Global Positioning System tracking systems can ensure the location and duration of each unit of work. Mobile devices that have the ability to take customers in and out of service, or the ability to perform tests that can be service disrupting, require authentication and access control mechanisms, along with confidentiality capabilities and anti-theft mechanisms.

5.1.4 Reflections on Past ITU Treatment of Managing Security

Whenever security mechanisms are deployed, some form of management capability is necessary. Security management is concerned with the management of security mechanisms to:

- provide operational efficiency and a unified methodology for managing security service/functions within the infrastructure;
- reduce operational complexity of, and operational training costs associated with, security-related administration;
- increase operational productivity, and minimize operational errors, during security-related administration; and
- facilitate and support a rapidly evolving communications and services infrastructure.

Unfortunately, the discussion of needed security management capabilities in ITU-T X.800, introduced in Chapter 1, is limited to enumerating a number of security management categories spanning system security, security service, and security mechanism management. Under system security management, the following areas are identified:

- overall security policy management without any further detail;
- interaction with other management functions without any further detail;
- interaction with managed element security service controls without any further detail;
- event handling management with a brief statement that this area includes reporting, alarm generation, and threshold management;
- security audit management with a brief statement that this area includes event logging, remote audit log and event collection, and reporting; and
- security recovery management with a brief statement that this area includes administration of suspected security event recovery reaction rules, remote reporting, and administrator activities.

However, no useful detail is provided for any of the aforementioned areas. Under security service management, the following areas are identified without any further detail:

- determination and assignment of service security protection mechanism;
- administration of security mechanism selection rules to protect a service;

- negotiation of available security mechanisms;
- invocation of security mechanisms; and
- interaction with other security management functions.

Under security mechanism management, the following areas are identified:

- key management with a brief statement that this area may include asymmetric and symmetric key generation, distribution, and replacement via either a key distribution center (KDC) or manual mechanisms;
- encipherment management with a brief statement that this area may include interaction with key management functions, algorithm selection, symmetric encryption synchronization, and administration of cryptographic parameters;
- digital signature management with a brief statement that this area may include interaction with key management functions, algorithm selection, protocol and third-party usage, and administration of cryptographic parameters;
- access control management with a brief statement that this area may include security attribute distribution (including access control or capability lists) and the use of access-control-related protocols;
- data integrity management with a brief statement that this area may include interaction with key management functions, algorithm selection, protocol usage, and administration of cryptographic parameters;
- authentication management with a brief statement that this area may include authentication credentials distribution (i.e., passwords, challenges, digital signatures, or other cryptographically processed information) and the use of authentication-related protocols;
- traffic padding management with a brief statement that this area may include administration of rules governing attributes such as data rates, padding mechanisms, and message characteristics;
- routing control management with a brief statement that this area may include link or sub-network selection based on specified criteria; and
- notarization management with a brief statement that this area may include notary information distribution, interaction between notaries, and the use of notarization-related protocols.

The point is made that "there exist strong similarities between digital signature management and encipherment management" (ITU-T X.800, clause 8.4.3) where, in fact, the application of digital signatures for achieving peer–entity authentication and data integrity is nothing more than a specific use of asymmetric encryption (encipherment) and should not be considered as separate from encipherment management where encipherment is basically the use of encryption to achieve Data-origin authentication, data confidentiality, or data integrity. It is noted that "When using cryptographic techniques for data integrity, there exist strong similarities between data integrity management and encipherment management" (ITU-T X.800, clause 8.4.5) where, in fact, data integrity always relies on the use of a protected message digest algorithm. There are three ways to provide data integrity, namely, receiving a clear-text message along with:

1. a message digest (output from a cryptographically secure hash algorithm) that is the result of processing the clear-text message along with a shared secret symmetric key by the selected hash algorithm; or
2. a symmetrically encrypted message digest that is the result of processing the clear-text message by the selected hash algorithm; or
3. a private-key-based asymmetrically encrypted message digest (a digital signature) that is the result of processing the clear-text message by the selected hash algorithm.

As can be seen, the message digest is protected using either a shared secret key directly, a shared secret key and a symmetric encryption algorithm, or a private key and an asymmetric encryption algorithm. Therefore, one should not necessarily draw a distinction between the key management needs for encipherment, digital signatures, and data integrity.

Some other points worth noting are that:

- Traffic padding is no longer considered a security mechanism in commercial environments;
- Routing control is no longer considered a security mechanism in commercial environments other than when specifying the use of IP security (IPsec) between specified communicating systems as part of IPsec policy configuration activities; and
- The concept of notarization services/mechanisms has been ignored within the commercial arena, although one could perhaps argue that PKIs or distributed Identity Management capabilities are possibly related to notarization concepts.

The ITU-T M.3050 eTOM documents do not consider security management, or security mechanisms, as part of their "Strategy, Infrastructure & Product" or "Operations" process areas. They only focus on security in the form of "Enterprise Risk Management" within the "Enterprise Management" process area. Consequently, eTOM does not address security management from an operational perspective and does not provide any additional detail or elaboration regarding security management beyond what is found in ITU-T X.800. ITU's recommendation (ITU-T M.3060) for the management of next-generation networks addresses the management of security by referencing ITU-T X.805 and ITU-T M.3016 and then states:

> To deal with the complexity of securing all of the NGN, including its management plane, there is a need to mechanize the application of various security services, mechanisms, and tools by employing operation systems to automate the process. Requirements and architecture for such operations systems, also known as Security Management Systems (SMS), is for further study. (ITU-T M.3060, Clause 9.5)

ITU-T M.3016 has already been discussed, so let us consider what is discussed within ITU-T X.805 (introduced in Chapter 1). ITU-T X.805 sets out a framework for addressing end-to-end network security and defines the concept of security dimensions that span eight aspects of security. The ITU-T X.800 Access Control, Authentication, Data Confidentiality, Data Integrity, and Non-repudiation services align with the ITU-T X.805 security dimensions of the same name. ITU-T X.805 specifies three additional security dimensions, namely:

- Communications Security (imported from the military security environment) which is of questionable value in a commercial context;
- Availability (which recognizes the relationship between security and network availability); and
- Privacy (which should not be considered as privacy is an objective of a subject to control access to information about said subject).

ITU-T X.805 partitions a telecommunications network into a three-layer hierarchy of equipment and facilities groupings comprising:

- the infrastructure security layer;
- the services security layer; and
- the applications security layer.

In addition, ITU-T X.805 defines the following three types of activities (security planes) that can occur at every layer as:

- management security plane;
- control/signaling security plane; and
- end-user security plane.

Unfortunately, ITU-T X.805 does not address the management of security other than to consider it as part of the management security plane. The third aspect of security noted by ITU-T M.3060, clause 9.5, the need for a Security Management System (SMS), is considered in Section 5.1.6 The management of security as presented in ITU-T M.3400 (introduced in Chapter 1) is organized around the concepts of prevention, detection, containment, and recovery and security administration. M.3400 provides the greatest degree of detail on security management of all the ITU-T documents discussed so far. However, as noted in Chapter 1, M.3400 does not provide any guidance on how to provide the security management capabilities.

5.1.5 Management of Security Services and Mechanisms Revisited

Following is a short discussion of security services and selected security mechanisms that are needed for protecting systems (both managed devices and associated MS) and their intercommunication.

5.1.5.1 Key Management. Key management is a critical service. The use of asymmetrical keys as the basis of peer–entity authentication is of great importance, while shared symmetric secret keys are crucial for efficient data integrity and data confidentiality. The proper management and centralization of symmetric and asymmetric keys will greatly reduce the complexity of rolling out new services and reduce the duplication of identities or, even worse, misidentification within the company. Beyond centralized key repositories, proper key management such as key rings, backup and restore, automatic key updates, and key signature management are critical services. Asymmetric public keys should be distributed and managed via a PKI. Shared secret symmetric keys should be dynamically generated by security protocols (i.e., IPsec, TLS/SSL, SSH) when possible, and other security protocols without dynamic key generation should rely on KDC systems such as Kerberos.

5.1.5.2 Non-repudiation. As data is moved back and forth between SP systems and wholesale partners, the capability to counter repudiation (denial) of requests is of high importance. Technologies that provide non-repudiation (i.e., IPsec, TLS, SSH) are being utilized today. But to provide a cohesive system, the ability to manage the archiving of secured data and signatures as well as the proper archival of the keys used to digitally sign data are also required.

5.1.5.3 Time-Stamping. The use of secure time-stamping is necessary and should be used to support security audit and logging, key management, notarization services, integrity verification, and many other areas. A common high-quality authenticable time source should be available to all MS and managed elements to facilitate time-stamp synchronization between audit logs and alarms. A common approach used to synchronize system time across multiple devices is the Network Time Protocol (RFC 5905 for NTPv4 or its predecessor RFC 1305 for NTPv3). NTPv3 has been in use for many years, with very few organizations using its message digest and secret-key-based authentication due to the lack of key management capabilities. NTPv4 was finalized just 2 years ago with a new authentication approach along with backward compatibility with NTPv3, but NTPv4 has not been widely deployed to date.

5.1.5.4 Privilege and Policy Management. The ability to manage user/administrator privilege and identities in a unified manner is a growing issue since systems by default implement their own identity, authentication, and authorization services. The ability to standardize on:

- a single authentication method, such as single sign on;
- a single method to create organizational user/administrator identities; and
- the use of standardized roles and responsibilities

for the management of security mechanisms will reduce errors and deter malicious activities. This not only reduces management "level of effort" but also assists in minimizing potential mistakes or mis-mapping of identities to capabilities. It will also reduce the amount of time required to map a new identity to the network and provide for the ability to immediately revoke capabilities or privileges. Finally, the ability to delegate responsibility for security administration allows for the seamless flow of work regardless of the need to delegate tasks for whatever the reason. With a single point of control, this task now becomes manageable in the face of the ever-growing number of managed devices.

5.1.5.5 Confidentiality and Integrity. For most enterprise systems, the need to provide confidentiality of data is not as important as authentication, authorization, and integrity capabilities, unless that data includes PII or other information that must be kept confidential as specified by legislation or regulation. The ability to monitor and manage confidentiality and integrity mechanisms with sufficient performance levels becomes very important. Beyond just communication channels, the confidentiality and integrity of management data are required.

5.1.5.6 Audit and Logging. Most, if not all, managed devices and MS generate copious amounts of security logging data and security audit trails. The ability to collect and maintain these data trails needs to be centralized for a single point of control and thereby a single point of contact to ensure proper repudiation and proper long-term storage. Core security management capabilities are the use of remote "syslog" functionality coupled with automated audit reporting and the use of security information event management (SIEM) tools.

5.1.5.7 Intrusion Detection and Prevention. Every organizational network and host device can be targeted for intrusion by an outside party that was not provided authorized access. The ability to detect and counteract intrusions is highly important due to the sensitivity of the data contained within these systems. As such, the proper management of intrusion detection and prevention systems to ensure for a cohesive policy for this feature will become paramount. Intrusion detection and prevention goes significantly beyond stateful packet filtering (aka firewalls) techniques. Firewalls are an excellent way to control the flow of network traffic between, and within, enterprise networks and sub-networks efficiently. Yet, firewalls are unable to detect many forms of attacks carried by valid and approved application protocols. Both network- and host-based intrusion detection and prevention systems are able to deal with far more forms of attacks and should be considered as a major security tool, especially when managed in a centralized and uniform manner.

5.1.5.8 Malicious Software Detection. The ability to detect and quarantine malicious software (malware) is crucial in modern organizations. A virus, worm, or other form of malware that is able to infect an enterprise's systems would be very dangerous and could create huge breaches in the security of the network. There are many entry points that malware can utilize, from classic network activities to removable media (i.e., thumb drives, CDs, and DVDs) to personal devices as in the Bring Your Own Device (BYOD) trend (letting employees use personally owned devices within the organization). Thus, anti-malware applications watching the OSs of both managed devices and MS are necessary, especially when BYOD is allowed. Such anti-malware applications need to be managed in a centralized manner, including the roll-out of software and anti-malware "signatures" and other detection rules. Another security management approach worth considering is to deploy device scanning technology that prevents a device (including BYOD equipment) from attaching to and using an organization's network infrastructure until the device has been remotely scanned for the presence of malware.

5.1.5.9 Secured Software Distribution. It is routine to see new versions, updates, and patches released for the OSs and most application software used within enterprise-deployed devices. Some MS provide mechanisms to automatically distribute software for self-upgrade or to elements provided by device vendors. In all cases, the management of software load integrity is very important. When a vendor ships a piece of software, the vendor should provide for the notarization of the new software, or patch/update, via a cryptographically secured hash digest or digital signature to ensure the validity of the load as provided by the vendor. Once the released software is validated, it should be first installed in a test environment, that reflects the software currently being used for production operations, and tested to ensure that the production software will not fail when the new software is rolled out into the production environment. Once validated and tested, the software should be transferred to an enterprise software repository and then distributed from the repository to production devices. Each production device should verify software updates coming from the repository via the same cryptographically secured hash digest or digital signature mechanism used to validate the initial receipt from the vendor.

5.1.6 A Security Management Framework

The third area discussed by ITU-TM.3060, clause 9.5, is the concept of an SMS. We focus on such a system here. Not long after the publication of M.3060, work began on the development of such a concept which led to the publication of ITU-TM.3410 in 2008 to document the functional requirements for such an SMS and was based on the ANSI Standard ATIS 0300074.2006. In M.3410, the concept of Security Management was broadened to include:

- Administrative login account management;
- Administrative authentication credentials management;
- Attack identification–recognition;
- Security service mechanism configuration management; and
- Element vulnerability analysis.

All these are addressed later in this section.

The intent of M.3410 was to present a framework for an integrated set of security management functionality that takes into consideration security management mechanisms that an enterprise may already possess. Figure 5.1 depicts the functional groups within the SMS framework. We will discuss the management functional groups a little later; some functional groups worth covering now are the:

- Communications Interface;
- Administrator Interface; and
- Security Management Information.

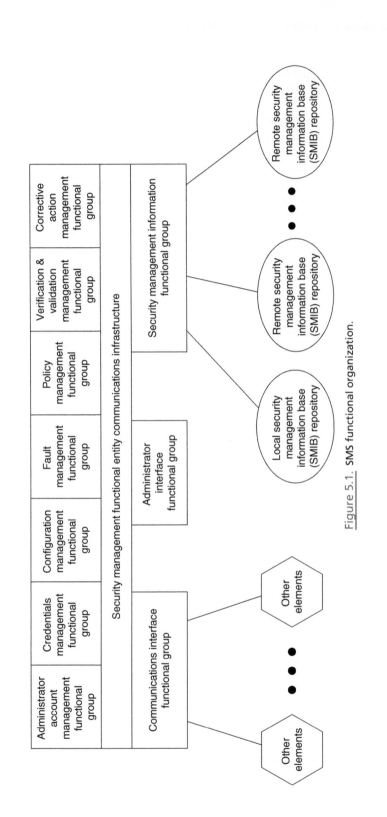

Figure 5.1. SMS functional organization.

The Communications Interface functional group is composed of different functional entities that support the different protocols needed for communicating with the variety of managed devices and systems within the infrastructure. Within this group of functions would be support for different versions of the management protocol SNMP, as well as the use of XML, telnet or preferably SSH, HTTP-based web interaction, and other approaches for remote management. The Administrator Interface functional group is composed of different functional entities that support different forms of user interfaces, such as a simple command line approach, an HTML/XML web approach, or other forms of human–system communication.

The Security Management Information functional group is responsible for providing storage of management information utilized by other SMS functions. Since the SMS will likely be deployed along with existing MS, which already maintain management information storage, this functional group needs to provide two sub-functions:

- Local SMS storage of management information and
- Tracking of, and access to, management information stored/maintained by existing EMS, NMS, OSS, and other MS.

As previously noted, an SMS is expected to augment existing MS and provide a unified approach to managing security across all organizational infrastructure components. This relationship is depicted in Figure 5.2.

Now let us consider the remaining SMS management functional areas for:

- Authentication Credentials Management;
- Security Configuration Management;
- Security Event, Fault & Attack Management;
- Corrective Action Management;
- Administrative Account Management; and
- Security Verification and Validation Management.

Authentication Credentials Management spans the creation, archiving, distribution, and revocation of digital credentials supporting authentication and authorization for a heterogeneous mix of managed elements, across the following areas:

- Subject authentication X.509v3 certificate request processing, public/private key generation, certificate creation, repository loading, archiving, and revocation (organization public key infrastructure);
- Shared authentication symmetric key generation, secure distribution, archiving/ escrow, and revocation (organization electronic key management services); and
- Subject authorization X.509v3 certificate request processing, certificate creation, repository loading, archiving, and revocation.

However, this function is not limited to PKI-based certificate management, although digital certificates and associated private keys for devices need management. This

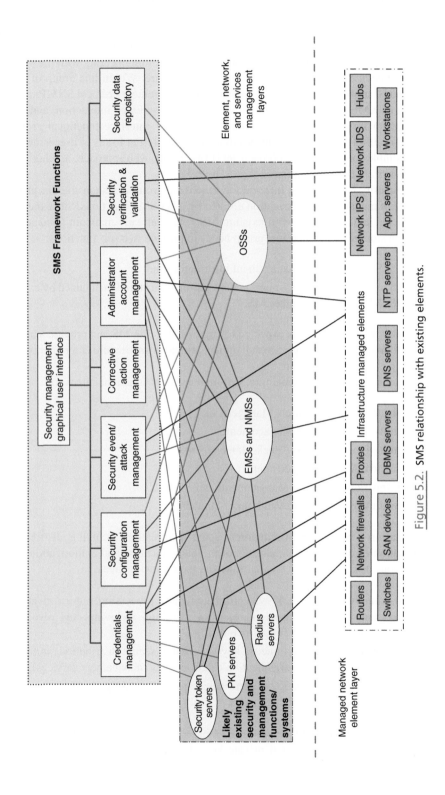

Figure 5.2. SMS relationship with existing elements.

function interacts with and manages existing credentials systems, such as Security Token usage, RSA SecureID products, Radius servers, and credentials (i.e., passwords), used for local device authentication.

Security Configuration Management spans the creation, archiving, downloading, validation, and modification of security-related configuration attributes, within a heterogeneous mix of managed elements and other MS for the following areas:

- Organizational policy definition and specification as machine-readable rules and tracking of said rules against other organization-security-related configuration attributes;
- Network and host located source/destination address and port packet filtering rules (i.e., firewalls);
- Network located application protocol packet filtering rules (i.e., an application proxy);
- Network and host located deep packet inspection rules (i.e., intrusion detection/ prevention);
- Managed element internal object access control rules, authentication, authorization, integrity, confidentiality, and logging/reporting default configuration parameters; and
- Organizational default symmetric and asymmetric encryption parameters, attributes, algorithms, Certificate Authorities (CAs), Registration Authorities (RAs), and directories.

Security Event, Fault & Attack Management for a heterogeneous mix of managed elements and other MSs capable of performing the following activities.

Security Event Management includes:

- event reception—collection, reporting, and archiving and
- managed element log retrieval, reporting, and archiving, which may include use of remote syslog systems/clients.

Security Fault Management includes:

- event analysis for attack indications;
- log analysis for attack indications; and
- alarm generation, distribution, tracking, and logging.

Attack identification–mitigation includes:

- identification of existing and or incipient attacks on infrastructure and
- attack tracking (similar to trouble ticket management).

The use of Security Event Management (SEM) and SIEM products can be considered as likely existing MS that this functional area interfaces/interacts with.

Corrective Action Management interacts with the Attack identification–mitigation component of Security Event, Fault & Attack Management to support system-generated recommendations on how to isolate, block, or mitigate existing and/or incipient attacks on infrastructure. This functional area could also interact with Security Configuration Management by issuing specific reconfiguration commands allowing automated isolation, blocking, or mitigation actions.

Administrative Account Management spans the creation, archiving, downloading, validation, and modification of accounts used by administrators, and associated privileges and attributes for a heterogeneous mix of managed elements within an enterprise, for the following areas:

- Individual administrative user account creation;
- Specification of administrative user identifiers;
- Resetting of administrative user passwords; and
- Specification and maintenance of administrative user access rights and privileges.

Security Verification and Validation Management works with and coordinates the use of external tools and systems focusing on:

- the auditing of managed element security-related configuration attributes;
- penetration testing of managed elements;
- network-based intrusion detection;
- host-based intrusion detection; and
- verification of managed element compliance to organizational security policies.

This function is expected to interface with tools that perform host and network scanning (i.e., ISS, Nessus, SAINT) and configuration change detection (i.e., Tripwire, OSSEC, AIDE, Samhain).

Although the functional requirements for an SMS are defined by M.3410, there are presently no currently available commercial products that provide an M.3410-compliant SMS. However, one should expect the availability of commercial management applications, based on M.3410, within a few years from now.

At this point we now consider security mechanisms, processes, and procedures that are appropriate for operations personnel and management when operating and maintaining an organization's information processing and communications infrastructure.

5.2 SECURITY OPERATIONS AND MAINTENANCE

Operations Security (OPSEC) focuses on ensuring compliance with an organization's information security programs and policies. Central to OPSEC is a well-thought-out and dynamic operational security compliance program that not only receives senior management support but has senior management involvement as discussed in Section 3.4.1.

5.2.1 Operational Security Compliance Programs

An Operational Security Compliance Program exists to ensure that all those business requirements, policy statements, and specific security dictates are being complied with. An organization should not consider its Compliance Program as all inclusive, nor should it be viewed as the full security program; rather it is a program that communicates, tracks, and monitors how well the enterprise fulfills its compliance statements. A Compliance Program is not a static process. Rather it is a cyclic process, as shown in Figure 5.3. Policies, standards, and regulations legislation drive requirements, the requirements drive selection, deployment, and operation of security mechanisms, and completing the cycle is verification of satisfying/complying with the requirements.

The enterprise security governance program and associated policy document(s) need to include statements and requirements for Security Compliance verification that articulate security requirements, should be "timeless" and independent of technology (as much as possible), and should be reviewed annually. A good "free" reference source is the Sans Policy Project at http://www.sans.org/resources/policies/

Some of the main standards or legislation/regulations that necessitate compliance verification are:

- HIPAA (Health Insurance Portability and Accountability Act of 1996);
- SOX (Sarbanes–Oxley Act of 2002);
- PCI DSS (Payment Card Industry Data Security Standard);

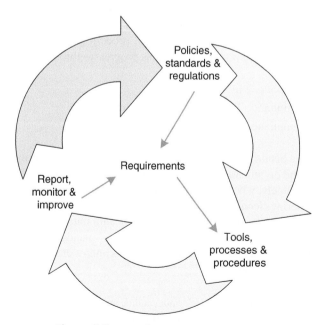

Figure 5.3. Compliance cycle major phases.

- PII Laws (now 46 states have enacted these laws); and
- FISMA (Federal Information Security Management Act of 2002).

Security Compliance Procedures should:

- articulate security requirements but be more detailed, as these procedures need to be followed by operations personnel regularly;
- be technology or process specific as necessary; and
- be reviewed annually, or as technology changes.

Some good "free" references (source) on compliance policies, procedures, and tools are:

- National Institute of Standards and Technology (NIST) at http://csrc.nist.gov/publications/PubsSPs.html
- Center for Internet Security (CIS)—Guides at http://www.cisecurity.org/
- Microsoft Developer Network (MSDN) at http://msdn.microsoft.com/en-us/library/ms998408.aspx

Appendix M contains an example operational hardening procedure for the Microsoft XP OS. As can be seen, this procedure is quite specific and provides detailed directions for configuring the XP OS to comply with the enterprise security policies.

There exist a number of Security Compliance Frameworks, some of which we have already discussed in Chapter 3 from a general security governance perspective. COBIT, ITIL, and FISMA are also excellent sources for procedures guidance and example procedures and OPSEC checklists that should be considered for inclusion within an Operational Security Compliance Program. The process of verifying an Operational Security Compliance Program for completeness progresses through three phases:

- Security Compliance Inventory;
- Security Compliance Tools and Checklists; and
- Security Compliance Report, Monitor, and Improve.

When conducting a Security Compliance Inventory, identify what is critical information and applications the organization depends on. Understand the way data flows through the organization, namely, who and what touches the data when, where, and why.

When considering Security Compliance Tools and Checklists, it is better to automate as much compliance checking as possible. If automation (full or partial) is not possible, then make it easy with checklists that are easy to understand and applicable to specific technology or processes. After selecting tools and/or checklists, determine, and document, the following points:

Who: roles and responsibilities for performing audits, analyses, adjudications, etc.
What: assets and processes are critical, non-critical?
When: how often to perform compliance checks and audits?
How: what to report, to whom, prioritization and remediation plans.

These items will need input from, and likely are controlled by, the organization's senior security and general management principals. The direct oversight of compliance verification checks and activities is commonly coordinated with personnel from the organization (or sub-unit) being reviewed/audited. Other situations require independent outside auditors. Selection of tools and checklists should be done based on how well they assist in verifying specific detailed security requirement or security policy statement compliance or degree of deviation.

Security Compliance Report, Monitor, and Improve activities cover the reporting of review–audit activities and analyses and the ongoing monitoring for compliance violations. The first time a set of compliance review–audit activities are conducted, the reports may seem to present an overwhelming picture that with remediation will improve over time. Prioritizing and developing remediation action plans with stable budget allocations is crucial to improvement. On the Monitor side, you should be looking for steady improvements and optimally obtain an understanding of trends that could provide early warnings or signify need for a change in requirements.

5.2.1.1 Tools. Following are a sample (far from inclusive) of tools used for numerous operational security tasks including compliance verification:

- Nessus: a proprietary comprehensive vulnerability scanning tool free of charge for personal use in a non-enterprise environment (www.nessus.org);
- Security Administrator Tool for Analyzing Networks (SATAN): a testing and reporting toolbox that collects a variety of information about networked hosts (www.porcupine.org/satan/);
- System Administrator's Integrated Network Tool (SAINT): a computer software used for scanning computer networks for security vulnerabilities and exploiting found vulnerabilities (www.saintcorporation.com/);
- Nmap: runs on Linux, Microsoft Windows, Solaris, BSD, and Mac OS X and used to discover computers and services on a computer network and may be able to determine various details about the remote computers, including OS, device type, uptime, software product used to run a service, exact version number of that product, presence of some firewall techniques, and, on a local area network, even vendor of the remote network card (www.nmap.org/);
- Security Event Manager (SEM): a computerized tool used on enterprise data networks to centralize storage and interpretation of logs, or events, generated by other software; also called Security Information Managers (SIMs) and Security Information and Event Managers (SIEMs). SEMs can help satisfy US regulatory requirements such as those of Sarbanes–Oxley Act which require that certain events, such as accesses to systems and modifications to data, be logged and that the logs be kept for a specified period of time;
- Professional Hackers Linux Assault Kit (PHLAK): a Linux distribution Live CD that focuses on providing network security tools including security tools such as nmap, nessus, snort, the coroner's toolkit, ethereal (now called Wireshark), hping2, proxychains, lczroex, ettercap, kismet, hunt, and brutus (www.sourceforge.net/projects/phlakproject/);

- DenyHosts: a security tool for SSH servers to prevent brute force attacks on SSH servers by monitoring invalid login attempts and blocking the originating IP addresses (www.denyhosts.sourceforge.net/);
- Network Security Toolkit (NST): a Linux Distribution Live CD/DVD that provides Network Security Administrators with a comprehensive set of Open Source security and networking tools to perform routine security and networking diagnostic and monitoring tasks within network computing environments (www.networksecuritytoolkit.org/nst/index.html);
- Yersinia: a network security/hacking tool for Unix-like OSs, designed to take advantage of some weakness in different network protocols, still under development with attack targets including Spanning Tree Protocol (STP), Cisco Discovery Protocol (CDP), Dynamic Trunking Protocol (DTP), Dynamic Host Configuration Protocol (DHCP), Hot Standby Router Protocol (HSRP), IEEE 802.1Q, IEEE 802.1X, and VLAN Trunking Protocol (VTP) (www.yersinia.net/);
- SekChek Local: defined as a set of automated computer security analysis and benchmarking tools to analyze security controls on hosts or domains across an organization's LAN and comprises of three built-in security analysis tools: SekChek SAM, SekChek AD, and SekChek for SQL (www.sekchek.com/SekCheklocalsw.htm);
- Netcat: a computer networking utility for reading from and writing to network connections on either TCP or UDP (netcat.sourceforge.net/); and
- Check Point Integrity: an endpoint security product designed to protect personal computers and networks from computer worms, Trojan horses, spyware, and intrusion attempts by hackers (www.checkpoint.com/products/endpoint_security/index.html).

All these tools can be used for good or bad; the very capabilities that make these tools useful for security engineering and administration lend themselves to Threat Agents as possible attack tools. A sound enterprise policy regarding these tools is to restrict possession and use to only authorized employees. It is strongly advisable to notify all employees that possession/use of these types of software is ground for serious disciplinary action which may include termination, unless an employee is authorized in writing that possession is necessary as part of the employee's job responsibilities.

5.2.1.2 CheckLists. As already noted, the use of checklists within an operational security compliance program is quite useful in ensuring uniformity of operations personnel activities. Currently there are 233 available checklists that can be retrieved from the URL: http://web.nvd.nist.gov/view/ncp/repository spanning the 28 product categories listed in Table 5.3.

The NIST checklists are based on commonly accepted technical security principles and practices, as well as SP 800-27 "Engineering Principles for Information Technology Security (A Baseline for Achieving Security)" and the NSA Information Assurance

TABLE 5.3. **NIST Available Checklist Categories.**

• Anti-virus software	• Applications servers	• Configuration management software
• Malware	• Desktop applications	• Desktop clients
• Directory services	• DNS servers	• Email servers
• Encryption software	• Enterprise applications	• General-purpose servers
• Handheld devices	• Identity management	• Database management systems
• Network switches	• Network routers	• Multi-functional peripherals
• Office application suites	• Operating systems	• Peripheral devices
• Security servers	• Firewalls	• Virtualization software
• Web browsers	• Web servers	• Wireless email
• Wireless networks		

Technical Framework (IATF), available at:http://oai.dtic.mil/oai/oai?verb=getRecord&metadataPrefix=html&identifier=ADA393328

The use of such checklists is advisable.

5.2.2 Security Operations Reviews and Audits

All organizations should have a single individual as the "Chief Security Officer" (CSO) who holds final responsibility for the security governance of the organization. The more independent this position is from the other groups within the organization requiring oversight, the more objective and consistent the results of security audits will be, thereby ensuring consistent policy compliance. There is a further advantage when the CSO reports into the management hierarchy at a sufficiently high level, namely, the CSO will have the necessary authority to enforce security policy compliance upon development and operations groups, as well as other enterprise units. An organization should adopt an approach for performing audits and technical/operational reviews by a group from within the CSO organization. The two major forms of security-related audits are life cycle security reviews and external compliance audits.

5.2.2.1 Life Cycle Security Reviews. Equipment, software, and process security reviews should occur throughout the deployment life cycle. More specifically at least once each year, each major area of an enterprise's infrastructure, and its associated operations activities, should undergo a security review by an operationally independent group. Appendices L, N, and O contain example audit procedures that can be used as part of these security reviews. The results, findings, and conclusions should, at a minimum, include the following:

- What vulnerabilities were uncovered;
- Recommendations for equipment modifications, changes, or upgrades that will reduce vulnerability exposure or further procedural or organizational changes that will reduce vulnerability exposure or further reduce the probability of attack success;
- Degree of operational staff cooperation or interference;
- Recommended timeframe for changes;

- Have new threats (agents and or attack types) appeared?
- Are all organizational security policies and procedures being complied with?

Review findings should be presented to the operations management team for the area being reviewed and to senior personnel within the CSO organization. Issues and conflicts regarding implementation of review recommendations should be escalated to the Senior Management Security Steering Committee. It is strongly suggested that any decision to ignore or deviate from the review recommendations requires documented Senior Management Security Steering Committee approval. These decisions should be based on sound risk versus benefit (cost vs. benefit) analyses.

Another aspect of life cycle reviews is to maintain a documentation trail that tracks initial deployed security capabilities, all security-related upgrades, improvements, modifications, and any security policy exceptions that may apply. This record should also note how equipment is used, the types of information that had been stored on it, along with information about authorized personnel.

A third advantage of doing periodic life cycle security reviews is how these reviews position the organization for getting through external compliance audits. Virtually all organizations will face security audits conducted by external third entities. These external security audits may be due to PCI-DSS compliance for continued approval to process credit card payments, HIPAA audits, SOX-driven financial audits and reporting, or FISMA compliance as part of bidding on government contracts. By performing periodic life cycle security reviews, the organization will know both the strengths and weaknesses present in its security posture (how well or lacking it is in complying with its security governance policies, associated external security mandates, and legislation/regulations) prior to an external compliance audit. By possessing an in-depth knowledge of its security posture, and action plans in place for mitigating deficiencies, prior to an external compliance audit, the organization is better positioned to respond to external audit negative findings.

5.2.2.2 External Compliance Audits. As already noted, external compliance audits are a reality organizations face. It is advantageous to have a Single Point of Contact (SPoC) group between the organization and the third-party external auditors. It is recommended that this SPoC group be located within the CSO organization, as discussed in Section 3.4.1. The SPoC group members can mediate interaction between the auditor personnel and organization employees to ensure bilateral cooperation during the audit process and facilitate effective communication. Since personnel from the CSO organization will be routinely involved in organizational life cycle security reviews and associated security posture mitigation planning, these personnel are well positioned to facilitate arriving at mutually agreeable audit outcomes.

5.2.3 Security Event Response and Incident Management

Security incident management is a function of managing and protecting computer assets, networks, and information systems in the course of dealing with security-related events or outright cyber attacks. As enterprise systems become more critical to the personal and economic welfare of our society, organizations (public and private sector groups, associations, and enterprises) should understand their responsibilities to the public good and to the welfare of their members and stakeholders. This responsibility includes having a program and procedures for mitigating the damage when the organization experiences a security event.

Computer security incident management involves:

- monitoring for, and detecting, security events within computers and network infrastructures;
- the development of a well understood and predictable response to damaging events such as computer intrusions; and
- the execution of proper responses to those events.

Incident management requires a process and a response team which follows this process. This definition of computer security incident management follows the standards and definitions described in the National Incident Management System (NIMS) (http://www.nimsonline.com/). Since organizations will differ in how they organize their personnel, we cannot go into any details about specific groups involved in event management other to say that:

- Customers, employees, or other individuals should report a problem to the enterprise "help desk";
- The "help desk" person should open (create) a "Trouble Ticket" that captures the initial information from the reporting party; or
- Operations staff within the enterprise Network or Security Operations Center (NOC or SOC) should identify a problem, as part of their administration, surveillance, and monitoring activities, and should open (create) a "Trouble Ticket" directly.

Each open Trouble Ticket should be tracked through a cycle of steps covering:

- Review to determine the criticality of the event based on the complexity of the problem, number of affected elements, services, and/or customers;
- Investigation of the "root cause" of the event;
- Determination of appropriate isolation, remediation, and restoration activities and evidence collection objectives;
- Performance of isolation, remediation, and restoration activities in conjunction with sound forensics procedures; and
- Confirmation that remediation has been completed successfully.

Quite often when reacting to a security event, the response team has to be concerned with the gathering of evidence/information as to who is responsible for the event occurring and was/is any damage occurring due to the event. This collection activity is called *computer forensics* and is the application of computer investigation and analysis techniques to gather evidence suitable for presentation in a court of law. The goal of computer forensics is to perform a structured investigation while maintaining a documented chain of evidence to find out exactly what happened on a computer and who was responsible for it.

Forensic investigators typically follow a standard set of procedures:

- After physically isolating the computer in question to make sure it cannot be accidentally contaminated, investigators make a digital copy of the hard drive;
- Once the original hard drive has been copied, it is locked in a safe or other secure storage facility to maintain its pristine condition; and
- All investigation is done on the digital copy.

Investigators use a variety of techniques and applications to examine the hard drive copy, searching hidden folders and unallocated disk space for copies of deleted, encrypted, or damaged files. Any evidence found on the digital copy is carefully documented in a "finding report" and verified with the original in preparation for legal proceedings that involve discovery, depositions, or actual litigation. Computer forensics has become a major area of specialization, with significant books and coursework available and various certifications issued.

The Computer Forensic Tool Testing project at the NIST has established a methodology for testing computer forensic software tools by development of general tool specifications, test procedures, test criteria, test sets, and test hardware. These results provide information for toolmakers to improve tools, for users to make informed choices about acquiring and using computer forensics tools, and for interested parties to understand the tools capabilities. A capability is required to ensure that forensic software tools consistently produce accurate and objective test results. Information about the Computer Emergency Response Team at Carnegie Mellon University operated under U.S. Government contract can be found at: http://www.cert.org/

5.2.4 Penetration Testing

Penetration testing is a method of evaluating security capabilities and vulnerabilities of a computer system or network by simulating an attack by a threat agent. This form of testing involves active analysis of the target for potential vulnerabilities that may result from:

- poor or improper system configuration;
- known and/or unknown hardware or software flaws; or
- operational weaknesses in process or technical countermeasures.

Penetration tests are carried out from the position of a potential attacker and can involve active exploitation of security vulnerabilities and issues found presented to system owner together with assessment of impact and often with a proposal for mitigation or a technical solution. The generic goal of these tests is intended to determine the feasibility of an attack and amount of impact or success. Tests can be performed as:

- Black-box testing: assumes no prior (zero) knowledge of the infrastructure to be tested and often done as an automated process; or
- White-box testing: relies on knowledge of infrastructure, such as network diagrams, source code, IP addressing information, etc.

There are numerous variations between the extremes of pure white-box or black-box testing. Penetration testing can be a labor-intensive activity and requires expertise to minimize the risk to targeted systems. While tests are underway, production systems and users may experience slow response time due to network and vulnerability scanning. One must consider the possibility that systems may be damaged in the course of penetration testing or may be rendered inoperable. To reduce the likelihood of negative impacts on production systems and services, while ensuring thorough testing, the testing team should follow a well-designed methodology. Table 5.4 provides some good pointers on methodologies. The OSSTMM is the more comprehensive of the four presented in the table.

TABLE 5.4. Example Penetration Testing Methodologies.

Methodology	Information About It
Open Source Security Testing Methodology Manual (OSSTMM)	http://www.isecom.org/osstmm/
	A peer-reviewed methodology for performing security tests and metrics
	Test cases divided into five areas which collectively test: information and data controls, personnel security awareness levels, fraud and social engineering control levels, computer and telecommunications networks, wireless devices, mobile devices, physical security access controls, security processes, and physical locations such as buildings, perimeters, military bases
	Focuses on the technical details of exactly which items need to be tested, what to do before, during, and after a security test, and how to measure the results
	Rules of Engagement define for tester and client how the test needs to properly run
	New tests for international best practices, laws, regulations, and ethical concerns are regularly added and updated
NIST discusses penetration testing in	http://csrc.nist.gov/publications/nistpubs/800-42/NIST-SP800-42.pdf
	http://csrc.nist.gov/publications/nistpubs/800-115/SP800-115.pdf
	Less comprehensive than OSSTMM
	More likely to be accepted by regulatory agencies
Information Systems Security Assessment Framework (ISSAF)	http://www.oissg.org/issaf
	Peer-reviewed structured framework from the Open Information Systems Security Group
	Categorizes information system security assessment into various domains and details specific evaluation or testing criteria for each of these domains
	Aims to provide field inputs on security assessment that reflect real-life scenarios
	Still in its infancy

Carrying out a penetration test can reveal sensitive information about an organization, so care is called for when deciding who will perform a penetration test. This work is frequently outsourced to a managed security service or security consulting enterprise. However, recognize that a penetration testing team is positioned to learn significant sensitive organizational information. Given that we are talking about organizational security and sensitive information assets, consider the possible risks associated with employing ex-black hat hackers[1] or firms that employ such individuals for penetration testing activities. Any contracted with firm should require their employees adhere to a strict ethical code, follow a structured penetration methodology, and ensure that all penetration testers are properly certified for performing penetration testing. There are several professional and government certifications that indicate a firm's trustworthiness and conformance to industry best practices. Three certifications have been produced by the EC-Council[2]:

- The Certified Ethical Hacker course;
- Computer Hacking Forensics Investigator program;
- License Penetration Tester program and various other programs; and

have received endorsements from various U.S. government agencies. There are also:

- The Global Information Assurance Certification (GIAC)[3];
- The NSA Infrastructure Evaluation Methodology (IEM);
- Open Web Application Security Project (OWASP)[4] that provides a framework of recommendations that can be used as a benchmark;
- Web Application Penetration Testing services that help identify issues related to:
  - Vulnerabilities and risks in applications;
  - Known and unknown vulnerabilities;
  - Technical vulnerabilities such as URL manipulation, SQL injection, cross site scripting, back-end authentication, password in memory, session hijacking, buffer overflow, web server configuration, credential management, etc.; and
  - Business Risks including day-to-day threat analysis, unauthorized logins, personal information modification, pricelist modification, unauthorized fund transfer, breach of customer trust, etc.

5.2.5 Common Criteria Evaluated Systems

A useful approach for specifying/purchasing systems, especially security-related systems, is the product type certification recognized by the U.S. government and known as the Common Criteria. The Common Criteria (CC):

---

[1] Someone who had engaged in malicious or criminal acts targeting the assets (including governance) of the target organization or entity.

[2] International Council of E-Commerce Consultants (EC-Council) http://www.eccouncil.org/

[3] GIAC at http://www.giac.org/

[4] OWASP at http://www.owasp.org/index.php/Main_Page

- is an international standard (ISO/IEC 15408) for computer security;
- includes participation by NIST and NSA; and
- evolved from European (ITSEC[5]) and U.S. (TCSEC[6]) security criteria efforts.

There are three parts to the CC:

- Introduction and General Model (Part 1),
- Security Functional Requirements (Part 2),
- Security Assurance Requirements (Part 3).

The Common Evaluation Methodology (CEM) expands on Part 3 supplying details on the conduct of assurance/test activities. Both the CC and CEM continue to evolve with use, with formal changes periodically made that have been mutually agreed by participating nations. The value of each part of the CC to the three major types of interested parties (Consumers, Developers, and Evaluators) is shown in Table 5.5.

TABLE 5.5. **CC Parts Related to Parties.**

	Audience		
	Consumers	Developers	Evaluators
Part 1: Introduction and General Model	For background information and reference purposes	For background information and reference for the development of requirements and formulating security specifications for TOEs	For background information and reference purposes Guidance structure for Protection Profiles (PPs)
Part 2: Security Functional Requirements	For guidance and reference when formulating statements of requirements for security functions	For reference when interpreting statements of requirements and formulating functional specifications for TOEs	Mandatory statement of evaluation criteria when determining whether TOE effectively meets claimed security functions
Part 3: Security Assurance Requirements	For guidance when determining required levels of assurance	For reference when interpreting statements of assurance requirements and determining assurance approaches of TOEs	Mandatory statement of evaluation criteria when determining the assurance of TOEs and when evaluating PPs

Note: Target of Evaluation (TOE) is that part of the product or system which is subject to evaluation.

---

[5] http://www.ssi.gouv.fr/site_documents/ITSEC/ITSEC-uk.pdf

[6] http://csrc.nist.gov/publications/history/dod85.pdf

TABLE 5.6. Evaluation Assurance Level Equivalency.

Common Criteria	TCSEC	ITSEC
EAL1—functionally tested	–	–
EAL2—structurally tested	C1: Discretionary Security Protection	E1
EAL3—methodically tested and checked	C2: Controlled Access Protection	E2
EAL4—methodically designed, tested, and reviewed	B1: Labeled Security Protection	E3
EAL5—semi-formally designed and tested	B2: Structured Protection	E4
EAL6—semi-formally verified design and tested	B3: Security Domains	E5
EAL7—formally verified design and tested	A1: Verified Design	E6

The CC framework also presents a systematic process for documenting and evaluating product security capabilities similar to the TCSEC and ITSEC rating systems, as shown in Table 5.6.

Part of the CC framework is the development of a product protection profile (PP) which documents an implementation independent set of security requirements which consider:

- a specific threat profile (a combination of threat situations spanning threat situations and types of attacks scenarios);
- product security objectives within a likely deployment context;
- security assumptions relative to a product's likely deployment context;
- specific security functional requirements; and
- security texting requirements and rationale for meeting the specified security functional requirements.

By using the CC framework, especially by issuing PPs, product purchasing organizations can identify what security capabilities are required and how said capabilities need to be evaluated for effectiveness. Product manufacturers can develop PPs to document a product's security capabilities and use the CC product certification process to inform purchasing organizations of the security capabilities of their products. Table 5.7 highlights the types of devices for which PPs have been developed.

For products to be evaluated according to the CC framework, the products must be submitted to an accredited testing laboratory where such laboratories must comply with ISO 17025, and certification bodies (CBs) will approve accreditation based on either ISO/IEC Guide 65 or BS EN 45011. Compliance with ISO 17025 is typically accredited by a national approval authority, such as:

- in Canada, the Standards Council of Canada (SCC) accredits Common Criteria Evaluation Facilities;
- in France, the Comité français d'accréditation (COFRAC) accredits CC evaluation facilities, commonly called Centres d'Évaluation de la Sécurité des

TABLE 5.7. Types of Products for Which PPs Exist.

Validated PP	Draft PP
Anti-Virus	Switches and Routers
Key Recovery	Biometrics
PKI/KMI	Remote Access
Biometrics	Mobile Code
Certificate Management	Secure Messaging
Tokens	Multiple Domain Solutions
DBMS	VPN
Firewalls	Wireless LAN
Operating System	Guards
IDS/IPS	Single-Level Web Server
Peripheral Switch	Separation Kernel
Smart Cards	

Technologies de l'Information (CESTI). Evaluations are done according to norms and standards specified by the Agence Nationale de la Sécurité des Systèmes d'Information (ANSSI);

- in the UK, the United Kingdom Accreditation Service (UKAS) accredits Commercial Evaluation Facilities (CLEF); and
- in the United States, the National Institute of Standards and Technology (NIST) National Voluntary Laboratory Accreditation Program (NVLAP) accredits Common Criteria Testing Laboratories (CCTL).

NIST has currently accredited the following laboratories within the United States:

- atsec information security corporation
- COACT Inc. CAFE Laboratory
- Computer Sciences Corporation
- CygnaCom Solutions, Inc.
- DSD Information Assurance Laboratory
- InfoGard Laboratories, Inc.
- SAIC Common Criteria Testing Laboratory
- Arca CCTL
- Booz Allen Hamilton Common Criteria Testing Laboratory

5.2.6 Accreditation and Certification

Accreditation and Certification are frequently confused terms and should be understood to mean:

- **Accreditation** is the act or process of examining the competency, authority, or credibility of organizations that issue credentials or are accredited by standards bodies, thus also known as "accredited CBs," to certify that other enterprises are compliant with official standards. The accreditation process focuses on verifying these accredited CBs are competent to test and certify third parties, behave ethically, and employ suitable quality assurance processes. Another example is the accreditation of testing laboratories and certification specialists that are permitted to issue official certificates of compliance with established standards.

- **Certification** refers to the confirmation of certain characteristics of an object, person, or organization and is often provided by some form of external review or assessment. The primary forms of certification impacting information security are product certification (as in CC certified products) and process certification (as in ISO 27001) that address the processes and mechanisms used to determine if a product, service, or operation meets minimum standards.

So let us start to discuss further the relevance of security-related certification and accreditation to industry participants (service providers, product developers, content developers, subscribers, and consumers).

The definition of Certification used here is:

> The technical evaluation of a system's security features, made as part of and in support of the approval/accreditation process, that establishes the extent to which a particular system's design and implementation meet a set of specified security requirements

The definition of Auditing used here is:

> The examination of networks and computer systems by an independent consultant/entity/ organization, within a defined scope which may include; determination of an organization's compliance to specified standards and best practices, determination of an organization's vulnerability to criminal invasion (crackers, virus impact on management, end-use and, control traffic on end-to-end solution, etc.) and determination of an organization's vulnerability to natural disasters (fire, tornados, earthquakes, etc.)

From a global industry perspective, the most well-known examples of certification for quality, management, and security are the ISO/IEC 9000/9001, ISO/IEC 14000, and ISO/IEC 27001 standards. ISO/IEC are publishers of standards and do not issue certifications of conformity to any standard. Certificates of conformity to specified standards are issued by certification/registration bodies, which are independent of ISO and of the businesses they certify. These registration bodies are accredited third parties which visit an organization to assess their management system which includes access to their processes, documentation, and issue certificates to show the organization meets the intent of the standard.

Separately, product certification is specific to the business it is used in. Like other certifications, product certification provides users and regulators information that the certified product complies with the standard(s) specified on the certificate. Product certification may be limited to compliance with one or more standards even though the product may be subject to many standards.

From a U.S. Government perspective, there are a number of guidelines issued by NIST which discuss the process of certification for the civilian government agencies.

These guidelines, for our purposes, should be considered best practice references to consider when doing business with government agencies. Examples of such documents are NIST 800-37, *Guide for the Security Certification and Accreditation of Federal Information Systems*, and the recent NISTIR 7359, *Information Security Guide for Government Executives*.

5.2.6.1 ISO 9000/9001. As already noted earlier, ISO does not itself certify organizations. Many countries have formed accreditation bodies to authorize CBs, which audit organizations applying for ISO 9000/9001 compliance certification. It is important to note that it is not possible to be certified to ISO 9000. Although commonly referred to as ISO 9000:2000 certification, the actual standard to which an organization's quality management can be certified is ISO 9001:2000. Both the accreditation bodies and the CBs charge fees for their services. The various accreditation bodies have mutual agreements with each other to ensure that certificates issued by one of the accredited CBs are accepted worldwide.

The applying organization is assessed based on an extensive sample of its sites, functions, products, services, and processes and a list of problems ("action requests" or "noncompliances") made known to management. If there are no major problems on this list, the CB will issue an ISO 9001 certificate for each geographical site it has visited, or if there are existing problems it will issue a certificate once a satisfactory improvement plan is received from the management showing how any problems will be resolved.

An ISO certificate is not a once-and-for-all award, but must be renewed at regular intervals recommended by the CB, usually around 3 years. In contrast to the Capability Maturity Model there are no grades of competence within ISO 9001.

Two types of auditing are required to become registered to the standard ISO 9001: auditing by an external certification body (external audit) and auditing by internal staff trained for this process (internal audits). The aim is a continual process of review and assessment, to verify that the system is working as it is supposed to, find out where it can improve, and to correct or prevent problems identified. It is considered healthier for internal auditors to audit outside their usual management line, so as to bring a degree of independence to their judgment. The ISO 9011 standard for auditing applies to ISO 9000.

5.2.6.2 ISO 27001/27002. Organizations may be certified ISO 27001 compliant by a number of accredited CBs worldwide. ISO 27001 certification usually involves a two-stage audit process:

- Stage 1 is a "tabletop" review of the existence and completeness of key documentation like the Security Policy, Statement of Applicability, and Information Security Management System (ISMS) program; namely can the requesting enterprise document that it has an information security program conforming to ISO 27001 requirements.
- Stage 2 is a detailed in-depth audit involving testing the existence and effectiveness of the controls stated in the ISMS as well as their supporting documentation.

Certification involves periodic reviews to confirm that the ISMS program continues to operate as intended.

5.3 WITHDRAWAL FROM SERVICE

Your marketing group has been using a file server for the last 4 years for storing sales and product planning information but now find that the machine is providing slow responses to queries, the model is being discontinued by the manufacturer, and support is being stopped. Your manager has decided to replace the server with a newer, faster machine. So what do you do with the old machine? Should you just throw it into the trash?

One of the most frequent sources of valuable information about an organization is frequently obtained from trash. There is even an attack called "dumpster diving" where threat agents dig through the trash looking for phone books, organization charts, computer storage media (i.e., magnetic tapes, floppies, CD, thumb drives, etc.), or anything else that provides sensitive or valuable information. Law Enforcement also uses trash as a source of information about a subject's activities and plans. Most enterprises recognize this threat, and their policies require secure disposal of printed information via shredding, and even sometimes burning. Few have policies for secure disposal of old computers and data storage devices; usually this material is just trashed or sold to scrap dealers/recyclers and then forgotten.

This machine we are discussing contains critical business information so it really should be "scrubbed" before being discarded. Do not rely on simply dragging files and folders into the trash and thinking all is well; it is not. When a file is put into the trash or is the object of a Unix "rm" command, all that occurs is a set of pointer links are modified within the file system linking the disk space occupied by the "deleted" file into a list of "now available to allocate free disk space." The contents of the newly freed disk space are not erased and can be recovered using low-level disk utilities/editors (a technique used in forensic investigations). However, there are available commercial applications which provide administrative staff the ability to de-allocate a deleted file's disk space and specify how the contents of the deleted file are to be overwritten making it unretrievable. Some OSs also have this capability, such as the Apple Mac OS-X product.

In 2006, NIST released a set of computer media sanitizing guidelines for U.S. Federal Government use, yet explicitly focused on a larger audience by stating:

> Protecting the confidentiality of information should be a concern for everyone, from federal agencies and businesses to home users. Recognizing that interconnections and information exchange are critical in the delivery of government services, this guide can be used to assist in deciding what processes to use for sanitization or disposal. (NIST SP800-88rev1.pdf, Section 1.3 Audience)

Although many businesses and other organizations may consider the NIST guidelines excessive or beyond their resources, each organization will benefit from at least being aware of what should be considered and then tailor the guidelines to more closely reflect individual security objectives. NIST provides access to a number of other guidelines useful to other organizations at the following URL:http://csrc.nist.gov/publications/PubsSPs.html

The U.S. Department of Defense has developed a clearing and sanitizing standard (DoD 5220.22-M) that recommends the approach "Overwrite all addressable locations with a character, its complement, then a random character and verify." Table 5.8 depicts the DoD recommended steps for clearing and sanitizing information on writable media.

TABLE 5.8. U.S. DoD 5220.22-M Clearing and Sanitization Matrix.

Media		Clear	Sanitize
Magnetic Tape	Type I	a or b	a, b, or m
	Type II	a or b	b or m
	Type III	a or b	m
Magnetic Disk	Removable/external hard disks	a, b, or c	m
	Floppies	a, b, or c	m
	Non-removable Rigid Disk	c	a, b, d, or m
	Removable Rigid Disk	a, b, or c	a, b, d, or m
Optical Disk	Read Many, Write Many	c	m
	Read Only		m, n
	Write Once, Read Many (Worm)		m, n
Memory	Dynamic Random Access memory (DRAM)	c or g	c, g, or m
	Electronically Alterable PROM (EAPROM)	i	j or m
	Electronically Erasable PROM (EEPROM)	i	h or m
	Erasable Programmable ROM (EPROM)	k	l, then c, or m
	Flash EPROM (FEPROM)	i	c then i, or m
	Programmable ROM (PROM)	c	m
	Magnetic Bubble Memory	c	a, b, c, or m
	Magnetic Core Memory	c	a, b, e, or m
	Magnetic Plated Wire	c	c and f, or m
	Magnetic Resistive Memory	c	m
	Non-volatile RAM (NOVRAM)	c or g	c, g, or m
	Read Only Memory (ROM)		m
	Static Random Access Memory (SRAM)	c or g	c and f, g, or m
Printers	Impact	g	p then g
	Laser	g	o then g

Where:

a. Degauss with a Type I degausser.

b. Degauss with a Type II degausser.

c. Overwrite all addressable locations with a single character.

d. Overwrite all addressable locations with a character, its complement, then a random character and verify.

e. Overwrite all addressable locations with a character, its complement, then a random character.

f. Each overwrite must reside in memory for a period longer than the classified data resided.

g. Remove all power to include battery power.

h. Overwrite all locations with a random pattern, all locations with binary zeros, all locations with binary ones.

i. Perform a full chip erase as per manufacturer's data sheets.

j. Perform i, then c, a total of three times.

k. Perform an ultraviolet erase according to manufacturer's recommendation.

l. Perform k, but increase time by a factor of 3.

m. Destroy, disintegrate, incinerate, pulverize, shred, or melt.

n. Destruction required only if classified information is contained.

o. Run five pages of unclassified text (font test acceptable).

p. Ribbons must be destroyed. Platens must be cleaned.

While the information in Table 5.8 may seem overly complicated, there are commercial products (such as Webroot's Window Washer anti-malware application) that make these capabilities accessible to users at all skill/knowledge levels. For more information regarding DoD 5220.22-M, "National Industrial Security Program Operating Manual," 2/28/2006, use the following URL:http://www.dtic.mil/whs/directives/corres/html/ 522022m.htm

Whether enterprises follow the NIST guidelines, the DoD standard, or some other approach, what is critical is to remember that simply throwing equipment into the trash is a major information vulnerability.

5.4 SUMMARY

In this final chapter, we provided an overview of modern network and infrastructure management as a context for the management of deployed security mechanisms. In this review we discussed the need for management mechanisms specific to the management of security at all layers within the TMN. We then progressed to a discussion of operational security, necessary mechanisms, including forensics, third-party access reviews, and certification. We concluded our treatment of security management with consideration of how to withdraw equipment from service without exposing information to unauthorized access. The third aspect of security management considered is that of compliance. Compliance links back to security policies and requirements that must be adhered to by operations and management personnel.

5.5 CONCLUDING REMARKS

Whether one is talking about managing security within current generation or next-generation network infrastructures, the foundation remains a sound information security governance program that involves all levels of enterprise staff regardless of primary job responsibilities. All organization employees need clear direction and active leadership from senior management as to the importance of information security to the organization. Employee responsibilities need to be clearly communicated through training and access to organizational information security policies and related security procedures. The primary difference between current and next-generation environments is an increase in third-party interconnectedness due to increased use of outsourced application services and cloud-based infrastructures. These relationships will increase the need for contract-based "flow-through" of security policy requirements onto external entities along with effective compliance auditing procedures that verify compliance with the policies of the contracting organization.

FURTHER READING AND RESOURCES

Aidarous, S., Plevyak, T. (1994) Telecommunications Network management; Into the 21st Century, IEEE Press
ANSI-ATIS T1.276 (2003) "American National Standard for Telecommunications—Operations, Administration, Maintenance, and Provisioning Security Requirements for the Public

Telecommunications Network: A Baseline of Security Requirements for the Management Plane," Alliance for Telecommunications Industry Solutions (ATIS)

ANSI Standard ATIS 0300074.2006 (2006) "American National Standard for Telecommunications—Guidelines and Requirements for Security Management Systems," Alliance for Telecommunications Industry Solutions (ATIS)

ICSA Labs (2010) Firewall Certification Criteria Baseline Module—Version 4.1x, ICSA Labs. Retrieved on October 27, 2010, from https://www.icsalabs.com/technology-program/firewalls/network-firewalls-document-library

ICSA Labs (2010) Firewall Certification Criteria Corporate Module—Version 4.1x, ICSA Labs. Retrieved on October 27, 2010, from https://www.icsalabs.com/technology-program/firewalls/network-firewalls-document-library

ICSA Labs (2010) Firewall Certification Criteria Enterprise Module—Version 4.1x, ICSA Labs. Retrieved on October 27, 2010, from https://www.icsalabs.com/technology-program/firewalls/network-firewalls-document-library

ICSA Labs (2010) Firewall Certification Criteria High Availability Module—Version 1.0, ICSA Labs. Retrieved on July 14, 2010, from https://www.icsalabs.com/technology-program/firewalls/network-firewalls-document-library

ICSA Labs (2011) Network Firewalls Certification Criteria VoIP Module Version 1.0, ICSA Labs. Retrieved on January 28, 2011, from https://www.icsalabs.com/technology-program/firewalls/network-firewalls-document-library

ICSA Labs (2011) Network Firewalls—Optional IPv6 Certification Criteria Module Version 1.0, ICSA Labs. Retrieved on August 10, 2011, from https://www.icsalabs.com/technology-program/firewalls/network-firewalls-document-library

ITU-T M.3010, "SERIES M: TMN AND NETWORK MAINTENANCE: INTERNATIONAL TRANSMISSION SYSTEMS, TELEPHONE CIRCUITS, TELEGRAPHY, FACSIMILE AND LEASED CIRCUITS: Telecommunications management network, Principles for a telecommunications management network," INTERNATIONAL TELECOMMUNICATION UNION TELECOMMUNICATION STANDARDIZATION SECTOR, 02/2000

ITU-T M.3016.0, "SERIES M: TELECOMMUNICATION MANAGEMENT, INCLUDING TMN AND NETWORK MAINTENANCE: Telecommunications management network, Security for the Management Plane: Overview," INTERNATIONAL TELECOMMUNICATION UNION TELECOMMUNICATION STANDARDIZATION SECTOR, 05/2005

ITU-T M.3016.1, "SERIES M: TELECOMMUNICATION MANAGEMENT, INCLUDING TMN AND NETWORK MAINTENANCE: Telecommunications management network, Security for the Management Plane: Security Requirements," INTERNATIONAL TELECOMMUNICATION UNION TELECOMMUNICATION STANDARDIZATION SECTOR, 04/2005

ITU-T M.3016.2, "SERIES M: TELECOMMUNICATION MANAGEMENT, INCLUDING TMN AND NETWORK MAINTENANCE: Telecommunications management network, Security for the Management Plane: Security Services," INTERNATIONAL TELECOMMUNICATION UNION TELECOMMUNICATION STANDARDIZATION SECTOR, 04/2005

ITU-T M.3016.3, "SERIES M: TELECOMMUNICATION MANAGEMENT, INCLUDING TMN AND NETWORK MAINTENANCE: Telecommunications management network, Security for the Management Plane: Security Mechanism," INTERNATIONAL TELECOMMUNICATION UNION TELECOMMUNICATION STANDARDIZATION SECTOR, 04/2005

ITU-TM.3016.4, "SERIES M: TELECOMMUNICATION MANAGEMENT, INCLUDING TMN AND NETWORK MAINTENANCE: Telecommunications management network, Security for the Management Plane: Profile Proforma," INTERNATIONAL TELECOMMUNICATION UNION TELECOMMUNICATION STANDARDIZATION SECTOR, 04/2005

ITU-TM.3050.0, "SERIES M: TELECOMMUNICATION MANAGEMENT, INCLUDING TMN AND NETWORK MAINTENANCE: Telecommunications management network, Enhanced Telecommunications Operations Map (eTOM)—Introduction," INTERNATIONAL TELECOMMUNICATION UNION TELECOMMUNICATION STANDARDIZATION SECTOR, 07/2004

ITU-TM.3050.1, "SERIES M: TELECOMMUNICATION MANAGEMENT, INCLUDING TMN AND NETWORK MAINTENANCE: Telecommunications management network, Enhanced Telecommunications Operations Map (eTOM)—The business process framework," INTERNATIONAL TELECOMMUNICATION UNION TELECOMMUNICATION STANDARDIZATION SECTOR, 03/2007

ITU-TM.3050.2, "SERIES M: TELECOMMUNICATION MANAGEMENT, INCLUDING TMN AND NETWORK MAINTENANCE: Telecommunications management network, Enhanced Telecommunications Operations Map (eTOM)—Process decompositions and descriptions," INTERNATIONAL TELECOMMUNICATION UNION TELECOMMUNICATION STANDARDIZATION SECTOR, 03/2007

ITU-TM.3050.3, "SERIES M: TELECOMMUNICATION MANAGEMENT, INCLUDING TMN AND NETWORK MAINTENANCE: Telecommunications management network, Enhanced Telecommunications Operations Map (eTOM)—Enhanced Telecom Operations Map (eTOM)—Representative process flows," INTERNATIONAL TELECOMMUNICATION UNION TELECOMMUNICATION STANDARDIZATION SECTOR, 03/2007

ITU-TM.3050.4, "SERIES M: TELECOMMUNICATION MANAGEMENT, INCLUDING TMN AND NETWORK MAINTENANCE: Telecommunications management network, Enhanced Telecommunications Operations Map (eTOM)—B2B integration: Using B2B inter-enterprise integration with the eTOM," INTERNATIONAL TELECOMMUNICATION UNION TELECOMMUNICATION STANDARDIZATION SECTOR, 03/2007

ITU-TM.3060, "SERIES M: TELECOMMUNICATION MANAGEMENT, INCLUDING TMN AND NETWORK MAINTENANCE: Telecommunications management network, SERIES Y: GLOBAL INFORMATION INFRASTRUCTURE, INTERNET PROTOCOL ASPECTS AND NEXT-GENERATION NETWORKS, Next Generation Networks—Network management, Principles for the Management of Next Generation Networks," INTERNATIONAL TELECOMMUNICATION UNION TELECOMMUNICATION STANDARDIZATION SECTOR, 03/2006

ITU-TM.3400, "SERIES M: TELECOMMUNICATION MANAGEMENT, INCLUDING TMN AND NETWORK MAINTENANCE: Telecommunications management network, TMN management functions," INTERNATIONAL TELECOMMUNICATION UNION TELECOMMUNICATION STANDARDIZATION SECTOR, 02/2000

ITU-TM.3410, "SERIES M: TELECOMMUNICATION MANAGEMENT, INCLUDING TMN AND NETWORK MAINTENANCE: Telecommunications management network, Guidelines and Requirements for Security Management Systems to Support Telecommunications Management," INTERNATIONAL TELECOMMUNICATION UNION TELECOMMUNICATION STANDARDIZATION SECTOR, 08/2008

ITU-T X.800, "DATA COMMUNICATION NETWORKS; OPEN SYSTEMS INTERCONNECTION (OSI); SECURITY, STRUCTURE AND APPLICATIONS, SECURITY ARCHITECTURE FOR OPEN SYSTEMS INTERCONNECTION FOR CCITT APPLICATIONS," INTERNATIONAL TELECOMMUNICATION UNION TELECOMMUNICATION STANDARDIZATION SECTOR, 1991

ITU-T X.805, "SERIES X: DATA NETWORKS AND OPEN SYSTEM COMMUNICATIONS, Security, Security architecture for systems providing end-to-end communications," INTERNATIONAL TELECOMMUNICATION UNION TELECOMMUNICATION STANDARDIZATION SECTOR, 10/2003

Rozenblit, M. (2000) Security for Telecommunications Network management, IEEE Press

APPENDICES

When composing this book, a number of points were recognized:

1. some of the appendices (notably appendices A, B, C and F) provided a review of material that was secondary to the main subject of managing security;
2. some of the appendices (notably appendices D, E, I and J) provided material that would best serve the reader if available in electronic form rather than printed form; and
3. to be able to offer this book at a reasonable price, the size of the printed book needed to be constrained wherever possible.

Therefore it was decided to make the following appendices available at http://booksupport. wiley.com

- *Appendix A: Role of Cryptography in Information Security*
- *Appendix B: Authentication of Subjects*
- *Appendix C: Network Security Mechanisms*
- *Appendix D: Example Company Security Policy*
- *Appendix E: Example Generic Detailed Security Requirements*
- *Appendix F: Securing Common Network Protocols*
- *Appendix I: Example RFP Security Appendix*
- *Appendix J: RFP Security Analysis of ABC Proposal*

While including the following appendices in the printed version:

- Appendix G: Security Mapping Between M.3400 And M.3050
- Appendix H: State Privacy Laws as of 2010
- Appendix K: Example Security Statement of Work
- Appendix L: Example Solaris Operating System Audit Procedures

Security Management of Next Generation Telecommunications Networks and Services,
First Edition. Stuart Jacobs.
© 2014 The Institute of Electrical and Electronics Engineers, Inc. Published 2014 by John Wiley & Sons, Inc.

- Appendix M: Example Procedure for Basic Hardening of a Windows XP Professional Operating System
- Appendix N: Example Network Audit Procedure
- Appendix O: Example Unix–Linux Operating System Audit Procedures

Consequently the first appendix found in the printed book is Appendix G.

APPENDIX G: SECURITY MAPPING BETWEEN M.3400 AND M.3050

This mapping of ITU-T M.3400 Security Function sets to ITU-T M.3050 eTOM Security Process Areas is based on the mapping in the 2004 version of M.3050 Supplement[1] with augmentation to identify the eTOM Process Identifiers used in the 2007 version of M.3050.2.[2]

M.3400 ID	Function Name	2007 eTOM Process ID	Process Name	2004 eTOM Process ID
5	Performance Management	1.3.2	Enterprise Risk Management	1.E.2
5.3	Performance Management Control	1.3.2.1	Business Continuity Management	1.E.2.1
5.3	Performance Management Control	1.3.2.4	Audit Management	1.E.2.4
5.3.1	Network traffic management policy function set	1.3.2.1	Business Continuity Management	1.E.2.1
5.3.6	Audit report function set	1.3.2.4	Audit Management	1.E.2.4

[1] M.3050 Supplement 3, "eTOM to M.3400 mapping," International Telecommunication Union, TELECOMMUNICATION STANDARDIZATION SECTOR, May 2004.

[2] M.3050.2, "eTOM—Process decompositions and descriptions," International Telecommunication Union, TELECOMMUNICATION STANDARDIZATION SECTOR, March 2007.

Security Management of Next Generation Telecommunications Networks and Services,
First Edition. Stuart Jacobs.
© 2014 The Institute of Electrical and Electronics Engineers, Inc. Published 2014 by John Wiley & Sons, Inc.

M.3400 ID	Function Name	2007 eTOM Process ID	Process Name	2004 eTOM Process ID
8	Accounting Management	1.3.2	Enterprise Risk Management	1.E.2
8.4	Enterprise Control	1.3.2.4	Audit Management	1.E.2.4
8.4	Enterprise Control	1.3.2.5	Insurance Management	1.E.2.5
8.4.2	Auditing function set	1.3.2.4	Audit Management	1.E.2.4
8.4.8	Insurance analysis function set	1.3.2.5	Insurance Management	1.E.2.5
9	Security Management	1.1.3.4	Resource Performance Management	1.A.3.4
9	Security Management	1.3.2	Enterprise Risk Management	1.E.2
9	Security Management	1.3.6	Stakeholder & External Relations Management	1.E.6
9	Security Management	1.1.1	Customer Relationship Management	1.OFAB.1
9	Security Management	1.1.2	Service Management & Operation	1.OFAB.2
9.1	Prevention	1.3.2.2	Security Management	1.E.2.2
9.1	Prevention	1.3.6.5	Legal Management	1.E.6.5
9.1	Prevention	1.1.1.5	Order Handling	1.F.1.5
9.1.1	Legal review function set	1.3.6.5	Legal Management	1.E.6.5
9.1.2	Physical access security function set	1.3.2.2	Security Management	1.E.2.2
9.1.3	Guarding function set	1.3.2.2	Security Management	1.E.2.2
9.1.4	Personnel risk analysis function set	1.3.2.2	Security Management	1.E.2.2
9.1.5	Security screening function set	1.1.1.5.2	Authorize Credit	1.F.1.5.2
9.2	Detection	1.3.2.2	Security Management	1.E.2.2
9.2	Detection	1.3.2.3	Fraud Management	1.E.2.3
9.2	Detection	1.1.4.6	S/P Interface Management	1.FAB.4.6
9.2	Detection	1.1.3.5	Resource Data Collection & Processing	1.O.3.1

(continued)

M.3400 ID	Function Name	2007 eTOM Process ID	Process Name	2004 eTOM Process ID
9.2	Detection	1.2.3	Resource Development & Management	1.SIP.3
9.2.1	Investigation of changes in revenue patterns function set	1.3.2.3	Fraud Management	1.E.2.3
9.2.2	Support element protection function set	1.1.3.5.1	Collect Resource Data	1.AB.3.5.1
9.2.2	Support element protection function set	1.1.3.5.2	Process Resource Data	1.AB.3.5.2
9.2.2	Support element protection function set	1.1.3.5.3	Report Resource Data	1.AB.3.5.3
9.2.2	Support element protection function set	1.1.3.5.4	Audit Resource Usage Data	1.AB.3.5.4
9.2.3	Customer security alarm function set	1.3.2.2	Security Management	1.E.2.2
9.2.4	Customer (external user) profiling function set	1.3.2.3	Fraud Management	1.E.2.3
9.2.5	Customer usage pattern analysis function set	1.1.3.5.2	Process Resource Data	1.AB.3.5.2
9.2.5	Customer usage pattern analysis function set	1.1.3.5.4	Audit Resource Usage Data	1.AB.3.5.4
9.2.5	Customer usage pattern analysis function set	1.3.2.3	Fraud Management	1.E.2.3
9.2.6	Investigation of theft of service function set	1.3.2.3	Fraud Management	1.E.2.3
9.2.6	Investigation of theft of service function set	1.1.1.9.3	Analyze and Manage Customer Risk	1.FAB.1.9.3
9.2.7	Internal traffic and activity pattern analysis function set	1.1.3.1.2	Enable Resource Performance Management	1.O.3.1.2
9.2.7	Internal traffic and activity pattern analysis function set	1.1.3.1.4	Enable Resource Data Collection & Processing	1.O.3.1.4

M.3400 ID	Function Name	2007 eTOM Process ID	Process Name	2004 eTOM Process ID
9.2.8	Network security alarm function set	1.3.2.2	Security Management	1.E.2.2
9.2.8	Network security alarm function set	1.1.3.1.4	Enable Resource Data Collection & Processing	1.O.3.1.4
9.2.9	Software intrusion audit function set	1.1.3.5.4	Audit Resource Usage Data	1.AB.3.5.4
9.2.9	Software intrusion audit function set	1.3.2.2	Security Management	1.E.2.2
9.2.10	Support element security alarm reporting function set	1.3.2.2	Security Management	1.E.2.2
9.2.10	Support element security alarm reporting function set	1.1.3.1.4	Enable Resource Data Collection & Processing	1.O.3.1.4
9.3	Containment and Recovery	1.3.2.1	Business Continuity Management	1.E.2.1
9.3	Containment and Recovery	1.3.2.2	Security Management	1.E.2.2
9.3	Containment and Recovery	1.3.6.5	Legal Management	1.E.6.5
9.3	Containment and Recovery	1.2.3.1	Resource Strategy & Planning	1.S.3.1
9.3.1	Protected storage of business data function set	1.3.2.1	Business Continuity Management	1.E.2.1
9.3.2	Exception report action function set	1.1.3.2.2	Configure & Activate Resource	1.F.3.2.2
9.3.2	Exception report action function set	1.1.3.2.4	Collect, Update & Report Resource Configuration Data	1.F.3.2.4
9.3.3	Theft of service action function set	1.3.2.2	Security Management	1.E.2.2
9.3.3	Theft of service action function set	1.3.6.5	Legal Management	1.E.6.5
9.3.3	Theft of service action function set	1.1.3.2.4	Collect, Update & Report Resource Configuration Data	1.F.3.2.4
9.3.4	Legal action function set	1.3.6.5	Legal Management	1.E.6.5
9.3.5	Apprehending function set	1.3.2.2	Security Management	1.E.2.2

(*continued*)

M.3400 ID	Function Name	2007 eTOM Process ID	Process Name	2004 eTOM Process ID
9.3.6	Service intrusion recovery function set	1.1.2.2.4	Implement & Configure Service	1.F.2.2.4
9.3.7	Administration of customer revocation list function set	1.3.2.2	Security Management	1.E.2.2
9.3.8	Protected storage of customer data function set	1.3.2.1	Business Continuity Management	1.E.2.1
9.3.9	Severing external connections function set	1.1.3.2.2	Configure & Activate Resource	1.F.3.2.2
9.3.10	Network intrusion recovery function set	1.1.3.2.2	Configure & Activate Resource	1.F.3.2.2
9.3.11	Administration of network revocation list function set	1.3.2.2	Security Management	1.E.2.2
9.3.12	Protected storage of network configuration data function set	1.3.2.1	Business Continuity Management	1.E.2.1
9.3.13	Severing internal connections function set	1.1.3.2.2	Configure & Activate Resource	1.F.3.2.2
9.3.14	NE(s) intrusion recovery function set	1.1.3.2.2	Configure & Activate Resource	1.F.3.2.2
9.3.15	Administration of NE(s) revocation list function set	1.3.2.2	Security Management	1.E.2.2
9.3.16	Protected storage of NE(s) configuration data function set	1.3.2.1	Business Continuity Management	1.E.2.1
9.4	Security Administration	1.1.2.5	Service & Specific Instance Rating	1.B.2.5
9.4	Security Administration	1.3.2.1	Business Continuity Management	1.E.2.1
9.4	Security Administration	1.3.2.1	Business Continuity Management	1.E.2.1
9.4	Security Administration	1.3.2.2	Security Management	1.E.2.2
9.4	Security Administration	1.3.2.4	Audit Management	1.E.2.4
9.4	Security Administration	1.1.4.6	S/P Interface Management	1.FAB.4.6

M.3400 ID	Function Name	2007 eTOM Process ID	Process Name	2004 eTOM Process ID
9.4	Security Administration	1.2.3.1	Resource Strategy & Planning	1.S.3.1
9.4.1	Security policy function set	1.3.2.2	Security Management	1.E.2.2
9.4.2	Disaster recovery planning function set	1.3.2.1	Business Continuity Management	1.E.2.1
9.4.3	Manage guards function set	1.3.2.2	Security Management	1.E.2.2
9.4.4	Audit trail analysis function set	1.3.2.2	Security Management	1.E.2.2
9.4.4	Audit trail analysis function set	1.3.2.4	Audit Management	1.E.2.4
9.4.5	Security alarm analysis function set	1.3.2.2	Security Management	1.E.2.2
9.4.5	Security alarm analysis function set	1.1.3.1.4	Enable Resource Data Collection & Processing	1.O.3.1.4
9.4.6	Assessment of corporate data integrity function set	1.3.2.2	Security Management	1.E.2.2
9.4.7	Administration of external authentication function set	1.3.2.2	Security Management	1.E.2.2
9.4.8	Administration of external access control function set	1.3.2.2	Security Management	1.E.2.2
9.4.9	Administration of external certification function set	1.3.2.2	Security Management	1.E.2.2
9.4.10	Administration of external encryption and keys function set	1.3.2.2	Security Management	1.E.2.2
9.4.11	Administration of external security protocols function set	1.3.2.2	Security Management	1.E.2.2
9.4.12	Customer audit trail function set	1.1.2.5.3	Analyze Usage Records	1.B.2.5.3
9.4.12	Customer audit trail function set	1.3.2.2	Security Management	1.E.2.2
9.4.12	Customer audit trail function set	1.3.2.4	Audit Management	1.E.2.4

(*continued*)

M.3400 ID	Function Name	2007 eTOM Process ID	Process Name	2004 eTOM Process ID
9.4.13	Customer security alarm management function set	1.3.2.2	Security Management	1.E.2.2
9.4.13	Customer security alarm management function set	1.1.3.1.4	Enable Resource Data Collection & Processing	1.O.3.1.4
9.4.14	Testing of audit trail mechanism function set	1.3.2.4	Audit Management	1.E.2.4
9.4.15	Administration of internal authentication function set	1.3.2.2	Security Management	1.E.2.2
9.4.16	Administration of internal access control function set	1.3.2.2	Security Management	1.E.2.2
9.4.17	Administration of internal certification function set	1.3.2.2	Security Management	1.E.2.2
9.4.18	Administration of internal encryption and keys function set	1.3.2.2	Security Management	1.E.2.2
9.4.19	Network audit trail management function set	1.3.2.2	Security Management	1.E.2.2
9.4.19	Network audit trail management function set	1.3.2.4	Audit Management	1.E.2.4
9.4.19	Network audit trail management function set	1.1.3.2.4	Collect, Update & Report Resource Configuration Data	1.F.3.2.4
9.4.20	Network security alarm management function set	1.3.2.2	Security Management	1.E.2.2
9.4.20	Network security alarm management function set	1.1.3.1.4	Enable Resource Data Collection & Processing	1.O.3.1.4
9.4.21	NE(s) audit trail management function set	1.3.2.2	Security Management	1.E.2.2
9.4.21	NE(s) audit trail management function set	1.3.2.4	Audit Management	1.E.2.4

M.3400 ID	Function Name	2007 eTOM Process ID	Process Name	2004 eTOM Process ID
9.4.21	NE(s) audit trail management function set	1.1.3.2.4	Collect, Update & Report Resource Configuration Data	1.F.3.2.4
9.4.22	NE(s) security alarm management function set	1.3.2.2	Security Management	1.E.2.2
9.4.22	NE(s) security alarm management function set	1.1.3.1.4	Enable Resource Data Collection & Processing	1.O.3.1.4
9.4.23	Administration of keys for NEs function set	1.3.2.2	Security Management	1.E.2.2
9.4.24	Administration of keys by an NE function set	1.3.2.2	Security Management	1.E.2.2

APPENDIX H: STATE PRIVACY LAWS AS OF 2010

State	Legislation or State Law	Requires
Alaska	A.S. 45.48.010 (July 1, 2009)	Notice to consumers of breach in the security of unencrypted, unredacted personal information in physical or electronic form, or encrypted information, where the encryption key may also have been compromised. No notice is required if a reasonable investigation determines there is no reasonable likelihood of harm to consumers. Written documentation of the investigation must be kept for 5 years. Entities subject to compliance with the Gramm–Leach–Bliley Act are exempt.
Arizona	A.R.S. 44-7501 (December 31, 2006)	Notice to consumers of breach in the security of unencrypted, unredacted computerized personal information. No notice is required if a reasonable investigation determines there is no reasonable likelihood of harm to consumers. If entity complies with federal rules, then it is deemed to be in compliance with Arizona law.
Arkansas	Ark. Code Ann. 4-110-101 to 108 (March 31, 2005)	Notice to consumers of breach in the security of unencrypted, computerized personal information and medical information in electronic or physical form. Notice is not required if there is no reasonable likelihood of harm to consumers. If entity complies with state or federal law that provides greater protection, and at least as thorough disclosure, then it is deemed in compliance.

Security Management of Next Generation Telecommunications Networks and Services,
First Edition. Stuart Jacobs.
© 2014 The Institute of Electrical and Electronics Engineers, Inc. Published 2014 by John Wiley & Sons, Inc.

State	Legislation or State Law	Requires
California	Civil Code Sec. 1798.80-1798.82 (July 1, 2003)	Notice to consumers of breach in the security, confidentiality, or integrity of unencrypted, computerized personal information held by a business or a government agency. If the person or business has own notification procedures consistent with timing requirements and provides notice in accordance with its policies, or if the person or business abides by state or federal law and provides greater protection and disclosure, then it is deemed in compliance.
Colorado	Co. Rev. Stat. 6-1-716(1)(a) (September 1, 2006)	Notice to consumers of breach in the security of unencrypted, unredacted computerized personal information. Notice is given unless investigation determines misuse of information has not occurred or is not reasonably likely to occur. If entity is regulated by state or federal law and maintains procedures pursuant to laws, rules, regulations, or guidelines, it is deemed in compliance.
Connecticut	699 Gen. Stat. Conn. 36a-701 (January 1, 2006)	Notice of security breach by persons who conduct business in the state and have a breach of the security of unencrypted computerized data, electronic media, or electronic files containing personal information. Notice is not required if the breached entity determines in consultation with federal, state, and local law enforcement agencies that the breach will not likely result in harm to the individuals. Governmental entities are not required to provide notice under this section. Entities are also deemed compliant if notification is in compliance with rules or guidelines established by the primary function of the regulator under the Gramm–Leach–Bliley Act.
Delaware	Del. Code Ann. Title 6 Section 12B-101 to 12-B-106 (June 28, 2005)	Notice to consumers of breach in the security of unencrypted computerized personal information if the investigation determines that misuse of information about a Delaware resident has occurred or is reasonably likely to occur. If the entity is regulated by state or federal law and maintains procedures for a breach pursuant to the laws, rules, regulations, guidance, or guidelines established by its primary or functional state or federal regulator, then it is deemed in compliance provided it notifies affected residents in accordance with the maintained procedures when a breach occurs.
District of Columbia	DC Code Sec 28-3851 et seq. (January 1, 2007)	Notice to consumers of breach in the security, confidentiality, or integrity of unencrypted, computerized, or other electronic personal

(*continued*)

State	Legislation or State Law	Requires
		information held by a business or a government agency. This section does not pertain to person or entity subject to the Gramm–Leach–Bliley Act. This section also does not apply to a person or business with its own notification procedures with consistent timing requirements in compliance with notification requirements of this section, and the person or business provides notice in accordance with its policies and which is reasonably calculated to give actual notice.
Florida	Fla. Stat. Ann. 817.5681 et seq. (July 1, 2005)	Notice to consumers of breach in the security, confidentiality, or integrity of computerized, unencrypted personal information held by a person who conducts business in the state. Notice is not required if, after appropriate investigation or consultation with law enforcement, a person reasonably determines breach has not and will not likely result in harm to individuals. Determination must be documented in writing and maintained for 5 years. It is deemed in compliance if person's own notification procedure is otherwise consistent with the timing requirements of this section, or "maintaining" notification procedures established by person's primary or functional federal regulator.
Georgia	Ga. Code Ann. 10-1-910 et seq. (May 24, 2007. Covers "information brokers and data collectors")	Notice of breach that compromises the security, confidentiality, or integrity of computerized personal information held by an information broker or data collector.
Hawaii	HRS Sec 487N-1 et seq. (January 1, 2007)	Notice when unauthorized access to and acquisition of unencrypted or unredacted records or data containing personal information where illegal use of the personal information has occurred, or is reasonably likely to occur, and that creates a risk of harm to a person. Notice under this section is not required by a financial institution subject to Federal Interagency Guidance on Response Programs for Unauthorized Access to Consumer Information and Consumer Notice or by any health plan or healthcare provider under HIPAA.

State	Legislation or State Law	Requires
Idaho	Id. Code Ann. 28-51-104 (July 1, 2006)	Notice to consumers of breach in the security of unencrypted, computerized personal information if, after a reasonable investigation, the agency, individual, or entity determines that misuse of information of Idaho resident has occurred or is reasonably likely to occur. Notice under this section is not required by a person regulated by state or federal law and who complies with procedures under that law.
Illinois	ILCS Sec. 530/1 et seq. (January 1, 2006)	Notice to consumers of breach in the security, confidentiality, or integrity of personal information of the system data held by a person or a government agency. Notice under this section is not required if entity maintains own notification procedures as part of an information security policy for the treatment of personal information and is otherwise consistent with the timing requirements of this act.
Indiana	Ind. Code Sec. 4-1-11 et seq. (June 30, 2006)	Notice to consumers of breach in the security, confidentiality, or integrity of computerized personal information held by a government agency.
Indiana	Ind. Code Sec. 24-2-9 et seq). (June 30, 2006)	Notice when a data collector knows, should know, or should have known that the unauthorized acquisition of computerized data, including computerized data that has been transferred to another medium, constituting the breach has resulted in or could result in identity deception, ID theft, or fraud. Notice is not required under this section if entity maintains own disclosure procedures, is under Federal USA Patriot Act, Exec. Order 13224, FCRA, Financial Modernization Act, HIPAA, or financial institutions that comply with the Federal Interagency Guidance on Response Programs for Unauthorized Access to Member Info and Member Notice.
Iowa	Iowa Code Chapter 2007-1154 (July 1, 2008)	Notice to consumers of breach in the security of unencrypted, unredacted personal information in electronic form. No notice is required if a reasonable investigation determines there is no reasonable likelihood of harm to consumers. Written documentation of the investigation must be kept for 5 years. Exempted are those with own notification procedures or procedures under state or federal law providing at least greater protection to personal information and at least as thorough disclosure requirements pursuant to the rules, regulations, procedures, guidance, or guidelines established by primary regulator or state or federal laws. Entities subject to compliance with the Gramm–Leach–Bliley Act are exempt.

(*continued*)

State	Legislation or State Law	Requires
Kansas	Kansas Stat. 50-7a01, 50-7a02 (January 1, 2007)	Notice to consumers about a breach in the security of unencrypted, unredacted computerized personal information if investigation determines misuse has occurred or is reasonably likely to occur.
Louisiana	La. Rev. State. Ann. Sec. 51 3071-3077 (January 1, 2006)	Notice of breach of the security, confidentiality, or integrity of unencrypted, computerized, personal information by persons doing business in the state. No notice if, after a reasonable investigation, the data holder determines that there is no reasonable likelihood of harm to customers. Notice is not required by financial institutions in compliance with federal guidance.
Maine	Me. Rev. Stat. Ann. 10-21-B-1346 to 1349 (January 31, 2006. Covers only information brokers)	Notice of breach of the security, confidentiality, or integrity of unencrypted, computerized, personal information if the personal information has been or is reasonably believed to have been acquired by an unauthorized person. Notice under this section is not required by persons regulated by state or federal law and who comply with procedures under that law.
Massachusetts	201 CMR 17.00 (March 1, 2010)	Notice of breach of unauthorized acquisition of unencrypted data or encrypted electronic data and the confidential process or key that is capable of compromising the security, confidentiality, or integrity of the personal information that creates a significant risk of identity theft or fraud.
Michigan	2006-PA-0566 (July 2, 2007)	Notice of breach of the security, confidentiality, or integrity of unencrypted, computerized, personal information by persons doing business in the state. Notice under this section is required unless person/agency determines security breach has not or is not likely to cause substantial loss, or injury to, or result in identity theft. It does not apply to financial institutions or HIPAA entities.
Minnesota	Minn. Stat. 324E.61 et seq. (January 1, 2006)	Notice of breach of the security, confidentiality, or integrity of unencrypted, computerized, personal information by persons doing business in the state. It does not apply to financial institutions or HIPAA entities.
Montana	Mont. Code Ann. 31-3-115 (March 1, 2006)	Notice to consumers of breach in security, confidentiality, or integrity of computerized personal information held by a person or business if the breach causes or is reasonably believed to have caused loss or injury to a Montana resident. Notice under this section is not required if the entity maintains own

State	Legislation or State Law	Requires
		notification procedures as part of an information security policy for the treatment of personal information and is otherwise consistent with the timing requirements of this section.
Nebraska	Neb. Rev. Stat. 87-801 et seq. (July 16, 2006)	Notice to consumers of breach in the security of unencrypted, computerized personal information if an investigation determines use of information has occurred or is reasonably likely to occur. It is deemed in compliance if person's own notification procedure is otherwise consistent with the timing requirements of this section, or if notification procedures are established by person's primary or functional federal regulator.
Nevada	Nev. Rev. Stat. 607A.010 et seq. (January 1, 2006)	Notice of breach of the security, confidentiality, or integrity of unencrypted computerized personal information by data collectors, which are defined to include government, business entities, and associations who handle, collect, disseminate, or otherwise deal with non-public personal information. Notice under this section is not required if the entity maintains own notification procedures as part of an information security policy for the treatment of personal information and is otherwise consistent with the timing requirements of this section, or is subject to compliance with the Gramm–Leach–Bliley Act.
New Hampshire	NH RS 359-C: 19 et seq. (January 1, 2007)	Notice of unauthorized acquisition if it is determined that likelihood information has been or will be misused. Notice must be given if there is a determination that misuse of information has occurred or is reasonably likely to occur or if a determination cannot be made. Notice under this section is not required if the entity maintains own notification procedures as part of an information security policy for the treatment of personal information and is otherwise consistent with the timing requirements of this section, or if the entity is a person engaged in trade or commerce under RSA 358-A:3 and maintains notification procedures established by its primary or functional regulator.
New Jersey	NJ Stat 56:8-163 (July 2, 2006)	Notice of breach of security of unencrypted computerized personal information held by a business or public entity. No notice is required if a thorough investigation finds misuse of the information is not reasonably possible. Written documentation of the investigation must be kept for 5 years. Notice under

(continued)

State	Legislation or State Law	Requires
		this section is not required if entity maintains own notification procedures as part of an information security policy for the treatment of personal information and is otherwise consistent with the timing requirements of this section.
New York	NY Bus. Law Sec. 899-aa. (December 8, 2005)	Notice of breach of security of computerized unencrypted, or encrypted with acquired encryption key, personal information held by both public and private entities.
North Carolina	N.C. Gen. Stat. 75-65 (December 1, 2005)	Notice of breach of security of unencrypted and unredacted written, drawn, spoken, visual, or electromagnetic personal information, and encrypted personal information with the confidential process or key held by a private business if the breach causes, is reasonably likely to cause, or creates a material risk of harm to residents of North Carolina. Financial institutions subject to compliance with Federal Interagency Guidance on Response Programs for Unauthorized Access to Member Info and Member Notice are exempt.
North Dakota	N.D. Cent. Code 51-30 (June 1, 2005)	Notice of breach of security of unencrypted, computerized, personal information by persons doing business in the state. It includes an expanded list of sensitive personal information, including date of birth, mother's maiden name, employee ID number, and electronic signature. Exception is for those financial institutions which are in compliance with federal guidance.
Ohio	O.R.C. Ann. 1349. 19 et seq. (February 17, 2006)	Notice of breach of security or confidentiality of computerized personal information, held by a state agency, political subdivision, or business where reasonably believed it will cause a material risk of identity theft or fraud to a person or property of a resident of Ohio. Notice under this section is not required by financial institutions, trust companies, or credit unions or any affiliate required by federal law to notify customers of information security breach and who is in compliance with federal law.
Oklahoma	Okla. Stat. 74-3113.1 (June 8, 2006)	State government agencies to give notice of breach of the security of the system following discovery or notification of the breach in the security of the data to any resident of Oklahoma whose unencrypted personal information was, or is reasonably believed to have been, acquired by an unauthorized person.

State	Legislation or State Law	Requires
		Notice is not required under this section by a state agency, board, commission, or unit or subdivision of government if the entity maintains own notification procedures as part of an information security policy for the treatment of personal information and is otherwise consistent with the timing requirements of this section.
Oregon	O.R.S. 646A.604 (October 1, 2007)	Notice when unauthorized acquisition of computerized data that materially compromises the security, confidentiality, or integrity of personal information maintained by the person. Notice is not required if after an appropriate investigation or after consultation with federal, state, or local agencies responsible for law enforcement, the person determines no reasonable likelihood of harm to consumers whose personal information has been acquired has resulted or will result from the breach. Determination must be in writing and kept for 5 years. Exempted are those with own notification procedures under state or federal law providing at least greater protection to personal information and at least as thorough disclosure requirements pursuant to the rules, regulations, procedures, guidance, or guidelines established by primary regulator, or state or federal laws, and financial institutions which are in compliance with federal guidance.
Pennsylvania	73 Pa. Cons. Stat. 2303 (June 30, 2006)	Notice of breach of the security or confidentiality of computerized personal information, held by a state agency, political subdivision, or business and is reasonably believed to have been accessed or acquired by an unauthorized person. Notice under this section is not required if entity maintains its own notification procedures as part of an information security policy for the treatment of personal information and is otherwise consistent with the timing requirements of this section. Financial institutions subject to compliance with Federal Interagency Guidance on Response Programs for Unauthorized Access to Member Info and Member Notice are exempt.
Puerto Rico	10 L.P.R.A. 4051 et seq. (January 5, 2006)	Notice of breach of the security, confidentiality, or integrity of unencrypted personal information, where access has been permitted to unauthorized persons or it is known or reasonably suspected that authorized persons have accessed the information with intent to use it for illegal purposes.

(continued)

State	Legislation or State Law	Requires
Rhode Island	RI Gen. Law 11-49.2-3 to 11.49.2-7 (March 1, 2006)	Notice of breach of the security, confidentiality, or integrity of unencrypted, computerized, personal information by persons and by state agencies if breach poses significant risk of identity theft when unencrypted personal information was, or is reasonably believed to have been acquired by an unauthorized person. No notice is required if after an appropriate investigation or after consultation with relevant federal, state, and local law enforcement agencies it is determined that the breach has not and will not likely result in harm to individuals. It does not apply to HIPAA entities or financial institutions in compliance with Federal Interagency Guidelines. Entities covered by another state or federal law are exempt only if that other law provides greater protection to consumers.
South Carolina	SC Code §1-11-490 et seq. (January 1, 2009)	Notice of breach of the security of computerized, unencrypted, and unredacted personal information, or encrypted information with a key that has also been compromised, when illegal use of the information has occurred or is reasonably likely to occur or use of the information creates a "material risk of harm" to the consumer. Notice under this section is not required if entity maintains its own notification procedures as part of an information security policy for the treatment of personal information and is otherwise consistent with the timing requirements of this section.
Tennessee	Tenn. Code. Ann. 47-18-21 (July 1, 2005)	Notice of the unauthorized acquisition of unencrypted computerized data that materially compromises the security, confidentiality, or integrity of personal information. It does not apply to persons subject to Title V of the Gramm–Leach–Bliley Act.
Texas	Tex. Bus & Com. Code Ann. 4-48-103 (September 1, 2005)	Notice of breach of the security, confidentiality, or integrity of unencrypted, computerized, personal information by persons who conduct businesses in the state. Notice under this section is not required if the entity maintains its own notification procedures as part of an information security policy for the treatment of personal information and is otherwise consistent with the timing requirements of this section.
Utah	Utah Code 13-44-101 et seq. (January 1, 2007)	Notice of breach of the security of computerized personal information that is not protected by a method that makes the information unusable. Entities covered by another state or federal law are exempt if the person notifies each affected Utah resident in accordance with law.

State	Legislation or State Law	Requires
Vermont	Vt. Stat. Tit 9 Sec. 2435 (January 1, 2007)	Notice if investigation reveals misuse of personal information for identity theft or fraud has occurred or is reasonably likely to occur. Notice is not required if the data collector establishes that misuse of personal information is not reasonably possible. It must provide notice and explanation to the Attorney General or department of banking, insurance, securities, and health care administration in the event data collector is a person/entity licensed with that department. Financial institutions subject to compliance with Federal Interagency Guidance on Response Programs for Unauthorized Access to Member Info and Member Notice are exempt.
Virgin Islands	14 V.I.C. 2208 et seq. (October 17, 2005)	Notice of breach of the security, confidentiality, or integrity of unencrypted, computerized, personal information reasonably believed to have been acquired by unauthorized persons. Notice under this section is not required if entity maintains own notification procedures as part of an information security policy for the treatment of personal information and is otherwise consistent with the timing requirements of this section.
Virginia	VA Code 18.2-186.6 (July 1, 2008)	Notice of any breach of the security of computerized, unencrypted, and unredacted personal information, or encrypted information with a key that has also been compromised, if an individual or entity reasonably believes such information has been accessed and acquired by an unauthorized person and has caused or will cause identity theft or other fraud. Notice under this section is not required if an entity maintains its own notification procedures as part of an information security policy for the treatment of personal information and is otherwise consistent with the timing requirements of this section, or if the entity has notification procedures established by a federal regulator. This section does not apply to any entity that is subject to compliance with the Gramm–Leach–Bliley Act.
Washington	RCW 42.17 et seq. (July 24, 2005)	Notice of a breach of the security, confidentiality, or integrity of unencrypted, computerized, personal information by persons, businesses, and government agencies. Notice is not required when there is a technical breach of the security of the system which does not seem reasonably likely to subject customers to a risk of criminal activity. Notice under this section

(continued)

State	Legislation or State Law	Requires
		is not required if entity maintains own notification procedures as part of an information security policy for the treatment of personal information and is otherwise consistent with the timing requirements of this section.
West Virginia	WV Code 46A-2A-101 et seq. (June 26, 2008)	Notice of any breach of the security of computerized, unencrypted, and unredacted personal information, or encrypted information with a key that has also been compromised, reasonably believed to have been accessed and acquired by an unauthorized person and has caused, or will cause, identity theft or other fraud. Financial institutions subject to compliance with Federal Interagency Guidance on Response Programs for Unauthorized Access to Member Info and Member Notice are exempt.
Wisconsin	Wis. Stat. 895.507 (March 16, 2006)	Notice to the consumer when personal information is taken in a security breach that is not encrypted, redacted, or altered in any manner rendering the information unreadable. This includes DNA and biometric data. Notice is not required if the acquisition of personal information does not create a material risk of ID theft or fraud.
Wyoming	W.S. 40-12-501 to 509 (July 1, 2007)	Notice of the unauthorized acquisition of computerized data that materially compromises the security, confidentiality, or integrity of personal identifying information of an investigation determines misuse of the personal identifying information has occurred or is reasonably likely to occur. Financial institutions subject to the Gramm–Leach–Bliley Act or credit unions under 12 USC §1752 are exempt from providing notice under this section.

APPENDIX K: EXAMPLE SECURITY STATEMENT OF WORK

I GENERAL

I.1 Overall Objectives

I.1.a Supplier acknowledges that a principal Purchaser objective is to:

I.1.a.1 identify the security-related vulnerabilities contained within the equipment Supplier sells or offers to sell to Purchaser under this Agreement;

I.1.a.2 identify the security-related vulnerabilities contained within the deployment architecture (including physical, geographical, and logical) of Purchaser's Network, as developed in connection with this Agreement; and

I.1.a.3 mitigate found vulnerabilities in a cost-effective and timely manner.

1.1.b Supplier agrees to use best efforts to support and cooperate with Purchaser in achieving those objectives.

1.1.c Supplier further acknowledges that Purchaser is still in the process of evaluating the security capabilities it will require for the Products procured under this Agreement. Supplier agrees to respond as promptly as possible to Purchaser inquiries with respect to: (i) what security capabilities are extant in the Products, and (ii) what capabilities are not now extant in the Products but may be incorporated in the foreseeable future consistent with product planning, roadmaps, estimated availability dates, cost implications to Supplier and Purchaser, and any proposed alternate capabilities.

I.2 Security Requirement Compliance

I.2.a Supplier shall be responsible for ensuring that its Products comply with the security requirements set forth in the following documents that are attached hereto and made a part hereof:

Security Management of Next Generation Telecommunications Networks and Services,
First Edition. Stuart Jacobs.
© 2014 The Institute of Electrical and Electronics Engineers, Inc. Published 2014 by John Wiley & Sons, Inc.

- Attachment A: Security Requirements Compliance Commitment Spreadsheet
- Attachment B: Additional Management System Security Requirements
- Attachment C: Additional Element Security Requirements
- Attachment D: Supplier Security Roadmap

Attachments A, B, and C represent generally accepted security practices in the information processing and data communications industry. Supplier shall incorporate functionality that conforms to such security requirements as part of Supplier's ongoing product development process during the term of this Agreement.

The Parties shall negotiate, in good faith, an amendment to Attachment B to specify such requirements.

I.2.b All Internet-Protocol-based management, control, and signaling messages that traverse between Supplier products and Purchaser management systems shall be protected through the use of the Internet Engineering Task Force (IETF) IPsec protocols as set forth in Attachment B.

I.2.c Purchaser and Supplier shall agree on IPsec configuration and functional details during follow-up meetings.

I.3 Purchaser-Furnished Equipment

I.3.a Purchaser will be providing the hardware and operating system software upon which the Supplier management application software will execute/reside.

II PURCHASER WINDOWS OPERATING SYSTEM HARDENING REQUIREMENTS

In the event Supplier supplies any computing equipment upon which Microsoft Operating System software is used, then Supplier shall comply with the requirements stated in this section. Purchaser will authorize exceptions to the requirements in this section only if Supplier demonstrates to Purchaser's satisfaction that compliance causes system or application failure. However, in such cases, Supplier agrees to seek and reasonably implement software fixes that eliminate any system/application conflicts with these requirements. Supplier agrees to provide a quarterly summary report of its progress in seeking and reasonably implementing software fixes that eliminate any system/application conflicts with these requirements.

II.1 All machines using a Microsoft-supplied operating system shall be configured using the concept of "least privilege" access. Only allowed services and protocols necessary for the business function of the machine shall be enabled.

II.2 The NTFS file system shall only be used.

Attached to Agreement No xxx

II.3 The latest available service pack shall be installed.

II.4 Supplier shall check to see that an account is built for each user including the System Administrator.

   a. Default Administrator account shall be renamed.

   b. Disable guest account.

   c. Eliminate all accounts not needed—duplicates, test accounts, retired accounts, etc.

II.5 The following security changes (in bold) shall be made in the registry—use the regedit command. The pre-approved general purpose Purchaser Warning Message is shown below. If appropriate, the word "network" may be used in place of the word "system."

Notice—proprietary system

This system is intended to be used solely by authorized users in the course of legitimate corporate business. Users are monitored to the extent necessary to properly administer the system, to identify unauthorized users or users operating beyond their proper authority, and to investigate improper access or use. By accessing this system, you are consenting to this monitoring.

---

   a. Install approved warning banner.
HKLM\Software\Microsoft\Windows NT\CurrentVersion\Winlogon\LegalNoticeCaption
is where "NOTICE—PROPRIETARY SYSTEM" goes.
HKLM\Software\Microsoft\Windows NT\CurrentVersion\Winlogon\LegalNoticeText
is where the banner message goes.

   b. Disable DirectDraw—prevents direct access to video hardware and memory and may impact some programs that require DirectX (games), but most business applications should be unaffected.
HKLM\SYSTEM\CurrentControlSet\Control\GraphicsDrivers\DCI and set the value for timeout REG_DWORD to 0

   c. Clear the Paging File at shutdown. Some programs store passwords and other sensitive information in memory; this will eliminate this information.
HKLM\SYSTEM\CurrentControlSet\Control\Session Manager\Memory Management
and change the data value of the ClearPageFileAtShutdown value to 1.

   d. Disable anonymous logons.
HKLM\SYSTEM\CurrentControlSet\Control\Lsa
and change value of **RestrictAnonymous=dword 00000002**

e. Protect against Trojan .REG files.
HKLM\Software\Classes\regfile\shell\open\command
and value= @="notepad.exe \"%1\""

f. Do not allow ICMP redirecting.
HKLM\SYSTEM\CurrentControlSet\Services\Tcpip\Parameters
and EnableICMPRedirect=0

g. Turn on SYN-ACK protection.
HKLM\SYSTEM\CurrentControlSet\Services\Tcpip\Parameters
and **SynAttackProtect=1**

h. TCP\IP filters all incoming UDP datagrams, raw IP datagrams, and TCP SYNs.
HKLM\SYSTEM\CurrentControlSet\Services\Tcpip\Parameters
and EnableSecurityFilters=1

i. Determine if system was loaded with Microsoft Internet Information Server (IIS). (This registry change must be made even if IIS is not being used.)
HKLM\Software\Microsoft\DataFactory\HandlerInfo
and HandlerRequired = 1

II.6 If present,

a. Remove OS/2 subsystem.
Remove or disable in the WINNT\System32 folder the following files:
Os2.exe, Os2srv.exe, Os2ss.exe

b. Remove POSIX subsystem.
Remove or disable in the WINNT\System32 folder the following files:
Psxdll.dll, Posix.exe, Pax.exe, Psxss.exe

II.7 Open Local Security Policies in Administrative folder and check/change the following:

Account policies—Password policies	Enforce password history = four passwords remembered
	Maximum password age = 90 days
	Minimum password age = 2 days
	Minimum password length = six characters (eight recommended)
	Passwords must meet complexity requirements = Enabled
Account policies—Account lockout	Account lockout duration = 30 minutes
	Account lockout threshold = three invalid logon attempts
	Reset account lockout counter after = 30 minutes

II.8   Security Policy. Administrative tools > Local Security Policy > Local policies > Security option

   a. Enable "Do not display last user name in logon screen."
   b. Enable "Clear virtual memory pagefile when system shuts down."
   c. Enable "Digitally sign server communication (when possible)."
   d. Disable "Allow system to be shut down without having to log on."

II.9   Enable auditing

Open Local Security Policies in Administrative folder and check/change the following:
Local policies—audit policies

Event	Level
Account logon events	Success, failure
Account management	Success, failure
Logon events	Success, failure
Object access	Success
Policy change	Success, failure
Privilege use	Success, failure

II.10 Access Control

To set access permissions at the directory or file level, right-click on the directory or file name. Select "Properties"; select "Security" tab.

• Add groups or individuals allowed access.
• Select Permissions appropriate for the group added.
• Remove the group "Everyone" whenever possible.

Users shall be granted access to files based on the concept of "least privileged" access. Group policies, based on access requirements, shall be implemented to accomplish this security goal.
   Protect "Special" binaries and system files using access controls. Protecting these executables and binaries consists of ensuring that only the "Administrators" group has executable access to the C:\WINNT\System32 directory, the C:\BACKUP directory, the C:\I386 directory, and the C:\DOS directory.
   Remove the default hidden share for all local drives if the Server Service is enabled (e.g., C$, D$, etc.).
The use of pcAnywhere for external remote access (dial up) is not allowed.

Attached to Agreement No xxx

II.11 Check security permissions in \WINNT folder.

    a. Remove "EVERYONE."

    b. Check security permissions in \WINNT\System32\Spool\Drivers. This prevents users from uploading "trojaned" drivers that would be distributed to other users.
- Remove "EVERYONE."
- Change "Users" to Read and Execute.

II.12 Shutdown unnecessary services. Many services are installed and started during installation. The following services are acceptable:

Computer browser	TCP/IP NetBIOS Helper	NTLM SSP	WINS
Microsoft DNS Server	Spooler	RPC Locator	Workstation
Netlogon	Server	RPC Service	Event Log
Window management	Task Scheduler	Plug and Play	Norton Services
Network connection			

II.13 Security Templates

Windows comes with a number of security templates. Caution shall be used when implementing the templates. Typically, security settings within the templates may require further modification to ensure appropriate security. The templates are located in the Windows root directory (normally WINNT) in \Security\Templates. The following templates are used in a high-security environment, such as the Purchaser Network. These provide additional security settings to the basic templates:

- Securedc.inf and Hisecdc.inf—for domain controllers
- Securews.inf and Hisecws.inf—for member servers and workstations

The following templates are used only in a low-security environment and, therefore, should not be used within the Purchaser Network.

- Basicwk.inf—for Windows 2000 Professional
- Basicsv.inf—for Windows 2000 Server
- Basicdc.inf—for Windows 2000-based domain controllers

Attached to Agreement No xxx

II.14 Limit the Number of Network Shares

    a. Restrict access to trusted groups and users.

    b. Right-click shared folder or drive and click Sharing.

    c. Click Permissions. Add or remove the appropriate users or groups.

II.15 A System Administrator (management) must be assigned.

II.16 Disable Dump File Creation Dump file can help troubleshoot unexplained crashes and provide potentially sensitive information to hackers. Feature can be turned on when needed.

Control Panel > System > Advanced > Startup and Recovery
and change the options for "write debugging information" to none.

II.17 The bios shall be password protected and accessed by the System Administrator only.

II.18 Change the boot order in the bios to make the C drive first in line.

II.19 Set screen saver for 15 minutes or less and password protect. This shall be set for all users.

II.20 Norton AntiVirus for Windows 2000/2003 shall be installed, enabled, and scheduled to update at least once a week.

II.21 Verify that all appropriate Microsoft patches and fixes have been applied.

II.22 No removable media (floppy disk, CD ROM, etc.) shall be enabled that would allow data downloads/uploads by anyone other than the System Administrator.

III PURCHASER IPSEC USAGE REQUIREMENTS

For network interfaces where IPsec is used, Supplier shall comply with the following requirements:

III.1 All elements shall implement the Internet Key Exchange (IKE) protocol as defined in IETF RFC2409 and the Internet Security Association Key Management Protocol (ISAKMP) as defined in IETF RFC2408.

III.2 The IKE/ISAKMP implementation shall support "Peer-entity" authentication via pre-shared keys.

III.3 The IKE/ISAKMP implementation shall support "Peer-entity" authentication via digital signatures and based on the RSA public key encryption and X.509v3 digital certificates.

Attached to Agreement No xxx

III.4   All elements shall implement a function that allows for loading pre-shared keys, RSA private keys, and X.509v3 digital certificates into the element.

III.5   Pre-shared and RSA private key loading shall support pre-shared and RSA private keys that are encrypted according to PKCS #10 Enveloped-data content type.

III.6   Pre-shared and RSA private key loading shall support RSA private keys and digital certificates that are encrypted according to PKCS #12 Enveloped-data content type.

III.7   Pre-shared and RSA private key loading shall require entry of a passphrase by an authorized administrator.

III.8   The IKE/ISAKMP implementation shall support "Aggressive Mode."

III.9   The implemented ISAKMP Protection Suite shall include IPsec ESP null encryption with HMAC-MD5-96 in transport mode.

III.10 The implemented ISAKMP Protection Suite shall include IPsec ESP null encryption with HMAC-SHA1-96 in transport mode.

III.11 All elements shall implement the RFC2410.

III.12 All elements shall implement the HMAC-MD5-96 as defined in IETF RFC2403.

III.13 All elements shall implement the HMAC-SHA1-96 as defined in IETF RFC2404.

III.14 All elements shall implement Dead Peer Detection as defined in IETF RFC3706.

IV LIST OF ATTACHMENTS

Supplier and Purchaser acknowledge and agree that the following attachments are hereby made a part of this Appendix A-3. In case of conflict between the requirements of this Appendix A-3 and those in an attachment to this appendix, the terms of this Appendix A-3 shall take precedence.

Attached to Agreement No xxx

Attachment	Title	Attachment File Name
A	Security Requirements Compliance Commitment Spreadsheets	APPENDIX A-3 Attachment A—SOW Requirements.xls
B	Additional Management Security Requirements	APPENDIX A-3 Attachment B—Management.doc
C	Additional Element Security Requirements	APPENDIX A-3 Attachment C—Elements.doc
D	Supplier Security Roadmap	APPENDIX A-3 Attachment D—Supplier Security Roadmap.doc

APPENDIX L: EXAMPLE SOLARIS OPERATING SYSTEM AUDIT PROCEDURES

1. Verify the host name, system type, system release, and version.
   - Type ***uname -a***
2. Logon to the system.
   - Was correct "Warning Banner" displayed before the login prompt?
   - Banner located in */etc/issue*.
     The authorized message for the banner can be found in the Operations Information Security Policy document.
3. Check umask.
   - Type ***umask***
     umask setting of 027 or higher is required.
     Set in */etc/profile* or */etc/default/login*.
4. Test user password. (Try to change to an illegal password.)
   - Type ***passwd***
     Password should be at least **eight** characters.
5. Obtain a list of */etc/passwd* and */etc/shadow*.
   - Verify that only one user account has UID of 0.
     If more accounts have UID of 0, they should be disabled.
   - Verify that all users have a password entry or are disabled.
   - Verify that users have unique UIDs.
     Check GECOS field for information not required.
     System Admin info should not be in GECOS.
   - All hosts should use the shadow file.
   - */etc/shadow* should not be world-readable. 400 file permission.
   - */etc/shadow*.

Security Management of Next Generation Telecommunications Networks and Services,
First Edition. Stuart Jacobs.
© 2014 The Institute of Electrical and Electronics Engineers, Inc. Published 2014 by John Wiley & Sons, Inc.

Check for password.

Check for password aging, 90 days or less.

* Check and turn off dormant accounts if not used in 6 months.
* Users should have the ability to change own password.
* System logins should be disabled if not needed.
* Verify that new users are forced to change password on initial login.
* FAILLIMIT option should be set to three (password is locked after three wrong attempts).

6. Obtain a list of */etc/group*.
   * Check to see that the password is disabled.

   No logins should have a system group like root.
   * Verify that there is no password in */etc/group*.
   * Check logins with GID of 0.

7. Check world-writable directories.
   * Type *find / -type d –perm –0002 –exec ls –ld {} \; > writable_dirs*

   The only world-writable directories should be spool/public directories and should have the sticky bit set.

   Look at system-owned directories.

8. Check world-writable files.
   * Type *find / -type f –perm –0002 –exec ls –l {} \;>writable_files*

   Look for system-owned files.

9. Obtain a list of the crontab file for root and all other account crontabs.
   * Type *pg /var/spool/cron/crontabs/root*

   Verify that permissions on files are 660.

   Type *ls –l /var/spool/cron/crontabs*

   Type *ls –l /var/spool/cron/atjobs*

   If only one crontab exists, verify permission restricted to superuser.

   Know the function of each program.

   Check the cron.allow, cron.deny, at.allow, and at.deny files.

10. Obtain a listing of the */etc/inittab* file used in start-up process.

    Type *pg /etc/inittab*

    Verify that the superuser's terminal is activated for single user.

    Check permissions. It should not be world-writable.

    /etc/inittab

    /etc/init.d

    /sbin/rcx where x = 0,1,2,3,6

    All start-up scripts should have a complete path description.

11. Obtain a listing of the sulog.
    * Type *pg /var/adm/sulog*

Verify that only authorized users have superuser access.

Look for failed attempts to gain superuser access.

- Check */var/adm/syslog* if used.
- Check */var/adm/loginlog* (failed login attempts).

12. Examine root's home directory.

    - Verify that the current directory (.) is not part of the default path.

    Type *echo $PATH*

13. No .rhosts files.

    Type *find / -name .rhosts –print*

14. No .netrc files.

    Type *find / -name .netrc –print*

15. Check hosts.equiv to make sure who is a trusted host.

    - Hosts.equiv should not have a + or - in the file and no usernames.
    - Only system administration hosts.

    Type *find / -name hosts.equiv -print*

16. Review */etc/default/login file*.

    CONSOLE=/dev/console

    To prevent direct login as root except at console.

17. Obtain a list of inetd.conf file.

    - Type *pg /etc/inetd.conf*

    Check for services—turn off services not needed.

    The following services should be turned off:

    echo   daytime chargen time   finger

    discard   rusers   wall   spray   rex

    Check for HTTPD service if using, otherwise turn off.

        Log access

    Check smtp (25) Sendmail

        S88smtpd in the */etc/rc2.d* and */etc/rc3.d*

        Turn off.

    Check uucp.

        Turn off if not needed.

        Files owned by uucp.

        No normal shell.

        Login and password.

    Check tftp.

        Run in secure mode.

Check nfs.

Type *showmount –e xxxx* where xxxx=host

Shows what files can be mounted.

Only place directories and files needed— read-only mode.

Type *pg /etc/dfs/dfstab*

Shows what files can be mounted and permissions.

Some hosts (where terminals are booting from) may need nfs or tftp. Turn off the one not needed and secure the other.

18. Obtain a listing of */etc/ftpusers*.

- This list contains the logins that cannot ftp.

  System logins should be on this list.

- Look for ftp in the */etc/passwd* file for anonymous ftp.

  No anonymous ftp.

  FTP version should be the latest version.

19. Home directories should not be writable except by owner.

- Type *ls –l /home*

  Check for unique home directories.

20. No system prompts for users, menu only except System Administrators.

- No telnet.

- No ftp.

- No "r" commands.

-----< End of Procedure >-----

APPENDIX M: EXAMPLE PROCEDURE FOR BASIC HARDENING OF A WINDOWS XP PROFESSIONAL OPERATING SYSTEM

1. Check operating system version.
   Ensure that NTFS file system is being used.
2. Install the latest service pack.
   Service Pack 3 or later.
3. User Accounts
   a. Check to see that an account is built for each user including the System Administrator (using standard organization employee IDs).
      Default Administrator account should be renamed.
   b. Disable guest account.
   c. Eliminate all accounts not needed—duplicates, test accounts, retired accounts, etc.
4. The following security changes are made in the registry—use the regedit command.
   a. Install the Operations Information Security Policy document approved warning banner.
      HKLM\Software\Microsoft\Windows\CurrentVersion\policy\system\LegalNoticeCaption
      (This is where NOTICE—PROPRIETARY SYSTEM goes.) **HKLM\Software\Microsoft\Windows\CurrentVersion\policy\system\LegalNoticeText**
      (This is where the banner message goes.)
   b. Disable DirectDraw—prevents direct access to video hardware and memory and may impact some programs that require DirectX (games), but most business applications should be unaffected.

Security Management of Next Generation Telecommunications Networks and Services,
First Edition. Stuart Jacobs.
© 2014 The Institute of Electrical and Electronics Engineers, Inc. Published 2014 by John Wiley & Sons, Inc.

HKLM\SYSTEM\CurrentControlSet\Control\GraphicsDrivers\DCI
and set the value for timeout **REG_DWORD to 0**

c. Clear the Paging File at shutdown. Some programs store passwords and other sensitive information in memory; this will eliminate this information.

HKLM\SYSTEM\CurrentControlSet\Control\Session Manager\Memory Management
and change the data value of the **ClearPageFileAtShutdown value** to 1.

d. Disables anonymous logons.

HKLM\SYSTEM\CurrentControlSet\Control\Lsa
and change the value of
RestrictAnonymous=dword 00000002

e. Protects against Trojan .REG files.

HKLM\Software\Classes\regfile\shell\open\command
and
value = @="notepad.exe \"%1\""

f. Does not allow ICMP redirecting.

HKLM\SYSTEM\CurrentControlSet\Services\Tcpip\Parameters and
EnableICMPRedirect=0

g. Turns on SYN-ACK protection.

HKLM\SYSTEM\CurrentControlSet\Services\Tcpip\Parameters
and
SynAttackProtect=1

h. TCP\IP filters all incoming UDP datagrams, raw IP datagrams, and TCP SYNs.

HKLM\SYSTEM\CurrentControlSet\Services\Tcpip\Parameters
and
EnableSecurityFilters=1

i. Determine if system was loaded with Microsoft Internet Information Server (IIS). (This registry change must be made even if IIS is not being used.)

HKLM\Software\Microsoft\DataFactory\HandlerInfo
and
HandlerRequired=1

5. Password Policy.

Administrative Tools>Local Security Policy>Account Policies>Password Policy

Enforce password history	Two passwords remembered or more
Maximum password age	90 days or more
Minimum password length	Six characters or more
Password must meet complexity requirements	Enabled

6. Account Lockout Policy.

   Administrative Tools > Local Security Policy > Account Policies > Account Lockout Policy

Account Lockout Duration	15 minutes
Account Lockout Threshold	Three invalid attempts
Reset account lockout counter after	15 minutes

7. Security Policy.

   Administrative Tools > Local Security Policy > Local Policies > Security Policy

Do not display last user name in logon screen	Enabled
Clear virtual memory pagefile when system shuts down	Enabled
Digitally sign server communication (when possible)	Enabled
Allow system to be shut down without having to log on	Disabled

8. Enable auditing.

   Administrative Tools > Local Security Policy > Local Policies > Audit Policies

Audit account logon events	Success, Failure
Audit account management	Success, Failure
Audit logon events	Success, Failure
Audit object access	Success, Failure
Audit policy change	Success, Failure
Audit privilege use	Success, Failure
Audit system events	Success, Failure

9. Event Viewer.

   Administrative Tools > Event Viewer

   Right-click log and go to Properties. If "Do not overwrite events" is checked, log must be cleared manually. Check logs routinely.

10. Shut down unnecessary services. Many services are installed and started during installation. The following services are acceptable Open Services in Administrative folder.

Computer Browser	TCP/IP	NetBIOS Helper
Microsoft DNS Server	Spooler	Netlogon Server
NTLM	SSP	WINS
RPC Locator	Workstation	RPC Service
Event Log	Plug and Play	Norton Services
Window management	Task Scheduler	Network connection

11. Limit the number of network shares.

    Restrict access to trusted groups and users.

    Right-click shared folder or drive and click Sharing.

    Click Permissions and add or remove the appropriate users or groups.

12. A System Administrator (management) must be assigned.

13. Disable Dump File Creation.

Dump file can help troubleshoot unexplained crashes and provide potentially sensitive information to hackers. If needed, feature can be turned on when needed.

Control Panel > System > Advanced > Startup and Recovery

and change the options for "**Write debugging information**" to **none**.

14. The bios must be password-protected.

It should be accessed by the System Administrator only.

15. Change the boot order in the bios to make the C drive first in line.

16. Set screen saver for 15 minutes or less and password-protect.

This has to be set for all users.

17. Install the RSA SecurID agent.

18. Norton AntiVirus for Windows XP must be installed, enabled, and scheduled to update at least once a day (preferably after 5 p.m.).

19. Provide physical security for the machine.

20. Verify that all appropriate Microsoft patches and fixes have been applied. As part of operational security audits, System Administrators must demonstrate familiarity with obtaining latest patches and must document that patches are applied in a timely manner. Such documentation must be retained and made available to Security Policy & Enforcement and Internal Auditing personnel.

21. No removable media (floppy disk, CD ROM, etc.) may be enabled that would allow data downloads/uploads by anyone other than the System Administrator.

22. Sniffing and scanning software tools are strictly prohibited.

Note 1: Adding software applications may enable system and network services. After adding any software, recheck to see if unnecessary or vulnerable services have been opened up.

Note 2: When implemented, the aforementioned recommendations provide only a "basic" security configuration.

Assessment of the local system may indicate the need for additional changes to reduce vulnerability. If the computer is used as a workstation and is not being used by a System Administrator, then all removable media must be disabled.

APPENDIX N: EXAMPLE NETWORK AUDIT PROCEDURE

N.1 INTRODUCTION

Effective security management procedures help to promote continued reliability and availability of computer resources. It is imperative that the level of security for all the computers directly or indirectly connected to the organization's networks meet, or exceed, a Minimum Security Baseline (MSB) established in the organization's information Security Policies. The MSB is established to ensure information in interconnected computers is not threatened from other systems in the network. This procedure relies upon a good technical understanding of systems and networks operation. This procedure:

- is written in technical terms;
- is operating system specific; and
- specifies MSB settings for networked components.

Security Audit and Compliance tools should be utilized to verify acceptance to the MSB.

N.1.1 Purpose of this Audit Procedure

The primary purpose of this audit procedure is to assist the organization's information security personnel to secure organization networks against unauthorized penetration, from outside as well as against malicious actions of those authorized to use the organization's information-processing-related assets, without significantly impacting the average user.

N.1.2 Applicability and Scope

This procedure applies to all components of the organization's distributed information processing infrastructure and seeks to prevent the unauthorized access to and misuse of the organization's distributed computers, networks, and data. This audit procedure is

Security Management of Next Generation Telecommunications Networks and Services,
First Edition. Stuart Jacobs.
© 2014 The Institute of Electrical and Electronics Engineers, Inc. Published 2014 by John Wiley & Sons, Inc.

applicable to all external network connections as well as systems that allow external access (e.g., via public networks).

This audit procedure does not address security aspects which are needed to ensure protection from threats such as fraud by authorized staff, theft, unavailability of resources, etc., which should also be considered by the organization's information security policies and procedures.

Where there is a conflict between this procedure and other organizational information security documents, this procedure shall be considered the authoritative document.

N.2 AUDIT CHECKLIST FOR EXTERNAL NETWORK SECURITY

N.2.1 Process

Vendor Installation and Administration Guides should be used as reference documents. If security tools are available on each system, an authorized system or security administrator should produce appropriate reports to aid in this audit. This checklist is intended to provide a guideline for the auditor to follow to ensure compliance to organization's information Security Policies.

N.2.2 Audit Checklist for External Network Connections

Verify the following for external connections to organizational networks (excluding firewalls):

1. Ensure that all external network connects adhere to the organization's information Security Policies.
2. Review information security operational documentation for who is responsible for the various network components.
3. Diagram the external connections to the network and ensure that the configuration is set up securely.
4. Review the physical security controls for all external network components.
5. Review the logical security controls for all external network components.
6. Verify modem connectivity.
   - Inbound and outbound access
   - SLIP
   - PPP
7. Review the router security guidelines and remote access process.
8. Review the external web server guidelines.
9. Discuss the use and controls in place for IP tunneling.
10. Review the PBX guidelines.
11. Review the FAX guidelines.

12. Review the mobile device (i.e., cellular phones, smart phones, tablet, PDA) guidelines.
13. Ensure that tools are in place to monitor external network components.
    - Collect output reports.
    - Determine if the reports are reviewed daily for security incidents.
14. Discuss the process for handling network intrusions with operational personnel.
15. Discuss the backup process for network components with operational personnel.
16. Review the process for security patches and ensure that the components are running current operating systems, applications, and microcode.

N.2.3 Audit Checklist for Firewalls

Verify the following for *each* organizational firewall:

1. Verify that the firewall is a commercial firewall product and not "home-grown."
2. Ensure that the firewall complies with the appropriate (Baseline, Corporate, Enterprise, VoIP, High Availability, or IPv6) ICSA Labs Firewall Certification Criteria Modules.
3. Review the operational authorization and approval process for Internet access.
4. Diagram the external and internal connections to the firewall and ensure that the configuration is set up securely.
5. Remove non-essential services within the *inetd.conf*, or equivalent, file.
6. Verify that *sendmail.cf*, or equivalent, is properly configured.
7. Reduce the functionality of the, or equivalent, printcap file (no *lpd* daemon).
8. Verify that no *.rhosts* files are in home directories.
9. Review the password file (look for minimal entries and verify that it is a shadow password file—C2 security enabled).
10. Review the screening rules and filtering for the firewall (all the applications enabled and their policies). Validate this information against a hardcopy from a previous date to determine changes.
11. Review the blocking and metering software that may be used on the firewall.
12. Verify which TCP and UDP packets travel though the firewall in both directions, and that the connections are via relays or proxies (also check what happens to rejected packets and is this logged).
13. Ensure that backups are done and restorable. Verify the procedures for log and alarm files. Especially check for the following files:
    - *sendmail.cf*
    - *fstab*
    - *rc.config*
    - */etc/namedb/** (all DNS files)
    - *syslog.conf*

- *inetd.conf*
- *screend.conf* (Gate only)
- *gated.conf*
- Auditing and accounting files

14. Review the nameservice (or *hosts* file) for proper configuration.

15. Ensure that log and alarm files are examined and appropriate reports produced.

16. Verify that "root" access is only allowed via the console. If remote access is required, it must be done by a limited number of hosts using handheld authentication or via encrypted tunnels.

17. Verify that no dialup access is available directly to the firewall.

18. Ensure that NFS is not configured or running on the firewall.

19. Ensure that UUCP is not configured or running on the firewall.

20. Verify that NTP is properly configured.

21. Verify that *xdm* is not running.

22. Verify that the firewalls are physically secured.

23. Ensure the live Internet connections to the backbone are labeled properly.

24. Review the */etc/motd* file only displays "Unauthorized Access is Prohibited" and ensure that no "Welcome" text is used.

25. Review the security tools running on the firewall and the latest reports from each tool.

26. Review the escalation procedure for an incident involving the firewall.

27. Ensure that the latest security patches are installed.

28. List the router security policy ensuring that the following are enabled:
    - Packet filtering
    - Access control rules
    - Console and remote access
    - Static routes

29. Ensure that NIS (Yellow Pages) is not installed or configured.

30. Ensure that Trivial File Transport Protocol (TFTP) is not installed or configured.

31. Review the configuration of the *inetd.conf* file for each gateway box to ensure:
    - On the Gate machine, all services are disabled except network traps on specific ports (to scan for network probing and to warn the Administrator)

32. Review the backup policy for the systems.

33. Ensure that the original backups of the initial firewall installation are available.

APPENDIX O: EXAMPLE UNIX–LINUX OPERATING SYSTEM AUDIT PROCEDURES

(Other variations of UNIX may have slightly different file names and locations.)

1. Verify the host name, system type, system release, and version.
   - Type *uname -a*
2. Logon to the system.
   - Was correct "Welcome" banner displayed before the login prompt?
   - Banner located in */etc/issue*
   - The authorized message for the banner can be found in the Operations Information Security Policy document.
3. Check umask.
   - Type *umask*

     umask setting of 027 or higher is required.

     Set in */etc/profile* or */etc/default/login*.
4. Test user password. (Try to change to an illegal password.)
   - Type *passwd*

     Password should be at least **eight** characters.
5. Obtain a list of */etc/passwd* and */etc/shadow*.
   - Verify that only one user account has UID of 0.

     If more accounts have UID of 0, they should be disabled.
   - Verify that all users have a password entry or are disabled.
   - Verify that users have unique UIDs.

     Check GECOS field for information not required.

     System Admin info should not be in GECOS.
   - All hosts should use the shadow file.

Security Management of Next Generation Telecommunications Networks and Services,
First Edition. Stuart Jacobs.
© 2014 The Institute of Electrical and Electronics Engineers, Inc. Published 2014 by John Wiley & Sons, Inc.

- */etc/shadow* should not be world-readable. 400 file permission.
- */etc/shadow*.

  Check for password.

  Check for password aging, 90 days or less.
- Dormant accounts—for SVR4—usermod—f 180 xxxx where xxxx=login can use last, finger, or loginlog.
- Users should have the ability to change own password.
- System logins should be disabled if not needed.
- Verify that new users are forced to change password on initial login.
- FAILLIMIT option should be set to three (password is locked after three wrong attempts).

6. Obtain a list of */etc/group*.
   - Check to see that the password is disabled.

     No logins should have a system group like root.
   - Verify that there is no password in */etc/group*.
   - Check logins with GID of 0.

7. Check world-writable directories.
   - Type *find/-type d –perm –0002 –exec ls –ld {} \; > writable_dirs*

     The only world-writable directories should be spool/public directories and should have the sticky bit set.

     Look at system-owned directories.

8. Check world-writable files.
   - Type *find/-type f –perm –0002 –exec ls –l {} \;>writable_files*

     Look for system-owned files.

9. Obtain a list of the crontab file for root and all other account crontabs.
   - Type *pg /var/spool/cron/crontabs/root*

     Verify that permissions on files are 660.

     Type *ls –l /var/spool/cron/crontabs*

     Type *ls –l /var/spool/cron/atjobs*

     If only one crontab exists, verify permission restricted to superuser.

     Know the function of each program.

     Check the cron.allow, cron.deny, at.allow, and at.deny files.

10. Obtain a listing of the */etc/inittab* file used in start-up process.
    - Type *pg /etc/inittab*

      Verify that the superuser's terminal is activated for single user.

      Check permissions. It should not be world-writable.

      /etc/inittab

      /etc/init.d

/sbin/rcx where x = 0,1,2,3,6

All start-up scripts should have a complete path description.

11. Obtain a listing of all SUID, SGID, and device files.

- Type *find/-perm –004000 –type f –print* to get SUID files
- Type *find/-perm –002000 –type f –print* to get SGID files

Check all SUID and SGID files for new files.

All device files should be in the */dev directory*.

Check permissions.

All device files should be owned by root.

All device files should be unreadable and unwritable by world except */dev/ null*, */dev/tty*, and */dev/console*.

12. Obtain a listing of the sulog.

- Type *pg /var/adm/sulog*

Verify that only authorized users have superuser access.

Look for failed attempts to gain superuser access.

13. Examine root's home directory.

- Verify that the current directory (.) is not part of the default path.
- Type *echo $PATH*

14. No .rhosts files.

Type *find/-name.rhosts –print*

15. No .netrc files.

Type *find/-name.netrc –print*

16. Check hosts.equiv to make sure who is a trusted host.

- Hosts.equiv should not have a + or - in the file and no usernames.
- Only system administration hosts.

Type *find/-name hosts.equiv -print*

17. Review */etc/default/login file*.

CONSOLE=/dev/console

To prevent direct login as root except at console.

18. Check

/var/adm/syslog

/var/adm/loginlog (failed login attempts)

/var/adm/acct/sum/lastlogin (last login of all users)

and other logs.

19. Obtain a list of inetd.conf file.

- Type *pg /etc/inetd.conf*

Check for services—turn off services not needed.

The following services should be turned off:

echo   daytime   chargen   time   finger   discard

Check for HTTPD service if using, otherwise turn off.

Most recent version, no cgi script; use cgiwrap

Log access

Check smtp (25) Sendmail

S88smtpd in the */etc/rc2.d* and */etc/rc3.d*

Turn off.

Check uucp.

Turn off if not needed.

Files owned by uucp.

No normal shell.

Login and password.

Check tftp.

Run in secure mode.

Check nfs.

Type ***showmount –e xxxx*** where xxxx=host

Shows what files can be mounted.

Only place directories and files needed—read-only mode.

Type ***pg /etc/dfs/dfstab***

Shows what files can be mounted and permissions.

Some hosts (where terminals are booting from) may need nfs or tftp. Turn off the one not needed and secure the other.

20. Obtain a listing of */etc/ftpusers*.
    * This list contains the logins that cannot ftp.

    System logins should be on this list.
    * Look for ftp in the */etc/passwd* file for anonymous ftp.

    No anonymous ftp.

    FTP version should be WU2.1.

21. Home directories should not be writable except by owner.
    * Type ***ls –l /home***

    Check for unique home directories.

22. SUID/SGID files.
    * Check for permissions—4711.
    * Run bash against baseline.

23. No system prompts for users, menu only except System Administrators.
    * No telnet.
    * No ftp.
    * No "r" commands.

24. X-win security.
  • Verify that a terminal lock ("screen saver") password is being used.
  • Verify that terminal configuration settings are protected by a password known only by the System Administrator.

-----<End of Procedure>-----

INDEX

Note: Page numbers in *italics* refer to Figures; those in **bold** to Tables.

Security Management of Next Generation Telecommunications Networks and Services,
First Edition. Stuart Jacobs.
© 2014 The Institute of Electrical and Electronics Engineers, Inc. Published 2014 by John Wiley & Sons, Inc.

Printed and bound by CPI Group (UK) Ltd, Croydon, CR0 4YY

27/10/2024

14580253-0001